Management for Professionals

The Springer series *Management for Professionals* comprises high-level business and management books for executives. The authors are experienced business professionals and renowned professors who combine scientific background, best practice, and entrepreneurial vision to provide powerful insights into how to achieve business excellence.

More information about this series at http://www.springer.com/series/10101

Bing Wang • Tobias Just
Editors

Understanding China's Real Estate Markets

Development, Finance, and Investment

 Springer

Editors
Bing Wang
Graduate School of Design
Harvard University
Cambridge, Massachusetts, USA

Tobias Just
IRE|BS
University of Regensburg
Regensburg, Bavaria, Germany

ISSN 2192-8096   ISSN 2192-810X   (electronic)
Management for Professionals
ISBN 978-3-030-49031-7   ISBN 978-3-030-49032-4   (eBook)
https://doi.org/10.1007/978-3-030-49032-4

This Springer imprint is published by the registered company Springer Nature Switzerland AG.
The registered company address is: Gewerbestrasse 11, 6330 Cham, Switzerland

Acknowledgments

This book began as a reflection on the development of the Chinese real estate market from its nonexistent stage in the late 1980s to its current transformation. However, as the book evolved, the work turned into a larger project aimed at addressing the more timely need to bridge the gap between real estate-based disciplinary knowledge and the practicalities of real estate practice in the Chinese context.

We owe a debt of gratitude to the contributors of this book, who are international and come from a spectrum of disciplinary backgrounds. Their dedication and patience made this publication possible. Some of them are distinguished policymakers, scholars, and real estate pioneers from China, with decades of experience working "on the ground," gleaning first-hand knowledge and insights. Others are located in different countries or continents, but have focused their attention on real estate and the Chinese context; the distance and their comparative perspectives shape their sensibility and unique angle for interpreting the subject.

Thanks should also be extended to the students who studied diligently in the graduate-level courses "Global Leadership in Real Estate and Design" and "Real Estate and City Making in China" over the years offered at Harvard University, and to students of the MBA program at the IRE|BS of the University of Regensburg in Germany who spent a few intensive weeks in Shanghai and Hong Kong. All these students' curiosity and rigorous discussions of how the specificities of real estate practice help shape contemporary cities in China frame several of the topics in this book.

Lastly, we thank the editorial team at Springer, especially its senior editor for the Business, Management, and Finance Department, Dr. Prashanth Mahagaonkar, who provided support and patience throughout the publication process. A special thanks also goes to Christian Braun, who helped manage many logistical details of this international book project.

Bing Wang
Tobias Just

Contents

Part III Finance and Investment for Real Estate Development

Part IV Real Estate as a Physical and Social Asset Type

Contributing Authors

Christian Braun is a research associate at the International Real Estate Business School in University of Regensbury. He works for the Chair of Real Estate analyzing a plethora of economic data, including the Chinese market. He holds a B.Sc. in Business Administration as well as an M.Sc. in Real Estate from Regensburg University. Currently, Christian is working on his Ph.D. dissertation researching connections between behavioral real estate and real estate aesthetics by means of discrete choice experiments.

Nova S. Y. Chan is a Partner and leads the valuation practices in Pricewaterhouse-Coopers (PwC) China. He has extensive experience in M&A advisory, due diligence, modelling, valuations, negotiation, post-deal integration, and divestiture. Nova served as a member of the International Valuation Standards Council's (IVSC) Standards Board from 2008 to 2012 and currently is a member of both Global and Asia Business Valuation Committees for the Royal Institute of Chartered Surveyors (RICS). He is a member of the Valuation Standards Technical Committee in China for more than a decade and has been deeply involved in drafting the Chinese Valuation Standards since 1998. He is an associate member of the Hong Kong Institute of Certified Public Accountants (HKICPA), a fellow member of Association of Chartered Certified Accountants (ACCA) and the Royal Institution of Chartered Surveyors (FRICS), and a Certified Public Valuer (CPV) in China.

Sean C. S. Chiao is President of Asia Pacific at AECOM, overseeing its APAC geography spanning across Greater China, Southeast Asia, Australia, and New Zealand, as well as its over 12,000 employees. He holds a Master of Architecture in Urban Design from Harvard University and a Master of Architecture from the University of California, Berkeley. Sean has played instrumental roles for the masterplans in many complex and multidisciplinary projects in Asia Pacific, such as the award-winning River of Life in Kuala Lumpur. Sean is a Fellow of the American Institute of Architects (FAIA) and a member of Harvard University's Master in Design Engineering (MDE) External Advisory Board and of the University of Southern California's Board of Advisors for the American Academy. He also serves as a global trustee of the Urban Land Institute (ULI), on the Board of

Governors for the American Chamber of Commerce in Hong Kong, and as an Executive Committee Member of Asia Society's Global Council.

Dave Chiou is the Senior Director of China Research for Colliers International. He works closely with Colliers' China business to strengthen and expand Colliers' China research platform. Dave's professional expertise mainly encompasses macroeconomic and real estate market research covering sectors such as investments, valuations, office, business parks, industrials, and consumer and retail. Dave spent many years as an equity analyst working for large international investment banks including Citigroup and Nomura Securities in Taipei and Hong Kong and focusing on the real estate and consumer/retail sectors. His research was highly ranked in surveys of major institutional investors such as GIC, Fidelity, and Blackrock.

Robert Ciemniak is a Hong Kong-based entrepreneur focusing on research, data analytics, and technologies. He is a specialist on China housing markets. In 2012, after his 13-year career with Thomson Reuters, including two major roles as Global Head of Real Estate Markets (London/Hong Kong) and earlier as Head of Corporate Foresight in Group Strategy, London, Robert founded Real Estate Foresight Ltd. and its sister venture Robotic Online Intelligence Ltd. in 2017. Real Estate Foresight (REF) provides the granular data-driven research on China housing markets, powered by the in-house technology, content from data partners, and alternative data. Robert serves on the board of directors of China Index Holdings (CIH). For the past 8 years, he has been a regular conference speaker, chair, and moderator at the industry events, in real estate as well as technology, in China, Hong Kong, and Singapore, and a contributor to specialist industry publications and media. Robert holds a dual MBA degree from London Business School and Columbia Business School, New York and MSc from the Warsaw School of Economics. He is also an international master in chess and an author of a book about the Internet and competitive strategy (1999).

Michael Crawford is the current Chief Executive Officer of the Johnson Controls Hall of Fame Village (JCHOFV) in Canton, Ohio. Crawford has held the position since December of 2018. Prior to coming to the JCHOFV, Crawford served as President of Portfolio Management at the Four Seasons Hotels and Resort and oversaw global project management functions. Crawford was also responsible for overseeing the product design and procurement of Four Seasons around the world. He served as the President of Four Seasons' Asia Pacific region from 2014 through 2016. Prior to Four Seasons, Crawford held various senior executive roles for the Walt Disney Company, including General Manager for the Walt Disney Shanghai Resort, President of the Walt Disney Holdings Company, General Manager of Disney World Orlando, Managing Director of Operations for Walt Disney Attractions Japan, Vice President of International Development, and Vice President of Business Development.

Christina Gaw is a Managing Principal of Gaw Capital Partners and in charge of global capital markets activities. She works closely with limited partners relating to capital raising and new product developments. Gaw Capital is a real estate private equity firm and has raised five commingled funds targeting the Greater China and APAC since 2005. Gaw currently commands assets of over US$23 billion under management. Prior to joining Gaw Capital, Christina has over 16 years of investment banking experience at Goldman Sachs and UBS as a Managing Director, with responsibilities as Head of Asia Equities Distribution and as Head of APAC Capital Introduction team within Prime Brokerage. She has rich experience in covering some of the largest institutional investors globally. Christina is also active in community and educational sector capacity work in Hong Kong. She is a board member of the Women's Foundation (HK), corporate member of the Cheltenham Ladies College UK, and executive committee member of the St. Paul's Co-Educational College Alumni Association (HK). She is also the school supervisor for the TWGH's S.C. Gaw Memorial College in Hong Kong.

Klaus-Jürgen Gern is Senior Researcher at the Forecasting Center of the Kiel Institute for the World Economy (IfW), which produces quarterly reports on the economic outlook for the German economy and the World economy and analysis of current economic problems with relevance to the public domain on a regular basis. He is responsible for the forecast and analysis of the international economy and commodity markets. His research interests include macroeconomic theory and policy, business cycle analysis, growth processes in emerging economies, international commodity markets, and social security in an international perspective. In 1999, he obtained his doctoral degree in economics from the University of Kiel on economic effects of a negative income tax in Germany. He has lectured macro- and microeconomics at the University of Applied Sciences Kiel, the Europa Universität Flensburg, and the Business and Information Technology School Hamburg.

Florian Hermann Hackelberg is a Professor for real estate economics and management at the HAWK University of Applied Sciences and Arts, Germany. Before joining HAWK, he was a Senior Manager with PricewaterhouseCoopers (PwC) based in Berlin and Shanghai. Florian spent over five years in China advising his national and international clients with their real estate investments in Asia. After studying civil engineering and management in Germany, England and China, Florian received his PhD in real estate economics from the Technical University of Berlin. He earned a master's degree at the University of Cambridge and was awarded the Madingley prize for his research work on Chinese foreign direct investments in Germany. He is a former scholarship holder of the Friedrich-Ebert-Foundation and the Carl-Duisburg-Foundation. Florian is a professional member of the Royal Institution of Chartered Surveyors (MRICS) and a member of the Professional Group Valuation of the Royal Institution of Chartered Surveyors. Florian is the author and co-author of a number of books and articles and is a frequent speaker on China-related real estate and business topics.

Philipp Hauber is a Research Associate at the Kiel Institute for the World Economy (IfW). He works in the Forecasting Center where he monitors the US economy as well as major emerging economies, including China. Prior to joining the IfW, Philipp worked as an economist for Oxford Economics forming part of the macroeconomic forecasting team with a focus on Asian economies. He holds a B.Sc. in Economics and Political Sciences from the University of Cologne as well as an M. Sc. from Universitat Pompeu Fabra, Barcelona. Currently, Philipp is enrolled in the University of Kiel's Ph.D. program "Quantitative Economics." His research focuses on short-term forecasting models and applied macroeconometrics.

Karen Ip is a Partner of Corporate Department in Herbert Smith Freehills Beijing office. Karen has over 20 years of extensive experience in advising clients doing business in China, including the establishment and operation of representative offices, wholly foreign-owned enterprises, and joint ventures in China. She is principally involved in private equity investment projects, M&A transactions, and greenfield investments in real estate, manufacturing, infrastructure, and financial institution sectors and advising on regulatory issues in China. Karen is named as the leading individual in corporate and M&A practice for five consecutive years (2013–2017) by Legal500 Asia Pacific, the leading individual in corporate and M&A practice by Chambers Asia Pacific 2016 and the leading lawyer in M&A practice by IFLR1000 for seven consecutive years (2010–2016). Karen is admitted as a solicitor in Hong Kong and the UK.

Qingjun Jin is the senior Partner of King & Wood Mallesons. Before joining King & Wood Mallesons in 2002, Mr. Jin served as a lawyer in Beijing C&C law firm from 1987 to 1993 and was the founding partner of Shenzhen Shu Jin Law Firm from 1993 to 2002. Mr. Jin is one of the first group of lawyers in China to obtain the qualification to engage in securities business, with expertise in real estate, securities, investment, company, bankruptcy, and litigation. Mr. Jin has been serving as directors of real estate and other listed companies, including but not limited to as independent director of Gemdale Group, Sino-Ocean Group Holding Limited, Times China Holdings Limited, Shenzhen Asiantime International Construction Co., Ltd., CSG Holding Co., Ltd., Guotai Junan Securities Co., Ltd., Bank of Tianjin CO., Ltd., and external supervisor of China Merchants Bank Co., Ltd. Mr. Jin is the adjunct professor of China University of Political Science and Law and Law School of Renmin University of China, co-tutor for graduate program of Law School of Tsinghua University, arbitrator of Shenzhen International Arbitration Institute, Shanghai International Arbitration Center, and Southern Africa Arbitration Foundation, and mediator of Shenzhen Securities and Futures Industry Dispute Mediation Center.

Tobias Just is Managing Director at the IRE|BS Immobilienakademie and professor of Real Estate at the University of Regensburg. Tobias studied economics in Hamburg and Uppsala (Sweden). In 1997, he started to work at the University of the Federal Armed Forces Hamburg. His Ph.D. dissertation was awarded the university science prize in 2001. For more than 10 years, Tobias worked at Deutsche Bank

Research. He headed the unit's economic sector and real estate team and was a member of Deutsche Bank's group-wide Environmental Steering Committee. In 2006, Tobias was Research Fellow at the American Institute of Contemporary German Studies at the Johns Hopkins University. Tobias published more than 200 papers in professional and academic journals and books. He is President of the German Society of Property Researchers and editor of the ZIÖ—*the German Journal of Real Estate Research*. In 2017, Tobias became Fellow of the RICS by nomination. His book *Es sind nicht nur Gebäude* was shortlisted for the German Prize for Finance Books 2016"—it was for the first time that a book on real estate was shortlisted.

Nanda Lau is a partner of Herbert Smith Freehills (HSF) based in Shanghai. Her practice covers a wide range of corporate and commercial work including M&A, foreign direct investment, private equity, joint ventures, corporate restructurings, competition law, and regulatory compliance matters in China. Nanda has extensive experience in cross-border transactions with a China element. She is the coauthor of various publications and articles published by HSF, including the "China Investment Guide 2015" and the China chapter of "Asia Pacific M&A Review 2017" and "Restructuring, Turnaround and Insolvency in Asia Pacific 2016." She regularly publishes e-bulletins relating to China-related M&A developments and investment issues.

Hannah Levinger is a senior economist with Deutsche Bank's macro-risk research team, where she focuses on economic, geopolitical, and societal developments in Asia, in particular China. Her responsibilities include assessing country-specific risks and analyzing economic and political trends in the region. She has published on a wide range of topics including China–EU relations, corporate bond markets, and infrastructure financing in Asia. Before joining Deutsche Bank in 2012, Ms Levinger worked at the European Bank for Reconstruction and Development in London. She holds a graduate degree in international economics from the University of Tübingen, Peking University, Beijing, and Tufts University, Boston.

Nancy F. Lin is Head of Strategy & Planning and Chief of Staff for President of Asia Pacific at AECOM. She is a civil engineer, architect, and urban designer. She received her Master of Architecture from the Graduate School of Design at Harvard University and her Bachelor of Science in Engineering from Princeton University in the USA. Professionally, Nancy's career before joining AECOM included leading her own architectural practice, serving as a landscape advisor for Taitung County and Taichung City, and 12 years of teaching architecture design studios at Tamkang University, Tunghai University, Ming Chuan University, and National Chiao Tung University in Taiwan. Immediately after joining AECOM, Nancy was the managing director for the Design, Planning and Economics Business in Hong Kong. Her projects as a practitioner span public space and plazas, schools, offices, and residential buildings. She is the Project Director for the Harvard University Graduate School of Design—AECOM Studio which was launched in 2012. Nancy's professional affiliations include being a Registered Architect of New York; a Member of the American Institute of Architects; a Member of the Board for the Chinese Institute of Urban Design in Taiwan; and a Founding Member of the Organization of Architecture Reformation in Taiwan.

Qian Ma joined Clifford Chance in 2011. Qian is Director and Co-Head of Clifford Chance China Desk in Germany. She obtained her Master of Laws (LL.M.) and Doctor (iur.) degree at the University of Saarland, Germany. She specializes in cross-border M&A, real estate transactions, capital markets, and intellectual property law. Qian is author and coauthor of numerous articles and books on German and Chinese M&A, real estate, Intellectual Property, and capital market issues. She is a regular speaker on international conferences and lecturer at the Goethe University Frankfurt am Main and the University of Applied Sciences Darmstadt in Germany.

Roger Nissim is an adjunct professor in the Real Estate and Construction Department at Hong Kong University. He qualified in the UK as Chartered Surveyor in 1968 and worked from 1973 until 1993 for the Lands Department in Hong Kong (former Crown Lands & Survey Office). During this time, his line of action encompassed overseeing land resumption and land disposal work. From 1993 until 2007, he worked for Sun Hung Kai Properties Limited (SHK) as manager of their Project Planning Department, a job which included premium negotiations and a wide range of land and real estate matters.

Baoxing Qiu is Counselor of the State Council, P. R. China, Director for the Chinese Society for Urban Studies, Chairman for the Chinese Committee of the International Water Association (IWA), and Ph.D. in Economics and Engineering. He is a former Vice Minister of Housing and Urban-Rural Construction of China, Mayor of the City of Hangzhou, Secretary of Jinhua Municipal Party Committee, Secretary of Yueqing County Party Committee, and also served as Deputy Head of the Workgroup for Reconstruction after the earthquakes in Wenchuan, Yushu, and Lushan, and as First Person in Charge for National Major Program for Water Pollution Control and Governance. Dr. Qiu is a specialist in Urban Planning and Construction. He was a visiting scholar at Harvard University and is currently faculty supervisor of doctoral research at Zhejiang University, Tongji University, Renmin University of China, Tianjin University, and Chinese Academy of Social Sciences. He is also an adjunct, visiting or honorary professor at Tsinghua University, Beijing University, Nanjing University, Fudan University, Hong Kong Polytechnic University, and Cardiff University, UK. He has won many international awards, including the International Water Association Chairman Award in 2006, the UNESCO Asia-Pacific Heritage Award in 2010, International Green Building Council Chairman Award as well as the International Water Association Global Award in 2014. Among many of his publications, the two books, *Harmony and Innovation: Problems, Crisis and Countermeasures in the Process of Rapid Urbanization* and *Urban Planning Reform in the Process of Urbanization in China*, have been translated into English and German and published internationally.

Friedemann Roy is the Global Product Lead Housing Finance at International Finance Corporation (IFC) Financial Institutions Group. He is leading IFC's offering in Housing Finance Advisory Services and is also involved in IFC's investment transactions in the area of housing finance. Having worked in more than 50 countries (emerging markets and developed countries), he has been involved in banking and housing finance transactions at different levels: advice to governments on regulatory issues and capital market instruments, investments in financial institutions, securitization transactions, and consulting to lenders on the management of retail and mortgage lending operations.

Megan Walters is the Global Head of Research at Allianz Real Estate based in Singapore. She was an International Director at JLL and Head of Research, leading a team of 170 researchers in Asia Pacific. Dr. Walters is a Fellow of RICS with a Ph.D. from the University of Hong Kong in Institutional Economics of Real Estate. Megan joined JLL in 2010 as Head of Research, Asia Pacific Capital Markets, a role responsible for advising investor clients and generating publications on office, retail, and industrial real estate trends in capital markets. Megan sits on the research committees of ANREV and APREA and is the ULI Women's Leadership representative for Asia Pacific on the WLI Global Committee. Megan held an Adjunct Associate Professor position at the National University of Singapore and served on the RICS International Governing Council from 2009 to 2015.

Bing Wang is Associate Professor and Faculty Head for Real Estate and the Built Environment at Harvard University Graduate School of Design (GSD). She is Faculty co-chair for Real Estate Management, a joint executive education program at the Harvard GSD and Harvard Business School. She also directs the advanced education for senior real estate executives, the Advanced Management Development Program in Real Estate at Harvard. Her publications include but not limited to the books *Prestige Retail: Design and Development*, *The Global Leadership in Real Estate and Design*, *The Architectural Profession of Modern China*, and *Nexus: Field Studies in Real Estate, Planning, and Design*. In 2016 and 2018, two of her works received the Best Manuscript Awards from the American Real Estate Society. Dr. Wang is on the Steering Committee of Harvard China Fund, on the board of the Chinese Society of Urban Studies and is a Board Director of the American Real Estate Society. She has been advising and taking executive leadership roles in multinational private organizations, national government agencies, and publicly listed real estate companies, headquartered in the USA, China, Japan, Singapore, Saudi Arabia, and the Netherlands.

Matthew Wong is a Partner and the practice leader of the China Financial Services Tax Group of PriceWaterhouseCoopers (PWC). He manages all major financial services and real estate clients in Shanghai and specializes in advising financial services and real estate sectors on China Tax and Investment. He has over 30 years of tax experience, 25 years of which is in China. The Shanghai Municipal Tax Bureau appointed Matthew as one of the members of its external supervising committee for the period 1996–1998. He chaired the tax committee of AmCham Shanghai in 2000. Matthew was voted as a top tax advisor in China in the surveys conducted by the International Tax Review in 2001 and 2002. He was also a member of International Advisory and Consultative Committee of Wuxi New District in 2006 and 2007. Matthew currently serves as Global Council Member of ACCA and Expert Panel Member of ACCA Central China. He is a committee member of the Financial Services Focus Group of British Chamber of commerce in Shanghai. He is also a member of the Chinese Institute of Certified Public Accountants (CICPA), ACCA, and HKICPA.

Haijun Xia is Vice Chairman and CEO of China Evergrande Group, a Fortune 500 company and one of the largest real estate developers in China. In this role, he is in charge of the company's overall operations and financial strategies. Since joining the company in 2007, Dr. Xia has successfully led all the company's fundraising and strategic developments, growing the company from a regional developer to a top national player with businesses in real estate development, healthcare, tourism, and financial services. China Evergrande Group is listed on the Hong Kong Stock Exchange with a market capitalization of approximately $50 billion and has over 120,000 employees today. Dr. Xia was recently awarded the Top CEO of China in the real estate industry in 2017, and currently serves as the Vice Chairman of the Chinese Real Estate Association. Dr. Xia holds an M.B.A. and a Ph.D. degree in Economics. He has over 30 years of experience in management and over 20 years of experience in real estate industry.

Joe Zhou is Executive Director, Capital Advisors Group of CBRE China. He was a regional director and the Head of Research for JLL in China before joining CBRE. He works with researchers across 13 offices in mainland China to cover the office, retail, residential, and industrial property sectors in the key Chinese cities. Joe joined JLL's Research team in 2005 and was taking a lead in the JLL's real estate research service in China: Real Estate Intelligence Service (REIS) and Logistics Intelligence Service (LIS). He has extensive experience in providing real estate advisory and consulting services to both international and Chinese developers, investors, and corporates. He is also a frequent commentator on China's real estate markets, appearing in print and broadcast media. He holds two postgraduate degrees: one is a master's degree in construction economics and management from the University College of London (UCL), while the other is a master's degree in housing from London School of Economics and Political Science (LSE).

Bing Zhu holds a Ph.D. in Real Estate Economics from the EBS Business School, Germany. Since August 2019, Dr. Zhu is a W2TT professor for Real Estate Development at the Technical University of Munich. Before that, she was a lecturer at the University of Reading and University of Cambridge in the UK, and University of Regensburg in Germany. She has published research on spatial econometrics and real estate economics in the *Journal of Banking and Finance*, *Real Estate Economics*, and the *Journal of Real Estate Finance and Economics*. She has also worked as a reviewer for several international journals, such as *Journal of Urban Economics*, *Cities*, *Real Estate Economics*, and *Journal of Real Estate Finance and Economics*. Her doctoral thesis received a grade of Summa Cum Laude and was awarded the 2011 Excellent Research Prize by German Real Estate Research Society (GIF). In 2015, one of her manuscripts received the "Thinking Out of the Box" Award from the American Real Estate Society (ARES).

Hui Zuo is Chairman of the board of Lianjia (Homelink as its English name) and Vice Chairman of Beijing Real Estate Agency Association. As a senior expert of the real estate agency industry in China, he has won the annual Leader Award and the Most Media Attention Industry Leader Award many times. Under his leadership, Homelink became the leading real estate service provider by engaging in high-quality services such as financial and capital management and acting as a real estate agent.

Understanding China's Real Estate Markets: A Brief Introduction

Bing Wang and Tobias Just

Abstract

This chapter serves as an introduction to this book. It highlights the unique context and original intentions for this book, which focuses on the transformation of China's real estate markets. It presents the book's organizational structure and briefly summarizes the content of each chapter. By looking closely at the conditions and characteristics of the various critical aspects of China's real estate markets, this book aims to establish a connection between the disciplinary knowledge and the practice of real estate while situating real estate in the context of China's overall economic outlook, its legal system, financing mechanisms, and asset-defined physical and social development patterns.

The Chinese real estate industry has acted as one of the most effective economic engines in the country, with direct effects on the political and social stability of society. It has also acted as a medium for materializing the unprecedented urbanization in the country. How can we understand the formation of China's real estate sector and its related practice in the context of the country's unique social, political, and economic forces within the confines of space and time? More importantly, how can we contemplate its future when the real estate industry is at a critical juncture, accompanying the country's slowing economic growth and dwindling urban expansion?

This volume *Understanding China's Real Estate Markets: Development, Finance and Investment* offers an examination of the complexity of China's real estate market

B. Wang (✉)
Graduate School of Design, Harvard University, Cambridge, Massachusetts, USA

T. Just (✉)
IRE|BS, University of Regensburg, Regensburg, Bavaria, Germany

© Springer Nature Switzerland AG 2021   1
B. Wang, T. Just (eds.), *Understanding China's Real Estate Markets*, Management for Professionals, https://doi.org/10.1007/978-3-030-49032-4_1

and accounts for its various aspects in development, investment, and finance from a multidisciplinary perspective, with the purpose of delineating a vista that may help explain some aspects of the "China puzzle". Given the size of the Chinese real estate market the country's economic and the complexity of its transitional nature that has led to the co-existence of many institutional structures in real estate practice, it is not an easy task to select and develop the focus of this book, which aims to facilitate a mitigation of the much-decried split between real estate disciplinary knowledge and "on-the-ground" practice.

This book situates real estate within the larger macro-context of China's unprecedented economic growth. It provides a close look at the conditions and characteristics of China's real estate market and articulates the connection marrying real estate practice and its disciplinary knowledge through the interrelationship between real estate and China's economic outlook, its legal system, financing mechanisms, and development patterns. Real estate is viewed as an investment asset, a product of the consumer market, and a typology of the physical and social embodiment.

Given the short history of its formalized existence, China's real estate market possesses certain unique qualities. This book synthesizes the present conditions and scenarios essential to the Chinese context, wherein a large quantity of real estate is developed, financed, and invested. Some characteristics of the Chinese market are particularly noteworthy. First, there is China's vast size, various geographic locations, and imbalanced regional developments that have led to many differentiated and fragmented submarkets. A total of 660 cities and towns are categorized into six different tiers based on overall real estate transaction volumes, prices, quality, and trends in residential real estate assets. Second, in China, the dichotomy of land use rights between urban and rural areas, the absence of a nationwide property tax, and the allocation of tax distribution between the central and local governments have all rendered its urbanization uniquely based on the land-financing system, which forms the country's fundamental mechanism for rapid urban growth. Third, given the role of the government in China and the absence of existing theories and practices suitable for guiding and regulating its real estate markets, experimental interventions from the Chinese government are often carried out and applied in a trial-and-error manner, which are at times conducive to the market and at other times have generated unexpected results and even backfired. Fourth, as real estate is located at the intersection between physical property and capital markets, given China's transitional nature in economic conditions, international and domestic capital markets have often had profound impacts on the developmental stages of its real estate market and corresponding performance. Although the rising middle class and less developed domestic capital markets in China have led to concentrated investments by retail investors in residential real estate, the globalization of capital market networks has impacted the flow of capital from international institutional investors to commercial real estate in major Chinese cities. Fifth, the mixed market structure reveals the pragmatism imbedded in the business and economic environment throughout China's reform era. Real estate companies take on various organizational forms, including private business, state-owned real estate development enterprises, publicly listed real estate companies on domestic or foreign stock exchanges, and even those listed simultaneously in multiple exchanges both within and outside China. Lastly, the complexity of China's real estate market often leads us to forget that real estate in China is still a young industry, with merely 40 years of history. The institutional infrastructure facilitating the development of the real estate industry is still in its infancy. A formalized real estate investment trust and real estate asset-backed securitization market are still absent and remain in the discussion stage. Many of these aspects of the Chinese real estate market are conveyed and delineated in detail in this volume.

Specifically, this book is a collection of articles from selected authors across a range of disciplines and practices. Each article has its own focus based on the author's expertise in the domain. Collectively, by linking the social, economic, legal, and physical aspects of the real estate market and industry, these articles reveal the relational characteristics of China's real estate market and form a lens to read China through the vicissitudes of its real estate sector, which is critical to the country's urbanization process, wherein unprecedented cultural, economic, and social transformations have taken place. The contributors are international and come from a spectrum of disciplinary backgrounds. Some are distinguished policymakers, scholars, and real estate professionals within China, with decades of experience, working "on the ground" so to speak, gleaning firsthand insights into and related to real estate in China. Others are located in a different country or continent, but have focused their attention on real estate and China; the distance and their comparative perspectives shape their sensibility and unique angle for interpreting the subject. Altogether, the authors' views and writings are instrumental in revealing the conditions and dynamics of real estate in China and help expand the potential for our collective knowledge of real estate and its interaction within defined institutional forms.

This book addresses four crucial aspects of real estate that the editors regard as central to understanding the Chinese real estate market. Part I, spanning from Chaps. 2 to 6, focuses on a contextual overview and macro-level examination of structural aspects of the real estate market in China. The five articles in Part I highlight the critical macro-level transformation in China's economy and its concurrent and consequential representation in the real estate market.

Bing Wang's chapter "The Evolving Real Estate Market Structure in China" delineates the overall trajectory of China's real estate sector, tracing its formation and transformative development over the past four decades from a market structure perspective. It addresses the transitional nature of the composition of market players and their strategic operational focuses when responding to various stages of the country's urbanization. Robert Ciemniak's chapter "Navigating the Property Data Landscape" defies the conventional outcry about the lack of data from China on economic performance and real estate transactions. Ciemniak argues that data have never been scarce in China; rather, an overwhelming amount of raw data is indeed available. The challenge is to apply practical and suitable methods and approaches that guide decisions when interpreting the data for gaining insights about the market.

With "China's Economy at the Crossroads," Klaus-Jurgen Gern and Philipp Hauber unfold a macro-economic outlook of the country and discuss the roots of its growth miracle as well as complications that have arisen in recent years as a result of a more challenging international environment and imbalanced growth in the domestic economy. The authors highlight the gradualism imbedded in the country's structural transformation and its global integration as the two critical institutional strategies for the country's international ascendancy. In "China's Provinces: Addressing the Discrepancies at the Local Level," Hannah Levinger and Christian Braun dissect China's development from a regional perspective and focus on the changes and challenges various provinces in China are facing as the shift to the "new normal" occurs in the economy. The authors also point out a dilemma for China's land-financed urbanization—namely, the risk of debt accumulated by the local central governments and the central government's efforts in deleveraging. Given its history and current status as a special administrative region in China, Hong Kong's land administration system and real estate market have unique characteristics. Roger Nissim's chapter provides a succinct yet comprehensive overview of the region's land and real estate-related structural and regulatory systems.

Part II of the book focuses on the legal and judicial frameworks for real estate transactions and operations in China. It covers four critical aspects of real estate investment and development operations that are most relevant to readers: the international real estate investment framework, real estate valuation methods, regulatory leasing environment, and taxation systems. In the discussion of the key legal frameworks guiding real estate development and investment in China, Qian Ma's chapter traces the historic development that established the foundation for land use rights in real estate, and the Constitution's epochal acknowledgement of protection for private property. She elaborates on the definition of property ownership, uniquely defined within China's legislative framework, and the recent legal and regulatory environment for international investments. In a subsequent chapter, "Real Estate Valuation in China," Florian Hackelberg and Nova Chan delineate detailed conditions regarding real estate valuation methods and approaches as well as standards and specifications. In addition, they lay out unique economic, regulatory, and property factors existent in the Chinese market that have rendered the real estate valuation methods at times different from those in other international contexts. Next, Karen Ip and Nanda Lau trace the specific steps taken in regulating the Chinese real estate leasing market and associated activities. Their description highlights the unified regulatory framework at the national level and points to the potential flexibility and variations at the local level. Given that real estate as an asset class derives its value from three key aspects (i.e., appreciation, cash flow, and tax benefits), the chapter by Matthew Wong categorizes the critical taxes centering on these three aspects associated with real estate investment in China and highlights the various possible investment entity structures, financing strategies, and exit channels for international real estate investments in the country based on a consideration of China's tax taxonomy.

Part III of this book collectively illustrates the various financing channels and mechanisms for real estate development and investment and provides a framework for understanding the intertwined relationship between China's capital markets and its real estate industry. "The Leverage Game: from Offshore to Onshore" provides a broad picture of financing mechanisms for real estate at both the property level and company level, highlighting the dynamics in the shifting choices between onshore and offshore funding. The discussion of perpetual bonds, trust firms, real estate investment trusts (REITs), commercial and residential mortgage-backed securities (CMBS and RMBS), peer-to-peer funding (P2P), and crowdfunding reflects the growth of relatively young capital markets experimenting the emerging financial tools for the real estate industry. Within this context and given the significance of residential real estate in China, with 68.4% of total real estate investment in the residential sector among all asset types, the subsequent article by Friedemann Roy "Housing Financing at the Crossroads: Access and Affordability in an Aging Society" delves deeper to address the role of the financial sector in balancing supply and demand for the residential real estate market.

Part III also includes articles addressing multiple formats in real estate that are engaging with capital markets, including public listings, mergers and acquisitions (M&As), real estate investment trusts, as well as real estate private equity investments. In the chapter "Listings and M&As of Chinese Real Estate Enterprises," Qingjun Jin provides detailed analyses of how real estate companies can create financing strategies via the pursuit of public listings in the domestic stock exchanges and how M&As are processed in China to enable companies to gain control through their expansion. The chapter "Scenarios of Real Estate-Backed Securitization and Financing in China" by David Chiou addresses how CMBS are introduced and repackaged in China as well as the rationales guiding some developers' choices on such mortgage-backed securities. Bing Zhu's chapter "The Development of REIT Markets in Greater China" provides an overview of the regulatory aspects of REIT markets in Greater China and highlights various performance outcomes of offshore REITs denominated by Chinese currency renminbi. Although China is still in the early stages of asset securitization, the market potential for such products could grow substantially over time. In the chapter "Real Estate Private Equity Investing in China: from a Practitioner's Perspective," Christina Gaw offers a vivid depiction of her experience and expertise gained from years of practice in private equity real estate, bridging between China's property market and the international funding mechanism. Her three case studies help illustrate approaches to and scenarios of private equity investments in China.

In the final section of the book, Part IV, real estate is depicted as a built product and an asset type imbued with economic, political, and social consequences. In the chapter "Sustainable Buildings and Practice in China," Sean Chiao and Nancy Lin chronicle the rise of green buildings and associated sustainable practice in the built environment of China. Their analyses articulate key market drivers and the continuing challenges within the milieu of contemporary real estate practice by buildings at various scales. With his manifesto "Thoughts on China's Real Estate Policies," Baoxing Qiu, the former vice minister of the Ministry of Housing and Urban-Rural Development in China, delivers recommendations for guiding regulatory principles to manage the growth of the real estate industry from a macro urban policy perspective. Qiu's advocacy is based on a legacy of experience as a policymaker and his insights into the diverse local economic conditions and scenarios. His predictions about the next phase of domestic urbanization are subsequently reflected in the implementations of real estate policies in the country.

The next three chapters discuss the physical development of real estate based on asset types, focusing primarily on residential and hospitality as the two dominant typologies in the Chinese market. In his chapter "Minding the Strategies: A Progressive Development Model," Haijun Xia, who has been leading one of the largest real estate enterprises for years, uses Evergrande Group as a case study to analyze its continually adjusted business strategies in the shifting macro market environment. Given the importance of residential real estate development in China, we extend the discussion to include Tobias Just and Hannah Levinger's article on the current state of residential markets. Michael Crawford, the former head of an international luxury hotel brand, discusses his approach in building hotels in China and the importance of striving for collaborations with local developers. Lastly, Hui Zuo, undoubtedly a leader in China's real estate brokerage industry, lays out the unique developmental path of the real estate brokerage industry in the country, using a comparative approach to differentiate the Chinese model from the brokerage prototypes in developed countries. Furthermore, he articulates his vision for and actions in constructing a platform-based cooperative network of brokerages and an information system that combines technology and real estate to nurture the often overlooked service-based subsector of the industry.

In a nutshell, this book assembles an extensive brain trust that introduces and delves into the conditions, scenarios, operations, and propositions of real estate practice in contemporary China. Critical modes of thinking and a diverse range of aspects involved in the process of real estate development, financing, and investment are addressed thematically through both analytical insights and personal accounts. As one of the first books to synthesize today's real estate praxis in China, this book highlights intentions and approaches to bridging the gap between the disciplinary knowledge of real estate and its forms of practice and institutional structure. The discussions and narratives herein reflect the transdisciplinary nature of real estate as it operates at the forefronts of financial markets, the production of spatial environments, and shifting social and cultural currents, across the globe.

Part I

Structural and Macro Economic Aspects of Real Estate in China

The Evolving Real Estate Market Structure in China

Bing Wang

Abstract

In recent decades, the real estate sector emerged as one of the key drivers of China's economic growth engine. However, limited work has sought to illustrate the evolving market structure and key players within this sector, especially from a historic perspective. This chapter provides an overview of the formational trajectory of China's real estate market structure over the past 40 years and characterizes two critical players of the industry: state-owned enterprises and publicly-listed real estate companies. The chapter highlights the complexity of the real estate market's institutional characteristics and introduces the intersection among China's urbanization, the evolving structure of its real estate sector, and the potential trajectory of critical real estate players.

1 Introduction

The uniqueness of China's real estate sector is reflected in not only the direct effects of its contribution to the country's economic growth and social stability, but also its acting as a significant medium in materializing the unprecedented urbanization process. Over the past four decades, China's real estate industry grew from being non-existent before the economic reforms to its current stage, with capital investment in real estate reaching US $1.73 trillion in 2018 and total sales of residential real estate comprising 1.6 trillion square meters in 2017 alone.[1]

---

[1] *China Statistical Yearbook 2019* and *China Statistical Yearbook 2018*, by the National Bureau of Statistics (NBS) of China. The conversion rate used was 6.9 Chinese Renminbi (RMB) to one US dollar.

B. Wang (✉)
Graduate School of Design, Harvard University, Cambridge, Massachusetts, USA

© Springer Nature Switzerland AG 2021
B. Wang, T. Just (eds.), *Understanding China's Real Estate Markets*, Management for Professionals, https://doi.org/10.1007/978-3-030-49032-4_2

Yet academic and professional publications focusing on the evolving market structure in China remain limited. Few formal accounts examine how the real estate industry initially emerged during the reform era and what constitutes the hybridity of the organizational hierarchies of real estate players in the market today. One explanation for such meager offerings in the literature could be the lack of relevant detailed records as well as the complexity embedded in the transitional nature of China's socioeconomic contexts, which have caused vagaries in the landscape of China's real estate sector during its formative stages.

As structural features of a market and its organizing mechanism help provide a better understanding of expected market productive capacities and help explain, if not directly, the dynamics among players and competitors in relation to the intrinsic characteristics of a market (Scherer and Ross 1990), this chapter focuses on the delineation of the market structure and categorization of the leading players in China's real estate industry.

This chapter consists of three sections. The first section begins with an introduction about the emergence of the Chinese real estate industry at the initial stage of the reform era, laying out the institutional background within which certain unique characteristics of the Chinese real estate market and industry formed. The second section proceeds to analyze the current dominant players in the industry, namely, state-owned enterprises and publicly listed real estate companies, the two players that largely shape the supply and orientation of the contemporary Chinese market. The last concluding section discusses the evolving business models of the real estate sector and highlights the upcoming trajectory of real estate companies.

2 Emergence of the Real Estate Sector

The formalization of China's real estate sector was a gradual process. The cornerstone of the overall economic reforms, such as the establishment of a household responsibility system[2] in the countryside and the Special Economic Zones (SEZs) in selected coastal regions in the late 1970s, formed the prerequisites for the emergence of the modern real estate industry in China. These two significant steps brought about a much larger socioeconomic reform agenda and unfolded an ideological prelude that later solidified the far-reaching potentials for commoditization in land use rights and the wide acceptance of profit sharing in society, where the land transaction market and private ownership of assets had been absent from the 1950s to the early 1980s.

Starting in the late 1970s, intensive theoretical discussions and debates emerged among intellectuals and policymakers to examine the potential measures for reforming the declining welfare housing system. The nationwide debates and

---

[2]The Household Responsibility System (HRS) was initiated in the countryside of An'Hui Province in an effort to redistribute agricultural productivity quotas to individual families instead of the communes, for profit sharing in the agriculture production system.

discussions were subsequently followed by a step-by-step enactment of state policies guiding the housing commodification. In 1987, Shenzhen, one of the salient special economic zones, became the first city to utilize the compensable offering of industrial land, converted from farmland, as the government's equity to participate in joint ventures with international investors. This method of exchanging land value to attract capital investments was soon expanded to other selected regions and formulated an unprecedented decentralization process where decisions on commercializing land were delegated to local governments at the county level (Xu and Xue 2016).

Soon after, a process of gradual privatization and decentralization through mainly trial-and-error measures at local municipal and county levels unfolded nationwide and formed some critical characteristics of China's economic reform, of which urban land reform was an important part. The commercialization of land use rights and privatization of housing were the two structural, yet parallel reforms that led to a budding real estate industry in the 1980s. Diverse players participated in a vibrant, if not tumultuous, real estate market as the country transitioned from a centrally planned economy to a market-oriented economy. Despite land ownership remaining intact, as stipulated by the Constitution, whereby urban land is owned by the State and rural land belongs to collectives in the countryside, the transformation of land use rights formed a foundation for a gradually active real estate market.

In the early 1980s, there were designated government agencies in charge of implementing the transition from a welfare housing system to the establishment of market-based channels for housing production and distribution, whereby urban residents purchased residential units that were originally allocated to them as rentals. Urban residents' acquisitions were initially subsidized by various levels of government. When expanded sources for housing capital investments were gradually widened to include contributions from individual families and work units, governmental liabilities over housing investments were largely reduced. The historic role of the state since the 1950s as a direct provider of housing started to evolve toward a process of housing privatization, wherein the state acts more as an administrator and coordinator, creating an enabling environment to guide market forces to meet various demands.

During this process, designated public agencies at various levels representing government managed a wide range of tasks involved in the transition toward housing privatization: from land acquisition, building construction and renovation, to property management and after-sales services. These government-owned agencies acted as affiliates to central ministries at the national level and to various government entities at the regional and local levels and functioned as the initial prototypes of real estate agencies in China. After 1993, when *The Company Law* was enacted, most of such agencies gradually converted to shareholding enterprises and became government-affiliated real estate companies. Thereafter, through rounds of restructuring, mergers and acquisition, as well as bankruptcy filings, etc., many such agencies eventually became either a public-private jointly-owned venture, a publicly listed company, a fully privatized non-listed company, or remained a subordinate of a state-owned enterprise (SOE), all with their dominant business in construction and real estate. Their lineages unavoidably entailed strong socialist traits.

Meanwhile, conversely, another lineage of today's real estate sector bears an imprint of a market system. In 1988, a critical amendment to the Constitution formally acknowledged the legitimate status of private enterprises, in which urban individuals were permitted to register independently to form business entities in commercial nature that were not necessarily affiliated with any state-owned enterprise or public institution (Zhang and Stough 2013).[3]

Within an increasingly liberated societal environment, privately-owned real estate enterprises started to emerge. Epitomized by Deng Xiaoping's visit to southern China in 1992, society embraced open and aggressive reform measures for economic pursuits. Shenzhen and Hai'nan played a significant role as cradles of Chinese entrepreneurship. Tracing back to the early 1980s, Shenzhen, as the first SEZ established in the reform era, attracted many young professionals and college graduates pursuing their entrepreneurial dreams. In the ensuing years, it thrived as the first city to implement the commodification of land use rights and subsequently issued mortgages for individual borrowers purchasing commercialized housing units. It was in Hai'nan, an island at the southern tip of China, with its newly gained status as a province in 1988, that those most lately formed private real estate companies with the expansiveness of cheap credits, zealously built and traded real estate and consequentially led to the first real estate bubble in 1993. This bubble soon expanded to Guangdong, Guangxi, and Fujian, the three nearby provinces along China's southeast coast. Between 1992 and 1993, the aggregated proportions of the leased yet unused land in these three provinces "were higher than those in the rest of the country" (Jiang, Chen and Isaac 1998).

As the construction bubble burst in Hai'nan, resulting in many unfinished buildings and non-performing loans filling the books of commercial banks, the involved entrepreneurs learned important lessons about the cyclic nature of real estate. This "bubble-burst" reality offered an involuntary training session for these young entrepreneurs pursuing real estate venture and imbued them the realization and initial understanding of market mechanism. Quite a few of the players in Hai'nan back then subsequently became prominent real estate developers, leading private and public real estate companies in China. It is not surprising that the three largest publicly-listed real estate companies in contemporary China—namely, Vanke, Evergrande, and Country Garden—are headquartered in Guangdong Province, where Shenzhen is located.

---

[3]There were time differences between the autonomy obtained by urban residents and that by privately owned township and village enterprises (TVE). The latter enjoyed its legalized privatization far earlier than their urban counterparts.

3 Hybridity in the Chinese Real Estate Market Structure

In 1988, with the establishment of the land leasehold system, private businesses in China were allowed to capitalize land use rights through land transfers. Ten years later, in 1998, a milestone marked the establishment of a formalized real estate market, wherein housing supply and consumption became market-driven activities without governmental financial assistance in any form (except for affordable and social housing). That being said, local governments remained the solely legalized party for land supply, that is, local governments are the only agency allowed to acquire farmland, convert them into various urban uses, and sell the use rights of converted land to development entities. Local governments' autonomy in land requisition and conversion unfolded an era of urbanization-led economic growth, whereby local fiscal revenues largely comprise land transaction earnings by and for the governments.

Subsequent economic growth led to the formation of a middle class. Their rising disposable income generated unprecedented market demand for housing. Total investments in urban fixed assets increased from 1.6 trillion renminbi in 1995 to 5.5 trillion renminbi in 2015, with an average annual growth rate reaching 19.73% over the span of twenty years.[4] From 2003 to 2015, investments in real estate development on average accounted for 26.8% of the total investments in urban fixed assets annually, reaching 28.7% in 2003 and 24.3% in 2015, which were the peak and trough respectively, during the 12-year period. In the meantime, the total completed area of construction (including both residential and commercial) on an annual basis increased from 1.46 billion square meters in 1995 to 3.55 billion square meters in 2014. With this staggering scale of construction and investment in real estate, the sector grew dramatically. The total number of employees in real estate development sector alone increased from 825,888 in 1998 to 2.7 million in 2015, a growth of 232% over a period of 17 years. The aggregated number of real estate companies increased from 24,378 to 93,426 during the same period, nearly four times that of 1998 when the market was initially formalized.[5]

Amidst this growth, China gradually transitioned from a centrally planned economy to a market economy, though with socialist characteristics (Xu 2011). Various types of business ownership developed and coexisted, forming hybridity of market structure for the real estate industry. These different ownership structures included state-owned real estate companies, privately owned domestic enterprises, quasi-public and private joint ventures, foreign-invested companies that include wholly foreign-owned enterprises (WFOEs) and joint ventures, as well as companies that had any combination of the above. In addition, since the early 1990s, with the establishment of China's capital markets, another form of ownership emerged:

---

[4]The total investments of urban fixed assets comprise investments in urban infrastructure and urban real estate.

[5]All data are from the National Bureau of Statistics of China, accessed on June 19, 2019, http://www.stats.gov.cn/english/pressrelease/201801/t20180126_1577671.html

publicly listed stock companies traded on one of the two domestic exchanges—
Shenzhen Stock Exchange and Shanghai Stock Exchange. Although the initial
intention for China's capital markets was to provide SOEs with an alternative
financing channel besides conventional bank debt, the Exchanges gradually opened
to all different types of enterprises (Zhen 2013).

Two critical players, among many, have significantly shaped the trajectory of the
Chinese real estate industry: those owned by or affiliated with various levels of
government (hereafter referred to as SOE real estate companies) and publicly listed
real estate companies on the two domestic Chinese stock exchanges.

SOE Real Estate Companies

Given the unique historical and social context, the lineage of the modern real estate
industry in China, as aforementioned, traces back to government agencies and state-
owned organizations. Hence, it is not surprising that many real estate companies in
China are owned, wholly or partially, either by central government agencies, local
municipalities or district governments, or affiliated in some manner with large-scale
government-owned enterprises. As China's economy still maintains certain
characteristics of resource planning, these SOE real estate companies often have
implicit, if not explicit, advantages in terms of access to financing channels, government subsidies, well-connected social networks, as well as a popular market perception of that they would be "too big to fail" due to their strategic importance to
China's overall economy.

As the price of land acquisition soared, so did housing prices as developers
shifted the increased cost to consumers. Especially in recent years, as many smaller
real estate enterprises were squeezed out of competition, the size and scale of these
real estate SOEs became an ever-increasing advantage. In March 2010, the State-
owned Assets Supervision and Administration Commission (SASAC) of the State
Council, in order to level the playing field and help curb soaring housing prices
caused by speculative capital investments, publicly announced that 78 central
government-controlled SOEs, whose primary business focuses were not real estate,
were banned from participating in land bidding and development upon the completion of their current real estate projects. As a result of this announcement, 16 central
government SOEs remained in the field whose dominant business were indeed in
real estate and construction (Lao 2017). In the following year, an additional five
central-government-controlled real estate companies were allowed to operate and
remain competitive in real estate. Altogether, 21 real estate companies, owned or
directly associated with central government agencies or entities, are currently major
players in the real estate sector. Measures, such as this, of adjusting the behaviors of
SOEs, often function as an extra mechanism for the central government to regulate
the real estate market, in addition to decisions on interest rates or quotas for land
supply. In a similar manner, in 2017, the SASAC announced that SOEs would no
longer be allowed to expatriate money to invest in real estate outside of China.

There are also numerous real estate companies owned and partially controlled by
various levels of government. On the one hand, they are in fierce competition for
market share and search for profitability in the same way as all other players in the

market; on the other hand, their operations reflect and are directly linked to intricate multilevel governmental hierarchies. Their advantages in competition are as evident as their disadvantages: they have access to low-cost financing and tax incentives, often possess large-scale land banking and have favorable consumer preferences. However, operational inefficiencies and a lack of performance incentives are also generated from their political affiliations. Sometimes the government's interference in operations could include requests for facilitation on tasks with administrative and social aims and intervention on executive appointments.

As contemporary China is now at a critical juncture in its economic transformation, the role of state involvement and that of the SOEs in industries, including real estate, has become a focus of many social and political debates. Given that real estate is both a commodity and a necessity of individual families, the balance between a fully market-oriented operation and government-driven intervention has been contested and pushed for a reexamination. Meanwhile, after four decades of economic reform, non-state-owned enterprises now contribute more than 60% of the total industrial production in the Chinese economy, and over 90% of Chinese employment are generated by non-state enterprises. This shift attests to the success of China's reform to a market-oriented economy in providing people's livelihood (Fung, Kummer and Shen 2006).

If SOE real estate companies are one critical player in the Chinese market, at the other end of the spectrum lie those publicly-listed stock companies that are the backbones of the real estate industry and whose transparency are demanded and regulated with efficiency by the public capital markets.

Publicly Listed Real Estate Companies
With the establishments of the Shanghai and Shenzhen stock exchanges in the early 1990s, capital markets formally emerged in China. In 1992, the State Council Office of Securitization was formed, which was soon followed by the appointment of the China Securities Regulatory Commission (CSRC) as its execution institution. The real estate company Vanke became the second publicly-listed company on the Shenzhen Stock Exchange and was soon followed by others in the industry. These subsequent listings included state-owned real estate companies as well as companies with private ownership and hybrid organizational structures.

Before the nationwide stock exchange reform in 2005, most publicly listed companies in China were SOEs. One-third of the outstanding shares of these listed companies were tradable A-shares and two-thirds were government-owned state and legal person (institutions) shares that were not legally tradable (Zhen 2013). It was not until mid-2006, as part of the implementation of the *Split Share Structure Reform*, that 94% of the listed companies in both stock exchanges, completed their conversions of non-tradable shares to legally tradable shares. Currently, the capitalization of all 3100 public companies listed on the Shenzhen and Shanghai stock exchanges exceeds 50 trillion renminbi. Among these companies, according

Fig. 1 Regional distribution of the publicly listed real estate companies in China. In this graph, the bar lengths are proportional to the number of companies represented. Source: © Author

to the categorization of real estate industry defined by the China Securities Regulatory Commission, 142 are real estate development companies.[6] Among these 142 companies, 14 are listed with both A-shares and B-shares, and 1 company has shifted from real estate to the infrastructure business only, focusing solely on bridges, tunnels and utilities. As such, there are 128 companies independently listed on the two Chinese domestic stock exchanges. Of these 128 companies, 21 are headquartered in Shanghai, 18 headquartered in Beijing, and sixteen in Shenzhen. Altogether, 43% of the real estate companies are concentrated in the three cities where economic growth has been spearheading the rest of the country for the past four decades. Figure 1 indicates the locations of the headquarters of 128 real estate stock companies publicly listed on the Shanghai and Shenzhen stock exchanges.

The dominant position of the publicly listed companies in the Chinese real estate industry is evident. By examining the top 50 publicly-listed real estate companies

---

[6]Based on the industry categorization defined by the China Securities Regulatory Commission in 2016.

based on market capitalization, while many of them possess distinct competitiveness in terms of capital operation capability and land reserve expansiveness, quite a few of them stand out as widely acknowledged market leaders of dominating a niche market with differentiated business strategies, and occupying a unique and valuable position in the sector.

4   Trajectory of Chinese Real Estate Companies

The vast scale of the Chinese real estate market, coupled with its significant contribution to the country's GDP, has prompted the need for a better understanding of the various business models of key real estate players. Chinese real estate companies, both large and small alike, have predominantly focused on capital-intensive ground-up developments. Three generalized evolving stages can be defined for the business trajectory of these companies in terms of their competing focuses and shifts when responding to overall market conditions.

The first stage spanned from 1998 to the early 2000s. The cornerstone of the competition among real estate companies was the expansiveness and scale of land reserves they possessed and their capacities to obtain land in attractive locations with desirable prices. During those years, a company's business competency was measured by its speed and efficiency in land assembly and entitlement process. Although this still largely remains the case today, the early 2000s to 2015 witnessed the subsequent second growth stage of real estate companies in China. During this stage, specialization in production process and quality of physical construction formed the competitive core. Many players expanded from a singular geographic location to a regional or even national scale. Leading companies often had projects located in more than 100 cities throughout the country. Large companies invested heavily in research and development, searching for advanced technologies to improve product marketability and construction efficiency.

Since 2015, due to declining economic growth, intensified competition, and increased regulatory control over land prices and financing channels, many real estate companies, whether SOEs or otherwise, have begun to search for alternative strategies and aimed for diversification, departing from the previous model that depended heavily on for-sale real estate production. This marked the third stage of the shifting business model. Leading real estate companies have pursued strategic diversifications, including: (1) expanding from for-sale products to include income-producing operations in order to generate long-term cash flow streams; (2) diversifying areas of expertise to include differentiated asset types and increased land reserve through mergers and acquisitions; and (3) investing in alternative high-growth business models that have less or minimal correlation with real estate cycles, such as operational tourism, technology, agricultural production and privatized sports management. All three directions demand knowledge of financial operations and skillful maneuvering within the capital markets, thereby leading to more intensified linkages between real estate and the capital markets in China's real estate industry.

Today, with many Chinese cities having developed rapidly into modernized service-oriented centers responding to market demands for high-quality office and residential as well as professionally managed retail asset types, the challenges for the next few decades for real estate companies will be focused not so much on quantitative expansion, but rather on qualitative improvement within their geographical hubs. Three main lines of future development are crucial. First, as much of the speed-driven office and residential space built in the 1980s and 1990s does not meet present market needs, significant refurbishments and replacements are called for based on the growth trajectory of macro economy and people's demands generated by increased living standards. Second, with urbanization rates still significantly lower than Western benchmarks and with coastal cities reaching their physical limits, the development of a broader and hierarchical urban network to include various tiers of cities, towns, and villages within China's macro growth trajectory is becoming imperative. Third, as coastal areas have already been developed and intensively used, the management of existing stock will increasingly afford leeway for real estate companies to specialize in and offer a more extensive set of services, focusing on lifestyle and the quality of livelihood. Improving companies' management capacities will need to precede the establishment of institutionalized investment vehicles, namely, real estate investment trust (REIT) and large-scale private equity, in alignment with international operations.

Increased sophistication of operations is expected, along with a transition to move from a development-focused real estate sector to a blended service-focused, development- and transaction-based sector. While the large real estate companies will be able to achieve specialization in wider markets, both geographically and functionally, smaller companies will have to choose a specific niche market to operate within an increasingly institutionalized context. In this sense, China's real estate markets will experience an era of specialization and dichotomization in the coming years.

In a nutshell, if the first stage of China's large-scale urbanization that occurred after 1978 prompted the emergence of an active real estate market, and the second stage of urbanization between 1998 and the early 2010s accelerated the unique formation of a hybrid real estate industry, the subsequent third stage of China's urbanization will likely prompt a real estate market that welcomes an era of quality-driven and service-focused specialization as well as a more institutionalized division among development, investment, and asset management.

References

Fung, H. G., Kummer, D., & Shen, J. J. (2006). China's privatization reforms: Progress and challenges. *The Chinese Economy, 39*(2), 5–25.

Jiang, D., Chen, J., & Isaac, D. (1998). The effect of foreign investment on the real estate industry in China. *Urban Studies, 35*(11), 2101–2110.

Lao, J. (2017). The regulations on real estate companies by SASAC had a good start, but an early withdrawal. *China Economic Weekly, 2017*(Z1), 63–65.

The National Bureau of Statistics of China. (2018). *China Statistical Yearbook 2018.* Beijing: China Statistics Press.

The National Bureau of Statistics of China. (2019). *China Statistical Yearbook 2019*. Beijing: China Statistics Press.

Scherer, F. M., & Ross, D. (1990). *Industrial market structure and economic performance* (3rd ed.). Boston: Houghton-Mifflin.

Xu, C. G. (2011). The fundamental institutions of China's reforms and development. *The Journal of Economic Literature, 49*(4), 1076–1151.

Xu, Y., & Xue, Z. F. (2016). *New land reform in Shenzhen*. Beijing: China CITIC Press.

Zhang, T., Stough, R. R., & Song, C. (2013). *Entrepreneurship and economic growth in China*. Singapore: World Scientific Publishing.

Zhen, Y. (2013). *China's capital market*. Oxford: Chandos Publishing.

Navigating the Property Data Landscape

Robert Ciemniak

Abstract

China property data, especially in the housing markets, is surprisingly rich, broadly available from both government and independent private sources, yet unstructured and highly nuanced to interpret correctly. The office, retail, industrial and niche sectors have less transparent data, mainly served by the established brokerage firms and industry associations. The increasing competition between developers in a more mature market, availability of alternative data, and China's big push for artificial intelligence all drive a growing interest in and supply of the data. This chapter provides a practical introduction to the China's property data landscape from an institutional (investor, fund manager, developer, and lender) perspective, focusing on the housing markets, in the context of decisions related to investments.

1 Property Data in China

The property data in China plays a vital role in supporting investment decisions and judgments, such as whether or when to enter and exit a market or city from a top-down perspective and in the in-depth bottom-up due diligence or market feasibility studies on potential transactions.

It may take less than 24 h from the moment a new home is sold in China, even in a lower-tier city, to when the data about the transaction gets posted publicly on a local government website. China is in a way a surprisingly transparent market with an abundance of data, especially in the housing markets—the focus of this chapter.

R. Ciemniak (✉)
Real Estate Foresight Ltd, Hong Kong SAR, China

21

B. Wang, T. Just (eds.), *Understanding China's Real Estate Markets*, Management for Professionals, https://doi.org/10.1007/978-3-030-49032-4_3

With over USD 1 trillion in annual sales each year over the 2015–2019 period,[1] the market for new home sales in China is the most sizeable and active property sector in the country. It is politically and economically sensitive as it, directly and indirectly, contributes to a substantial share of economic output (IMF 2017), can be highly leveraged, and therefore creates systemic risks, and it also shapes consumer sentiment as the home purchase remains one of the primary consumer goals. The sheer size of the sector and the need to watch it result in greater availability of the data from the central and local governments, central bank, as well as various ministries, as the housing data serves as key economic indicators. In addition, in response to the demand from developers, independent private data providers serve the market.

In contrast, the data on the commercial property sectors—office, retail, or industrial—practically comes from established domestic and foreign brokerage firms such as the well-known JLL, CBRE, Cushman & Wakefield, Savills, Colliers, or Knight Frank. They facilitate the investment or leasing transactions and capture the "data exhaust" from such transactions as well as the private market intelligence. The public disclosure in commercial real estate is very limited except for specialist sector publications by the government-related organizations, for example, the publications by the Chinese Academy of Social Sciences (CASS),[2] the specialist industry yearbooks such as China Logistics Development Report by the China Society of Logistics, and some global sector specialists such as STR in the hotel sector, with the internationally standardized metrics. This chapter discusses the data directly related to physical property, as opposed to the data representing factors that may impact the property market such as demographic, economic, or financial data.[3] However, for the commercial real estate sectors, such factor data can be an important proxy for the assessment of the conditions and the outlook for the sector in the absence of the well-grounded underlying property data, for example, the e-commerce sales and transportation data for the logistics sector, employment data for the office sector, tourism and travel statistics for the hospitality sector, or a range of retail sales data or even housing data as macro factors for the retail sector. The following sections focus on the housing markets.

2   China's Housing Market Data

The typical analysis of the China housing markets by developers and investors boils down to the assessments of the property-level data and factors that capture the dynamics of:

---

[1]Measuring the reported sales by developers of "commercialized residential" housing: RMB 7.3, 9.9, 11.0, 12.6 and 13.9 trillion for 2015, 2016, 2017, 2018, and 2019, respectively (National Bureau of Statistics of China 2020).

[2]CASS publishes regular annual "blue books" on real estate market, including the competitiveness rankings of cities (CASS 2018).

[3]Statistical analysis of the determinants of the house price growth in China has been a subject of various academic papers including Zhang et al. (2012) and Ming (2017).

- Average house prices
- Sales volumes (demand)
- Inventory and land sales (supply)

It is helpful to keep in mind the following attributes of the data, to ensure the definition remains clear and the data is used appropriately.

THE METRICS AND MEASURES—What does the data aim to capture, what exactly does it describe? To understand the demand for new homes, one might look at the growth rate of sales volumes. Sales volumes dynamics can be measured in various ways, by looking at the GFA sold in square meters, RMB transaction value, or the number of units sold, and the growth rate may be expressed as monthly year-on-year, year-to-date year-on-year, or a range of multi-month moving averages year-on-year.

THE COVERAGE—What area does the data cover? The data can refer to a geographic area (e.g., national, province, city, district, set of specific projects) or aggregates of these (e.g., Tier-2 cities, the Pearl River Delta region) or specific segment (e.g., luxury or villas) or unit sizes, e.g., 120–140 square meter units in high-rise buildings.

THE FORMAT—What raw or derived metrics are most meaningful? The data can come in a raw format, e.g., a level of available for sale GFA in a city in GFA terms, or as a derived data, e.g., months-to-clear (MTC) at a 6-month pace of sales— computed as the available for sale GFA at a point in time divided by the average monthly GFA sales volume over a 6-month period. Such MTC explains how many months it would take to clear existing inventory at the prevailing pace of sales over recent months.

THE COMPARISON—What timeframe and what point of comparison make the most sense? For example, it may make a big difference in discussing the increase in future supply from the latest land sales in China, if one looks at the land acquisitions (in construction area) by developers as a year-on-year change comparing 2017 and 2016 (+16%) vs. comparing the same 2017 figure as a change vs. the 5-year average of annual land sales (−18%).[4]

THE SOURCE—Who publishes the data and how is the raw data gathered in the first place? In China, most of the housing data is still published by the central or local governments and ministries or their related agency bodies, though there are several established private sources. What matters about the source in this context is the level of credibility and transparency as to the methods of collection and calculation of the data.

THE FREQUENCY—How often is the data updated? While it is possible to capture some "real-time" data and the daily updates to major private databases are a norm, in practice, the housing data comes out to investors at the weekly, monthly, quarterly, or annual frequency.

---

[4]Data sourced from National Bureau of Statistics (2018) and compiled and processed by Real Estate Foresight (2018).

Following that logic, an example of a fully specified data helping avoid ambiguity could be:

> To gauge the house price growth in Tier-2 cities in 2019, one can compute the average of the average growth rates for all Tier-2 cities. The growth rate for each city would be the change between the average price reported for that city for December 2019 and compared to December 2018, with the average price computed as the ratio of the total RMB value sold to the total GFA sold for the core urban districts of the city, excluding the affordable housing from the data. These two underlying monthly metrics are sourced from CREIS database.

Such precision would be ideal. In practice, though, one needs to accept a level of ambiguity in the data, as both the government and private sources rarely provide in-depth definitions of all the data features.

3   Traditional Data Sources for Housing Markets

Table 1 presents the non-exhaustive but major public (government) sources of data and the types of metrics that can be obtained from them as of early 2020.

Also, important research and some data sets are published by the government think tanks, such as the National Development and Reform Commission (NDRC) or Chinese Academy of Social Sciences (CASS), in the form of annual "blue books," "green books," and special reports. The central bank publishes a range of monthly and quarterly statistics on mortgage lending as part of the broader reports on the monetary situation. The Ministry of Housing and Urban-Rural Development and the Ministry of Land Resources determine critical policies for the housing markets and also publish related information. Locally, many cities have their own industry associations for developers that serve as platforms for exchanging detailed property information and transaction data contributed by the members but also only available to such members.

Among the private providers and aggregators of the underlying data, Beijing-based China Index Holdings[5] with its China Real Estate Index System (CREIS), is the leading independent data firm. It provides a comprehensive set of databases on cities, projects, developers, and land, available on a commercial license basis, covering over 2300 cities many with detailed project, unit, and product type level information with transaction and asking prices, volumes, and inventory data. The closest competitor to China Index Academy is Shanghai-based CRIC (China Real Estate Information Corporation),[6] a division of E-House, a major real estate brokerage firm. The two major national providers vary in their coverage by city

---

[5]More background information in English: http://chinaindexholdings.com/en/data. Since May 30, 2019, the author has been an independent director of China Index Holdings (CIH). However, any opinions or comments expressed in this article are in a personal capacity, and not on behalf of CIH.

[6]More background information in English: http://www.ehousechina.com/cric/index?name=EN

Table 1 Major public (government) sources of data

Source	Data type coverage	Maximum frequency of updates	Scope of coverage	Most useful for	comments
National Bureau of Statistics (NBS)	House prices, sales volumes, construction indicators, land sales	Monthly	National, regional, province, city	National-level data, 70 cities price indices	Most consistent but limited granularity
City Statistical Yearbooks by NBS local branches	Extensive macro, demographic, property, investment, fiscal, etc. statistics	Yearly	City and districts, counties	Longer-term city attractiveness assessment	Very rich data but published with a 1–2 year lag
Local City Housing Bureaus	Development project information, permits for sale, sales status of new homes	Daily	City and districts, counties	Local project-level analysis, monitoring of project sales	Data availability and format can vary widely by city
Local City Land Bureaus	Land sales, auctions, land supply plans information	Daily	City and districts, counties	Analysis of the land market	The format of the data and level of depth varies by city

Source: Own compilation

and data type, but both provide a range of opinion-shaping research reports and city-level indices. The underlying data is typically updated on an ongoing basis, but the main data updates and reports have a monthly and some a weekly frequency. Domestic brokerages and online property listing businesses, such as Lianjia, Fang, Anjuke, Fangdd, and Beike, also serve as rich sources of information.

Internationally, at the institutional level, the Bank for International Settlements (BIS) and the International Monetary Fund (IMF)[7] regularly research and report on the housing markets in China from a perspective of financial stability, risks, and reforms. Finally, both domestic and foreign independent research firms, investment banks, law firms, and accounting and consulting firms provide a layer of value-added analysis and reports on the market.

---

[7]Including the IMF Working Paper Understanding Residential Markets in China (2015), available at http://english.gov.cn/news/top_news/2018/02/05/content_281476037070464.htm

4   Alternative Data

As the traditional data gets increasingly commoditized and becomes broadly available (at least in the major cities), the developers look at the new types of data in their
search for a competitive advantage to better gauge the size of the demand and the
buyers' preferences.

Mobile location data, or smartphone app usage data, can be helpful in understanding the patterns of people movements in a city or a district. Used frequently in
the retail sector, it can also inform the popularity of locations and profile of the
people in the target development area for the new homes. Country Garden, one of the
largest Chinese developers, uses services from a company providing such types of
services Talking Data, according to the Talking Data website.[8] Baidu, the leading
Internet company and search engine in China, provides the live heat-map overlays
onto their maps for the mobile devices, where the color intensity corresponds to a
higher population density.[9] Search volume indices capture the online search engine
users' activity and some research shows that such data in some cities may have
predictive power for subsequent house price movements (Wu and Deng 2015; Han
et al. 2013), also demonstrated as anecdotal evidence for some cities in the 2016
up-cycle.[10] Web scraping techniques can be used to capture changes in the asking
prices on the property listings websites, providing early indicators for changes in
market sentiment. Many cities post their local newspaper content in a digitized
format online and enable programmatic mining of such text information to identify
crucial local developments before they get picked up by the national or major media
or to better gauge the local sentiment on the market.[11]

5   Data Twists, Traps, and Caveats

Certain technicalities about the China property data may make it harder to interpret
correctly for an analyst pursuing a true and fair view of the market.

---

[8]As disclosed on the website https://www.talkingdata.com/about-us.jsp?languagetype=en_us

[9]Some disclosure of the details of the data and how it is collected is available at https://baike.baidu.
com/item/%E7%99%BE%E5%BA%A6%E7%83%AD%E5%8A%9B%E5%9B%BE/3098963
(in Chinese).

[10]Can Online Searches Predict Price Hikes In China Property Markets? Forbes online article
available at https://www.forbes.com/sites/robertciemniak/2017/01/03/can-online-searches-predict-
price-hikes-in-china-property-markets/#5a00492449c1

[11]Asian investors boost use of unorthodox data sources in battle to beat benchmarks. Reuters online
article available at https://www.reuters.com/article/us-investment-asia-data-analysis/asia-investors-
boost-use-of-unorthodox-data-sources-in-battle-to-beat-benchmarks-idUSKBN17R32L

Fig. 1 The major cities' share in national new home sales in gross floor area sold. Source: analysis by Real Estate Foresight based on data from NBS

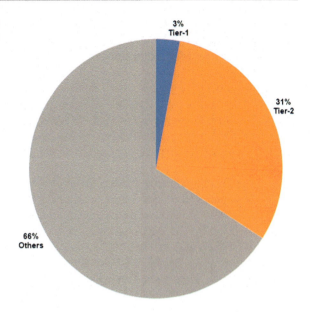

Cities Without Data

While locally the housing market data can be surprisingly rich and available (if one spends sufficient time on understanding the city), such data does not come in a format that would allow consistent comparisons or even aggregations across the cities, especially regarding the supply of housing and inventory situation. The consistent and comprehensive data, including historical data, is available for around 30–40 major cities, at best the 4 Tier-1 and 36 Tier-2 cities, though some data such as the land sales is available even for over 300 cities. Figure 1 shows that the Tier-1 and Tier-2 cities combined only make up 34 percent of the national sales volumes, leaving 66 percent as "cities without (consistent) data," as measured by the NBS data.

Therefore, trying to draw any conclusions about the overall national market based on an understanding of only, e.g., Shanghai or a group of Tier-2 cities would not be meaningful. Similarly, a great insight at a macro level may be meaningless for a specific situation in, e.g., a Tier-2 city like Ningbo. To analyze a market in a smaller city outside of the major 70–100 cities, one needs to rely more on local sources and on-the-ground research, while the Statistical Yearbooks and local housing and land bureaus and local media may also provide useful information.

To-Date or Not to-Date

Major government statistics related to property, such as monthly new home sales, fixed asset investment, or land acquisitions by developers, are in China published at source primarily on a year-to-date year-on-year basis (YTD Y/Y), a different practice from, e.g., the USA where the similar data would be presented on an annualized and seasonally adjusted basis.[12] Compared to a monthly year-on-year (Y/Y) calculation, YTD Y/Y gives a fairer picture for the full year as it unfolds but also downplays the information value of the latest months' data, especially toward the end of the year.

Practical experience suggests that a robust approach would include decumulating the YTD data and then calculating a range of rolling averages, for example, a 12-month rolling moving average year-on-year (12MMA Y/Y) for a longer-term view or a 3MMA Y/Y for a shorter perspective, though the specific decision context should still determine what the right metric for the job is.

The Spring Festival and the Golden Week

During the Chinese New Year (or the Spring Festival) period, the new sales tend to be extremely low, where most people spend time dining with families or traveling across the country. The data challenge comes from the fact that each year the Chinese New Year holiday break falls on different dates, for example, February 16–25 in 2018 versus January 28–February 5 in 2017. Any Y/Y calculations might get distorted through the base effect in the weeks surrounding this period. In contrast, the Golden Week of the National Day Holiday typically shows the seasonally higher new home sales every year. It falls on the first week of October but the actual holiday period may vary from year to year. How should the data be adjusted for these differences in the weekly or monthly data? One approach is to set the week of the New Year (or Golden Week) as Week 0 and refer to the surrounding weeks as Week −1, Week +1, etc. and make Y/Y computations on that basis rather than the calendar days.

Dealing with the City Boundaries

With China's urbanization level at 60.6% (2019),[13] many cities are in a constant development and expansion mode. This means new districts are being created, the meaning of "city core area" may embrace greater suburbs, or a county-level city may be administratively brought in as a district of the prefecture-level city, changing its status. The property data such as average house prices or new home sales do not normally get adjusted backward (as one would do with some financial markets indices). Chengdu in 2017 provides a good illustration. A seemingly clear decline in average house prices for the core city area was, in fact, the result of including six additional districts into the "core." As the prices further away from the city center are normally lower, the six new districts effectively brought down the new average price for the new core, and without adjusting the base of the prior year, the new average would be even lower than the year earlier, resulting in the headline-level Y/Y

[12] For example, see the data release on new residential sales by the US Census Bureau: https://www.census.gov/construction/nrs/pdf/newressales.pdf

[13] According to Xinhua news agency quoting data from National Bureau of Statistics: http://www.xinhuanet.com/english/2020-01/19/c_138718450.htm

price drop. In practice, this means a thorough understanding of the local city boundaries and major changes is needed to draw accurate insights from the data.

When the Music Stops

Revisions to how major economic indicators are calculated and published are common across all countries, but in a rapidly developing China, such changes can be significant. For example, the widely watched index of 70 major cities in China published by the NBS was discontinued from 2011, on NBS's own concerns about whether the index was reflective of the reality on the ground. For the individual 70 cities, the NBS changed the underlying data from developer-reported data to registered transaction data. Reuters, Bloomberg, The Wall Street Journal, etc. followed with their calculations to maintain some aggregate 70-cities measure to report on. After November 2016, at the peak of the market cycle, Fang (SouFun), the major private source of house price indices, stopped publishing their widely watched indices for 100 cities, citing concerns about the selective use of data by the Chinese media, influencing consumers without providing full context, according to The Wall Street Journal article.[14] Avoiding the overreliance on one single source of data can help to some degree remedy such situations. For analysts deeply involved in the market, coming up with their own internal-use-only "indices" based on raw underlying data could also be a viable solution.

6   House Price Indices

House price indices tend to be the single most important measures of the property markets, and when a US analyst tries to gauge the China house prices, the natural question emerges, "Is there a Case-Shiller-like index in China?".[15] The short answer is no, and the reasons behind it are very illuminating for the fundamental differences between the housing markets in the two countries.

The US new home sales market is dominated by the single-family homes, whereas China is all about the condo sales (if we put it in US terms, putting aside the technicalities of ownership vs. leasehold). The USA has a substantial secondary home sales market, while in China, except for some major cities, the vast majority of transactions take place in the primary market. The USA has a well-developed multifamily or apartment sector, whereas, in China, the big reforms pushing for the development of the rental housing only really began in 2017. As a result, the repeat-sales index for single-family homes viable in the USA may be hard to replicate in a meaningful way consistently across China. Instead, focusing on the

---

[14] Available at https://www.wsj.com/articles/chinas-property-market-has-a-new-blind-spot-1487065745

[15] The full name of this index series for the US house prices is S&P CoreLogic Case-Shiller Home Price Indices, for details see https://us.spindices.com/index-family/real-estate/sp-corelogic-case-shiller

price dynamics of the newly built "condos" covers the most significant parts of the market currently in China.

7   House Price Data in Action

Of all the metrics for the housing markets, the measures of the house price growth remain the most important data points for China markets as not only do they capture the market dynamics but also tend to be a trigger for policy shifts between the policy tightening and easing, as the policy makers respond to the overall price movements. Figures 2, 3, 4, 5, 6, and 7 below demonstrate the richness of the data for the major cities and the types of analysis for institutional investors as well as the historical cyclicality of the market.

The house price indices from NBS or from CREIS help gauge where the overall market (70 or 100 major cities) is in the cycle, looking at the Y/Y and M/M monthly changes in the relevant indices. The breakdown by tier and by region helps understand the key drivers of the overall growth. Drilling further into the city-level data uncovers the more detailed patterns and how the individual cities move through their cycles.

Data visualization can be helpful in understanding the China house price growth patterns over time. Each row in Fig. 6 represents one of the 70 major cities and each column 1 month from January 2011 to May 2020, for the total of 7910 data points

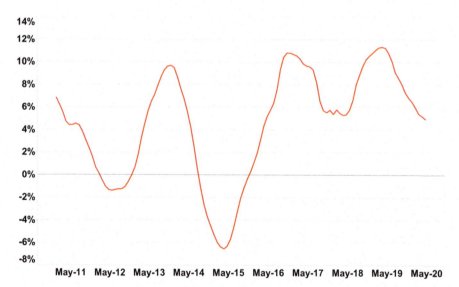

Fig. 2 Y/Y house price growth and M/M house price growth (right). Average for 70 cities. Source: analysis by Real Estate Foresight based on data from NBS

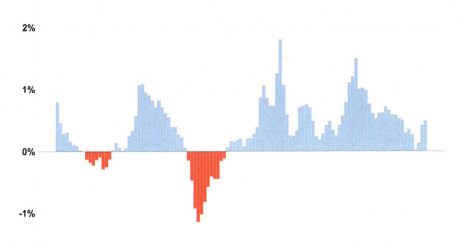

Fig. 3 M/M house price growth. Average for 70 cities. Source: analysis by Real Estate Foresight based on data from NBS

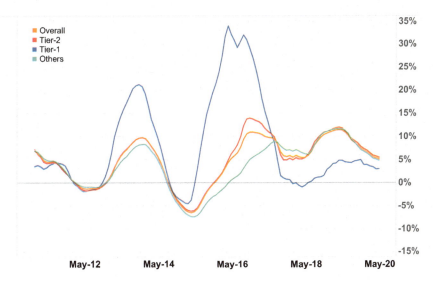

Fig. 4 Y/Y house price growth by tier. Source: analysis by Real Estate Foresight based on data from NBS

where each data point is a year-on-year change in the NBS house price index for the given city and month. The green color represents a positive and red a negative growth, with the color-coding applied across all the data points.

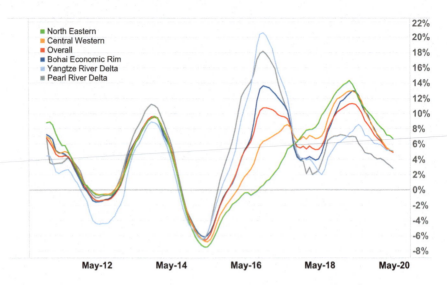

Fig. 5 Y/Y house price growth by region. Source: analysis by Real Estate Foresight based on data from NBS

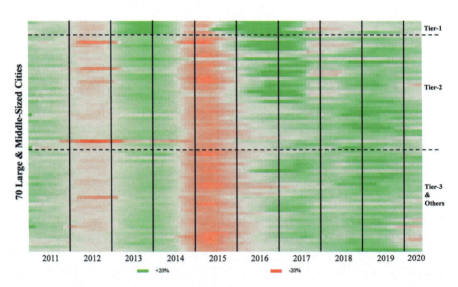

Fig. 6 House price growth patterns January 2011–May 2020, monthly Y/Y price growth for 70 major cities. Source: analysis by Real Estate Foresight based on data from NBS

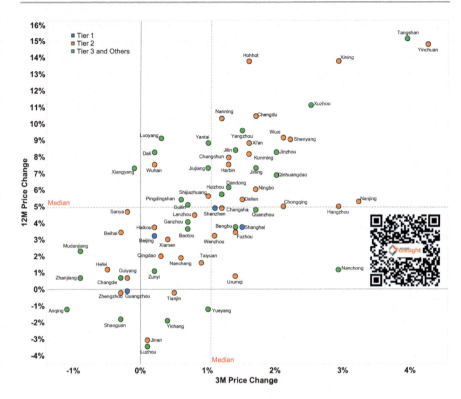

Fig. 7 Y/Y vs. 3-month price growth by city, data for May 2020. Source: analysis by Real Estate Foresight based on data from NBS. Scan the QR code to watch the animation of the monthly house price movements for 70 major cities on a map from January 2012 to May 2020

8   Why Data Will Be Key to Success

The nature of competition between property developers in China is changing. A combination of high land prices, the limited supply of land and tighter policing of the development practices, and the more discerning and knowledgeable buyers (increasingly upgraders) lead to a requirement for the finer assessment of specific development opportunities and the product design. Data that helps developers better gauge what the right product mix should be, the timing of the launch, realistic price, or sales velocity can become a source of competitive advantage. This contrasts with the prevailing reality in China over many years, where securing a piece of land in a sensible location would itself guarantee sufficiently attractive, even if not maximized, profits.

In addition to China's already rich property-related data landscape, the country's quest for dominance in artificial intelligence (AI) is likely to produce large volumes of new data sets as the side effect, be it related to self-driving cars, drone-collected images, smart cities, or people movement monitoring with facial recognition and mobile phone data. In December 2017, the Ministry of Industry and Information Technology of China released the 3-year action plan to develop the AI industries in China over the period 2018–2020,[16] following the earlier stated goals of rapid development of AI. Such data, if commercially available, could significantly enhance the speed and ways in which the developers assess the land or project acquisition opportunities and how they understand what the buyers ultimately want.

References

CASS. (2018). Major publications list. Retrieved March 12, 2018 from http://casseng.cssn.cn/research/research_publications/research_reports/

Han, S., Wang, P., & Wang, B. (2013). A study on correlation between web search data and housing price evidence from Beijing and Xi'an in China. In *2nd International conference on science and social research (ICSSR 2013)*. Retrieved March 12, 2018 from https://www.atlantis-press.com/proceedings/icssr-13/7788

IMF. (2017). People's Republic of China. *IMF country report no. 17/248*. Retrieved March 12, 2018 from https://www.imf.org/~/media/Files/Publications/CR/2017/cr17248.ashx

Ming, Q. (2017). The determinants of Chinese property prices. *International Journal of Economics and Finance, 9*(1), 194–201.

National Bureau of Statistics of China. (2020). Data sourced from http://data.stats.gov.cn/english/easyquery.htm?cn=A01

Wu, J., & Deng, Y. (2015). Intercity information diffusion and Price discovery in housing markets: Evidence from Google searches. *The Journal of Real Estate Finance and Economics, 50*(3), 289–306.

Zhang, Y., Xiuping, H., & Liang, Z. (2012). Exploring determinants of housing prices: A case study of Chinese experience in 1999–2010. *Economic Modelling, 29*(6), 2349–2361.

---

[16]The announcement was widely covered by the media and industry magazines, including https://www.technologyreview.com/the-download/609791/china-has-a-new-three-year-plan-to-rule-ai/

China's Economy at the Crossroads

Klaus-Jürgen Gern and Philipp Hauber

Abstract

The Chinese economy has experienced impressive growth since the late 1970s, driven by ongoing market-based reforms as well as integration into the world economy. However, growth has been biased toward the industrial sector, investment, and exports. The recent buildup of private sector debt, rising inequality, and increasing environmental problems are casting shadows over the economic outlook. The chapter discusses the roots of the growth miracle as well as complications that have arisen in recent years as a result of a more challenging international environment, imbalanced growth in the domestic economy, and limited appetite to implement further liberalization.

1 Introduction

China's economic growth stands out for both its speed and duration: over a period of more than 30 years, from 1978 to 2010, real GDP growth averaged 10% per annum; over the same period, GDP per capita relative to the USA climbed from 5% to over 25%. While growth has moderated somewhat more recently, to around 7%, it is still impressive by international standards. Over the past decades, China has turned from one of the poorest countries to the largest economy in the world, today accounting for more than 18.5% of world GDP at purchasing power parities (the share is slightly less at market exchange rates)[1] and roughly one third of global growth in the years

---

[1]Valuation of GDP at purchasing power parities is typically used in international comparisons and aggregation of GDP and adjusts for the different levels of prices between countries. Because of a lower level of prices (of non-tradables in particular), real GDP in developing countries is typically

K.-J. Gern (✉) · P. Hauber
Institut für Weltwirtschaft, Kiel, Germany

© Springer Nature Switzerland AG 2021   35
B. Wang, T. Just (eds.), *Understanding China's Real Estate Markets*, Management
for Professionals, https://doi.org/10.1007/978-3-030-49032-4_4

after the global financial crisis. This chapter briefly discusses the causes of China's economic ascent, focusing on the role of market reforms in the late 1970s and the ensuing structural transformation (Sect. 2). Section 2 focuses on the integration into global markets and supply chains. More recent macroeconomic developments are treated in Sect. 3, starting with the first official acknowledgment of imbalances in the Chinese growth model to China's response to the global financial crisis as well as the current attempts to "rebalance" the Chinese economy toward a more sustainable growth path. We proceed with projections of medium-term growth (Sect. 4) and discuss risks to the outlook—in particular the rapid buildup of private sector debt in Sect. 4.1—before we conclude.

2   China's Structural Transformation and Global Integration

Prior to Deng Xiaoping's reforms in 1978, China was a planned economy effectively shut off from global markets. Virtually all prices were set by the state with little or no role for market forces. State-owned enterprises accounted for nearly three quarters of industrial output and employment; agricultural production was largely collectivized. Initial reforms focused on the primary sector, ending collectivization and allowing farmers to sell surplus product on the market. This led to rapid gains in productivity and freed up labor to reallocate to other sectors: total factor productivity—the growth in output that cannot be accounted for by increases in the factors of production such as capital or labor—in the agricultural sector grew by over 6% per year between 1978 and 1984; over the same period, the share of the labor force employed in agriculture dropped rapidly from nearly 70 to just above 50%, while at the same time per capita agricultural production and consumption levels increased (Zhu 2012). In the words of Young (2003, p. 1260): "Along with rising participation rates, educational attainment and capital investment, the transfer of labor out of agriculture, whether driven by productivity growth in that sector or the equalization of labor's marginal product with other sectors of the economy, has played a [. . .] significant role in fueling the growth of the People's Republic."

The steep rise in productivity in agriculture and relocation of labor from the farms was key to the rapid growth of the Chinese economy in the early years. However, as the economy grew and agriculture accounted for a smaller and smaller share of output (Fig. 1), additional boosts to productivity had to come from elsewhere.

State-owned enterprises (SOEs) and the underdeveloped private sector were natural candidates. Reforms allowed free entry into previously sealed-off industries with the associated increase in competition and the decentralization of investment decisions in state-owned firms. This was instrumental in achieving further improvements in resource allocation, shifting resources to the growing light-industry, export-oriented manufacturing sector. Brandt and Zhu (2010) argue that

---

inflated relative to real GDP in advanced economies compared to a conversion of GDP into a common currency (usually the US dollar) at market exchange rates.

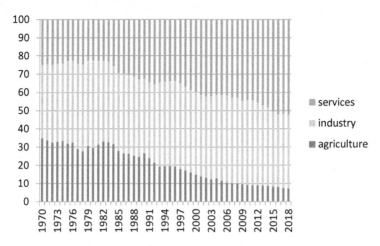

Fig. 1 Gross value added by sectors (percent). Source: World Bank World Development Indicators (WDI)

more than anything else the reallocation of labor and capital from the non-agricultural state to the non-agricultural non-state sector can explain China's rapid productivity growth. Based on counterfactual simulations from a three-sector model, they conclude that virtually all the gains in total factor productivity that accrued outside of the primary sector can be attributed to the non-state sector and half of the increase in overall labor productivity was accounted for by firms outside of the state sector.

As revolutionary as the transformation of the Chinese economy may appear in hindsight, it is important to note that China did not liberalize its economy in one step with a big bang but rather followed an approach of evolutionary reform implementing market elements gradually. For example, similar to the reforms in the agricultural sector, official prices and production quotas for SOEs were not abandoned from one day to another but initially replaced by the so-called dual-track system where only inputs and outputs over and beyond these quotas were allowed to be traded at market prices. Special economic zones were set up allowing policy makers to introduce liberalization measures such as first on a small scale before extending them to the wider economy. "Trial and error" was an important component in Chinese economic policy in the reform process (McMillan and Naughton 1992).

Despite the gradualist approach to economic reforms, the transition from a planned, centralized, to a competitive market economy progressed swiftly as judged by the share of prices determined by market forces. While government interference into the price mechanism was virtually omnipresent on the eve of reforms in 1978,

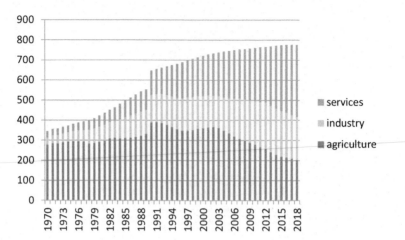

Fig. 2 Employment by sector (millions). Source: Chinese Ministry of Human Resources and Social Security

roughly 70% of consumer goods transactions involved market-determined prices by 1991 (Lardy 2014).[2]

The gradual but steady increase of the role of market forces in the economy was the decisive factor driving improvements in resource allocation as well as sectoral transformation and can hardly be overestimated when accounting for China's stellar growth experience. After the reforms, per capita GDP growth more than doubled; total factor productivity, which on average contracted by 1% per year in the three decades prior to the reforms, grew by 3% per annum. The structural transformation of the Chinese economy was also reflected in a rapid urbanization and in changing employment patterns. In the 1970s, as much as 80% of the population lived in rural areas and the same percentage of the labor force was employed in agriculture. By 2018, the share of rural population had dropped to below 50% and the share of agriculture in total employment declined consistently to around 25%, although employment in agriculture in absolute terms started to fall significantly only in the 2000s (Fig. 2).

In the first two decades of the economic transformation, price developments were quite volatile, with spikes of inflation in the end of the 1980s and in the mid-1990s (Fig. 3). Inflation moderated substantially after the peak of consumer price inflation at 24% in 1994, which in part had been a response to a drastic one-off devaluation of the Chinese currency as Chinese policy makers aligned official and black market exchange rates. Since 1997, consumer price inflation has been remarkably stable, at 1.9% on average and with limited fluctuations from year to year that were to a large

---

[2]The share for agricultural and producer goods was, however, considerably lower (55 and 45%, respectively). By 2003, however, most prices were market-determined. Notable exceptions include the price of water, electricity and other utilities, interest rates, and natural gas, crude oil, as well as refined oil products.

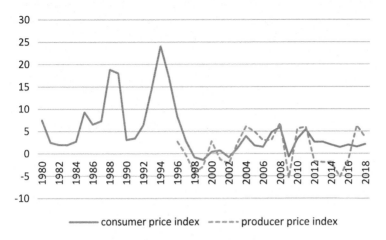

Fig. 3 Price dynamics in China 1980–2015 (change over previous year percent). Source: National Bureau of Statistics

extent driven by transitory developments in food prices. Producer price inflation has followed a very similar path until 2012 when prices at the factory level temporarily moved into deflationary territory due to a combination of lower commodity prices and excess capacities in basic industries such as coal, cement, and steel production.

Another important element of Deng Xiaoping's economic program of "reform and opening up" was the integration of China into global markets. Similar to the introduction of market reforms, trade liberalization was a gradual process: average tariffs which stood at a 50% on average in 1980 still exceeded 30% in the early 1990s before falling sharply in 1996 and yet again after 2001, when China joined the World Trade Organization (WTO). In 2014 the average tariff applied to goods was 7.5%. As a result of this gradualism, in the first 20 years of the transformation, Chinese exports actually grew at lower rates than those seen during the industrialization and global integration of other Asian economies such as Japan, Korea, or the "tiger" economies of South East Asia (Rumbaugh and Blancher 2004). The share of China in total world trade nevertheless rose steadily from less than 1% in 1980 to 4% in 2000. The process of integration into the global economy really took off, however, following China's accession to the WTO in December 2001. By 2015 the share of China in global trade has reached 10% for imports and even 13.5% for exports, according to IMF figures (Fig. 4).

Over the course of three decades, China has thus turned from an economy almost completely separated from the rest of the world into a manufacturing and exporting hub for the global economy and by 2009 had surpassed both the US and German economy as the world's largest exporter. With the economy maturing, the momentum of trade growth has, however, slowed down during the past decade. In the past couple of years, the share of Chinese exports in world total has even decreased. The share of exports and imports in Chinese GDP peaked already in 2006, reflecting the growing size of the domestic economy and a rising share of the service sector.

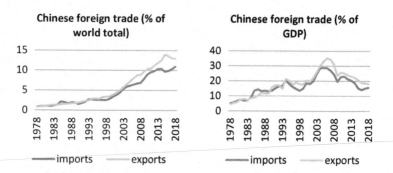

Fig. 4 Development of Chinese trade. Source: International Monetary Fund Direction of Trade Statistics, International Financial Statistics

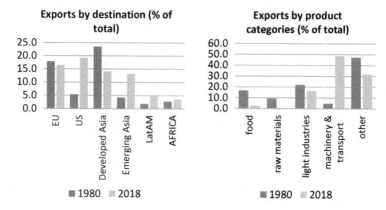

Fig. 5 Chinese exports by destination and product categories. Source: China Customs, International Monetary Fund Direction of Trade Statistics

There were also substantial qualitative changes in China's foreign trade over time—both in terms of exports products and destinations. In line with China's comparative advantage—an abundance of cheap and unskilled labor—exports were initially concentrated in low-skill sectors such as textiles and toys. These light industries accounted for nearly 20% of exports in 1980 (Fig. 5). Exports of primary goods were also important with food commodities accounting for 15% of exports and raw materials for another 10%. In 1980, imports were distributed relatively evenly across product categories, with imports of machinery and equipment representing the largest share. This presumably linked to China's undergoing industrialization and its reliance on the import of capital goods from developed countries such as the USA, Japan, or the EU. Imports of food and raw materials together accounted for over 30% of total imports. By 2018, the picture had changed quite drastically: exports of raw materials have become negligible, while imports of raw materials still account for a substantial share (and have strongly risen in absolute terms).

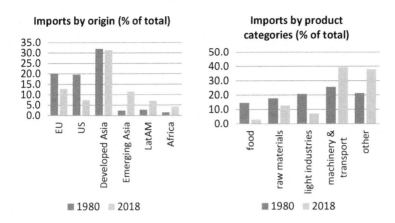

Fig. 6 Chinese imports by origin and by product categories. Source: China Customs, International Monetary Fund *Direction of Trade Statistics*

At the same time, the importance of machinery and transport equipment has increased even further now accounting for nearly 50% of total exports (Fig. 6). These figures seem to suggest that Chinese exports have graduated on to more skill-intensive sectors such as electronics and machinery equipment. However, Amiti and Freund (2010) point at the fact that a lot of the export activity in manufacturing merely consists of assembling imported intermediate inputs, i.e., export processing. Looking only at non-processing manufacturing exports, they find little change in the skill content of Chinese exports over the period from 1992 to 2005. The importance of global value chains and re-exporting in understanding Chinese trade patterns is also made apparent by the large rise in the share of imports from these sectors (40%). Koopman et al. (2012) note that, while the share of domestic content in Chinese exports rose between 2002 and 2007, sophisticated industries such as electronics and telecommunications equipment are those industries with a particularly high foreign value-added component.

However, rising investment in research and development over the past years as well as a larger human capital stock have led China to catch up to advanced economies in terms of product sophistication (Deutsche Bundesbank 2018). China's ambitions to close the technological gap are reflected in the "Made in China 2025" industrial strategy, which aims to make China the world's leading manufacturer by 2045 in a range of sectors, ranging from robotics to the production of ships and airplanes as well artificial intelligence.

Geographically, these developments are reflected in growing trade shares with Western consumer markets, particularly in the USA. While exports to the USA accounted for a mere 5% of total exports in 1980, by 2018, the figure had increased nearly fourfold to close to 20%. At the same time, China's role in global manufacturing chains led to an intensification of regional trade in Asia. China's imports from developed economies in Asia such as Japan, South Korea, or Taiwan accounted for over 30% of total imports in 2018; those from emerging Asian economies, e.g., Indonesia and Malaysia, increased to more than 10% over the period of 1980–2018. The increase in Chinese imports from emerging and developing economies in Africa or Latin America largely reflects rising Chinese demand for raw materials.

Over the past few years, a frequent claim has been that China's stunning export growth was fueled by an undervalued exchange rate. Indeed, Cline and Williamson (2009) survey a range of studies and find that in real effective terms the undervaluation of the renminbi was on average close to 20% between 2000 and 2007. Only one estimate found the renminbi to be close to its fair value over this period. Notwithstanding the considerable uncertainty embedded in estimates of real equilibrium exchange rates, it seems safe to say that the renminbi was undervalued for a considerable period of time.

What is less clear is how important an undervalued exchange rate was in boosting Chinese exports. Rodrik (2008) argues that a real undervaluation is a significant feature of the so-called export-led growth in low-to-medium income countries as it compensates for market failures or institutional deficiencies in the tradable sector typical of developing economies. In the case of China, however, a substantial part of any gains from an undervalued exchange rate would have been offset by higher import prices owing to central role of importing and reprocessing intermediate goods in China's growth model. There is also evidence that the division of labor in global value chains, which is at the heart of the rise of China to a global trade goliath, is the reason why manufacturing exports have become less sensitive over time—particularly since the early 2000s—to changes in the real exchange rate (Ahmed et al. 2015). While these studies suggest that the role of an undervalued exchange rate might be overstated, empirical evidence from previous episodes of renminbi appreciation indicates that there is still some role for the exchange rate in explaining Chinese trade as a stronger currency tends to depress demand for final goods exported from China (Eichengreen and Tong 2015).

Lastly, foreign direct investment (FDI) played an extremely important role in explaining the rapid growth of the Chinese economy and particularly Chinese exports. Between 2000 and 2010, foreign-invested firms were responsible for over half of Chinese goods exports. Foreign firms bridged the technological gap while also creating managerial spillovers to Chinese firms. Virtually absent up until 1980, FDI inflows peaked in the mid-1990s relative to GDP at close to 6%. Inflows have moderated since in relative terms but remained elevated in absolute numbers and continue to be crucial to China's exports. More recently, as the Chinese economy is catching up to the technological frontier, Chinese firms themselves are looking abroad for investment opportunities: according to World Bank data, outward FDI in relation to GDP have been on a steady upward trajectory in the past few years, though still falling short of inflows which reached 1.5% of GDP in 2018.

China's reintegration into the world economy has reached another stage with the Belt and Road Initiative, a combination of existing and new infrastructure projects in over 50 countries aimed at fostering trade and growth. While the Initiative is arguably motivated in part by geopolitical considerations, it will serve to further intensify China's economic ties with the rest of the world.

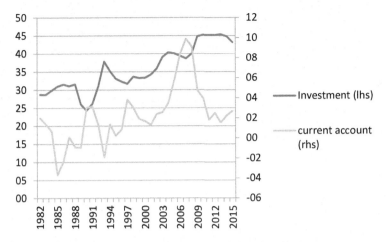

Fig. 7 Investment and current account balance as a share of GDP. Source: International Monetary Fund *World Economic Outlook Database*, October 2016

---

3   Recent Developments

Notwithstanding China's impressive growth performance in the past decades, there were increasing concerns about the long-run viability of its growth model. In a now famous speech, given at the National People's Congress in 2007, former Prime Minister Wen Jiabao described the Chinese economy in remarkable clarity as "unsteady, imbalanced, uncoordinated, and unsustainable."[3] Specifically, he was referring to China's overreliance on investment and exports as "engines of growth": investment as a share of GDP averaged close to 40% over the period of 1990–2007, while the current account balance had steadily risen since 2001 and was the world's largest in 2007, amounting to 10% of GDP (Fig. 7). On the production side of the economy, these imbalances manifested themselves in an extremely large industrial sector accounting for nearly half of GDP and a relatively underdeveloped services sector.

Per se, such developments do not necessarily constitute imbalances, however. For a country like China, in which capital is relatively scarce, high rates of investment make economic sense.[4] Indeed, massive capital accumulation played a key role also in the economic development of the other Asian miracle economies such as Hong Kong, Taiwan, Singapore, or Korea (Young 1995). Current account surpluses, i.e., higher domestic savings than investment, are more difficult to reconcile with

---

[3]Quote from Lardy (2012, p. 1).

[4]See Batson and Zhang (2011) for a comparison of China's capital stock compared to other countries at different stages of development. They conclude that in per capita terms, China's capital stock is still low compared to the advanced economies.

economic fundamentals, however, given that countries with less capital per worker should in theory be net capital importers not exporters. Lardy (2012) identifies two key distortions that were responsible for the overreliance on exports and investment and lead him to consider the Chinese growth model as imbalanced.

Firstly, an undervalued exchange rate boosted profits in the tradable (manufacturing) sector relative to the non-tradable (service) sector, channeling investment into the manufacturing sector, and at the same time depressed household's disposable income and private consumption. Secondly, prices of key production factors such as capital, land, and energy were largely determined not by market forces but rather by state policy. By setting these prices too low, the tradable sector, which uses these inputs more intensively than the non-tradable sector, is in effect subsidized, giving rise to a distorted production structure and an overreliance on investment and exports.[5] Other developments fueling political concern about the feasibility of the growth strategy were a rise in income inequality—according to World Bank estimates, the Gini coefficient increased from 0.3 in 1990 to 0.43 in 2005, a serious process of environmental degradation and widespread corruption. Policy makers increasingly acknowledged that in order to escape the infamous middle-income trap and join the ranks of advanced economies, adjustments to the prevailing growth model would be necessary.

3.1 China's Response to the Global Financial Crisis

In 2008, the world economy experienced the sharpest downturn since the Great Depression. Global growth had started to slow early on in the year, but it wasn't until after the bankruptcy of the American investment bank Lehman Brothers and the subsequent collapse of the interbank credit and money markets that the cyclical downswing turned into a full-blown financial crisis. Like most emerging economies, China's direct exposure to US subprime mortgage-backed securities was limited. However, the Chinese economy was also severely hit by the shock to global activity and the drastic fall in world trade. Faced with a sharp contraction in external demand, exports plummeted, while industrial production—hitherto expanding by around 15% year-on-year—recorded unprecedented low growth of just above 5%. Overall economic activity as measured by GDP reached its trough in the first quarter of 2009 expanding by just 6.2% on a year-on-year basis, less than half the rate reported for the fourth quarter of 2007 (13.9%). As drastic and sudden as the collapse in activity was, it also proved to be rather short-lived. Growth in GDP and industrial production returned to double digits already in the course of 2009; nominal exports continued to fall—on a year-on-year basis—but bounced back at the end of the year. The drop in consumer prices that followed the weakening of demand was more persistent: CPI

---

[5]With respect to the current account imbalance, he notes that the rise in savings relative to investment was a phenomenon occurring across all sectors—households, firms, and government—of the economy.

inflation had averaged 6% in 2008—partly due to rising commodity prices (especially food prices) at the start of the year—but stayed in deflationary territory for most of 2009.

The quick rebound from the global financial crisis was in large part due to an aggressive policy response by the Chinese authorities. Monetary policy, after successive tightening in response to frothy real estate markets, was reversed: the central bank cut its lending rate and lowered reserve requirement ratios to historical lows. More significant in stabilizing output, however, was a fiscal stimulus program announced in November 2008 totaling 4 trillion yuan, or roughly 13% of 2008 GDP, to be implemented over the following 2 years, a large share of which was designated for investment in infrastructure. Only about a quarter of the program was financed by the central government budget directly. Shih (2010) estimates that the actual amount of stimulus was far greater than that: according to his calculations, local governments raised off-balance sheet debt via local investment companies to finance additional investment projects bringing the total stimulus to above 11 trillion yuan. This explains the fact that while Chinese general government debt as a percentage of GDP hardly increased during the crisis, private sector debt ballooned: domestic credit to nonfinancial corporations had increased by nearly 30% of GDP by the end of 2010; corporate bond credit—though far less important in absolute terms—also more than doubled in 2009 and 2010. Issuance of offshore bonds, in particular in sectors such as real estate and mining, saw a sharp increase with firms taking advantage of low interest rates in advanced economies to fund activities back home (Chivakul and Lam 2015). These developments were mirrored in soaring fixed asset investment which saw average growth rates of over 30% in 2009 with the bulk of expansion concentrated in the heavy-industry sectors.

On the whole, China's response to the global financial crisis was widely judged as having been successful in containing the direct economic fallout from the global recession.[6] Some observers, however, emphasized the risks of rising overcapacities in heavy industries and the large expansion of private sector debt, both of which could contribute to financial instability and inefficient factor allocation (European Chamber of Commerce 2009). Furthermore, the fiscal stimulus exacerbated China's overreliance on investment, making the transition toward a more consumption-based and services-oriented economy more difficult (Pettis 2010).

3.2   Rebalancing the Economy

While the collapse in world trade and the subsequent weak recovery in advanced economies reduced the role of exports for China's growth performance, the enormous fiscal and monetary stimulus by the Chinese authorities—though successful in stabilizing growth—only aggravated the imbalances because of the heavy reliance

---

[6]See Lardy (2012) and Fardoust et al. (2012) for overall positive assessments of China's stimulus measures.

on investment to stimulate growth.[7] Policy makers were well aware of this. The 12th Five-Year Plan, approved in 2011, envisioned lower growth targets for GDP (7% per annum) and set out a number of other targets to address economic, social, and environmental imbalances. For example, the plan stipulated that the growth contribution from services to GDP should rise to 47% (from 44% in 2010). Furthermore, it set limits on the emission of greenhouse gases. It also identified seven priority industries including green energy and high-tech IT whose contribution to GDP should be increased from 2 to 8%. Spending on research and development should increase to 2.2% of GDP. As such, the National People's Congress interpreted rebalancing as leading to lower but more inclusive and qualitatively higher growth.

These goals were supplemented by the Third Plenum of the National People's Congress in 2013 which included reform proposals for more than 60 areas ranging from state-owned enterprises to the hukou system and the one-child policy. The most exciting detail probably was the statement that markets were to play a "decisive" role in resource allocation, indicating a liberalization of sectors still dominated by state-owned enterprises and more market-determined prices of water, transport, telecommunications, electricity, and oil. Far-reaching reforms to financial markets were also part of the Plenum in order to improve the efficiency of resource allocation, including interest rate and capital account liberalization. As bold as the reforms looked on paper, their implementation has, however, been modest: the European Chamber of Commerce in China and US-China Business Council have found that progress in most areas has been stalling.

The latest Five-Year Plan, approved in early 2016, broadly continues in the direction of its predecessor: the growth target for GDP was again lowered but remains ambitious, and the new plan includes a—equally ambitious—labor productivity target in key sectors such as high-end manufacturing. Furthermore, the issue of excess capacities in state-owned enterprise-dominated sectors like coal, steel, glass, and cement is to be tackled head-on: consolidation in these sectors is expected to result in around 5 million job losses. Roach (2016) detects a change in paradigm in the latest Five-Year Plan, arguing that it focuses more on reforming the structure of the economy rather than increasing private consumption and boosting domestic demand, as previous ones did. Looking back on the history of China's development, this sounds promising. But its success will, of course, depend crucially on implementation.

Lardy (2019) takes a skeptical view, highlighting the rising share of investment by state-controlled enterprises at the expense of private firms since 2015. Given the lower profitability of state-owned enterprises, this development does not bode well for China's medium-term growth prospects. As the fundamental impediment to more market-orientated reforms, he identifies political causes: Chinese leaders are

---

[7]It is noteworthy, however, that the fiscal stimulus also did include measures aimed at boosting domestic consumption either directly through subsidies for the purchases of durable electronic goods or indirectly via the provision of affordable housing or health care services.

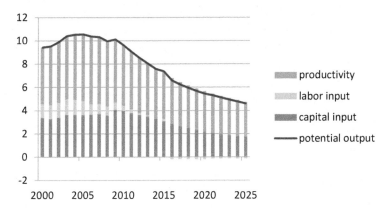

Fig. 8 Factor decomposition of potential output growth (percent). Source: World Bank *World Development Indicators*, United National *Population Projections*, National Bureau of Statistics, Penn World Tables 9.0, Kiel Institute calculations

convinced that dominant state-owned enterprises are instrumental in maintaining the position and control of the Communist Party.

---

4   Economic Outlook: Risks and Challenges Ahead

The rate of growth that can be achieved over the medium term crucially depends on the development of potential output—the production that can be sustained without leading to inflationary or deflationary pressures in the economy. In estimating the potential growth rate of China, we closely follow Burns et al. (2014) who estimate potential output in emerging markets based on a neoclassical production function. Their methodology is well-equipped to deal with a lack of reliable data on the capital stock, unemployment, or the participation rate that is typically a problem in emerging economies. For example, they take the working-age population as a proxy for labor input and compute the capital stock with the perpetual inventory method based on national accounts gross fixed capital formation (GFCF) data.[8] Forecasts for the working-age population are taken from the United Nations population projections. The results are presented in Fig. 8.

Total factor productivity that has been the most important driver of potential growth in China is expected to remain so over the coming years as well. In absolute terms, however, the contribution is expected to decline. The same holds for capital accumulation: its contribution to potential growth is likely to halve from the high values seen during the investment boom of the stimulus years 2008–2010 to around

---

[8]It is in the latter regard that we differ slightly from their approach: whereas they compute their own estimate of the initial capital stock using the properties of the production function, we rely on data from the Penn World Tables. We find that this delivers a more sensible capital-output ratio, in particular at the start of the sample.

2% points by 2025. Up until 2005 there have also been sizeable contributions to potential growth from a rise in working-age population, but this demographic dividend has largely been paid out and the contribution has been diminishing in recent years. In the projection period, the working-age population will start shrinking and actually be a (admittedly minor) drag on potential growth.

In this context, a word of caution regarding the reliability of Chinese statistics is in order. It has long been questioned whether official Chinese statistics deliver an adequate depiction of the economic reality (Koch-Weser 2013). Doubts arose for technical reasons. For example, China publishes its GDP figures with only a 2-week delay after the end of each quarter—given the vast size of its economy an extraordinary feat. Also, headline GDP growth is quite smooth compared to other emerging economies (and also most advanced economies), suggesting that official figures may not adequately reflect business cycle dynamics. Furthermore, there is evidence that Chinese officials manipulate local statistics to enhance their odds of being promoted within the party ranks, leading to inaccurate figures at the aggregate level.[9] Doubts over the reliability of GDP figures grow when alternative activity indicators such as energy consumption, freight traffic, or credit growth are taken into account, for example, by looking at the so-called Keqiang Index, a simple weighted average of the aforementioned variables.[10] Empirical evidence in the literature is not conclusive. While Fernald et al. (2013) and Holz (2014) find no compelling evidence that Chinese policy makers falsify official statistics, Nakamura et al. (2016), using a different approach, conclude that Chinese statistics have in recent years been overstating growth and understating inflation by several percentage points per year and—similar to Koch-Weser (2013)—emphasize the lower volatility of official figures. Chen et al. (2019) estimate that between 2008 and 2016 the growth rate of national GDP was overstated by on average 1.7%, mainly due to inflated growth figures at the local government level that the National Bureau of Statistics insufficiently adjusted for. Users of Chinese macroeconomic data should thus be aware of the limitations in data quality, although it is unlikely that official figures are completely disconnected from reality.

4.1   Is China in for a Hard Landing?

The above projections assume a gradual and smooth transition of the Chinese economy toward a more sustainable level of economic growth. In the policy debate, this is referred to as the "soft landing" scenario. Conversely, a "hard landing" would see a sharp deceleration in domestic demand, possibly triggered by a rise in

---

[9]Serrato Suarez et al. (2016), for example, document the manipulation of birth figures by Chinese mayors in order to comply with the one-child policy and secure promotions.

[10]See Economist (2010) for details. It should, however, be noted that by construction the "Keqiang Index" is an imperfect proxy for overall economic activity, or GDP, as it is biased toward the heavy-industry-related sectors.

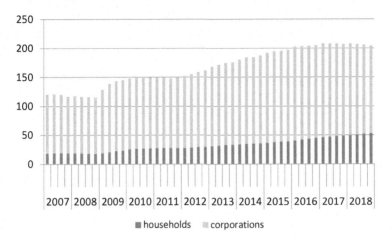

Fig. 9 Private sector debt (% of GDP). Source: Bank for International Settlements

non-performing loans, distress in the banking sector, and ultimately a financial crisis. Indeed, for advanced economies, Schularick and Taylor (2012) have shown that rapid credit expansions are often a precursor of financial crises. This does raise concerns in light of the massive buildup of debt in the Chinese economy with overall private sector liabilities having increased to over 200% of GDP with a particularly rapid expansion of corporate sector debt until 2016. More recently, the private debt-to-GDP ratio has leveled off, partly in response to a crackdown on shadow banking by the authorities (Fig. 9). To put these figures into perspective, the Bank for International Settlements estimates that private sector debt as a share of GDP in the USA or Germany amounts to 150 and 100%, respectively. China's debt levels, thus, do not merely stand out among emerging economies but can be considered high even when compared to more advanced economies with sophisticated financial systems.

But there are good reasons to believe that Chinese growth will not come to a sudden stop in the immediate future. As public debt is still relatively low in China, the central government has ample policy space to intervene and dampen the fallout from such a financial crisis and ensuing recession. A less dramatic but nevertheless worrying scenario is described by Heilmann (2015). He views "repeated stimulus and prolonged stagnation" as the most likely outcome: lacking the political will to embrace structural transformation (and consolidate sectors with overcapacities), thus freeing up resources, the government is likely to counter slowing growth with fiscal stimulus and further expansion of credit. While boosting growth in the short-term, overcapacities, and inefficiencies would only increase as a result of the stimulus, bad debt would be rolled over and not written off holding back the creation of new, productive investments, and growth would soon start slowing again. Chinese authorities would then respond with another round of stimulus and so on and so forth. In this sense, there are clear analogies to developments in Japan in the 1990s after the bursting of the financial bubble which led to a "zombification" of the economy—overleveraged, unproductive firms were kept afloat by insolvent banks who were unwilling to recognize losses on their loans, thus impeding a reallocation of resources and eventually producing prolonged stagnation.

More recently, the trade conflict with the USA poses a threat to the Chinese economy. Against the backdrop the large US trade deficit vis-à-vis China and a generally more protectionist US trade policy approach, in early 2018 the Trump administration started to impose tariffs on imports from China to counter what it considered unfair trade practices. By fall 2019, more than half of imports were covered, with the average tariff on Chinese goods having risen from around 3 to 20%. Exports from China to the USA contracted in response, as did Chinese imports from the USA—partly due to retaliatory measures on US goods imposed by the Chinese government. The trade conflict has slowed growth in China, and the Chinese authorities have responded with expansionary fiscal and monetary policies in the form of tax cuts and lower interest rates and capital reserve requirements. But in light of the aforementioned risks, the size of the stimulus is not comparable to the measures taken after the global financial crisis.

5   Conclusions

The Chinese economy has experienced impressive growth since the late 1970s, turning it from one of the world's poorest countries into a cornerstone of the global economy. Ongoing market-based reforms as well as integration into the global economic system played a key role in this spectacular performance. But growth in the past decades has been biased toward the industrial sector and investment and exports, and a huge buildup of debt, rising inequality, and increasing environmental problems are huge challenges policy makers are currently facing. Will China overcome the "middle-income trap" and join the ranks of advanced economies in due course? There are reasons to be optimistic. After all, summing up modern Chinese economic history, Zhu (2012, p. 119) notes that "whenever the effect of one set of reforms on productivity seemed to be exhausted, the Chinese government found a way to initiate new reforms that reignite growth". However, given the long list of obstacles highlighted in this chapter—the rapid buildup of debt, inefficient and unprofitable SOEs, as well as overregulated and underdeveloped financial markets— only time will tell whether this optimism was justified.

References

Ahmed, S., Appendino, M., & Ruta, M. (2015). Depreciations without exports? Global value chains and the exchange rate elasticity of exports. In *World Bank policy research working paper (7390)*. World Bank: Washington, DC.

Amiti, M., & Freund, C. (2010). The anatomy of China's export growth. In R. Feenstra & S. J. Wie (Eds.), *China's growing role in world trade*. Chicago, IL: University of Chicago Press.

Batson, A., & Zhang, J. (2011). Capital stock: How much is too much? *China Economic Quarterly, 15*(3), 46–49.

Brandt, L., & Zhu, X. (2010). Accounting for China's growth. IZA Discussion Paper No. 4764.

Burns, A., van Rensburg, T. J., Dybczak, K., & Bui, T. (2014). Estimating potential output in developing countries. *Journal of Policy Modeling, 36,* 700–716.

Chen, W., Chen, X., Hsieh, C. T., & Song, Z. (2019). A forensic examination of China's national accounts. In *BPEA conference draft.* Springer.

Chivakul, M., & Lam, R. (2015). Assessing China's corporate sector vulnerabilities. In *IMF working paper 15/75.* International Monetary Fund: Washington, DC.

Cline, W., & Williamson, J. (2009). Estimates of the equilibrium exchange rate of the RMB: Is there a consensus and if not, why not? In M. Goldstein & N. Lardy (Eds.), *Debating China's exchange rate policy.* Washington, DC: Peterson Institute for International Economics.

Deutsche Bundesbank. (2018). Die Neuausrichtung der chinesischen Wirtschaft und ihre internationalen Folgen. *Monthly Bulletin,* July 2018.

Eichengreen, B., & Tong, H. (2015). Effects of renminbi appreciation on foreign firms: The role of processing exports. *Journal of Development Economics, 116,* 146–157.

European Chamber of Commerce. (2009). *Overcapacity in China: Causes, impact and recommendations.* Beijing.

Fardoust, S., Lin, J. Y., & Luo, X. (2012). Demystifying China's fiscal stimulus. In *Policy research working paper 6221.* Washington, DC: World Bank.

Fernald, J., Malkin, I., & Spiegel, M. (2013). On the reliability of Chinese output figures. *FRBSF Economic Letter, 8,* 1–15.

Gern, K. J., Hauber, P., & Potjagailo, G. (2015). Economic slowdown in China – Current assessment and global implications. In *Kiel policy brief* (Vol. 94). Kiel: Kiel Institute for the World Economy.

Heilmann, S. (2015). China unter Abwärtsdruck. In *China policy brief.* Berlin: Mercator Institute for China Studies.

Holz, C. (2014). The quality of China's GDP statistics. *China Economic Review, 30,* 309–338.

Koch-Weser. (2013). The reliability of China's economic data: An analysis of national output. In *Proceedings of the U.S.-China economic and security review commission staff research project.*

Koopman, R., Wang, Z., & Wie, S. J. (2012). Estimating domestic content in exports when processing trade is pervasive. *Journal of Development Economics, 99,* 178–189.

Lardy, N. (2012). *Sustaining China's economic growth after the global financial crisis.* Washington, DC: Peterson Institute for International Economics.

Lardy, N. (2014). *Markets over Mao.* Washington, DC: Peterson Institute for International Economics.

Lardy, N. (2019). *The state strikes back.* Washington, DC: Peterson Institute for International Economics.

McMillan, J., & Naughton, B. (1992). How to reform a planned economy: Lessons from China. *Oxford Review of Economic Policy, 8*(1), 130–142.

Nakamura, E., Steinsson, J., & Liu, M. (2016). Are Chinese growth and inflation too smooth? Evidence from engel curves. *American Economic Journal: Macroeconomics, 8*(3), 113–144.

Pettis, M. (2010). China is misread by bulls and bears alike. *Financial Times,* February, 25 2010. London.

Roach, S. (2016). China's strategic challenges amid a daunting transition. *Caixin,* 31.3.2016. Retrieved October 20, 2019 from http://english.caixin.com/2016-03-31/100926957.html

Rodrik, D. (2008). The real exchange rate and economic growth. In D. W. Elmendorf, N. G. Mankiw, & L. H. Summers (Eds.), *Brookings papers on economic activity, fall 2008* (pp. 365–412). Washington, DC: Brookings Institution.

Rumbaugh, T., & Blancher, N. (2004). China: International trade and WTO accession. *IMF working paper 04/36.* Washington, DC

Schularick, M., & Taylor, A. M. (2012). Credit booms gone bust: Monetary policy, leverage cycles, and financial crises, 1870-2008. *American Economic Review, 102*(2), 1029-1061.

Shih, V. (2010). Local government debt: Big rock candy mountain. *China Economic Quarterly, 14* (2), 26–32.

Suarez Serrato, J. C., Wang, X. Y., & Zhang, S. (2016). The limits of meritocracy: Screening bureaucrats under imperfect verifiability. In *NBER working paper no. 21963*.

The Economist. (2010). *Keqiang ker-ching*. December 09, 2010, London. Retrieved October 20, 2019 from http://www.economist.com/node/17681868

Young, A. (1995). The tyranny of numbers: Confronting the statistical realities of the East Asian growth experience. *Quarterly Journal of Economics, 110*(3), 641–680.

Young, A. (2003). Gold into base metals: Productivity growth in the People's Republic of China during the reform period. *Journal of Political Economy, 111*(6), 1220–1261.

Zhu, X. (2012). Understanding China's growth: Past, present, and future. *Journal of Economic Perspectives, 26*(4), 103–124.

China's Provinces: Addressing the Discrepancies at the Local Level

Hannah Levinger and Christian Braun

Abstract

As China embarks on a path of economic rebalancing, regional differences in dealing with slowing growth, volatile property prices and changing investment and consumption patterns have moved into focus. It is often local challenges—such as Zhengzhou's coping with a fading housing boom or Hainan's growing debt burden, that shape the perception of China's economic health. In fact, while all 31 provinces are affected by China's transition, regional differences remain substantial. Not only is there huge variation in the provinces' ability to stem China's planned shift from investment-driven growth towards more sustainable and consumption-led development. But provincial risks are often at the root of China's current reform trends, too, notably with regard to fiscal reform and the recent push to establish a functioning local government bond market.

1   Introduction

Over the past 5 years, China has embarked on a path of economic rebalancing. At its centre stands the challenge to move away from the legacy of a debt-fuelled investment boom and towards more sustainable growth. The changes that come with this shift hold implications for the country as a whole as well as for the development of China's provinces. Given China's vast stretch of land, the challenges may look quite different in steel-producing Hebei than in real estate-reliant Hainan. Notably, the

H. Levinger (✉)
Deutsche Bank AG, Frankfurt, Germany

C. Braun
University of Regensburg, IRE|BS, Regensburg, Bavaria, Germany

© Springer Nature Switzerland AG 2021   53
B. Wang, T. Just (eds.), *Understanding China's Real Estate Markets*, Management
for Professionals, https://doi.org/10.1007/978-3-030-49032-4_5

provinces in the north-eastern "rust belt" have borne the brunt of China's economic adjustment over the past years and continue to be heavily dependent on state investment. Inland provinces, as opposed to the tech-oriented coast, increasingly have to confront competition with other low-cost manufacturing hubs in Asia.

Provincial finances have been at the root of China's fiscal risks, stemming from an overreliance on local governments' income from land sales and a mismatch between local responsibilities for managing revenues and expenditures. Measures to expand local government bond financing are a positive step towards reducing fiscal risks and accumulation of debt at the local level. Property markets have seen a rollercoaster ride with volatility, increasing notably since early 2014. As economic activity slowed, the squeeze on property prices was felt across China, and property sales and investment slowed or declined throughout the country, particularly in the north-eastern provinces. But the diversity of local markets is huge and so has been the development since mid-2015. Some local property markets, especially around the large tier-1 cities, have staged a tremendous recovery, which in turn has raised doubts about sustainability. By contrast, property markets in structurally weak regions still reflect stagnant demand. China's diverse property market complicates efforts to adequately respond to the problems in the sector on a nationwide basis.

Finally, China's ongoing endeavour to expand cross-border trade and investment via the "New Silk Road" has yielded benefits for provinces at the western and southwestern border as well as inland provinces' connectivity. However, convergence of some of these provinces to the living standards in the richest ones has effectively come to a stillstand. This chapter gives an overview over some of the most pressing opportunities and challenges faced by China on the provincial level.[1]

2   China's "New Normal" at the Provincial Level

China's thirty-one provinces could count as outright "countries" in terms of their population or economic output, let alone land area.[2] Figure 1 depicts a map of the provinces. China's most populous provinces Guangdong, Shandong and Henan with around 100 m inhabitants each nearly reach the population size of Egypt or the Philippines. Together, these three provinces alone are home to almost as many people as the United States. Xinjiang, Tibet and Inner Mongolia all have land areas of more than 1 million (mn) square kilometres, comparable to South Africa or Colombia. In terms of provinces' nominal GDP numbers, Guangdong, Shandong and Jiangsu have remained the heavyweights of China's economy over the past years with economic output between USD 1 and 1.25 trillion (tr) in 2017—roughly comparable to Spain or Mexico. At the other end of the spectrum are Ningxia, Qinghai and Tibet whose individual nominal GDP amounted to less than USD 50 billion (bn) in 2017. China's ten strongest provinces account for 60% of the

---

[1]The basis of this article is a Deutsche Bank report of China's provinces—see Levinger (2015).

[2]The 31 provinces referred to include 22 provinces, 5 autonomous regions and 4 self-governed municipalities.

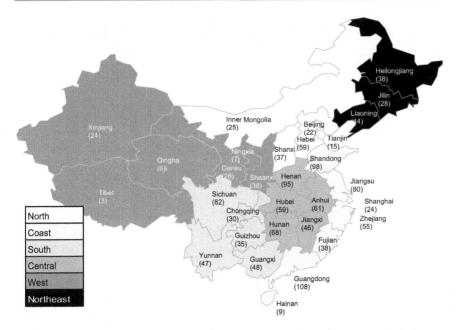

Fig. 1 Map of China's provinces and population. Population in millions, rounded (2015). Source: Deutsche Bank

national economic output but only 20% of its land area. The sheer dimensions mask the dramatic changes that China's provinces have undergone in previous years.

In the course of the reform and open door policy, launched in the late 1970s, China promoted economic growth by allowing market orientation in specific areas with proximity to trading partners. Special economic zones (SEZs) were granted preferential treatment with regard to tax policy and import tariffs. Industrial parks were set up, and foreign direct investment (FDI) was encouraged. Spatial agglomeration successfully triggered development along the coast, making the eastern provinces China's growth stars. However, this policy approach also contributed to the emergence and rapid growth of regional disparities as reflected in divergent paths of GDP per capita.[3]

In the early 2000s, the central government reacted to persistent regional inequality by launching the "Development of the West" programme. The initiative—often dubbed the "go West" strategy—focused on promoting infrastructural projects, improving the investment environment and encouraging domestic- and foreign-funded business formation. Preferential policies on taxation and finance were implemented to generate incentives for business activity. This strategy specifically targeted provinces in the West and South. Notwithstanding the unprecedented

---

[3]See Dyck and Levinger (2010) for a more detailed discussion of provinces' structural changes in the early 2000s.

development, regional disparities persist not only with regard to economic indicators but also structural and social factors. The development of infrastructure of China's remote regions has been a key ingredient of the "go West" strategy along with improvement of rural livelihoods.

2.1   Adjustment Not Uniform Across China

China's real GDP growth has moderated considerably in recent years. The slow-down is observable across China's provinces. In 2018, growth rates were lower by 6.81 pp on average compared to their peak levels in 2010–2018 (Fig. 2).

Economic growth has proven relatively resilient in the coastal provinces such as Guangdong, Zhejiang and Shanghai. For city-states such as Beijing and Chongqing, the slowdown has been orderly. Also, the poorer provinces of Xinjiang, Tibet and Guizhou continued to record high growth rates. Growth rates slumped most in the "rust belt" provinces in the north-eastern provinces of Jilin, Liaoning and energy-producing Heilongjiang (where one of China's largest oilfields is located) and in those reliant on bulk materials such as Shanxi and Inner Mongolia. It is not far-fetched to say that some of these provinces have already undergone the kind of sharp growth deceleration that has been labelled a "hard-landing" on the national level. The island province of Hainan also slowed from a peak of 16%, albeit less sharply than the commodity producers. Notably, inland provinces which experienced bumper growth rates during the global financial crisis (when export-dependent coastal provinces were hard hit) now face the largest loss in momentum.

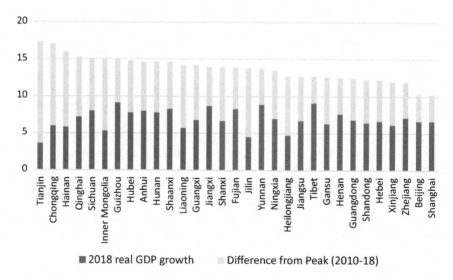

Fig. 2 Growth has slowed across provinces. Real GDP growth, % year-on-year. Source: National Bureau of Statistics

2.2　Convergence in Provincial Incomes Per Capita

Building on a large-scale infrastructure push, the "go West" strategy has been successful in lifting per capita GDP in less wealthy provinces. As a result, discrepancies in provincial income have declined over the past decade (Fig. 3). Nonetheless, including the rich Coast region, the gaps remain considerable. Especially interesting is the time span since 2015. While the north and north-east weren't able to keep up with the income growth of the poorer regions, the dominant position of the Coast remains relatively untouched. Therefore one can rather observe a convergence from rich to poor than the other way round.

In addition, while hundreds of millions of people have been lifted out of poverty, China's rapid development has not always produced equitable outcomes. In fact, income inequality in China is among the highest globally as measured by the Gini coefficient. As of 2017, China's national statistics office put the Gini coefficient at 0.467—a level ranking China as one of the least equal 20 percent of countries worldwide (World Bank). Alternative data, such as from the Standardized World Income Inequality Database (SWIID) which includes the net Gini coefficient after taxes and transfers, reach similar conclusions about China's income distribution (Solt 2016). An important driver of less equitable incomes seems to have been the shift from upper-middle incomes to higher incomes (Dabla-Norris et al. 2015). China's urban-rural divide concurrently contributed to a widening income gap within provinces (Xie and Zhou 2014). Zhang et al. (2015) find that the differences between provinces' stages of development remain huge with respect to social or structural indicators such as life expectancy, health and the quality of education.

This is confirmed by a simple comparison of the old-age dependency ratio across provinces. The share of the population aged 65 or older relative to the 15–64 year olds shows relatively high variation from one province to another. As of 2017, Chongqing had the highest ratio, while autonomous provinces with large minority

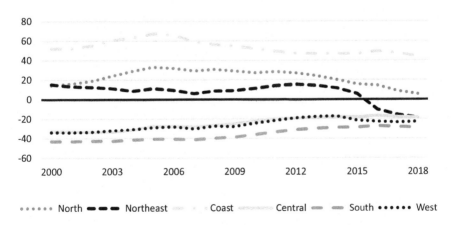

Fig. 3 Long-term decline in income discrepancies between regions. GDP per capita by regions, % deviation from national average. Source: National Bureau of Statistics

populations such as Tibet and Xinjiang had the lowest ratio (Fig. 4). Natural growth rates—the difference between a province's birth and death rate—also show significant variations (Fig. 5). The relaxation of the one-child policy since 2015 may smooth the slope of old age dependency but is unlikely to cope with the society's rapid ageing. The implementation of the two-child-policy introduced in 2015 has been declared a matter of the provinces. Guangdong province, for example, was the first to publish local legislations. The north-east is still faced with the lowest birth

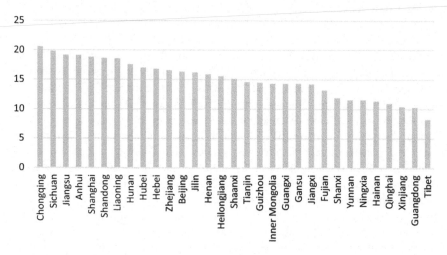

Fig. 4 Old age dependency ratio. Share of the population aged 65 or older relative to those aged 15–64, % (2017). Source: National Bureau of Statistics

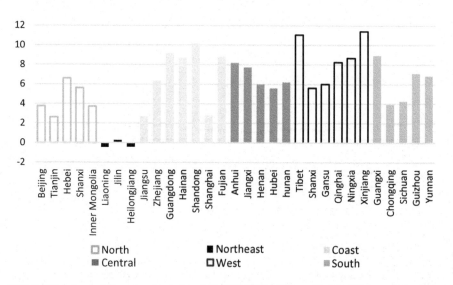

Fig. 5 Natural population growth rate by region. ‰ (2017). Source: National Bureau of Statistics

rates—a reflection also of the economic downturn in the region over the past years. As a result, discrepancies are expected to remain sizeable over the medium term.

2.3 A New Phase of Urbanisation

Despite their large and diverse challenges, Chinese provinces have many success stories to tell. Urbanisation has made rapid progress in underdeveloped regions. Transport infrastructure has expanded massively, with the result that China now boasts more than 140,000 km of expressways. By the end of 2017, China also recorded a railway network of close to 130,000 km—the largest globally and an increase from less than 90,000 km in 2008—with a share of 19.8% of high speed railway network. Notably, railway network continued to be built at a pace of more than 8% annually in 2014 and 2015, which is faster than in previous years despite the broader economic slowdown. In 2016 and 2017, however, the network expansion process slowed down to roughly 2.5% annually. Regions with the largest increase in high-speed networks since 2008 include vast and remote provinces such as Inner Mongolia and Xinjiang but also geographically and economically important hubs like Guangdong, which connects the mainland and Hong Kong. Although China has come a long way expanding physical infrastructure, considerable gaps in the supply and quality of rail and road density as well as municipal and environmental infrastructure remain.[4]

Moreover, China's evolving agenda to expand investment and trade in Asia and globally via the "New Silk Road" economic belt importantly include China's domestic provinces in the south-west and west (via the Chongqing-Xinjiang-Europe international railway) as well as coastal provinces for the maritime "road" connecting China and Europe. Provinces close to the national or sea border are well placed to benefit from expanding cross-border trade and investment thanks to existing infrastructure, new transport links and easing regulations. Manufacturing hubs have emerged outside the traditional powerhouses along the Pearl and Yangtze deltas. That is because unit labour costs in the manufacturing sector remain the highest along the coast (Economist Intelligence Unit 2014). While inland provinces are catching up fast, some provinces like Jiangxi, Henan and Hebei have retained low unit labour costs that enable them to compete with countries such as Thailand, the Philippines and Vietnam.

2.4 Foreign Direct Investment and the Consumer Class

China has become one of the world's largest recipients of foreign direct investment (FDI) as well as a source of significant investment abroad. According to UNCTAD

---

[4]For an overview of China's and other Asian countries' infrastructure financing challenges see also Hansakul and Levinger (2016).

(2017), China's inward stock of foreign investment amounts to more than USD 135 billion (USD 240 billion when Hong Kong is included). China's coastal provinces continue to record the highest amount of actually utilised investment. Shanghai is also a top recipient of FDI both in nominal terms and as a share of the province's GDP. Investment has also been lured into inland regions, in particular as labour cost advantages relative to the costlier coast become apparent. FDI into inland provinces Anhui and Henan more than doubled as a share of GDP over the past decade. Nevertheless, projections that rapid wage rise along the coast would lead to the less developed provinces superseding traditional magnets of foreign investment have proven largely premature.

At the same time, the inland shift is apparent in the spread of China's middle class. According to a McKinsey and Company (2013) report, economically and politically less viable cities such as Leshan located in Sichuan province or Yulin in Shaanxi with less than 5 million inhabitants are poised to account for the largest increase in China's upper-middle class population.[5] By 2022, the report estimates, third- and fourth-tier cities, will account for roughly 40% of China's total middle class from just 18% in 2002.

2.5 Rebalancing the Provincial Growth

Much light has been shed on China's transition to a new, sustainable growth model, shifting from industry to services and from investment to consumption as drivers of supply and demand.[6] The transformation of the economy is borne out of necessity, with the old model having contributed to massive debt accumulation, resource misallocation and growing environmental deficiencies. China's progress towards successfully rebalancing its economy is often assessed by the shifting contributions of consumption (demand side) and services (supply side) to its national GDP. While progress at the national level has been mixed, this is differently reflected at the provincial level, where some regions have traditionally relied less on industries or saved less (and consumed more) than others.

On the supply side, most provinces continue to rely heavily on investment as key engine of growth. Gross fixed capital formation, a proxy of investment, averaged 62% of GDP across provinces in 2017. The provinces which have relied more on investment-driven growth over the past years include Qinghai, Tibet, Ningxia and Xinjiang, where development needs remain sizeable, and the property-dependent province of Hainan. The rate of private consumption as a proportion of GDP by contrast averaged 39% of GDP across provinces in 2017 and has increased by 6% points since 2011. A moderate rise in the consumption rate was seen in all but five

---

[5]The authors' definition of economic and political importance is based on nominal urban GDP as of 2010 with tier-3 and tier-4 cities up to RMB 120 billion.

[6]See, for example, Zhang (2016) and Frieden (2016) for a broader view on China's rebalancing process and its implications.

provinces. The provinces which increased consumption but reduced investment as a proportion of GDP are for the most part either located at China's consumer savvy coast or large metropolitan areas in China's inland. This may be taken as a sign that already more advanced regions remain at the forefront of driving China's rebalancing. Slowly inland provinces are starting to shift from investment to consumption as well.

Retail sales, a higher-frequency indicator capturing private consumption dynamics, confirm the mixed picture. Since 2011, sales of consumer goods have slowed significantly in all parts of the country. While growth rates on the national level are still declining, the decline has slowed down since 2015. In 2018 growth fell below two-digit rates for the first time since the early 2000s.[7] Although the slowdown was most prominent in north and north-eastern provinces, where the economy sputtered the most, there are provinces across the country which realised negative growth rates. According to the Ministry of Commerce, growth in 2019 was driven by online retail sales as well as the service sector and is attributed to the strong purchasing power of central and western regions (China Watch 2020). Overreliance on investment is evident across Chinese provinces by the rapid expansion in capital spending in recent years. Indeed, investment in fixed assets, which includes land purchases,[8] expanded by 24% p.a. on average in 2010–2013. Industrial overcapacity surged as a result of years of buoyant investment in industrial equipment and related industries, facilitated by easy credit to state-owned enterprises, which dominate China's heavy industry (European Chamber of Commerce 2016).

By sector,[9] the slowdown in fixed asset investment was led by manufacturing, which slackened across the country. Mining-related investment slowed or declined in resource-rich provinces such as Inner Mongolia, Shaanxi, Shanxi and Liaoning. Real estate investment, which accounted for a quarter of total fixed investment on average across provinces, rose moderately in two out of three provinces but dropped sharply in northern and north-western provinces as well as Sichuan, Yunnan, Gansu, Ningxia and Xinjiang. Moreover, lower investment in upstream industries (cement, steel, construction materials) contributed to a slowdown in other areas of investment in the supplier provinces.

The provinces where investment contracted most typically suffer from a high build-up in industrial overcapacities. In February 2016, the State Council declared dealing with overcapacities a national priority, followed by stricter guidelines for local governments in June. Nevertheless, authorities' efforts to shut down unprofitable firms have proven difficult, notably in steel and coal sectors. On the provincial level, consolidation efforts are challenged by local governments' reliance on company tax revenues and the overarching preference for social harmony. Nevertheless

---

[7]According to official sources, the retail sales growth rate in 2018 was 9%; however, our own calculations with the underlying data indicate a growth rate of slightly above 4%.

[8]Defined by NBS as construction projects and purchases of fixed assets (incl. fees) with a total planned investment of min. RMB 5 m in urban and rural areas but excluding rural households.

[9]Data available until 2014 only.

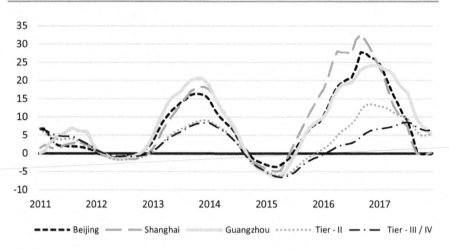

Fig. 6 Property prices in selected cities. Prices of newly constructed residential buildings in 70 city index, % change year-on-year. Source: National Bureau of Statistics

China has cut its crude steel capacity by more than 150 million metric tonnes[10] (MMT) and coal capacity by 810 MMT since 2016 but is still facing an overcapacity problem in these two sectors (China Daily 2019). In contrast, while overcapacity was reduced, the actual output increased significantly. Although the national capacity cutting targets in the steel and coal industries was met 2 years ahead of time—at the end of 2018 instead of 2020—provinces like Hebei and Shandong are looking to further decrease overcapacities (Reuters 2019; China Daily 2020). Moreover, the aim to curb China's heavy reliance on fixed investment stands in sharp contrast to heavy infrastructure investments at the provincial level (Hsu 2019).

3   Different Provinces, Different Challenges

The property market is of high importance for the Chinese economy. In 2014, residential property alone accounted for 15% of urban employment and around 20% of bank lending (Chivakul et al. 2015). Property is used as collateral for corporate borrowing and constitutes a relevant source of revenues for local governments (see next section). In 2015, construction, sale and outfitting of homes contributed 15.1% of GDP. It comes hardly as a surprise that the housing market was at the forefront of China hard-landing concerns when real estate prices started to decelerate in mid-2014. A disorderly correction in prices and sales, and stalling urbanisation rates, could pose a drag to the real economy and imply risks for the

---

[10]Given China's crude steel capacity of roughly 1130 MMT in 2015, this cut equals a reduction of about 13.3%.

financial sector, given the high linkages between banks, local government finances and real estate developments. Precisely this high dependence on the property markets also makes the sector an effective channel for stimulating growth. Property prices stabilised in most provinces in late 2015 and into 2016, but the rapid price surge in some cities has fuelled concerns of a housing bubble which persists to date. China's ability to withstand boom and bust in the property market comes down to the local level. Due to the sheer size of the country, there exist not one but many property markets that may face quite different supply and demand trends and require differentiated policy responses.

Due to the highly diverse nature of urban and rural settlements within China, price trends are generally measured on a city level rather than by province. The widely used 70-city index encompasses the large municipalities as well as sub-provincial and prefecture-level cities. First-tier cities such as Beijing, Shanghai, Tianjin, Shenzhen and Guangzhou have generally witnessed above-average price increases over the past years (Fig. 6).[11] By contrast, second-tier cities have faced much larger price variations. Despite considerable differences between local markets, the turn in the property price cycle has been visible across regions. Cities located in the north-east, the north and along the coast were among the first to experience price declines. The drop has also been much sharper than in cities located elsewhere. Conversely, China's central and coastal cities were the first to recover. Meanwhile, the largest cities from Beijing to Shenzhen recorded high double-digit annual gains in prices for both new and existing residential property.

The fluctuation in the property market has brought about countercyclical policy responses. The downturn was met by incremental relaxation of restrictions, not just in Beijing and Shanghai. Plans for nationwide residential property taxes were shelved and home-purchase restrictions reversed, some of which had been in place since 2010 (Just and Dyck 2011). Moreover, the government introduced financial incentives to boost sales; further easing of mortgage restrictions were rolled out in April 2015, and minimum down payment ratios were slashed in several cities. Eighteen months on, overheating concerns in some cities prompted resumption to tightening measures on a city-by-city basis. These were not confined to first tier markets but included mid-tier cities such as Chengdu, Jinan, Wuhan and Zhengzhou—the latter once famous for being home to China's largest ghost town.

---

[11]Chinese cities are typically divided into four categories. Tier-1 cities include Beijing, Guangzhou, Shanghai and Shenzhen. Tier-2 cities comprise of Beihai, Changchun, Changsha, Chengdu, Chongqing, Dalian, Fuzhou, Guiyang, Haikou, Hangzhou, Harbin, Hefei, Hohhot, Jinan, Kunming, Lanzhou, Nanchang, Nanjing, Nanning, Ningbo, Qingdao, Sanya, Shenyang, Shijiazhuang, Suzhou, Taiyuan, Tianjin, Urumqi, Wenzhou, Wuhan, Wuxi, Xiamen, Xi'an, Yinchuan and Zhengzhou. Smaller cities are grouped into Tier-3 and Tier-4 categories.

4   Provincial Debt and Deleveraging

Tightly linked to the developments in the property market is the health of provinces' fiscal balance sheets. Local governments' finances have been subject to an inherent mismatch between centralised revenue generation and local spending responsibilities for many years (Dyck and Levinger 2010). This mismatch is illustrated by the fact that the share of local to total fiscal expenditures (around 85% on average in 2011–2018) by far exceeded the share of local to total revenues (between 51 and 55% on average in 2011–2018) and is also much higher than in developed countries (Lu and Sun 2013). As a result, local governments resorted to off-budget funds and land sales for propping up budget revenues, while expenditures remained highly localised and often channelled through special purpose vehicles. This imbalance became more apparent in recent years as budgetary performance deteriorated. All provinces faced significantly slower growth in budget revenues in the period after 2012, relative to previous years (Fig. 7).

Among the provinces that saw the sharpest revenue drop is "rust belt" Jilin as well as coal producer Shaanxi and relatively poorer provinces such as Guizhou. Arguably, in 2017 revenue trends evolved differently from province to province. Some places observed a notable recovery in revenues, while some of the hardest hit regions experienced a further double-digit contraction.

Besides their budgetary fiscal incomes, China's provincial governments draw on off-budget income from government-managed funds. Fund revenues account for 40% of total revenues at the local level, making them a key source for provincial spending. Crucially, around 80% of government fund revenues are in turn derived

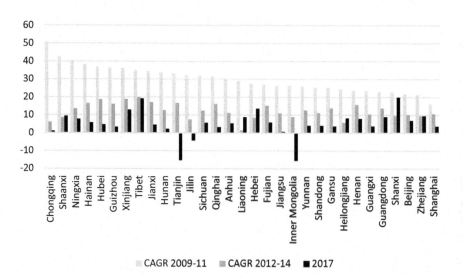

Fig. 7 Local government revenues growing more slowly. Annual average growth and compound annual growth rate, %. Note: Refers to budgetary revenues before transfers. Source: National Bureau of Statistics

from the sale of state-owned land use rights. Land sales slowed significantly in 2014 as a result of lack of demand for land and sluggish real estate development. This trend continued in 2015 when land sales revenues declined sharply from the previous year. Accordingly, local governments recorded rebounding sales when the property market stabilised in 2016. Moreover, budgetary income sources such as tax revenues may also depend quite strongly on the real estate market (e.g. through land appreciation tax, farmland occupation tax and deed tax) or are little diversified altogether, hence revealing provinces' sensitivity to changes in the property cycle on local finances. This includes, for example, Chongqing and Hubei, as well as primarily coastal provinces.

Financing of real estate and infrastructure projects is a local responsibility. Confronted with the dilemma to fund centrally induced investment increases while being banned from direct issuance of debt, local governments either relied on the central government to issue bonds on their behalf or resorted extensively to off-budget channels, i.e. special purpose local government financing vehicles (LGFVs), which in turn borrowed from banks, wealth management products (WMP), trusts or the bond market.

LGFVs in turn have faced deteriorating finances (Zhang 2015). With mounting concerns about the lack of transparency and fiscal risks as well as the higher borrowing costs associated with informal local financing, regulations on LGFVs and WMP have tightened on a provincial and national level in the course of 2014.[12] Shandong province imposed a ban on new debt issues by LGFVs altogether. China's fiscal reform plans have followed the "open the front door, close the back door" approach to steer local government financing away from LGFVs and the shadow-banking sector and towards direct borrowing on the bond market. In the face of the growth slowdown, however, shutting the "back door" is at best a gradual process. LGFVs remain a powerful funding tool, as the decision by the Chinese government in mid-2015 to resurrect bank support to existing LGFV projects and prop up local governments' spending ability revealed. Stricter rules' enforcement has definitely yielded results. On a national level, non-bank or "shadow" financing (via bankers' acceptance bills, trust products and entrusted loans) as a share of total credit flows declined from 30% in 2013 to 18% in 2014 and further to 9% in 2015. In 2018 only Inner Mongolia and Gansu had positive "shadow" financing credit flows (Fig. 8).

Arguably, the central government's fiscal capacity to smooth shortfalls on the local level is substantial. Owing to the system of interregional transfers, local governments that run budget deficits receive net transfers and tax rebates from the central government, while those with budget surpluses remit funds back to the centre. In recent years, operating budgets have diminished in many provinces, thus driving up reliance on transfers from the centre. Provinces' ability to stem these fiscal challenges differs, not just due to varying degrees of revenue diversification and reliance on land sales for funding. It also depends on their availability of (liquid)

---

[12]LGFV borrowing costs are on average twice as high as government bond yields. See also Zhang and Barnett (2014).

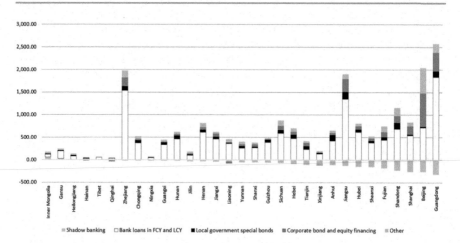

Fig. 8 Shadow banking—new financing mostly via bank loans and bonds. Net new financing, RMB billion (2018). Source: People's Bank of China

assets, for example, in the form of stakes in state-owned enterprises which could be sold in case of financial distress.

4.1   Provincial Debt and the Bond Swap Programme

Local governments have accumulated significant debt in sync with rising house prices and rapid expansion of local government financing schemes. By the end of 2015, regional and local governments' (short RLG) direct debt amounted to RMB 16 trillion or 23% of GDP according to China's National Audit Office. More importantly, the debt level has risen rapidly over the course of few years. The stock of direct debt owed by RLG increased only 4% from end-2014 (RMB 15.4 billion) but nearly 50% since a previous audit in mid-2013 (RMB 10.9 trillion) and more than doubled from 2010 (RMB 6.7 trillion). In addition, explicitly and indirectly guaranteed debt was estimated at RMB 8.6 trillion at end-2014 or 13% of China's GDP. As provinces are now barred from extending new guarantees, out-standing obligations will be run down gradually. Of the total debt at the end of 2014, nearly a quarter was invested in land reserves and social housing, and nearly 40% was guaranteed to be paid back land sales revenue (Liao et al. 2016).

Provinces, too, are required by the Ministry of Finance to disclose their direct debt to the public. As of 2015, the ratio of debt to provincial GDP reached as high as 87% in the case of Guizhou, while central Henan and some coastal provinces boasted a debt share below 20% of provincial GDP (Fig. 9). A substantial share of the local governments' debt burden is linked to infrastructure development and the property sector. LGFVs accounted for c. 39% of the National Audit Office's RMB 17.9 trillion debt estimate in 2013 or 12% of GDP—obligations for which local governments bear ultimate payment responsibility, given their arm's length borrowing through LGFV platforms (OECD 2015).

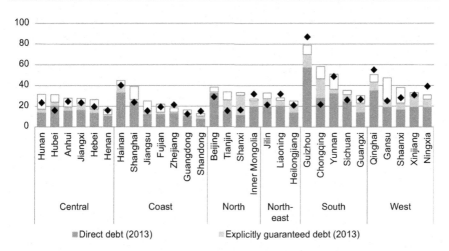

Fig. 9 Provincial government debt burden highest in south and West. % of provincial GDP. Source: Provincial audit offices and Moody's

The launch of the 3-year local government debt-for-bond swap programme in March 2015 marked an important step towards improving local government finances and mitigating short-term refinancing risks. Local governments received permission to convert short-term debt (mostly LGFV bonds) into lower-interest and longer-term municipal or provincial bonds. The rapid expansion of the local government bond market, especially in its early stages, also entailed some risks. Provinces were given the option of placing local bonds directly with existing creditors such as banks, trusts and insurances. These debt swap bonds now make up about 50% of the outstanding stock of local government bonds. Aside from the debt swap programme, the issuance of local government bonds has significantly increased in recent years. Especially the issuance of "special bonds" (meant for specific infrastructure investments), compared to "general bonds", has increased recently (Holmes and Lancaster 2019). After its initial difficulties[13], China's local government bond market is now the world's largest municipal bond market, even exceeding the USA. In addition, it is also the largest bond market in China with about USD 4 trillion outstanding bonds, roughly 30% of the Chinese GDP (Holmes and Lancaster 2019). In 2017, local government debt was comprised of about 90% bonds compared to only 7% in 2014. The increase can be regarded as a sign of greater transparency in local government borrowing but is also a reflection of the national government's use of this channel to stimulate growth via infrastructure investment. At the same time, regional and local governments are increasingly faced with stretched finances, and the broader

---

[13]For example, implementation challenges occurred during the initial kick-off of the swap plan, when Jiangsu and Anhui provinces had to postpone planned debt auctions amid weak investor demand and limited ability to use local government paper as collateral—until the central government determined their eligibility as collateral for central bank lending.

defined—or "augmented"[14]—fiscal deficit has crossed the 10% of GDP mark (IMF 2019).

5   Conclusion

As China embarks on a path of economic rebalancing, regional differences in coping with slowing growth, volatile property prices and changing investment and consumption patterns have moved into focus. It is often local challenges—such as Zhengzhou's coping with a fading housing boom or Hainan's growing debt burden, that shape the perception of China's economic health. In fact, while all 31 provinces are affected by China's slowdown, regional differences remain substantial. Not only is there huge variation in provinces' ability to stem China's planned shift from investment-driven growth towards more sustainable and consumption-led development. But provincial risks are often at the root of China's current reform trends, too, notably with regard to fiscal challenges and the recent push to establish a functioning local government bond market.

Across regions, the provinces in the north-eastern "rust belt" continue to be most vulnerable in the context of China's gradual growth slowdown due to their role as suppliers of heavy industry. Moreover, the north-east appears to be still stuck in the old model influenced by high reliance on fixed investment. Similarly, provinces located in the resource-rich north have felt the squeeze from weak commodity prices and waning demand, while investment dynamics vary across provinces. Coastal provinces are still among China's richest, but their lead is diminishing. Although the shift to consumption-led growth is perhaps most observable along China's coast, local rebalancing is challenged by the cyclicality in the housing market, low affordability and high labour costs, coupled with relatively higher use of non-bank channels for financing. Provinces in the south are among those who have accumulated the highest amount of debt. They are also at the lower end in terms of per capita income, thus raising questions about the financing of future development. Against this backdrop, new challenges arise in addressing the stalling rate of convergence between provinces. While provinces at the western and south-western border have benefitted from China's increased cross-border trade and investment agenda, new drivers need to be found for inland provinces' catching up to the higher-productivity coastal region to continue.

---

[14]Augmented fiscal data expand the perimeter of government to include local government financing vehicles and other off-budget activities.

References

China Daily. (2019). China to step up efforts to cut overcapacity in 2019. Retrieved January 13, 2020 from http://www.chinadaily.com.cn/a/201905/10/WS5cd51fa1a3104842260baff9. html

China Daily. (2020). China's steel base Hebei to further cut overcapacity. Retrieved January 13, 2020 from https://www.chinadaily.com.cn/a/202001/07/WS5e1444b0a310cf3e3558303b. html

China Watch. (2020). Retail sales of consumer goods set to top $5.73trn in China. Retrieved February 04, 2020 from https://www.telegraph.co.uk/china-watch/business/china-retail-sales-growth-2019/

Chivakul, M., et al. (2015). Understanding residential real estate in China. *IMF working paper no. 15/84*, Washington, DC.

Dabla-Norris, K., et al. (2015) Causes and consequences of income inequality – A global perspective. *IMF discussion note no. 15/13*, Washington, DC

Dyck, S., & Levinger, H. (2010). China's provinces - Digging one layer deeper. In *Deutsche Bank research current issues*, Frankfurt am Main.

Economist Intelligence Unit. (2014). *Still making it – An analysis of manufacturing labour costs in China.*

European Chamber of Commerce. (2016). *Overcapacity in China – An impediment to the party's reform agenda.*

Frieden, J. A. (2016). Macroeconomic rebalancing in China and the G20. *China & World Economy, 24*(4), 15–33.

Hansakul, S., & Levinger, H. (2016) Asia infrastructure financing – Getting it right would lift medium-term growth. In *Deutsche Bank research current issues*, Frankfurt am Main.

Holmes, A., & Lancaster, D. (2019). China's local government bond market. *Reserve Bank of Australia Bulletin*, June 2019.

Hsu, S. (2019). China's industrial production, fixed asset investment underscore slowdown. Retrieved December 12, 2019 from https://seekingalpha.com/article/4249537-chinas-industrial-production-fixed-asset-investment-underscore-slowdown

IMF. (2019). People's Republic of China. 2019 Article IV Consultation. *International monetary fund country report no. 19/266.*

Just, T., & Dyck, S. (2011). China's housing markets – Regulatory interventions mitigate risk of severe bust. In *Deutsche Bank Research Current Issues*, Frankfurt am Main.

Levinger, H. (2015) China's provinces – Mapping the way forward. In *Deutsche Bank Research Briefing*. Retrieved November 07, 2016 from https://www.dbresearch.com/PROD/DBR_INTERNET_EN-PROD/PROD0000000000356963/China's_provinces%3A_Mapping_the_way_forward.PDF

Liao, M., Sun, T., & Zhang, J. (2016). China's financial interlinkages and implications for inter-agency coordination. *IMF working paper no. 16/181*, Washington, DC.

Lu, Y., & Sun, T. (2013). Local government financing platforms in China. *IMF working paper no. 13/243*, Washington, DC.

McKinsey and Company. (2013). Mapping China's middle class. *The McKinsey Quarterly*, June 2013, New York.

OECD. (2015). *OECD economic surveys: China 2015* (p. 29). Paris: OECD Publishing.

Reuters. (2019). China's Shandong province plans further coal usage cuts over next five years. Retrieved January 13, 2020 from https://www.reuters.com/article/us-china-coal-shandong/chinas-shandong-province-plans-further-coal-usage-cuts-over-next-five-years-idUSKCN1TX1AW

Solt, F. (2016). The standardized world income inequality database. *Social Science Quarterly, 97*, 1267. https://doi.org/10.1111/ssqu.12295.

South China Morning Post. (2016). *Beijing struggles with local governments on industrial overcapacity*. Retrieved August 05, 2016.

UNCTAD. (2017). World investment report 2017 – Investment and the digital economy. In *United Nations conference on trade and development*, Geneva.

Xie, Y., & Zhou, X. (2014). Income inequality in today's China. *Proceedings of the National Academy of Science of the United States of America, 111*(19), 6928–6933.

Zhang, Z. (2015). China's unexpected fiscal slide. *Deutsche Bank Research.*

Zhang, L. (2016). Rebalancing in China—Progress and prospects. *IMF working paper no. 16/183,* Washington, DC.

Zhang, Y. S., & Barnett, S. (2014) Fiscal vulnerabilities and risks from local government finance in China. *IMF working paper no. 14/4,* Washington, DC.

Zhang, H., Zhang, H., & Zhang, J. (2015). Demographic age structure and economic development - Evidence from Chinese provinces. *Journal of Competitive Economics, 43*(1), 170–185.

Hong Kong: A Review of Its Land System, Real Estate Market, and Related Matters

Roger Nissim

Abstract

This chapter aims to review and help explain the land administration system and real estate market in Hong Kong, as well as what has changed and, just as importantly, what has not changed during the twenty-three years since Hong Kong's handover to China. The significant role that the Hong Kong Special Administrative Government (HKSARG) has on the local real estate business, together with its regulatory functions, is examined. Hong Kong's inevitable convergence, and in some cases divergence, with its neighboring cities located in mainland China north of the border, are also discussed.

1   Introduction

Hong Kong was a British colony from 1841 up until the handover back to China in 1997. The fundamental point that led up to the handover was the expiry in June 1997 of the lease for the New Territories, which can be seen from the map below (Fig 1) constitutes about 90% of Hong Kong's total land area. Because the shortage of developable land has been a problem from day one up until today, the administration's land management is of paramount importance as it has a very strong influence on the economy. All land in Hong Kong remains leasehold. For the government, land premiums and property-related stamp duties are an important source of revenue; and for developers the cost of land, which is usually more than half the total cost of any particular project, has a major impact on development decisions. The implications of these facts are considered further.

R. Nissim (✉)
University of Hong Kong, Hong Kong, SAR, China

© Springer Nature Switzerland AG 2021   71
B. Wang, T. Just (eds.), *Understanding China's Real Estate Markets*, Management
for Professionals, https://doi.org/10.1007/978-3-030-49032-4_6

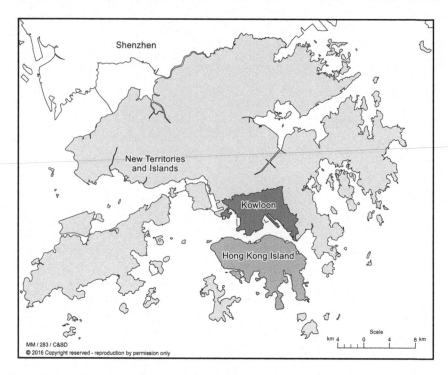

Fig. 1 Map of Hong Kong. Source: Base Map from Survey and Mapping Office, Lands Department, Hong Kong Special Administrative Region Government (HKSARG)

Hong Kong is situated at the southeastern tip of the mainland of China, with a total area of about 1106.7 square kilometers covering Hong Kong Island, 80.7 square kilometers, Kowloon 46.9 square kilometers, and the New Territories and Islands 979 square kilometers. By end-year 2018, the number of inhabitants in Hong Kong stood at slightly over 7.48 million and the predicted figure for 2024 is 7.8 million. It is expected that the population will peak at 8.22 million in mid-2043 and thereafter decline to 7.72 million by mid-2066 due to the aging of society.

2 Land Ownership

Hong Kong Island and Kowloon Peninsula were ceded to Britain on a permanent basis in 1841 and 1860, respectively, whereas the New Territories and Islands were leased from China for 99 years from 1898. It was the expiry of the New Territories lease in 1997, which covers nearly 90% of Hong Kong's total land area that led to the negotiations between Britain and China which resulted in the handover of Hong Kong, as a whole, to China on 1 July 1997.

During these negotiations between the governments of China and Britain, the Chinese leader Deng Xiaoping promised that there would be 'no change for 50 years' and articulated the concept of 'one country, two systems', whereby Hong Kong would be returned to Chinese sovereignty but would be allowed to continue its capitalist economic system, retain its own currency as well as common law rules and principles with the judiciary independent and separated from the central administration. The framework for this was set out in the *Sino-British Joint Declaration on the Question of Hong Kong* (the Joint Declaration) that was signed between the Chinese and British Governments on 19 December 1984, and was then embodied in the *Basic Law of the Hong Kong Special Administrative Region* (the Basic Law) that was adopted on 4 April 1990 by the Seventh National People's Congress (NPC) of the People's Republic of China (PRC). The Basic Law is, in effect, Hong Kong's mini constitution.

For example, Article 2 of the Basic Law authorizes the Hong Kong Special Administrative Region (HKSAR) to exercise a high degree of autonomy and will enjoy executive, legislative and independent judicial power, including that of final adjudication. Article 5 states that the socialist system and policies shall not be practised in the HKSAR and the previous capitalist system and way of life shall remain unchanged for 50 years. Article 6 requires that the HKSAR shall protect the right of private ownership of property in accordance with the law, and Article 8 states that the laws previously in force in Hong Kong, that is, the common law, rules of equity, ordinances, subordinate legislation and customary law, shall be maintained, except for any that contravene the Basic Law and subject to any amendment by the legislature of the HKSAR. These four articles laid the foundation for the continuation of pre-1997 land administration and practice, as well as town planning and property development controls that existed in Hong Kong to continue, broadly speaking unchanged, post-1997. This high degree of certainty that the rules of the game for property development were not going to be changed was a vital component towards ensuring a smooth handover as the development industry could continue to play its very important part in the economy of Hong Kong.

Apart from St. John's Cathedral on Hong Kong Island, all private land is held on leases of varying length from the government. On the permanently ceded parts of Hong Kong Island and Kowloon, there are a mixture of 999-year, 99-year and 75-year leases, with some renewable, some not, leases. In the New Territories, the leases were granted for 75 years with a right of renewal for a further 24 years up until 1997. Following the signing of the Joint Declaration, which included an entire Annex 3 related to *land leases*, all the leases that were expiring in 1997 were renewed by statute with the passing of the *New Territories Leases (Extension) Ordinance (Cap 150)* on 21 January 1988 with all such leases being extended for 50 years up until 30 June 2047 without requiring the payment of a premium just with an enhanced government rent (ground rent) calculated at 3% of the rateable value of the property.

In accordance with, and from the date of, the Joint Declaration, all new land granted or sold by the Hong Kong Government, up until the handover in 1997 was for a term expiring on 30 June 2047. A further commitment to there being no forced changes was the recognition in Annex 3 of the Joint Declaration that all leases of land granted before the Joint Declaration were signed and came into force, and which extend beyond 30 June 1997, which would include all the very long early leaseholds, and shall continue to have their rights recognized and protected under the law.

During the very first hours of 1 July 1997, the Hong Kong Reunification Ordinance, No. 110 of 1997, was enacted to ensure a seamless legal and administrative transfer from the old to the new administration. As regards land administration, Section 32 relates to lease or grant of land and natural resources and says that 'the chief executive may on behalf of the Government of the HKSAR lease or grant land and natural resources within the HKSAR which are state property'. Interestingly since the handover, all land sold or granted throughout Hong Kong has been for a uniform period of 50 years such that a lease granted in 1998 will expire in 2048, a lease granted in 2000 will expire in 2050 and a lease granted in 2019 will expire in 2069 which would indicate that when 2047 comes, there is a very good chance that all those expiring leases could be renewed again as Hong Kong now seems to have evolved into a system of perpetual leaseholds. Today, 22 years after the handover, all land leases continue to be written in English, all legislation is written in English and all court decisions are written in English based on the common law of legal system and principles which taken together is a very powerful testament to Deng's promise that there would be no change for 50 years.

3   Economy

Right from the founding of Hong Kong in 1841, it has been a free port which has thrived on free trade. This still holds good today with duty being charged on only very few products such as tobacco. In the 1950s, Hong Kong began to develop as a manufacturing centre, at first on the basis of cotton textiles and then adding woollen, man-made fibres and made-up garments as the major part of its domestic exports. Subsequently, electronic and electrical products, watches and clocks, toys, plastics and other light industries became major contributors. There were further surges in population with many fleeing the privations of the communist PRC to seek their fortune in Hong Kong in the mid-1960s and throughout the 1970s when the population was growing at around a million per decade such that by 1981 it had reached 5.1 million.

China's open door policy, announced by Deng in December 1978, followed by the setting up of the Special Economic Zones (SEZs) in 1980, including Shenzhen, which is situated immediately to the north of Hong Kong, had a profound effect on the local economy. China's economic policy was to positively encourage and support foreign trade and direct inward investment. These SEZs had favourable tax regimes and low wages that together with cheap land enabled them to attract capital and business from adjacent overseas Chinese communities such as Hong Kong. Hong Kong's manufacturers rapidly took advantage of these benefits to set up their factories in the Pearl River Delta (PRD) such that at its peak there were between

10 and 12 million people working in Hong Kong-owned factories in the PRD compared with the 800,000 that worked in Hong Kong factories prior to the opening up of the PRD. To handle the resulting phenomenal increase in output, our container port was rapidly expanded, and between the years of 1987 to 1989, from 1992 to 1997 and from 1999 to 2004, it was the world's busiest container port. Today it ranks sixth.

Hong Kong meanwhile transformed itself into to an entrepot role, a centre for finance and insurance, research and design, sales and tourism, which was boosted by the opening of Hong Kong Disneyland in September 2005, and other business-related activities were conducted here, whilst the manufacturing was done across the border. This transformation into a service centre rather than a manufacturing centre is such that today over 92% of the economy is service related as indicated in Table 1 which gives a breakdown of GDP by economic activity at current prices, noting that since October 1983, the Hong Kong dollar has been linked to the US dollar at the fixed exchange rate of HKD 7.80 to USD 1.00. Hong Kong's open-door policy has enabled it to become one of the world's largest trading economies and an international financial and commercial centre serving the Asia-Pacific region and the mainland of China. The cornerstone of this approach is a strong and credible multilateral trading system as evidenced by the fact that on 1 January 1995, Hong Kong became a founding member of the World Trade Organization (WTO). Hong Kong has continued its separate membership of the WTO since 1 July 1997 using the name 'Hong Kong, China', and has always been an active participant. In addition,

Table 1 Percentage contribution of economic activities to GDP at basic prices (%)

GDP by economic activity at current prices	2013	2016	2017
Agriculture, fishing, mining and quarrying	0.1	0.1	0.1
Manufacturing	1.4	1.1	1.1
Electricity, gas and water supply and waste management	1.7	1.4	1.4
Construction	4.0	5.2	5.1
Services	92.9	92.2	92.4
Import/export, wholesale and retail trades	25.0	21.7	21.5
Accommodation[a] and food services	3.6	3.3	3.3
Transportation, storage, postal and courier services	6.0	6.2	6.0
Information and communications	3.6	3.5	3.4
Financing and insurance	16.5	17.7	18.9
Real estate, professional and business services	10.8	11.0	10.8
Public administration, social and personal services	17.0	18.1	18.2
Ownership of premises	10.4	10.7	10.3
Total	100.0	100.0	100.0
GDP at basic prices (HK$ billion)	2098.1	2417.9	2556.2

Source: Hong Kong in Figures, 2019 Edition, Census and Statistics Department, HKSARG. www.censtatd.gov.hk
[a]Accommdation services cover hotels, guesthouses, boarding houses and other establishments providing short-term accommodations

again using the name 'Hong Kong, China', Hong Kong belongs to the Asia-Pacific Economic Cooperation as well as the Asian Development Bank. Currently Hong Kong's major trading partners in terms of imports, exports and re-exports and in order of financial importance are the mainland of China, the European Union, the USA, Japan and Taiwan.

In June 2003, the mainland and Hong Kong Closer Economic Partnership Arrangement (CEPA) was signed, introducing the first free trade agreement ever concluded between the two signatories. CEPA has opened up huge markets for Hong Kong goods and services with ten Supplements signed between 2004 and 2013, expanding market liberalization and further facilitating trade and investment. In November 2015, a new agreement on trade in services was signed which extended the geographical coverage for the basic liberalization of trade in services from Guangdong to the whole of the Mainland. CEPA also encourages foreign investors to establish businesses in Hong Kong to leverage the CEPA benefits enabling them to tap into the vast opportunities of the Mainland market. The financial secretary announced in his 2016–2017 budget that Hong Kong is actively pursuing further trade and investment agreements in order to expand our commercial and trading partnerships. The Hong Kong-ASEAN Free Trade Agreement (FTA) and an FTA with Georgia were signed in November 2017 and June 2018, respectively. FTA negotiations have begun with other trading partners such as Australia. Currently, the economic focus is turning towards two visionary and aspirational initiatives that will result in even greater integration with the mainland economy and which tie in with two major transport infrastructure projects which were both completed in the second half of 2018; the 55-km-long Hong Kong-Zhuhai-Macao Bridge and the 26-km-long Guangzhou-Shenzhen-Hong Kong Express Rail Link. The first initiative is the Guangdong-Hong Kong-Macao Greater Bay Area (GBA) which plans to bring together the two Special Administrative Regions of Hong Kong and Macao and nine municipalities in the Guangdong Province. Covering 56,000 square kilometers (about three times the size of the San Francisco Bay Area), the GBA has a combined population of 69 million people with a GDP of around USD 1.5 trillion (comparable to that of Tokyo Bay Area and New York Metropolitan Area). The GBA aims to harness the collective strengths through coordinated economic development with I&T as the key focus as well as financial, legal and professional services. With its mature economy and skilled work force, Hong Kong is well positioned to both participate and benefit from this initiative to develop this exciting new global economic zone. Secondly is the Belt and Road Initiative launched in 2013 as the Silk Road Economic Belt and the twenty-first-century Maritime Silk Road (B&R). The aim is to promote cooperation among countries and regions in areas of policy coordination, facilities connectivity, unimpeded trade, financial integration and people-to-people bonds. Again Hong Kong is seen as a key B&R link, and with central authority policy support, it can capitalize on its unique advantages to provide a two-way connection for the Mainland and B&R regions in areas such as international project financing, the internationalization of the renminbi (RMB), professional services, as well as economic and trade cooperation. Table 2 below from HKF 2019

Table 2 Regional headquarters, regional offices and local offices in Hong Kong representing parent companies located outside Hong Kong

	2013	2017	2018
Number of regional headquarters	1379	1413	1530
Number of regional offices	2456	2339	2425
Number of local offices	3614	4473	4799

Note: Figures refer to the first working day of June of the year. Source: Hong Kong in Figures, 2019 Edition, Census and Statistics Department, HKSARG

gives the figures of regional headquarters, regional offices and local offices in Hong Kong representing parent companies located outside Hong Kong.

The continuing growth in these numbers is a positive vote of confidence by the international business community in choosing Hong Kong as their preferred location to conduct their business no doubt due to a combination of factors such as its proximity to China; world-class infrastructure; free flow of information; no restrictions on inward or outward investment; no foreign exchange controls; no nationality restrictions on corporate or sectoral ownership; and simple, low tax regime and world financial hub. Indeed this is supported by the World Economic Forum's 2019 Index of Economic Freedom which again ranks Hong Kong at No.1, citing the implementation of prudent economic policy within a stable and transparent legal environment as being the cornerstone of Hong Kong's continuing achievement in maintaining the world's freest economy.[1]

However, the latest Worldwide Cost of Living survey conducted by the Economist Intelligence Unit published in 2018, which is designed to assess the material cost of living as it relates to compensation packages for expatriates, showed that Hong Kong is now equal with both Singapore and Paris as being the three most expensive cites globally. All three are 7% more expensive to live in than New York. Hong Kong's linked currency with the strong US Dollar was identified as the major reason for the volatility in ranking changes, and it will be interesting to see if this has any impact on the number of new overseas companies wishing to locate here.

4 Taxation and Public Finances

Hong Kong has a predictable tax system. The city only imposes three direct taxes and has generous allowances and deductions which reduce the taxable amount required: 1) Profits tax is capped at 16.5 percent; 2) Salaries tax is a maximum of 15 percent; 3) Property tax is 15 percent. More important are the taxes that Hong Kong does not impose: No sales tax or VAT, no withholding tax, no capital gains tax, no tax on dividends and no estate tax (Invest HK, HKSARG). Article 107 of the Basic Law requires the HKSAR to follow the principle of keeping expenditure

---

[1]Source: www.heritage.org/index/country/hongkong

within the limits of revenues in drawing up its budgets and strive to achieve a fiscal balance, avoid deficits and keep the budget commensurate with the growth rate of its gross domestic product.

The government has consistently recorded an annual budget surplus since the handover such that by the end of 2018, they had accumulated sufficient to give Hong Kong a very substantial and healthy fiscal reserve of HKD 1.16 trillion. These fiscal reserves are the mainstay to support the local economy and help to ensure the stability of the Hong Kong dollar and to help withstand the challenges being posed by the uncertainties surrounding the current global economic landscape. The breakdown of the composition of these figures is shown in Figs. 2 and 3 below which are stated in HK dollars. Hong Kong has already developed and, as indicated in the breakdown of expenditure in the last budget given above, continues to develop a sophisticated and reliable infrastructure that allows the city to operate very efficiently. The provision of this infrastructure can be traced over the past decades as follows:

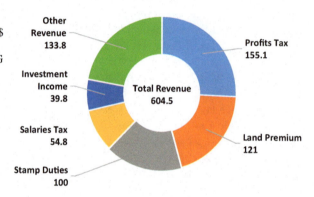

Fig. 2 Hong Kong government revenues. In HK$ billion. Source: 2018–2019 Budget Highlights, HKSARG

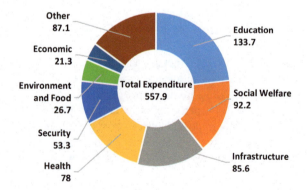

Fig. 3 Hong Kong government expenditures. In HK$ billion. Source: 2018–2019 Budget Highlights, HKSARG

- 1950s–1960s—Meeting basic needs such as water supply and public housing
- 1970s–1980s—Accommodating the growing population, building new towns and mass transit railway
- 1990s—Building of the new airport together with the airport express rail link and the container port facilities
- 2000s—Strengthening cross-border integration with the Lok Ma Chau Spur Line and the Shenzhen Bay Link Road
- 2009–2018—Strategic links between the east and west banks of the Pearl River Delta region with the construction of the 55-km-long Hong Kong-Zhuhai-Macao Bridge and to the north the 26-km-long Guangzhou-Shenzhen-Hong Kong Express Rail Link

Hong Kong's advanced transportation system means that 90% of all daily commuter journeys in the city are done on the railway networks, bus and minibus routes, tram rides, taxis and ferry services. Hong Kong International Airport has been ranked as the world's best airport for eight of the past 15 years. In the 2019 Skytrax rating of the world's top 100 airports, Hong Kong was fifth, but when viewed in the category of 70 million plus passengers, it came second. The recently completed Hong Kong-Zhuhai-Macao Bridge will make the nearby cities on the west side of the PRD accessible by road in just 30 min and the express rail link to the north will further enhance economic ties as well as help speed up the commute to China's populous southern cities. It will also connect Hong Kong with China's national high-speed rail system.

5   Government's Role in the Real Estate Market

With Hong Kong's leasehold land system the government has a very significant role to play in the real estate market, not only as the provider of the regulatory framework of planning and building control but as the principal supplier of land both for public as well as private sector development. Premiums from land sales and other land transactions have always been a major contributor, typically 20%, to the government's annual revenue, as Fig. 2 shows. Therefore, a properly regulated land supply has the twin objectives of meeting both the needs of the market as well as providing a significant revenue stream for the government.

The economic cycles have also had a big impact on the demand side with consequential adjustments being made by the government on the supply side which can best be illustrated with reference to the chart of Price Indices for Hong Kong Property Market from 1997 until 2019 (Fig. 4). Figure 4 shows clearly how prices initially peaked in 1997, but then, as a consequence of the Thai Baht induced Asian financial crisis of 1998, which was followed by the severe acute respiratory system (SARS) pandemic which hit Hong Kong in 2003, all sectors of the market dropped significantly with the domestic price index dropping from a high of 180 down to 100 by 1999 and then lower to 60 in 2003. The government's response to this was to significantly curtail land supply by ceasing to hold their regular

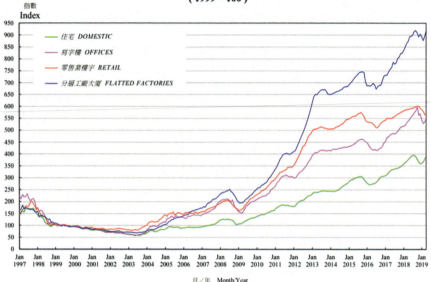

香港物業售價指數
PRICE INDICES FOR HONG KONG PROPERTY MARKET
(1999 = 100)

Fig. 4 Price Indices for Hong Kong Property Market. Source: Hong Kong Rating and Development Department

bi-monthly land auctions replacing it with a land application system, whereby the land was only put forward for sale once a developer had guaranteed to bid a pre-agreed minimum price. Understandably there was a significant drop in the amount of land sold even as the market recovered until the Lehman Brothers banking collapse resulted in another financial crisis in 2008–2009 when the domestic/residential price index dropped from 125 down to 100. The land application system, in fact, remained in place until 2013 when the government re-introduced its former policy of announcing and publishing its annual Land Sale Programme with sites being offered for sale by public tender in a regular and predictable manner.

This curtailing of land supply has had a long-lasting impact of private sector housing supply. The following figures tell the story: in 2013, after a number of years of limited land supply, only 8300 residential units were completed compared with 17,800 in 2017 and 21,000 in 2018, once a proper healthy land supply was restored. For private sector housing, the financial secretary in his 2019 budget estimates that government's land supply for private housing in the coming 3–4 years will be sufficient to produce 93,000 units. In addition the 2019/2020 Land Sale Programme includes 7 commercial/hotel sites capable of producing 814,600 square meters of floor space.

A detailed analysis carried out by Credit Suisse (Hong Kong) Ltd., a leading financial services company, and published by them on 18 November 2014 predicted that three of the biggest local developers, in terms of market share by the number of residential units built for sale, for the years 2015–2020, would account for 51% of the total supply. The dominant position of these three companies is unlikely to be challenged in the short- to medium-term because the high cost of land makes it very difficult for smaller companies, let alone new companies, to outbid them let alone enter the market. In addition these three companies are also sitting on huge land banks of undeveloped agricultural land which they can choose to develop, subject to agreement with government on the land premium for the change of use, at any time they consider the market conditions to be right which further consolidates their dominant position.

In recent years China-based developers have started to challenge the dominance of the local companies but with only limited success. DBS Bank (HK), a leading financial services group headquartered in Singapore, reported on 14 January 2019 that during 2018, local developers had bought most of the land put up for sale by the government. China-based developers had become less active in land banking in Hong Kong after the state council restricted domestic enterprises from making overseas real estate investments. In 2018 only three residential lots went to Chinese developers representing 21% of land sales. Today housing is the most important livelihood issue that needs to be addressed. Exorbitant property prices, high rentals, small living spaces, the proliferation of subdivided flats and the record high numbers on the waiting list for public rental housing mean that housing is at the top of the government's policy agenda. A review of the present position reveals that as of March 2018, the Hong Kong Housing Authority, government owned, and the Hong Kong Housing Society, government aided, had built 813,000 public rental housing units which house 29% of the population. In addition to this, these two organization provisions of 409,000 subsidized sale flats occupied by a further 14.6% of the population, and it is evident that the government has already provided housing for a significant percentage of the population.

In the 2018–2019 budget, it was announced that the government has adopted a public housing supply target of 100,000 units for the next 5 years, demonstrating its ongoing commitment to this type of provision. The remainder of the population, 56.4%, live in a mixture of owner-occupied or rented permanent private accommodation totalling 1,582,000 units, over half of which have no mortgages outstanding. As of March 2018, there were a total of 2.804 million permanent living quarters of all types in Hong Kong. At that time the population was just over 7482.5 million which gives an average household size of 2.67. Allowing, say, a 4% vacancy rate, this average would come up to 2.8 which is still lower than the current average household size of 2.91. On the basis of these statistics (HKF 2019), it could be argued that, overall, there is no real housing shortage in Hong Kong.

The real issue is not so much one of housing supply but one of affordability. Hong Kong has the dubious distinction, according to the 15th Annual Demographic International Housing Affordability Survey carried out in the third quarter of 2018 for middle-income housing, of having the most seriously unaffordable market out of 91 major metropolitan areas surveyed worldwide with a rating of 20.9, where moderately affordable is rated at 3.1–4, seriously unaffordable is rated at 4.1–5 and severely unaffordable is anything over 5 times the multiple of the median house price divided by median household income.[2] The unfortunate reality is that Hong Kong, on its own, cannot significantly engineer the correction to the market that is required for the affordability levels to drop in a meaningful way. The government in 2009 attempted to dampen the demand side by introducing a double stamp duty payment for flat purchasers who do not possess a permanent Hong Kong identity card which is given after 7 years residency. On the supply side, since 2013, the government has significantly ramped up the supply of land, but in spite of all of these efforts, prices continued to inexorably rise. There was a minor correction on residential pricing during 2016, but 2017 saw the inexorable rise resume and then another minor correction during 2018, which has again been wiped out in 2019. Probably the biggest factor was the decision by the Federal Reserve during this time to start raising interest rates, which, because of the linked currency, Hong Kong would have no choice but to follow. This immediately had an impact on buyers' affordability. For the time being the Federal Reserve seems unlikely to further raise interest rates in the short term so that should help stabilize sentiment. As Hong Kong enters uncharted waters, there will need to keep under review the full impact on the market over the coming months to properly assess the situation. Also, the uncertainty over the US-China trade war continues to hang heavily on the local economy.

6   The Local Development Regulatory System

There are basically three regulatory government departments involved in controlling the building industry in Hong Kong: the Lands Department, the Planning Department, and the Buildings Department. Within the government structure, overseeing the work of these three departments is the Development Bureau which is responsible for policy guidance and advice. The execution of the government's Land Disposal Programme is one of the principal functions of the Lands Department. They are responsible for preparing the land lease tender documents which will stipulate the obligations and duties of the purchaser and the planning, engineering and development requirements that need to be met. The following lease terms are typically included: 1) Lease term – normally 50 years from the date of grant or sale, with an annual rent assessed at 3 percent of rentable value. 2) Permitted uses – these generally correspond to the land use zoning on the relevant Outline Zoning Plan. For example, in residential zones usually only private residential use will be permitted. If the site is zoned for commercial/residential use, then mixed uses are permitted and the user clause will be written allowing non-industrial uses but excluding petrol filling stations. 3) Maximum building height permitted. 4) Minimum and maximum gross floor area permitted. 5) Maximum site coverage permitted. 6) A Building Covenant is always included specifying the time in which the minimum gross floor area permitted in new building, usually 60 percent of the maximum figure, is expected to be completed. For normal sized sites 48 or 60 months may be given

---

[2]www.demographia.com

and longer periods such as 72 months for larger sites. 7) Master Layout Plan requirement for larger sites over two hectares. 8) Design, Disposition and Height control for smaller sites. 9) Car parking, loading and unloading requirements. 10) Restrictions on vehicular ingress and egress. 11) Landscaping, tree felling and other environmental requirements. 12) Provision of recreational facilities in residential sites. 13) Deed of Mutual Covenant requirements to ensure there is a legally binding structure for the long-term management and maintenance of the new building and that these costs are fairly shared by all the new owners.

In addition to land sales, the Lands Department also handles requests for lease modifications and land exchanges which arise when new land use zoning plans result in there being conflicts with some of the sites governed by older, out of date, lease conditions. For example, a lot of pre-war residential leases were typically written with a 35-foot height restriction which today has been superseded by an outline zoning plan that permits, say, a 170-foot-high building. The owner of this land can apply for a lease modification to permit the new higher building, and if approved and, subject to the agreement to the modification premium, can redevelop. The lease modification document will contain conditions very similar to those in the land sale documents set out above. The modification premium is assessed by professional valuers in the Lands Department and is the difference in the value of the land with the benefit of the 170-foot height limit, known as the 'after' value minus the value of the land with the original 35-foot height limit, known as the 'before' value. The resultant figure being the premium needs to be paid to the government which is another valuable source of revenue. In the case of approved private not-for-profit organizations such as schools and hospitals, arrangements are made for land to be granted by private treaty, usually without payment of premium. Interestingly the Lands Department's authority over land is not covered by statutory control but by administrative law which has, and continues to evolve over time as more case law comes along.

Going back to the landmark 1981 case of Hang Wah Chong Investment Co. Ltd v Attorney General, and reaffirmed by the courts over subsequent years, the broad principles that have been established are that where a tenant seeks a concession from his landlord and, in this context, the government is seen to be acting in a private not a public capacity, in relation to the development of land leased, the landlord is entitled to make the granting of that concession conditional upon payment of a premium. Perhaps more importantly there is no requirement for the government to establish reasonableness in the exercise of its discretion as landlord, whether or not to grant such modification and what level of premium it may wish to charge. In addition the Lands Department are, broadly speaking, immune to judicial review proceedings. Notwithstanding the Lands Department's seemingly invincible position, they do recognize the need to provide a service to the development industry and the public which is spelled out in their vision and mission statements together with a number of performance pledges. A series of practice notes are published from time to time to advise the development industry and professional practitioners such as surveyors and architects of any policy changes, and all these can be viewed on their website.

The principal body responsible for statutory planning in Hong Kong is the Town Planning Board (TPB). It is formed under the Town Planning Ordinance and is served by the Planning Department. The local planning system comprises development strategies at the territorial level and various types of statutory and departmental plans at the district/local level. The most frequently referred to statutory plans are the Outline Zoning Plans (OZP's), now covering most of the urban and suburban areas of Hong Kong, which show the land use zones, development parameters and major road systems of an individual planning area. Areas covered by OZP's are in general zoned for uses such as residential, commercial, industrial, green belt, open space, government/institution/community uses or other specified purposes. Attached to each OZP is a schedule of notes showing the uses which are always permitted in a particular zone and other uses for which a prior permission from the TPB must be sought.

Building applications are controlled under the Buildings Ordinance and handled by the Building Authority whose approval is required before the commencement of any private sector development construction work. Such applications will only be accepted if submitted by an authorised person (AP), as defined in the Buildings Ordinance, usually a suitably qualified and registered architect, structural engineer or surveyor. The scope of control under the Buildings Ordinance includes, inter alia: (1) Control on all new building developments, e.g. offices buildings, residential blocks and other associated works such as foundations, demolition, structural and drainage works; (2) Control of renovation projects in respect of existing buildings for which structural elements and/or means of escape in case of fire will be altered in such projects; (3) Control of works such as erection of hoardings, covered walkways and demolition; (4) Control on specialized use of existing buildings such as kindergartens, homes for the elderly, cinemas and restaurants by a system of licensing; and (5) Control on unauthorized building works by means of prosecution and enforcement.

One important and critical link with the planning system is the power the Building Authority has, under Section 16 (1) (d) of the Buildings Ordinance, to refuse consent or approval to carrying out building works that would contravene any approved or draft plan prepared under the Town Planning Ordinance. The regulatory functions of the three departments described above have, broadly speaking, remained unchanged since the handover in 1997, ensuring certainty and continuity for the development industry and related professionals.

Locally, there remain significant uncertainties, and the timing of the final resolution of the USA-China trade war has put the government on the back foot. Hong Kong is waiting rather nervously to see how the government, developers and the real estate and financial markets respond in this uncertain and volatile environment.

References

Census and Statistics Department Hong Kong Special Administrative Region Government. (2019). Hong Kong in figures - 2019 edition. Retrieved June 24, 2019 from www.censtatd.gov.hk

Colliers International HK. (2019). Q1 2019 | Hong Kong | Residential. Retrieved July 04, 2019 from https://www.colliers.com/-/media/images/apac/hong%20kong/2019_images/quarterly/2019_q1/colliers_hong_kong_residential_q1_2019_20190415.pdf?la=en-gb

Credit Suisse (Hong Kong) Ltd. www.credit-suisse.com

DBS Bank Hong Kong. (2019). HK Property: Local developers dominated land market. Retrieved July 04, 2019 from https://www.dbs.com.hk/treasures/aics/templatedata/article/generic/data/en/GR/012019/190114_insights_hk_property.xml

Rating & Valuation Department, Hong Kong Special Administrative Region Government. (2019). June 2019 property review monthly supplement. Retrieved June 24, 2019 from www.rvd.gov.hk

Savills Hong Kong. (2019). Office leasing – Rental momentum continues in Q1. Retrieved July 04, 2019 from https://pdf.savills.asia/asia-pacific-research/hong-kong-research/hong-kong-office/off04-2019-1.pdf

South China Morning Post. (2019a). Demand for office space in Hong Kong cools by the most in five months, but rents edge higher. Retrieved April 15, 2019 from https://www.scmp.com/property/hong-kong-china/article/3006269/demand-office-space-hong-kong-cools-most-five-months-rents

South China Morning Post. (2019b). Hong Kong developer walks away from HK$11.1 billion Kai Tak project, citing 'social contradiction and economic instability'. Retrieved June 11, 2019 from https://www.scmp.com/business/article/3014075/hong-kong-developer-walks-away-kai-tak-project-citing-social-contradiction

South China Morning Post. (2019c). Hong Kong developers slash home prices by up to 20 per cent to kick some tempo back into the downbeat property market. Retrieved June 21, 2019 from https://www.scmp.com/business/article/3015427/hong-kong-developers-hope-put-recent-setbacks-behind-them-they-launch

South China Morning Post. (2019d). Chinese developers snap up discounted Kai Tak land as Hong Kong's mood for property sours amid protest rallies and trade war. Retrieved June 26, 2019 from https://www.scmp.com/business/article/3016205/chinese-developers-snap-discounted-kai-tak-land-hong-kongs-mood-property

South China Morning Post. (2019e). Hong Kong's retail sales will drop 5 per cent this year amid fall in numbers of mainland Chinese tourists, says PwC. Retrieved June 27, 2019 from https://www.scmp.com/business/money/market-snapshot/article/3016219/ong-kongs-retail-sales-will-drop-5-cent-year-amid

South China Morning Post. (2019f). What truce? US-China trade war uncertainty still weighing on global growth, Morgan Stanley says as it cuts outlook. Retrieved July 01, 2019 from https://www.scmp.com/business/china-business/article/3016819/what-truce-us-china-trade-war-uncertainty-still-weighing

Trade and Industry Department. (2019). Retrieved June 24, 2019 from www.tid.gov.hk

Part II

Legal and Regulatory Environment for China's Real Estate Markets

Legal Framework for Real Estate Investment in China

Qian Ma

Abstract

While the past few years witnessed muted foreign investor activity in Chinese real estate due to governmental restrictions and fierce competitions from domestic capital, a change is now underway. China's enormous population and differing residential requirements clearly distinguish it from other countries. Before investors jump into the fray of the Chinese market, it is important to know the unique rules and regulations regarding acquisition of Chinese property. In this chapter, the reader will learn about the legal framework for investors and the differences that characterize the Chinese real estate market. This chapter is based on recent relaxation of restrictions on foreign investments in the Chinese real estate market.

1 Introduction

Real estate investment is a significant pillar of the Chinese economy. However, before investors dive into the fray of the Chinese real estate market, it is important to bear in mind China's real property law. In 1988, China amended its constitution to allow the creation of transferable land-use rights in real property. This constitutional change effectively opened the flood to real estate development in China (Stein 2013). The current constitution of the People's Republic of China, as amended in 2004 (Constitution[1]), clearly provides for the protection of private property.

---

[1]Constitution of the People's Republic of China.

Q. Ma (✉)
Clifford Chance, Frankfurt am Main, Germany

© Springer Nature Switzerland AG 2021
B. Wang, T. Just (eds.), *Understanding China's Real Estate Markets*, Management for Professionals, https://doi.org/10.1007/978-3-030-49032-4_7

According to Article 13 of the Constitution, citizens' lawful private property is "inviolable" (Zhang 2015a). The law for the first time protected the interests of private investors to the same extent as that of state interests.[2] Most notable is the property law which came into effect on 1 October 2007 (Property Law[3]). The Property Law established a framework for the protection of property rights and addressed the establishment, alteration, transfer and elimination of property-related ownership rights and the registration and delivery of real property rights (Law Library of Congress 2015).

In 2006, China significantly tightened the rules on foreign investment in the real estate sector in an effort to prevent overseas "hot money" from flowing into China and to cool the real estate market that was seen to be overheating (Zhang 2015c). These measures, coupled with the overall economic slowdown, led to a considerable drop in foreign investment in the real estate market (Zhang 2015c). In order to reverse the trend and continue the general policy of relaxing foreign ownership restrictions in real estate, China issued the Notice on Adjusting the Policies on the Entry into and Administration of Foreign Investment in the Real Estate Market on 19 August 2015 (Linklaters 2015). Furthermore, in order to attract more foreign investment, the Ministry of Commerce of China (MOFCOM) released a draft version of the Foreign Investment Law on 19 January 2015 for public consultation (Clifford Chance 2015). On 26 December 2018, the First Draft FIL was revised by the National People's Congress. On 15 March 2019, the National People's Congress passed the new draft of the Foreign Investment Law (Clifford Chance 2019). On 1 January 2020, the new FIL entered into force and became the basic law regulating all foreign investment activities in China, significantly changing the previous regulatory regime.

This article introduces the Chinese legal framework for real estate asset classes. It is divided into two main sections: (1) the legal framework for domestic investors in China and (2) the legal framework for foreign investors in China. The first section includes an introduction to the real property rights regime and procedures when engaging in property investments. The recent relaxation of restrictions on foreign investment in the real estate market, together with its influence and significance for foreign investors, is addressed in the second section.

---

2   Legal Framework for Domestic Investors

The protection of private property is fundamentally provided for in the Constitution. The state protects the rights of citizens to private property and to its inheritance (Article 13 of the Constitution) (Zhang 2015b). Further, the PRC Property Law

---

[2]Article 13 of the Constitution: The state protects the right of citizens to own lawfully earned income, savings, houses and other lawful property. The state protects the right of citizens to inherit private property by law.

[3]Property Law of the People's Republic of China, adopted at the Fifth of the Tenth National People's Congress of the Peoples Republic of China on 16 March 2007.

established a framework for the protection of property rights. It addresses the establishment, alteration, transfer and elimination of property-related ownership rights and the registration and delivery of movable and real property rights (Zhang 2015b). In addition to the PRC Property Law, China regulates real property through a series of other laws and regulations, such as the Law on Land Management, the Interim Regulations on Real Estate Registration, the Law on the Administration of Urban Real Estate, etc. (Zhang 2015b).

2.1 Real Property Rights

Real property rights in China can generally be divided into three types: (1) ownership rights, (2) usufructuary rights and (3) security rights. Ownership rights are protected under Article 39 of the Property Law which gives the owner the right to possess, utilize, dispose of and obtain profits from the real property.[4] Generally speaking, rural collectives own agricultural land, and the state owns urban land. However, a property owner enjoys exclusive ownership of the part of the building exclusive to such owner and enjoys co-ownership of the common areas and adjacent ancillary facilities such as internal roads and green space (Article 70 Property Law[5]) (Lawrence 2007).

Pursuant to Article 117 of the Property Law, the owner of usufructuary rights has the right to possess, use and benefit from real property owned by others.[6] The land-use right in China is a "usufructuary right" since it allows the holder of the right, the usufructuary, to legally possess, use and benefit from property owned by someone else (Lawrence 2007). The owner may not intervene in the exercise of rights by the holder of the usufructuary right.[7] Usufructuary rights include (1) the right to the contracted management of land, (2) construction land-use right, (3) right to use house sites and (4) easement (Wang 2011). The contracted management of land enables a contractor of the right to possess, utilize and obtain profits from agricultural land. The construction land-use right exists only with regard to state-owned land, and the owner of the right is allowed to build buildings and their accessory facilities. With regard to an easement, it is governed by the terms of the contract. The owner of the easement has the right to use the real property of others to benefit his

---

[4]Article 39 of the Property Law: The owner shall have the right to possess, use, seek profits from and dispose of the real or movable property in accordance with the laws.

[5]Article 70 of the Property Law: Property owners shall enjoy ownership of the special parts within a building, such as the residential units and the units for business purposes, and shall enjoy the right to share and jointly manage the common parts other than the special parts.

[6]Article 117 of the Property Law: A usufructuary right holder shall, according to law, have the right to possess, use and benefit from the immovables or movables owned by another.

[7]Article 120 of the Property Law: In exercising his rights, the usufructuary right holder shall observe the provisions of law governing the protection and reasonable exploitation and utilization of resources. The owner shall not interfere with the exercise of rights by the usufructuary right holder.

own real property.[8] Thus, China was able to establish a foundational legal framework which functioned to stimulate growth in the rural areas and real estate development in the urban areas (Wang 2011).

Security rights are generally classified as mortgages (for real property, fixtures and equipment), pledges (for movable property) and liens. In order to ensure that obligations are met, owners of security rights have priority over assets if a debtor defaults on his obligation. Security rights cannot exist independently without a valid principal claim and become invalid when the debt lapses (Lawrence 2007). Article 179 of the Property Law provides that if a debtor or a third party mortgages property to a creditor in order to secure performance of a debt obligation without transferring possession thereof and the debtor fails to repay the debt on maturity or a circumstance provided for in the mortgage for its realization occurs, the creditor shall have the right to repayment from such mortgaged property on a priority basis (Lawrence 2007). As noted above, the Property Law generally requires the registration of the creation, change, transfer and termination of interests in immovable property in order to be effective and enforceable.[9] A mortgage must also be registered. The mortgage interest is created as of the date of registration.[10] Article 10 of the Property Law provides that registration shall occur at the place where the property is located.[11] The pledge of movable property is delivered to the creditor to secure the performance of a debt obligation (Lawrence 2007). The pledge of rights comes into existence after registration with a "credit investigation institution".[12] If a debtor fails to perform its matured debt obligation to a creditor, the creditor may place a lien on movable property of the debtor legally in the possession of the creditor and receive payment therefrom on a priority basis (Lawrence 2007).

2.2   Procedures for Property Investments

According to the Constitution, individuals cannot privately own land and natural resources in the country. The Constitution provides that land in urban areas must be

---

[8]Article 156 of the Property Law: Easement holders shall, according to the stipulations in the contract, have the right to use another person's immovable property to get better results from his own immovables.

[9]Article 9 of the Property Law: The creation, alteration, transfer or extinction of the property right shall become valid upon registration according to law; otherwise it shall not become valid, unless otherwise provided for by law.

[10]Article 187 of the Property Law: Where the property specified in subparagraphs (1), (2) and (3) or the buildings under construction specified in subparagraph (5), under the first paragraph of Article 180 of this Law, are mortgaged, such mortgage shall be registered. The mortgage interest is created as of the date of registration.

[11]Article 10 of the PRC Property Law: Registration of the immovables shall be handled by the registration authority at the place where they are located.

[12]Article 228 of the Property Law: Where the accounts receivable are pledged, the parties concerned shall conclude a contract in written form. The interest to the pledge is created at the time when the pledge is registered with the credit information service.

owned by the state, whereas land in rural and suburban areas must be owned by the state or local collectives (Law Library of Congress 2015). Although individuals cannot privately own land, they may obtain transferrable land-use rights for a number of years for a fee. Land-use rights can be obtained from the land administration department by agreement, tender or auction. A land grant contract should be signed by the land user and the land administration department at the municipal or county level (Law Library of Congress 2015). Under the current rules prescribed by the State Council, land may be used for residential purposes for up to 70 years; for industrial purposes for 50 years; for education, science, culture, public health and physical education purposes for 50 years; and for commercial, tourist and recreational purposes for 40 years (Zhang 2015a). Under the Property Law, when the term for land-use right expires, it will be automatically renewed.[13] However, the law does not clarify whether the state would charge granting fee at the time of renewal or how such a fee at the time of renewal would be determined (Zhang 2015a).

Under the Urban Real Estate Law, when real estate is transferred, the land-use rights of the land on which the buildings are situated and ownership of houses/apartments are transferred simultaneously (Zhang 2015a). Restrictions that may apply to the transfer of real estate include prohibiting transfer when the land-use rights are reclaimed by the state in accordance with law or when the property has not been properly registered and certificates of ownership have not been obtained (Law Library of Congress 2015).

All interests in land must be recorded in the official government registry. The Property Law provides that registration of real property must be performed by the registration authorities in the region where the property is located (Zhang 2015b). Both land-use rights of urban land and ownership of houses/apartments must be registered by municipal authorities at or above the county level. Certificates of ownership should be issued to confirm the rights and ownership (Law Library of Congress 2015). The Property Law only offers a general guideline, while the Interim Regulation on Real Estate Registration provides the specific official procedure and rules on registration. In the event that rights over immovable property are created, modified, transferred or eliminated, Article 6 of the Property Law requires a general

---

[13] Article 149 of the Property Law: The term of the right to use land for construction for dwelling houses shall be automatically renewed upon expiration.

The term of the right to use land for construction not for dwelling houses shall be renewed according to legal provisions. Where there are stipulations about the ownership of houses and other real properties on the aforesaid land, such stipulations shall prevail; if there is no such stipulation or the stipulations are not explicit, the ownership shall be determined according to the provisions in the laws and administrative regulations.

Article 41 of Interim Regulations of the People's Republic of China Concerning the Assignment and Transfer of the Right to the Use of the State-owned Land in the Urban Areas: Upon expiration of the term of use, the land user may apply for its renewal. Where such a renewal is necessary, a new contract shall be signed in accordance with the provisions in Chapter II of these regulations, and the land user shall pay the fee for the assignment of the right to the use of the land and undertake registration.

registration.[14] Article 10(2) of the Property Law provides for a unified registration system for all real property rights, which is however only adopted by first-tier cities such as Beijing and Shanghai.[15] The implementation of the unification of interests in a single registry in smaller cities is still lacking. The Public Notary Office is a subordinate agency of the Ministry of Justice, and it is responsible for issuing certifications for property titles.

3   Legal Framework for International Investors

All land in China belongs to the state or the collectives. Like all domestic investors, foreign investors may only obtain land-use rights, rather than land ownership (Zhang 1999). The general procedure for purchasing real property in China is as follows.

First of all, foreign buyers need to submit an official offer letter (through an agent if used) once the buyer or the buyer's agent has found a suitable property. The offer letter sets out the agreed purchase price, payment schedules and other conditions of purchasing the targeted property. A deposit of 1 percent of the agreed purchase price should be paid to the seller upfront (Sinojobs 2015). If necessary, the buyer can also start to make financing arrangements at this point. Some foreign banks provide mortgage facilities for foreigners purchasing property in China. Second, the agency or legal representative will carry out checks on the property and owner or developer. For some properties, it is necessary to apply for the approval of the government and the public security bureau in order for the sale to proceed (International Living 2016). Next, the seller and the buyer will enter into an official sales contract. This contract has to be notarised by the foreign buyer in China. Unlike domestic investors, foreign investors are supposed to contact their local Foreign Office to have the purchase approved by the government. If a mortgage is needed, a deposit of 29% of the purchase price (in RMB) is payable as a down payment to the seller, i.e. in addition to the 1% deposit which has already been paid. Finally, on the payment of the relevant fees and taxes, an application needs to be submitted to the Government Deed and Title Office for the transfer of the deed from the seller to the buyer. Upon the issuance of the ownership certificate after a few weeks, the outstanding 70% of the purchase price should be paid to the seller (International Living 2016). It is important to note that the Chinese governmental authority is also involved in the real estate investment process. In China, land-use ownership, the real

---

[14] Article 6 of the Property Law: The creation, alteration, transfer or extinction of the property right of the immovables shall be registered in accordance with the provisions of law. The property right of the movables shall be created or transferred upon delivery in accordance with the provisions of law.

[15] Article 10 of the Property Law: Registration of the immovables shall be handled by the registration authority at the place where they are located. The state practices a unified system of registration in respect of the immovables. The scope of unified registration, the registration authority and the measures for registration shall be stipulated by law and administrative regulations.

estate development process and foreign investment in real estate are all subject to multiple layers of governmental laws, regulations and controls at local, provincial and national levels (Rothstein 2013), which are not dissimilar to those in many other countries. For example, in Beijing, foreign institutions (except those approved to engage in real estate) have to set up branches or representative offices before they are allowed to purchase non-residential real property. In Shanghai, foreign individuals can only buy residential real estate. Foreign investors navigating the investment landscape often discover that the interpretation and implementation of laws, rules and regulations can vary significantly from jurisdiction to jurisdiction. The Chinese legal system is still in the process of integrating with international markets. Through regulatory oversight and approvals, the government achieves macro-control of the real estate market (Rothstein 2013).

3.1   Recent Relaxation on Foreign Investment

Restrictions on property sales to foreigners were first introduced on 11 July 2006 through the Opinions on Regulating the Entry into and Administration of Foreign Investment in the Real Estate Market (Opinions 171), rolling out restrictions specifically targeting foreign investment in the real estate sector. These included minimum equity ratios in Article 2, restrictions on debt financing in Article 7 and limits on property purchase in Article 10 of Opinions 171 (Zhang 2015c). In an attempt to boost the slowing economy, China has relaxed rules on property sales to foreigners since 2015. On 19 August 2015, six Chinese ministries jointly issued a notice to relax certain controls they imposed in 2006 (He 2015). The Notice set out the changes which remove or loosen certain restrictions on real estate investment by foreign investors.

Previously, a foreign company that wished to invest in and purchase real estate in China had to establish a foreign-invested real estate enterprise (FIREE), while a foreign investor's onshore entity, branch or representative office for other types of operations was eligible to purchase commercial property for their own office use (Zhang 2015c). The Opinions 171 imposed a higher debt-to-equity ratio for FIREEs. A FIREE was required to have a registered capital of not less than 50% of its total investment amount for any real estate investment of more than USD 10 million. The central government raised the equity ratio to 70% if the total investment amount was no more than USD 3 million. This ratio between the registered capital and total investment has been reduced by the Notice and brought in line with the rules that apply to foreign invested enterprises, so that the ratio ranges from one-third (e.g. if the total investment amount is USD 30 million or more) and 70% (e.g. if the total investment amount is no more than USD 3 million) (Zhang 2015c). For investments greater than USD 10 million, FIREEs in the real estate sector are allowed to have a lower level of equity than before and are allowed to maintain a higher level of leverage.[16]

Previously, a FIREE was required to have its registered capital paid in full before it could raise onshore or offshore loans or convert the proceeds of overseas loans (or any combination of these). In addition, it had to obtain the land-use right certificate and inject funds in the amount of 35% or more of the project's total investment in the real estate project (He 2015). The Notice has abolished the requirement of full payment of the registered capital of the FIREE as a precondition for raising onshore or offshore loans or for the conversion of foreign exchange loans into RMB (or any combination of these) (Zhang 2015c). However, other restrictions remain in place, such as having a valid state-owned land-use certificate and, for a real estate project, having equity funds of at least 35% of the project's total investment.

Under the Opinions 171, individual foreign buyers are allowed to buy property if they can demonstrate that they have studied or worked in China for at least 1 year and are buying the residence for self-use. The Notice removes the 1-year restriction. Foreign individuals who are working and studying in China may buy property in China for self-use at any time. Foreign individuals may also buy more than one property (Zhang 2015c). However, it should be noted that such purchases continue to be limited to owner occupation and the relaxation does not affect the application of city-level restrictions on property purchases (Linklaters 2015). According to the new policies, FIREEs are no longer required to make a foreign exchange registration of direct investment with the State Administration of Foreign Exchange (SAFE). Instead, they may complete the required formalities directly with a bank. Such change is in line with earlier reforms triggered by the SAFE which applied to all foreign invested enterprises (He 2015)

Another positive sign of the Chinese government's determination to relax restrictions on foreign investment is seen in the First Draft FIL. At the end of 2015, the First Draft FIL was submitted to the Legislative Affairs Office of the State Council as a necessary step in the legislative process. Thereafter, the bill would be introduced to the National People's Congress (Wang and Yang 2016). On 26 December 2018, the National People's Congress published the *New Draft FIL* in order to solicit public opinion. The New Draft FIL is significantly shorter than the earlier version, comprising just 39 articles, compared with the 170 articles that made up the First Draft FIL. On 15 March 2019, the National People's Congress passed the New Draft FIL, and the New FIL has been implemented since 1 January 2020, which makes investment in China more straightforward for foreign parties. Currently, there are three key pieces of legislation governing foreign-invested enterprises: the Sino-Foreign Equity Joint Venture Law, the Sino-Foreign

---

[16]Article 3 of Provisional Regulations for the Proportion of Registered Capital to Total Amount of Investment of Joint Ventures Using Chinese and Foreign Investment: If the total investment of a Sino-foreign joint venture is between USD 10 million and USD 30 million (including USD 30 million), its registered capital shall account for at least 2/5 of the total investment.

If the total investment of a Sino-foreign joint venture is more than USD 30 million, its registered capital shall account for at least 1/3 of the total investment.

Contractual Joint Venture Law and the Wholly Foreign-Owned Enterprise Law (WFOE Law). These three laws, promulgated in the late 1970s and 1980s, have led to some issues for regulators, adjudicators and investors. They were created by different government agencies without much inter-agency coordination, and there are conflicts and inconsistencies between them and the Company Law of 1993. After the New FIL became effective, the three laws have been replaced and simplified to a great extent. The New FIL is expected to consolidate and unify the raft of laws and regulations governing foreign investment in China and resolve these issues as well as bringing all various types of foreign investments into one consolidated framework (Miller Canfield 2015). The FIREEs would need to comply with the corporate governance requirements under the Company Law or the Partnership Enterprise Law, as applicable.

Another major change introduced by the New Draft FIL is the adoption of a "negative list" approach in respect of foreign investment approval (Clifford Chance 2019). Under the current regime, most of the governmental approvals required by FIREEs for foreign investments are not required for domestic enterprises (Wang and Yang 2016). Under the New FIL foreign investors will no longer be subject to a separate regulatory regime for investments in China and will be treated in the same way as Chinese investors. New foreign investments outside the "negative list" will enjoy the same national treatment as domestic companies in terms of market entry. In other words, a foreign investor will no longer be required to obtain prior approval of MOFCM to set up a new company in industries outside the "negative list". This will reduce the timeline required for foreign investment projects and offer foreign parties greater flexibility in structuring their investment. The "negative list" will set out industry sectors in which foreign investment is restricted as well as the specified investment thresholds (Mayer Brown 2015). Foreign investments in restricted industries on the "negative list" will be subject to prior approval from MOFCOM based on MOFCOM's review of the nature of the investment from a public interest perspective rather than the contracts underlying such investments.

3.2   Significance for International Investors

With the Opinions 171, the Chinese government progressively tightened overseas access to China's property market, making it much more difficult to introduce overseas capital into the market in the ensuing 7 years (South China Morning Post 2015). In an attempt to attract more foreign investment, the Chinese government has initiated reforms to the current laws governing foreign investment in order to introduce consistency and to eliminate uncertainties. The Notice and the New FIL represent a significant shift in the government's position.

The directives of the Notice allow foreigners to have a higher leverage ratio, easier access to financing and eased rules on purchases by foreign enterprises and individuals. It is a positive move and signals that China welcomes foreign investments. The changes proposed by the New FIL show China's effort to rational- ize its foreign investments regulatory regime. It is seeking to create a stable, transparent and predictable legal environment for foreign investors through restructuring the approval, supervision and governance mechanisms (Wang and Yang 2016). The New FIL will likely facilitate the creation of a clearer legal framework and a more level playing field for foreign investors in China. This is in line with China's general reform policy—to streamline its approval system and grant national treatment to all foreign investments, except those that fall under the negative list. The relaxations should boost investors' confidence and create a positive impact on market sentiment (South China Morning Post 2015). The latest rule change would likely have a bigger effect among individual homebuyers, rather than institutional buyers. Foreigners don't have to spend at least 1 year studying or working in a Chinese city before they can buy a home for self-use (The Wall Street Journal 2015).

However, the actual impact might be small, since overseas buyers make up only a microscopic proportion of China's housing market. Non-Chinese homebuyers accounted for 0.5% of existing home transactions in Shanghai 2015 (Bloomberg 2015). Despite a strong recovery in demand since 2015 (due to the aforementioned rule changes), many cities are still facing high inventories and downward pressure on housing pricing. It is unlikely that purchases by foreigners will be able to make any meaningful change to the market fundamentals and thus affect housing prices (JLL 2015). In addition, investment in China's real estate market is less compelling than it was before. Ten years ago, it was attractive for foreign investors because both housing prices and the currency were seen as providing room for further growth. Over the last decade, housing prices have risen steeply and are now seen as having less room for further growth. Especially for institutional investors, the country's real economy and financial markets play a bigger role in their investment decisions than the lower administrative hurdles. Foreign buyers typically also focus on the first-tier cities such as Beijing, Shanghai and Guangzhou, which still implement restrictions on home purchases. The overall change at the state-level on foreign investments does not automatically indicate a change at the individual municipality-level.

Although the relaxation of the Notice may not be strong enough to have a dramatic effect in the huge mainland market, it may facilitate selective investments by foreign investors seeking to take advantage of the additional flexibility. The first- and the second-tier cities are always the best placed for international real estate investments because they have large expatriate contingents, high security, more government regulation, well-developed infrastructure, international airlines, high density of amenities and higher-quality developments with professional property management. As success in the Chinese real estate market becomes more dependent on investment savvy and less on having access to deals, China's real estate investment will become both easier for foreigners from a regulatory perspective but more difficult for everyone as the market continues to become more competitive (Blumenfeld et al. 2016). There is no one single path or structure for accomplishing a successful investment in the Chinese real estate market. Investors who have enjoyed success have relied upon creativity, flexibility and patience to find the path that fits each particular investment opportunity (Rothstein 2013).

4 Conclusion

Taken together, the Chinese real estate market is neither heaven nor hell for foreign investors. Like all foreign investments, real estate in China presents many potential risks and also offers possible rewards. Although the central government has taken the initiative to boost the real estate market through relaxation of certain restrictions, the market remains challenging due to the concerns over soaring prices, slower economic growth, RMB depreciation and the overall market weakness (Zhang 2015c). Therefore, it is best for investors to proceed with caution and realistic expectations. The Notice by itself is unlikely to have a dramatic effect in stimulating foreign investment in Chinese real estate markets, but it may still be significant as a signal that the Chinese government is continuing to loosen real estate investment restrictions. There is no sign that the central government will soon relax the restrictions on property purchases by foreigners on a nationwide basis. However, it is believed that the Chinese government will adopt a step-by-step approach in further relaxing other barriers to foreign investment (Zhang 2015c). The SAFE has been continuously easing its registration requirements to facilitate the settlement of foreign currencies for international investors. The next logical loosening step might be that China authorises foreign real estate enterprises the right to access overseas shareholder loans. With all the effort, the real estate sector could benefit from a "new norm" that embraces a more open and transparent market in China for foreign investors (He 2015).

References

Bloomberg. (2015). China eases foreign purchase rules for property after Yuan depreciation. Retrieved November 07, 2016 from http://www.theedgemarkets.com/my/node/227800

Blumenfeld, D., Ma, W., & Guan, P. (2016). Some overlooked market trends in China real estate investment. Retrieved November 07, 2016 from https://www.paulhastings.com/publications-items/details/?id=0231e869-2334-6428-811c-ff00004cbded

Canfield, M. (2015). China's draft foreign investment law could be a game changer? Retrieved November 07, 2016 from https://www.millercanfield.com/resources-448.html

Clemens, U., Dyck, S., & Just, T. (2011). China's housing markets: Regulatory interventions mitigate risk of severe bust. In *Deutsche Bank research current issues*. Frankfurt am Main.

Clifford Chance. (2015). China proposes new foreign investment law. Retrieved November 07, 2016 from https://www.cliffordchance.com/briefings/2015/02/china_proposes_newforeign investmentlaw.html

Clifford Chance. (2019). China's new foreign investment law – What does this mean for foreign investors in China. Retrieved August 27, 2019 from https://www.cliffordchance.com/briefings/2019/03/china_s_new_foreigninvestmentlawwhatdoe.html

He, S. (2015). China relaxes foreign investment in real estate after 8 years of restriction. Retrieved November 07, 2016 from http://www.blplaw.com/expert-legal-insights/articles/china-relaxes-foreign-investment-real-estate-8-years-restriction

International living. (2016). Buying real estate in China. Retrieved November 07, 2016 from https://internationalliving.com/countries/china/buying-real-estate-in-china/

JLL. (2015). Easing of foreign investment restrictions will have minimal impact on China's real estate market. Retrieved November 07, 2016 from http://www.joneslanglasalle.com.cn/china/en-gb/news/489/easing-of-foreign-investment-restrictions

Law Library of Congress. (2015). China: Real property law.

Lawrence, R. H. III. (2007). China's new property law, selected notes and commentary.

Linklaters. (2015). China further relaxes foreign investment in its real estate sector. Retrieved November 07, 2016 from https://www.linklaters.com/en/insights/publications/asia-news/china-update/2015/china-further-relaxes-foreign-investment-in-its-real-estate-sector

Mayer Brown, J. S. M. (2015). Draft foreign investment law: Fundamental change to foreign investment regime in China. Retrieved November 07, 2016 from https://www.mayerbrown.com/files/Publication/c7e56576-38b5-4ed3-8e2c-4b07e1df01bb/Presentation/PublicationAttachment/aa023dbe-b0c0-4244-ba86-538b3e6647e1/150128-PRC-Draft-ForeignInvestmentLaw.pdf

Rothstein, J. (2013). What's next for China inbound real estate investment? Retrieved November 07, 2016 from http://www.paulhastings.com/publications-items/details/?id=1003de69-2334-6428-811c-ff00004cbded

Sinojobs. (2015). Purchasing properties in China as a foreigner. Retrieved November 07, 2016 from https://www.sinojobs.com/en/career-job-application/laws-salary/pension/purchasing-properties-in-china-as-a-foreigner.html

South China Morning Post. (2015). Foreign investors shift focus back to China's real estate market after investment restrictions eased. Retrieved September 13, 2015.

Stein, G. M. (2013). *Modern Chinese real estate law: Property development in an evolving legal system*. New York: Routledge.

The Wall Street Journal. (2015). The verdict on China's easing of foreign property rules? http://blogs.wsj.com/chinarealtime/2015/08/28/the-verdict-on-chinas-easing-of-foreign-property-rules-a-resounding-meh/

Wang, K. (2011). Whatever-ism with Chinese characteristics: China's nascent recognition of private property rights and its political ramifications. *The University of Pennsylvania East Asia Law Review, 6*(1), 43.

Wang, D., & Yang, M. (2016). Status of the new foreign investment law. Retrieved November 07, 2016 from http://www.elexica.com/en/legal-topics/commercial/27-status-of-the-new-foreign-investment-law

Zhang, X. (1999). Real estate investment in China - Legal review and analysis of foreign investors' participation. *Murdoch University Electronic Journal of Law, 6*(2).

Zhang, L. (2015a). Chinese law on private ownership of real property. Retrieved November 07, 2016 from https://blogs.loc.gov/law/2015/03/chinese-law-on-private-ownership-of-real-property/

Zhang, L. (2015b). China: Real property law. Retrieved November 07, 2016 from https://www.loc.gov/law/help/real-property-law/china.php

Zhang, V. (2015c). China relaxes foreign investment in the real estate market.

Real Estate Valuation in China

Florian Hackelberg and Nova Chan

Abstract

Property valuation has become increasingly important in China due to growing merger and acquisition (M&A) activities. Although the same internationally accepted valuation approaches are applied in real estate valuation in China, a number of local particularities need to be considered, including the special regulatory environment and the unique ownership structure, such as the so-called land use rights, as well as volatility in market developments.

1   Introduction

Before the introduction of political and economic reforms in the early 1980s, real estate in China was primarily owned and managed by the Chinese government. A market-oriented property market was nonexistent, and consequently, the valuation of property was an unnecessary exercise. Since that time, the introduction of political reforms has turned over the former state-owned allocation of property into private hands, and a prospering private property market has emerged. The size of the Chinese property sector, as well as promising investment opportunities available, has attracted international investors. As a result, property valuation has become an increasingly important topic. Even though the Chinese property market exhibits more and freer market characteristics, it is far away from being an open market, as governmental influences and controls still prevail. While property valuation in China follows internationally accepted valuation approaches, especially through the

F. Hackelberg (✉)
Hochschule für angewandte Wissenschaft und Kunst, Hildesheim, Germany

N. Chan
PricewaterhouseCoopers, Shanghai, China

© Springer Nature Switzerland AG 2021   101
B. Wang, T. Just (eds.), *Understanding China's Real Estate Markets*, Management for Professionals, https://doi.org/10.1007/978-3-030-49032-4_8

practice of international market participants, Chinese specifications need to be adequately taken into consideration in property valuations.

The following chapter will start with a general introduction to value and the typical purposes for which a valuation is conducted in China. Afterwards, special economic, regulatory, and property factors of the Chinese property market will be explained. Moreover the most commonly used valuation methods for special Chinese land use rights (LUR) and properties in China will be outlined, and recommendations are made how to adequately consider special Chinese market conditions in each method.

2   Value Concept and Purpose of Valuation

The definition of value found in the existing Chinese literature as well as relevant Chinese valuation standards is largely based on its international counterparts such as fair value and market value (CVS 2019). It is important to note, however, that there is not only one value that can be assigned to a particular object. Depending on the valuation purpose defined by the economic event, intended use as well as premise of the valuation and basis of the value, the resultant value of one and the same object can drastically differ. The desire for real estate valuation can arise for various reasons and be used for various purposes. In real estate valuation in China, one must distinguish between two main types of valuation. The first is used to serve the sole purpose of economic decision-making, such as transactions, mergers, and/or financing activities. The second type is used when the valuation has to comply with regulatory requirements, including taxation purposes, or for transactions involving state-owned enterprises (SOEs). When the second type of valuation is considered, it is usually referred to as a statutory valuation. In addition to the nature of the property being valued, the valuation purpose has a significant impact on the resultant valuation procedures and method as well as the nature of and type of the value to be determined (Wyatt 2013).

Statutory Valuation
When valuing an object for transaction purposes, whether it be for a purchase, a sale, the merging of two companies or company parts, or for the listing of a company, the fair value or the maximum price that would be paid for or at least achieved for the object is always needed (PwC 2014). Only rarely, however, do the negotiating parties have a mutual idea of the price of the object at the beginning of the transaction. Valuation therefore serves as the basis for sound decision-making. As mentioned, there are valuation purposes that exist in the legal sphere of China where a valuation is not only recommended for making sound transparent economic decisions but also because it is legally required. Statutory valuations are especially common for the purpose of transactions involving objects wherein SOEs have a stake but also when the transaction is needed for taxation purposes (PwC 2012).

Carrying out a statutory valuation is regulated in detail in terms of both the valuating firm as well as the valuation itself. Certified public valuers (CPV) are constrained to a set of detailed procedure as well as an extensive amount of due care and documentation when executing a statutory valuation. For instance in a statutory valuation environment, the so-called desktop valuations are forbidden, and an on-site inspection of the object to be valued is compulsory.[1] Depending on the type and scope of the transaction, the Chinese administratives such as the State-owned Assets Supervision and Administration Commission (SASAC) must be well integrated into the valuation process (CVS 2013). The scope of the valuation and the valuation method must be approved before the valuation can be compiled. A valuation work plan must also be handed in prior to beginning the valuation project. It is advisable to include all relevant governing bodies in an early stage to avoid last minute surprises (Hackelberg 2015).

Expert Practice

In addition to international organizations foremost the Royal Institution of Certified Surveyors (RICS) and the American Society of Appraisers (ASA), since the early 1990s, various state-organized associations have been established due to the ongoing market liberalization and the increasing complexity of real estate issues facing Chinese real estate professionals. Besides developing generally accepted professional and technical standards, these valuation professional organizations (VPO) provide initial and further education to their certified members. Memberships at VPOs are subject to credentialing as well as periodical surveillance checks and

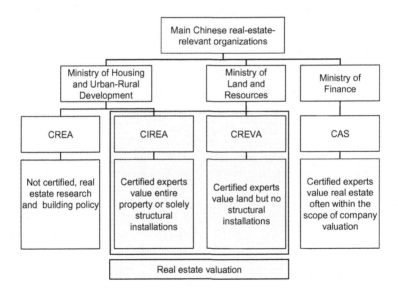

Fig. 1 Chinese real estate organizations. Source: according to Hong and Liu (2002)

---

[1]If the valuation is planned to take place for a longer duration or if the reporting date of the value changes, a new on-site inspection is required.

practice reviews. As illustrated (see Fig. 1), the certification of valuators are carried out by the Chinese Ministry of Housing and Urban-Rural Development or the Ministry of Land and Resources depending on whether the involved party is to become a valuer of real estate (i.e., property and structure) or of land.

The main local real estate-relevant organizations in China include China Real Estate Association (CREA), China Institute of Real Estate Appraisers and Agents (CIREA), China Real Estate Valuers Association (CREVA), and China Appraisal Society (CAS). In order to execute a real estate valuation project in China, a certification through professional associations is not necessarily needed. Instead, the valuation purpose and the background of the valuation and any pertinent regulatory provision define the required qualification of the valuer (Hackelberg 2010).

Chinese Valuation Standards

The Chinese Valuation Standards of the China Appraisal Society is the relevant regulatory framework for local Chinese appraisers controlled by the Ministry of Finance stream. They clarify obligations when adopting expert work, the relevant information, and disclosure requirements. The standards are mainly in line with their international counterparts (such as International Valuation Standards). Besides general guidelines regarding the valuation process itself, they contain ethical standards. Specifically, they are composed of the following parts (CVS 2019):

- General valuation standards and valuation ethical standards (General guidelines and ethical principles)
- Valuation practicing standards (specifications for valuations procedure and process)
- Practice notes (guidelines for assessing individual assets)
- Valuation guidance notes (including instructions for special assets and valuation purposes)

In addition to those Chinese Valuation Standards in Chinese valuation practice, valuers are following internationally accepted standards including the International Valuation Standards (IVS) or the Red Book published by the RICS.

3 Market Conditions

As already mentioned at the beginning of the chapter, the special conditions of China's real estate market impact the application of internationally accepted valuation methods. This section will therefore present the framework conditions separated into three main categories: economic influential factors, regulatory influential factors, and property inherent influential factors. Some factors are exclusively China-specific, and others are typically encountered for the so-called emerging market countries, i.e., also China.

Economic Influential Factors

Market volatility and a lack of market transparency are the most crucial influential economic factors in China. Although China's so-called Tier I and Tier II cities are becoming more transparent, according to the latest Global Real Estate Transparency Index published by Jones Lang LaSalle (JLL 2016), the markets in its Tier III cities as well as rural areas have a significantly lower level of transparency.[2] Progressive development of the real estate market gives hope for an improvement in data transparency. High market volatility and low market transparency do not directly affect the methodical procedure or certain input determinants of the valuation, rather they involve practical circumstances which require an increased amount of attention. This means that the researched valuation parameters, especially the comparable transactions, as well as for the income approach comparative rents, and discount rates need to be quite close to the reporting date, and the resulting value itself will have a short duration of validity.

Regulatory Influential Factors

The regulatory framework in China improved significantly over the last decades. However there are still special local regulatory implications to be considered in the real estate valuation. Among the most important are the so-called land use rights (LUR). While the construction portion of a property might be within private ownership, outright private ownership of land in China is disallowed under prevailing laws. All land is owned either by the state or by collectives. Certain land use rights may be acquired by private parties and transferred in accordance with Chinese laws. In China, different approaches should be assessed to determine the value of LUR. The term "land use right" refers to a right to use a specified piece of land for a particular purpose. Generally, Chinese law distinguishes between two different forms of LUR: allocated LUR and granted LUR. The most important features of allocated LUR are that the user has no right to transfer LUR and the state may reclaim the land at any time when needed without paying compensation for the land allocated. On the other hand, granted LUR can be transferred, and government reclamation is much more limited (Hackelberg 2010).

All LUR must be initially granted by the state, who acts as the landowner. In this regard, collectively owned land must be converted to state-owned land before LUR can be granted. Upon granting, a contract must be signed between the user and the state (normally this will be the competent local government). The contract sets forth the conditions under which the land may be used. The grantee is required to pay a land granting premium and an annual nominal ground rent. The grantee also needs to register the contract with the local land administration authority within a specified period of time. Land for which grant procedures have not been carried out and for which no grant fee has been paid (such as administrative allocated land) cannot be assigned, transferred, leased out, or mortgaged unless the occupant has paid the land

---

[2]Ranking out of 108 "Real Estate Transparency Tiers": China Tier I Cities (33), China Tier II Cities (55) and Tier III Cities (66).

grant premium to convert the land into granted land or obtained a special permit/ approval from the competent authorities.

The LUR has a significant impact on the valuation of real estate. This includes the risk of a denied extension of an LUR, a lack of clear regulation when dealing with emerging extension costs, and unclear escheat rules (and/or unclear building compensation). These issues have an increasing impact on real estate valuation in China, especially for those properties with a continuous useful life and therefore a shortened time to maturity. In practice, it is often argued that because of their short useful life and their usual low quality of construction, at the expiration of a 40–50 year LUR, there is no significant residual value left of the construction portion of the property itself. Although such arguments can be correct for any given individual case, the problematic nature of valuation is more significant than before, when a new building is constructed on a second-hand purchased LUR with a reduced useful life. Buildings related to LURs with a time to maturity of less than 20 years are often regarded as unsaleable.

Valuation issues attributable to the system of LURs usually arise in practice, often in the case of joint ventures between foreign and former SOEs. It is not rare to see that years after the venture is established, the land introduced as a capital- equivalent contribution from the Chinese side has not been sufficiently converted to a granted LUR. This does not only considerably influence the original value of the Chinese-side contribution but also legally impacts the existing buildings or planned extensions on the land. The often inadequate regulatory environment in China leads to practical problems in the valuation of real estate. This causes the seemingly easy-to-answer question of "who is the owner of a property" often become difficult. Although there are many offices in China where a document similar to a land register exists, the details are still not always clear. Reasons for this can mainly be found in the historical state allocation of properties and also when SOEs were transformed into semi-private or private enterprises. During this transformation, the ownership structure of properties was not always clearly governed. Often, investigations are needed in order to locate the actual legal owner of an LUR or a building.

Property Influential Factors

Property inherent factors refer to property location as well as architectural and structural aspects. The building quality of Chinese real estate does not yet meet Western standards, despite constant improvement over the last few decades. This fact has a profound impact on the entire life cycle of any given building and its economic and technical useful life. These circumstances cause the expenditure and revenue side of things to become negatively noticeable at more expedient rate than the fact that the property has a short useful life. On the revenue side of things, lower rents will be realized because of the poor building quality. To maintain the building, there will also be higher costs, which directly impact the value of the property.

In practice, it is often difficult to determine reliable property data as a basis for real estate valuation. Data regarding the square footage of Chinese properties sometimes do not correspond to uniform international standards. Usually, the gross area forms the basis of the valuation. To ensure the obtainment of reliable data used as a basis in the valuation, verification of the provided quantity structure based on the floor plans is recommended.

4   Valuation Methods

Similar to internationally accepted valuation procedures, valuation in China is typically executed via three methods (see Fig. 2): the market approach which focuses on market prices, the income approach which focuses on profits generated from the property, and the cost approach which calculates costs occurred in building the replacement property (Koller et al. 2010; CVS 2019 and valuation practicing standard – real estate, valuation approaches). This section will introduce and explain each method with particular focus on the consideration of local Chinese influential factors.

4.1   Recommendations for Chinese Real Estate Valuation

The Market Approach
The market approach is a statistical valuation method primarily used in the valuation of simple real estate types for the purpose of acquiring or selling or for renting out properties (Withe et al. 2003). Assuming a sufficient number of comparable transactions at the reporting date, the comparative method is the easiest valuation method. In the literature, it is considered the most preferred method, because of its direct link to the market conditions (Wyatt 2013).

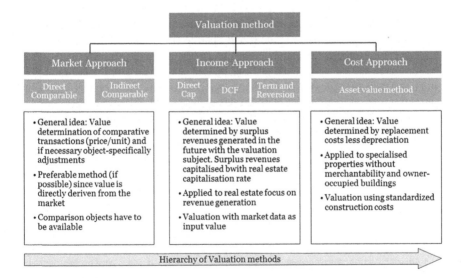

Fig. 2 Valuation methods. Source: according to Hackelberg (2010)

The basis for the comparative method is the existence of a sufficient number of comparable transactions performed close to the reporting date, which often are not available due to the heterogeneity of the market. Officially published data is usually limited to Tier I cities. The valuation therefore requires comprehensive market research, including a thorough examination of comparable transactions. The comparative method is often used in valuation of residential or undeveloped property, because the comparable aspects tend to be homogenous for these types of properties in China (Gondring 2009). Those transactions that have the highest possible conformity of comparative aspects can also be valued under the comparative method. Moreover, when selecting comparable transactions, a matching of their residual values should be ensured. If this is not the case, the comparable transactions may need to be adjusted to compensate for deviations. The basic scheme and the necessary calculations are simple compared to other more sophisticated methods. The total square footage multiplied by the adjusted price per square meter results in the value of the property.

The Income Approach

The income approach or investment method is usually used in the case of investment property. "The investment method" is an umbrella term that entails various income-oriented valuation methods which depend on the valuation purpose and any prevailing circumstances applicable at the valuation date. Essentially, these methods include the direct capitalization method, the term and reversion method, and the discounted cash flow (DCF) method. The basic idea of each method is that the value of the object being valued is derived from the present value of all future profits generated by the property and/or their capitalized values (Withe et al. 2003). The estimation of cash flows to be generated and their capitalized values are of particular importance. In order to derive these estimations, the valuer has to have acquired sufficient knowledge of the property being valued as well as of the prevailing market situation at the reporting date (Thomas and Schulte 2007).

Against this background and in regard to LURs, the unlimited life of an LUR presents the case of a never-ending useful life of the object being valued. This is implicitly assumed in all variants of the investment method but is actually inappropriate given that the finite nature of LURs is not considered. Because future revenues generated by Chinese real estate are only secured over the duration of the LUR, the limited useful life should be reflected within the valuation, i.e., the revenues should only be discounted until the end of the LUR's useful life. Even in practice, any references to future legal adjustments cannot be accepted due to the principle that mandates the use of pertinent information at the reporting date (Gärtner and Hackelberg 2010). The term and reversion method is used much less in China because the duration of rent contracts are much shorter than in Europe or in the USA.

The Cost Approach

Internationally, the depreciated replacement cost method is a substance-oriented method where the associated costs are much more prevalent than future earnings. The basic idea is that a potential buyer is not willing to pay more for an existing property than that what it would cost to build his own (RICS 2007). This method is primarily used for specialized properties (e.g., schools, churches, and hospitals) or industrial properties (e.g., properties used for refining oil or for chemical factories), which both do not have an actual identifiable market due to their unique characteristics (Thomas et al. 2000).

Because there is no precise market for industrial property rents that can be used for comparison purposes in China, the value of such properties is usually calculated using the cost approach. The method is done in two steps. First, the value of the land and the value of any structural installations are separately ascertained. The two values are then added together to give the total value. The estimation of the construction costs is executed under the assumption that the building will be established using the latest construction techniques and that it is in compliance with the latest regulations. It is not necessary to replicate the building as an exact copy with the exact same architecture, rather only to maintain an equivalent capacity of use (Withe et al. 2003).

Although the depreciated replacement cost method is prevalently used in some cases,[3] it is often labeled the "method of last resort" due to its lack of reference to market conditions and its history-oriented view (RICS 2007). Since the market value does not take into account what a property is worth based on its technical aspects but rather what the market is ready to pay at the reporting date for that property, it should only be used when the property type has no defined market and no other method can be applied (IVSC 2017). As previously mentioned, there are no clear regulations in China regarding compensation of any existing structural installations in the case of an escheat. Clearly, in such a case, an impact will be seen in the value. As shown in Fig. 3 "cost approach," an age reduction that considers the use of a building to be longer than the duration of the LUR implicitly imputes compensation of the market

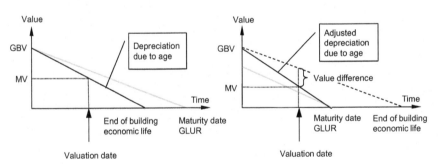

GBV: Gross book value (Historical costs of acquisition and production)
MV: Market value

Fig. 3 Cost approach. Source: Hackelberg (2010)

---

[3]These include, for example, the mortgage lending value or a reveiew of the appraisal used for insurance purposes (Cp. Kleiber, Wolfgang [2007], p. 207).

value of the structural installations should the case be that the LUR is not extended. The ratio of total building service life to building remaining useful life and also the remaining term of the land use right is therefore no longer a decisive factor in the reduction of the age of the LUR. If the remaining useful life of the structural installments exceeds the remaining useful life of the LUR, the latter will be crucial in determining the extent to which the age of the LUR will be reduced. Total useful lives should be more conservatively translated for Chinese properties than for properties in Western markets. Table 1 below provides a guideline of total useful life applied in the cost approach. Principally, the cost approach is only used in exceptional cases, e.g., when a lack of marketability of the property exists.

4.2   Valuation of Land Use Rights

In China, land is normally valued by considering three different valuation methodologies: the market comparison approach, the cost approximation approach, and the residual approach (Fig. 4).

Market Comparison Approach
The market comparison approach seeks to determine the current market land value by referencing recent comparable transactions. The valuer may make adjustments to those recorded transactions by taking into account factors such as differences in the date of sale/transfer, location, site services, and available infrastructure. If properly applied, this approach provides a fair and reasonable result. Its application is

Table 1 Proposed total useful life

Type of use	Proposed total useful life (years)
Office and administrative buildings	20–40
Shopping centers and department stores	15–20
Residential buildings with multiple floors (according to their quality)	30–50
Industrial buildings and warehouses (in accordance with their how they were constructed)	15–30

Source: Hackelberg (2013)

Fig. 4 Valuation of land use rights. Source: according to Chan and Hackelberg (2008)

however limited to certain types of land transactions in more well-developed areas of major cities and special development zones, as well as subject to the availability of sufficient and reliable public market data.

The following table shows examples of specific adjustments that may have to be considered for each of the comparable cases when applying the market comparison approach. The analysis result is generally derived from the average of the adjusted land price of each comparable case (Fig. 5).

Notes
- $P' = P \times F1 \times F2 \times F3 \times F4$
- F1: The factor is estimated to reflect the differences of specific transaction situations between the comparable case and the subject land.
- F2: The factor is calculated to reflect the price change from the transaction date of the comparable case to the valuation date.
- F3: The factor is generally estimated with reference to various location differences between the comparable case and the subject land (including transportation convenience and infrastructure facilities). This factor may be judgmental.
- F4: The factor is generally estimated to reflect other differences between the comparable case and the subject land (including land shape, area and basement, and tenure of the LUR).

A special version of the market comparison approach is the so-called adjusted benchmarking land price scale approach. Normally, land in the urban and suburban areas of a city in China is categorized into different zones or grades in accordance with its respective geographic location, infrastructure facilities, transportation convenience, industrial base, and other characteristics. The local government normally sets a benchmarking land price scale (BLPS) system for each grade of land, which

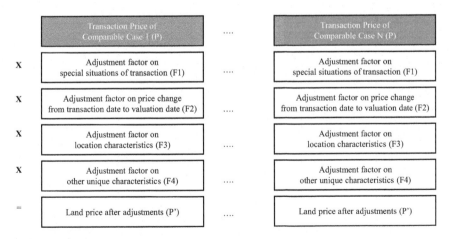

Fig. 5 Market comparison approach. Source: Hackelberg (2010)

gives an average base price suggested by the government for land-granting transactions. This average base price per grade can be used as a reference by a valuer to ascertain the value of a piece of particular granted land after considering proper adjustments. Whether this process reflects a true value of a particular piece of land is highly dependent upon the land valuer's judgments on those adjusting factors. This process can be highly subjective, and in some cases, it may be biased.

Cost Approximation Approach

The cost approximation approach is generally applied to the valuation of industrial land allotments, as sufficient market data are not usually available in most cases. This approach recreates the total cost of granted LUR on the assumption that the subject land is converted by the government from a piece of agricultural purpose land to a piece of industrial purpose land. Normally, the total cost includes land acquisition cost, site development/improvement cost, and land premium (the premium charged by the government for granting the land use rights). After considering all necessary costs mentioned above, the valuer will need to make further adjustments to reflect the remaining tenure of the subject land use rights. This approach is widely adopted by local Chinese valuers, as the cost comparison approach overcomes the general lack of publicly available comparable sales records (Fig. 6).

- The land acquisition cost includes the compensation and resettlement expenses paid for the loss of land and crops, buildings, structures, and other attachments and taxes and surcharges required to be paid in connection with the land requisition according to government rules and regulations.

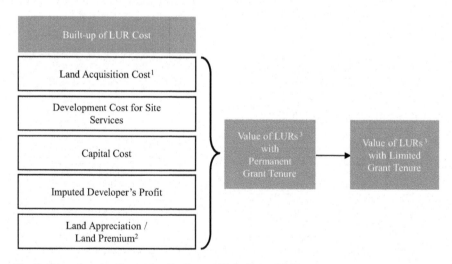

Fig. 6 Cost approximation approach. Source: Hackelberg (2010)

- Land premium refers to the portion of land value appreciation as a result of land development to be shared with the owner of the land, i.e., the state. It is normally calculated as a percentage of total economic costs (e.g., acquisition cost plus development cost plus capital cost plus imputed profit) for developing the land.
- This is the value of a piece of granted land. For non-granted land, a grant premium should be excluded from the value of the granted land.

Residual Approach

The residual value approach is an internationally recognized method preferentially utilized by investors that serve to determine the most acceptable land price. In this approach, the market value of the completed project is compiled based on market conditions and experience. After deduction of all development costs including the developer's profit, a balance remains (residuum) that corresponds to the value of the undeveloped land. Assuming that the developer will aim for the best usage concept by considering existing economical and legal environment (highest and best use) factors, the residual value can be compared with the market value. The residual method can be described as a combination of different valuation methods, as the value of the completed project is calculated by applying the market and income approaches, whereas deductible costs are calculated using the cost approach (Chan and Hackelberg 2008).

5   Conclusion

As outlined above, property valuations should always result in market values which are achievable at the date of valuation. The applied valuation method must reflect the local market environment, including the specifics of supply and demand as well as the specific Chinese market conditions outlined in this article. This often leads to a situation in which a valuer's adjustments and individual judgment highly affect the valuation result. As such, a transparent valuation approach containing sufficient explanation of any assumptions made and adjustments considered is highly recommended for the real estate valuation process.

References

Chan, N., & Hackelberg, F. (2008). Challenges in valuing land use rights in China. *Asset Management News*, 35–36.

CVS. (2013). *Chinese valuation standards 2013 (CVS)* (China appraisal society). Hongkong: Wolters Kluwer CCH.

CVS. (2019). *Chinese valuation standards 2019 (CVS)* (China appraisal society). Hongkong: Wolters Kluwer CCH.

Gärtner, S., & Hackelberg, F. (2010). Immobilienbewertung in China. *Der Immobilienbewerter - Zeitschrift für die Bewertungspraxis*, 13–17.

Gondring, H. (Ed.). (2009). *Immobilienwirtschaft-Handbuch für ftudium und Praxis* (2nd ed.). Munich: Verlag Franz Wahlen.

Hackelberg, F. (2010). *Immobilienbewertung in China – unter besonderer Berücksichtigung der wirtschaftlichen, regulatorischen und materiellen Einflussfaktoren.* Wiesbaden: Wiesbaden IZ Verlag.

Hackelberg, F. (2013). Immobilienbewertung in China. In G. Bobka & J. Simon (Eds.), *Handbuch Immobilienbewertung in internationalen Märkten.* Bonn: Bundesanzeiger-Verlag.

Hackelberg, F. (2015). Compliance Risiken in der Unternehmensbewertung. In P. Senff & B. U. Stucken (Eds.), *Compliancemanagement in China - Praxishandbuch für Manager.* Freiburg: Haufe Verlag.

Hong, Z., & Liu, H. Y. (2002). Real estate research in China. In K. W. Schulte (Ed.), *Real estate education throughout the world: Past, present and future, research issues in real estate* (Vol. 7). Massachusetts: Kluwer Academic.

IVS. (2017). *International valuation standards (IVS; "White Book").* London: International Valuation Standards Committee.

JLL. (2016). *Taking real estate transparency to the next level, global real estate transparency index.* Chicago: Jones Lang LaSalle.

Kleiber, W., & Simon, J. (2007). *Verkehrswertermittlung von Grundstücken.* Köln: Bundesanzeigerverlag.

Koller, T., Goedhardt, M., & Wessels, D. (2010). *Valuation – Measuring and managing, the value of a company* (5th ed.). New Jersey: Wiley.

Li, L. H. (1995). The official land value appraisal system under the Chinese land use right reforms in China. *The Appraisal Journal*, 102–110.

Pratt, S. P., & Niculita, A. V. (2008). *Valuing a business – The analysis and appraisal of closely held companies.* New York: McGraw Hill.

PwC. (2012). *PricewaterhouseCoopers, China tax news flash issue 22 on the topic of "fair value under spotlight like never before for China tax purposes".* Beijing: PricewaterhouseCoopers.

PwC. (2014). *PricewaterhouseCoopers, doing business and investing in China.* Frankfurt am Main: PricewaterhouseCoopers.

RICS. (2007). *RICS valuation standards "Red Book".* London: RICS.

RICS. (2014). *RICS Bewertung – Bewertungsgrundsätze Januar 2014 unter Berücksichtigung der Internationalen Bewertungsstandards der IVSC ("Red Book").* London: Royal Institution of Chartered Surveyors (RICS).

Song, C., Zhou Gan, Z., Xie, J., et al. (2007). *Study book for real estate valuer qualification in China – Theory and methods of real estate appraisal.* Beijing: China Institute of Real Estate Appraisers and Agents (CIREA).

Thomas, M., Leopoldsberger, G., Waldbröhl, V., & Schulte, K.-H. (2000). *Immobilienökonomie.* Oldenbourg: De Gruyter.

Thomas, M., & Schulte, K.-H. (2007). *Verkehrswert nach WertV und anderen Verfahren.* Munich: Studienbrief vdp.

Withe, D., Turner, J., Jenyon, B., & Lincoln, N. (2003). Internationale Bewertungsverfahren für das Investment von Immobilien (3rd ed.). Wiesbaden: IZ Verlag.

Wyatt, P. (2013). *Property valuation.* Oxford: Wiley-Blackwell.

The Regulation of Leasing Activities

Karen Ip and Nanda Lau

Abstract

Chinese law provides a national-level regulatory framework for leasing. Variation, however, can occur among different localities in respect of local regulations. Moreover, different customs exist in different localities, which can affect matters such as the amount of the rental bond, frequency of rental payments and whether subleasing is acceptable. In this chapter, we outline China's national-level regulatory framework for leasing activities. Local regulations and practices are also discussed, though no attempt has been made to systematically address local regulations and practices.

The leases discussed in this chapter involve the periodic payments of rental for the occupation of real estate premises, similar to leasing arrangements made elsewhere in the world. This is to be distinguished from the granting land use rights in China, which can also be referred to as leasing from the government. As discussed below, all land in China is owned either by the government or rural collectives. Government-owned land may be transferred to an individual or company for a certain period of time (between 40 and 70 years, depending on the usage) in exchange for the payment of money. This arrangement is sometimes referred as granting of the land use right or lease of land. For the purpose of this chapter, our discussion does not include the granting of land use rights, which is regulated under a different regulatory regime.

K. Ip (✉) · N. Lau
Herbert Smith Freehills, London, UK

© Springer Nature Switzerland AG 2021
B. Wang, T. Just (eds.), *Understanding China's Real Estate Markets*, Management for Professionals, https://doi.org/10.1007/978-3-030-49032-4_9

1   Lease Term

In practice, leases generally have a term of two or three years for commercial leases (see below) and 1 year for residential leases in China. Chinese law, however, permits leases to a much longer time frame, but still imposes limits.

Under Chinese law, lease terms cannot exceed 20 years. If a lease contract does specify a term longer than 20 years, then the excess term beyond 20 years is invalid. A lease may be renewed, provided that renewed term does not exceed 20 years. If a term is not specified, or the term is unclear under the lease contract, then the lease will be without a fixed term and either party may terminate the lease at any time. The landlord, however, can only terminate the lease upon giving reasonable notice to the tenant. If a tenant continues to occupy the premises after expiration of the term, and the landlord does not object, then the lease will continue without a fixed term.

2   Land Use Rights and Planning Requirements

All land in China is either owned by the state or owned by collectives. If the land is state-owned land, then usage rights for that land will be either allocated or granted. Allocated land use rights are generally given to state-owned enterprises, the military, public schools and similar enterprises or units. Granted land use rights, on the other hand, allow the use of land (typically for private enterprise purposes) for a specific purpose for a fixed term.

Only buildings that are built on granted state-owned land may be lawfully leased. If premises are built on state-owned land that is subject to only allocated land use rights, then any rental charged under a lease must be paid to the state, and not to the purported landlord. The effect of this rule is that tenants should always seek assurance that the land upon which premises are built are subject to granted state-owned land rights. Although the law does not specifically invalidate a lease for premises on allocated state-owned land, a landlord that is not permitted to retain collected rent cannot be expected to maintain the premises or satisfy other obligations under the lease. Collectively owned land in an urban area can only be used for real estate development and operations after it has been requisitioned and converted to state-owned land. This typically means that premises built in urban areas on collectively owned land cannot be lawfully leased. The situation in rural areas, however, is more complex with different localities having different local regulations and practices. China intends to unify the urban and rural construction land market by permitting rural collectively owned construction land to be transferred and leased directly without first being requisitioned and converted to state-owned land. So far, however, no state-wide laws or regulations have been issued.

Premises being offered for lease must satisfy governmental planning requirements. Premises that are built in violation of planning permits are considered illegal, and illegally constructed buildings cannot be leased lawfully. If a lease contract is entered for premises that are in violation of planning permits, then the lease contract will be invalid. However, if the violations are corrected prior to the closing of arguments in the court of first instance, then the lease contract may be deemed valid by the People's Court.

If a building does not meet town planning requirements prior to commencement of construction, then the developer would not be able to obtain a permit for planned use of land for construction, a planning permit for construction or a construction commencement permit. These three certificates, among other materials, are required in order for the developer to obtain a real property ownership certificate for the building. Accordingly, the holding of a real property ownership certificate should be evidence that town planning requirements have been satisfied.

It may still be the case, however, that a premise with a real property ownership certificate may still be in violation of town planning requirements. This may occur if the government granted the real property ownership certificate without due regard to the violations or if town planning requirements changed following issuance of the real property ownership certificate. Accordingly, a tenant should conduct its own due diligence on town planning requirements. If town planning requirements have changed after issuance of the real property ownership certificate and the government intends to use the land for other usages, then generally the government will take steps to expropriate the property. A tenant wishing to guard against this possibility should ensure that compensation is specified in the lease contract. Depending on the local regulations and practice, a tenant may negotiate with the local government for compensation.

3   Lease Agreement

Chinese law requires that all real estate leases must be in writing. This not only allows due registration of a lease but provides evidence of the agreement between the landlord and tenant in the event of future disputes. A lease must contain clauses such as the location and size of the leased premises, usage of the premises, term of the lease, rental charges (including time and method of payment) and maintenance obligations. It is, however, usual for leases to contain much more. Government-issued standard lease forms are common in China. Shanghai, for instance, has a standard form lease contract for residential usages and another standard form lease contract that may be used for business usages. Both Beijing and Shenzhen have standard form leases that may be used for either residential or business usages. The use of a standard form lease is not compulsory under national rules, and parties may register leases that are not in the standard form. However, it is not uncommon for registration authorities to prefer that standard form leases be used. When used, standard form leases typically may be negotiated. That is, the parties to the lease may negotiate additional terms and may also negotiate changes to the standard lease. Amendments to the standard lease will typically be set out in an addendum to the standard lease contract.

All leases must be registered. Specifically, the lease contract shall be filed for registration and record at the relevant local real estate administration department. For example, in Shanghai, lease contracts for business usage are filed with the district real property transaction centre, and residential leases are filed with sub-district office. In Shenzhen, all lease contracts are filed with sub-district office. In Beijing, business leases are filed with the district housing administration bureau, and residential leases are filed with sub-district office. Stamp duty is payable on executed lease contracts, with the general rate being set at 0.1% of the rental charge. National-level rules provide for an exemption from stamp duty if the lease contract is signed by individuals. Various localities, including Beijing, Shanghai and Guangdong, extend this exemption in favour of all residential leases, including those signed by a company.

4   Usage of Lease

The usage of the premises will typically be negotiated between the landlord and tenant. In many localities in China, it is a legal requirement that the negotiated usage of the premises under the lease must be consistent with the usage of the building approved during the construction phase. The validity of a lease contract is not affected if the lease contract is silent or ambiguous as to usage. Rather, Chinese law provides a mechanism for the usage of the premises under the lease to be determined or deemed. For leases that are silent or ambiguous regarding the usage of the premises, Chinese law indicates that the parties should enter a supplementary lease to clarify usage. Chinese law is also pragmatic enough to recognize that the parties might not be able or willing to agree to a supplementary lease. If the parties do fail to enter a supplementary lease, then Chinese law states that the usage of the premises should be determined from other provisions of the lease contract or from trade practices. Finally, if neither the provisions of the lease contract, nor trade practices clarify the usage of the premises, then the tenant must use the premises in a manner that is consistent with nature of premises. The nature of the premises will largely be determined by the approved usage of the building. As a general rule, and as noted above, the usage of premises must be consistent with the government-approved usage of the building as set out in the real property ownership certificate or planning permit for construction. This is explicitly required in both Shanghai Municipality and Guangdong and Zhejiang Provinces. If the usage of the premises is inconsistent with the government-approved usage, then three possible consequences must be considered as listed below.

   If the usage of premises set out in the lease contract is inconsistent with the usage in the real property ownership certificate, then the premise should not be leased as to do so would be deemed as a change in the nature of the use of the premise. However, if the change of usage requires modifications that result in a change of the nature of use of the premise, then the premises cannot be leased at all unless the owner/landlord completes the procedures to change the town planning-related permits. In some localities, however, such as in Zhejiang Province, the usage of premises can be changed temporarily for up to 5 years. An applicant for such a temporary change may need to pay extra land transfer fees. However, if the premises are expropriated, then compensation will be calculated based on the original usage. The registration authority may refuse to register a lease contract if the usage set out in the lease contract is inconsistent with the government-approved usage of the premises. Some localities, such as in Shenzhen, have a policy to actively reject the registration of any lease contract if the usage of the premises violates any legal requirements.

The real estate authority may order rectification within a certain time if the usage of premises is inconsistent with the government-approved usage. A fine of up to RMB 5000 may also be imposed. If illegal proceeds are gained, then the fine may be up to three times the illegal gain or RMB 30,000, whichever is smaller. If the tenant changes the usage of the premises without the landlord's consent, then the tenant may face administrative punishment from different government authorities, including departments in charge of planning, construction, land and resources, housing administration, public security, environmental protection and the safety administration.

Rent is payable in accordance with the negotiated terms of the lease. There are no price controls for rental charges in China, with rent typically being set at market rates. It is not uncommon for leases of retail space to set rent charges as greater as a turnover rent and fixed rent. If the lease contract is silent or unclear as to timing of rental payments, the parties cannot agree to a supplementary lease and trade practices are unclear, then the rent is payable annually or (for leases shorter than 1 year or if the remainder of the lease is less than 1 year) at the expiration of the lease. Chinese law does not provide any restrictions over how rental charges may be reviewed. In practice, however, rent is usually set and, for multi-year leases reviewed, annually. Reviews may be determined in accordance with market rates or may be subject to a review mechanism (such as CPI increases) set out in the lease contract. Security deposits are subject to negotiation and industry practice. In many areas in China, security deposits are set at 3–6 months of rent payable prior to the tenant taking possession of the leased premises.

5   Rights and Obligations of the Landlord and the Tenant

The landlord should ensure that appropriate access is available for any leased premises. A prudent tenant should also ensure that adequate due diligence is undertaken if there is any risk of access being obstructed by a neighbour. In the event of a problem arising, Chinese law states that a neighbour must grant access rights. However, these access rights are granted to the landlord. The tenant should ensure that the lease confers on the tenant the right to direct that the landlord pursues any request for a right of access on behalf of the tenant.

Access to real estate (including leased premises) is protected by a general obligation of neighbours to maintain proper neighbourly relations in respect of such matters as water supply, drainage, physical access, ventilation and lighting. In particular, if any obstruction is caused, then the obstructing neighbour must cease the infringement and eliminate the obstruction. The obstructing neighbour may also be responsible for the payment of compensation to any neighbour who has suffered loss. If access to leased premises requires access through a neighbouring property, then the neighbour must permit that access. However, the neighbour may also claim compensation if the grant of the access results in any loss.

During the term of the lease, and subject to the lease contract, the tenant is entitled to all proceeds resulting from the possession of the leased premises. This means, for instance, that any intention to charge turnover rent must be clearly expressed in the lease contract. If a tenant is unable to enjoy the benefits of the lease premises due to a claim by a third party, then the tenant may demand a reduction of or an exemption from rental payments. Subleases are permitted but only with the landlord's consent. The tenant will, however, be liable to the landlord for any damage caused by the subtenant. If a sublease is created by the tenant without the landlord's consent, then the landlord may terminate the lease. In such a situation, the tenant may also be liable to the subtenant for breach of the sublease contract.

During the term of the lease, the landlord must ensure that the leased premises remain fit for the contracted use. This includes a general obligation on the landlord to maintain the leased premises, though the lease contract may provide otherwise. Subject to the lease, a tenant may request the landlord to take care of maintenance and repairs within a reasonable time. If the landlord fails to maintain or repair the leased premises within a reasonable time, then the tenant may repair and charge the expenses to the landlord. If the maintenance and repair issues affect usage of the leased premises, then the rent may be reduced.

The tenant has a corresponding obligation to preserve the leased premises and will be liable for any damage or loss resulting from a failure to preserve the leased premises. Depending on the circumstances, this would likely include requiring the tenant to take care in using the leased premises and to take action to limit losses or further damage that may arise from things in need of maintenance. Generally speaking, the tenant is not liable for reasonable wear and tear, provided that the tenant's usage either complies with the lease contract or (if usage is not specified) is consistent with the nature of the leased premises. If the tenant's usage is inconsistent with the lease contract or the nature of the leased premises and such usage causes damage to the leased premises, then the landlord may terminate the lease and claim compensation for the damage. Any alteration by the tenant can only be implemented with the consent of the landlord. It would be usual in such situations for the landlord to request detailed plans showing the extent of the alteration before giving approval. Unless the lease contract says otherwise, there is no obligation on the landlord to approve any such request, and the landlord is not subject to any reasonableness test in deciding whether or not to approve the alteration. If the tenant goes ahead without the landlord's consent to the alteration (whether or not approval was sought), then the landlord may require the tenant to restore the leased premises to its original state. The landlord may also claim compensation for any loss caused.

A landlord may mortgage leased property, with the priority between lease and mortgage being determined largely according to the timing of the lease and mortgage. If the landlord leased the premises before mortgaging it, then the lease is not affected by the mortgage. However, if the landlord leased the premises after already having mortgaged the property, then the lease will be subject to the lawful interests of the registered mortgagee.

The transfer of leased premises during the term of the lease does not affect the validity of the lease. This means that a buyer of the leased premises will acquire ownership subject to the existing lease. Subject to the lease, however, the new owner does not have any obligation to renew the lease. The landlord must notify a tenant within a reasonable time prior to any sale of the leased premises. The tenant then has a right of first refusal to purchase the leased premise upon equal conditions offered by the proposed purchaser. In practice, it is not uncommon for the lease contract to include a tenant's waiver of the right of first refusal.

6 Expiration and Termination

There are no national-level rules that grant tenants a right to renew a lease the term for which is about to expire. However, some local-level regulations do offer such a right. For example, current tenants in Shanghai have a right of first refusal for any lease being offered to another prospective leasee. Similar regulations exist in places such as Beijing and Xiamen. Zhejiang Province once also had such a rule; however, the rule has been repealed. Such a right of first refusal may also be negotiated and included in a lease contract.

Leases may be terminated under the terms of the lease contract or in accordance with rights granted at law. Termination by mutual agreement is also permitted. If the tenant wishes to terminate, then termination by agreement will typically involve the tenant paying a penalty to the landlord, with the specific amount either being set out in the lease contract or negotiated at the time of the early termination. Chinese law also allows contracts (including lease contracts) to be terminated for various reasons, including: force majeure, pre-emptive breach, and persistent failure to fulfill contractual obligations.

A landlord may terminate a lease contract if rental payments are not made. However, prior to issuing a termination notice, the landlord must give notice to the tenant to pay the rent within a reasonable time limit. Termination is then only permitted if the rent is not paid within that time limit. Landlords should, however, be cautious to terminate a lease contract on the basis of a notice for non-payment of rent. Caution is particularly required if there is any suggestion that the tenant is delaying the payment of rent due to any alleged breach of the lease contract by the landlord. If in such a situation the tenant is subsequently found justified in delaying or withholding rental payment, the landlord may be found in breach for having given a termination notice. For similar reasons, a landlord with a late-paying tenant should not cut off supplies of water and electricity prior to obtaining a favourable court judgement. Without a court judgement, the landlord itself might be liable in damages to the tenant for breaching the lease contract. The landlord may terminate a lease contract if leased premises are not used in a manner consistent with the lease contract or the nature of the leased premises and the landlord suffers loss. In such a case, the landlord may also claim compensation from the tenant. Termination by the landlord is permitted if the tenant subleases the leased premises without the consent of the landlord. A tenant may terminate a lease if damage to the leased premises makes it impossible to achieve the purpose of the lease contract. This, however, is only applicable if the damage to the leased premises is not attributable to the tenant. Tenant may terminate the lease contract at any time if the leased premises endanger the tenant's health or safety. This applies even if the tenant knew or ought to have known the condition of the leased premises prior to entering the lease. The tenant must return the leased premises to the landlord upon expiration or termination of the lease. Generally, the leased premises must be returned to the landlord in the same condition as when it was leased. Nevertheless, if the landlord agrees, a tenant may leave partial or complete decorations in the leased premises.

7 Expropriation

The government will usually pay compensation to the owner of premises for expropriations. National regulations define the owners of buildings being expropriated as "the parties being expropriated". While the regulations provide for compensation for the business disruption, the regulations do not take into consideration the situation where the owner has leased the premises out and is not the business operator. The result is that if the tenant has neglected to require expropriation compensation in the lease contract, then it will be very difficult for the tenant to claim compensation from either the government or the landlord for the interruption to its business operations caused by expropriation. From the government's perspective, the tenant does not hold any granted land use rights for the leased premises. From the owner's perspective, the tenant's loss was not caused by the owner but rather by government action. Zhejiang Province is one place that has legislated the availability of compensation for tenants of leased premises that have been expropriated. In Zhejiang Province, tenants in leased premises suffering loss from the suspension of business resulting from an expropriation may claim compensation by submitting, among other things, materials proving profit in the past 3 years before expropriation and tax payment receipts. The government department and the tenants will then jointly entrust a valuation institution to assess the loss, and the government department will pay compensation to the tenant based on the result of assessment.

However, if a building is regarded as illegal, then the owner may not get any compensation. Unless the lease contract provides otherwise, it is also unlikely that the tenant of such leased premises can receive any compensation for the loss arising from the suspension of operation caused by expropriation when the owner cannot get such compensation. As a general principle, governments refer to the area registered on the owner's real property ownership certificate as a basis to calculate the compensation. That said, as practice differs from localities, it is likely that other factors (such as common areas of the premises) would be considered on a case-by-case basis.

8   Leasing for Business Usage

Leases for business usages are largely subject to negotiation between the parties and the general rules outlined above. There are, nevertheless, various matters specific to leases for business usages that should be taken into account during negotiations. Prior to establishment of any foreign investment enterprise (FIE), a foreign investor must have secured premises for that FIE. The premises must be secured in order for the FIE to have a registered address upon registration.

Typically, the foreign investor will be required to either buy or lease premises for the purpose of registering an FIE. In some localities, a letter of intent to lease premises will be acceptable. A further option, which has historically been most attractive for certain industrial sectors, has been to buy land and build premises that have been designed for the intended operations. It is also possible to have a built-to-lease solution. With real estate capital costs having increased dramatically over the last 10 years, leasing has become a more attractive option even for those industries that might traditionally have chosen to buy. If a lease or land purchase is required (rather than merely a letter of intent), then foreign investors are faced with a timing dilemma when setting up a new FIE in China. That is, a lease contract or purchase contract is required before the formal establishment of the FIE; however, the FIE cannot itself enter into any contract prior to establishment. The timing issue is more significant for FIEs engaging in activities or sectors that appear in China's "negative list". If the activities of an FIE fall into the negative list, then the FIE will be (i) prohibited or (ii) subject to approval by the Ministry of Commerce or its relevant local branch (MOFCOM). This involves a longer establishment process of approval and then registration. If, however, the activities of an FIE are not in the negative list, then the FIE does not require MOFCOM approval and may be established through a registration process with the relevant local Administration for Market Regulation (AMR). In terms of timing, a registration process with the AMR is much faster than a MOFCOM approval process combined with AMR registration. In terms of timing, this means:

- FIEs requiring MOFCOM approval (i.e. FIEs covered by the negative list) may be required to pay rent for multiple months before the FIE can start business. This is because the lease must be submitted to MOFCOM as one of the application documents for approval to establish the FIE. MOFCOM will then have up to 90 days to approve (or disapprove) the establishment of the FIE (although MOFCOM is typically much faster than this). After approval, the FIE will still need to be registered with the AMR before it can start business.
- For FIEs that may be registered directly by the AMR (i.e. FIEs not covered by the negative list), it may be possible for the FIE to start business within weeks of applying for establishment. If there are any delays in the AMR registration process, however, rent will still be payable while the causes of the delay are being resolved.

The other timing issue that arises out of a lease being required prior to the FIEs establishment is the party to the initial lease. The FIE cannot enter a lease (or any contract) until it is established. The lease, however, can be required prior to establishment. The usual solution to this problem is that the foreign investor, or a nominee of the foreign investor, will enter the initial lease contract. For this solution, care must be taken to include the following provisions in the lease:

• The lease, including all rights and obligations of the foreign investor (or nominee), should be transferred to the FIE upon establishment.
• The lease should prohibit the initial tenant from running any business in the leased premises, except for the purpose of establishing the FIE; this is to minimise the foreign investor's exposure to Chinese tax that might arise if the leased premises were to be deemed a permanent establishment.

The lease should be immediately transferred to the FIE once established. A flexible landlord that is familiar with the FIE establishment process can help this process to be smoother and possibly grant a longer than usual rent-free period. Commercial landlords will generally have standard leases for their premises. This is particularly the case for retail space in China's shopping centres. It is a market practice, particularly in places like Shanghai and Beijing, that there is limited scope for negotiating such standard leases, except if the tenant will occupy a significant proportion of the landlord's premises. As a general rule, the bigger the proportion of space to be leased, the more flexible the standard terms become.

9 Leasing for Residential Usage

In the residential market, expatriates in China typically prefer to lease as their time in China is generally limited to the duration of a job posting. The rapid increase in the capital cost of residential property over recent years has also made leasing more common for Chinese nationals.

Premises may only be leased for residential usages if the construction of the premises was carried in compliance with relevant laws and regulations, and the premises are used in accordance with their approved usage. Fines of up to RMB 5000 may be imposed for a violation of these requirements. And if illegal income is gained, then fines of up to three times the illegal income may be imposed. A tenant may only use the leased premises in accordance with the usage agreed in the lease contract. A tenant may not make any modifications without the consent of the landlord. A lease for residential premises must contain the following minimum clauses: (1) Names and addresses of the parties, (2) Location, area, structure, ancillary facilities and indoor furnishings, (3) Rental charges, deposit and payment method, (4) Usage and usage requirements, (5) Safety features of the premises and indoor furnishings, (6) Term of the lease, (7) Maintenance responsibilities (typically belonging to the landlord), (8) Responsibility for payment of property services and utilities, (9) Dispute resolution and (10) Liability for default. In addition, the lease should also address issues of compensation in the event that the leased premises are expropriated or demolished. Subleasing is permitted but only with the consent of the landlord. Any period of the sublease that exceeds the term of the main lease will be invalid. Subleasing without consent of the landlord is a ground for the landlord to terminate the lease. However, the landlord must object within 6 months when the landlord knew or ought to have known of the sublease. If the landlord does not object within 6 months, then the landlord will lose its right to object to the sublease.

A transfer of ownership of the leased premises does not affect the validity of the lease. That is, the buyer of leased premises will ordinarily take the premises subject to the lease. However, if the leased premises are sold following foreclosure by a mortgagee and the mortgage was entered prior to the lease, then the buyer of the leased premises may take it free of the tenant's interests under the lease. As noted above, a tenant has a right of first refusal if the leased premises that they lease are being sold by the landlord. The landlord must notify the tenant with a reasonable time if a sale of the premises is contemplated. A tenant that fails to respond to any such notice within 15 days will be deemed to have consented to the sale by the landlord. If the landlord fails to so notify the tenant, then the tenant may seek compensation from the landlord, and such a claim must be supported by the court. A right of first refusal, however, cannot be enforced against a good faith purchaser who has completed the post-purchase registration procedures. Leases for residential premises must be registered at the relevant local authority within 30 days of the lease being signed. The following materials are required for registration: the lease contract, identity documents for both landlord and tenant, ownership certificate for the premise being leased, and any other materials requested by the local officials.

Provided the materials are in order and the identity documents for both tenant and landlord match the parties set out in the lease contract, the relevant local real estate administration department will issue a registration receipt. A registered lease will take priority over a conflicting unregistered lease. However, an unregistered lease will still take priority over a registered lease if the tenant of the unregistered lease is in lawful occupation of the premises. Violations of the registration requirements may result the imposition of fines. If the violating party is an individual, then the fines may be up to RMB 1000. If the violating party is an entity, then the fines may be more than RMB 1000 and up to RMB 10,000. The parties may agree that validity of the lease is conditional on due registration. However, absent such an agreement, a lease that is not registered will still be valid. If an individual tenant dies during the term of the lease, then anyone who lived in the leased premises along with the deceased tenant may require the original lease to continue. In such a situation, the landlord will remain bound by the original lease.

10   Concluding Remarks

Leases in China are subject to both national-level laws and various local regulations, which can lead to different practices in different localities. Leases in China can be freely negotiated, but some mandatory provisions of Chinese laws must be complied with in order to ensure the validity and enforceability of the lease. These mandatory provisions include lease term, requirements on land use right and town planning, requirements on written lease form and registration, etc. Care and due diligence should be taken to tailor a lease agreement to suit a particular usage and to ensure adequate contractual protection to the parties concerned.

Tax Framework for Accessing Real Estate Asset Classes

Matthew Wong

Abstract

Real estate investment in China provides an enormous opportunity for significant capital appreciation and rewarding returns to foreign investors. Yet, the regulatory and tax regime governing foreign investment in China's real estate sector is complicated. Respectable return on a successful real estate project could be easily wiped out by uncertain or unexpected taxation rules. Thus, in order to avoid pitfalls, robust tax considerations are essential throughout the life cycle of different types of real estate projects. The purpose of this chapter is to highlight the application of taxation frameworks for international investors, in particular key tax challenges when investing in the real estate sector in China.

1 Overview of China Real Estate Taxation

China imposes multiple levels of taxes on real estate transactions along the investment cycle, from acquisition, holding, to the final exit stage. The China taxation regime mentioned in this chapter applies equally to different real estate asset classes regardless of whether they are commercial buildings, residential units, hotels properties, or logistic real estates. Meanwhile, this Chapter focuses on the tax impacts on international institutional investments.

Institutional investors acquiring of real estate assets or land use rights in China are subject to the following two types of taxes: (1) Deed tax: 3–5% on the acquisition price and (2) Stamp duty: 0.05% on the contract value. Thereafter, holding real estate assets in China for leasing attracts the following taxes: (1)

M. Wong (✉)
PricewaterhouseCoopers, Shanghai, China

© Springer Nature Switzerland AG 2021   127
B. Wang, T. Just (eds.), *Understanding China's Real Estate Markets*, Management
for Professionals, https://doi.org/10.1007/978-3-030-49032-4_10

Value-added tax (VAT): 5%[1] or 9%[2] on rental, (2) Real estate tax: 12% on rental income; or 1.2% on original value of the building × (1 − deduction rate), (3) Urban and township land use tax: RMB0.6~RMB30 per square meters on yearly basis, (4) Stamp duty: 0.1% on each leasing contract and (5) Corporate income tax (CIT): 25% on net profit. Finally, sales of real estate assets in China are subject to another five levels of taxes: (1) Value-added tax: 5%[3] or 9%[4] on net disposal gain, (2) Land appreciation tax (LAT): 30–60% on the appreciation value from property transfer, (3) Stamp duty: 0.05% on transfer price, (4) Corporate income tax (CIT): 25% on net gain and (5) Dividend withholding tax: 10% on repatriation of dividend. It is apparent that sale of real estate assets is not a tax efficient way to exit given the above laundry list of potential heavy taxes to be imposed on the seller. This mode of exit may only be adopted in residential development projects targeting a large number of domestic buyers on residential housing units.

Deed tax, generally at rates from 3% to 5%, may be levied on purchases or sales, gift, or exchange of ownership of land use rights or real estate properties. The transferee/assignee is the taxpayer. Stamp duty is imposed on dutiable documents executed in China. Typical dutiable documents include sales and purchase contracts, loan contracts, and leasing contracts. Rates vary between 0.005% and 0.1% on the contract value and are generally applicable to all parties in the contract. For sales of real estate, stamp duty at 0.05% is imposed on both the buyer and seller. For leasing of real estate, stamp duty at 0.1% on the total rental amount is imposed on both the lessor and the lessee. A flat amount of RMB5 applies to certification of real estate of ownership and land use certificates.

Sales or rentals of real estate assets are subject to VAT, effective from 1 May 2016. VAT is assessed on the gross sales proceeds of disposed real estate assets. It is also assessed on rental incomes from leasing of real estate assets. The applicable VAT rate is either 9% or 5% depending on the status of the taxpayer and the real estate assets. For general VAT taxpayers, input VAT incurred may be credited against output VAT in computing the VAT payable. Urban construction and maintenance tax is imposed at a certain rate on the amount of China's VAT payable by the taxpayer. Effectively, the VAT taxpayers are also the taxpayers of urban construction and maintenance tax. It is charged at three different rates depending on the taxpayer's location: 7% for urban areas, 5% for county areas, and 1% for other areas. Educational surcharge is imposed at 3% on the amount of China's VAT payable by the taxpayer. Again, the VAT taxpayers are effectively the taxpayers of educational surcharge. Local educational surcharge is imposed at 2% on the amount of China's VAT payable by the taxpayer. Again, the VAT taxpayers are effectively the taxpayers of local educational surcharge.

---

[1]There are also various VAT surtaxes, including urban construction and maintenance tax and education levies that would be imposed in parallel with VAT.

[2]See footnote 1.

[3]See footnote 1.

[4]See footnote 1.

Real estate tax is a tax imposed on the owners, users, or custodians of houses and buildings. The tax rate is 1.2% of the original value of buildings. A tax reduction of 10–30% is commonly offered by local governments. Alternatively, real estate tax may be assessed at 12% of the rental value. Urban and township land use tax is levied on taxpayers who utilize land within the area of city, country, township, and mining districts. It is computed, on an annual basis, based on the space of area actually occupied by a taxpayer, multiplied by a fixed amount per square meter that is determined by the local governments.

Real estate development or investment companies in China are subject to corporate income tax (CIT) on net operating income. The CIT rate is 25%. Prior to completion of construction, a real estate developer in China may be allowed to "presell" its incomplete properties through a process called "presale" by obtaining a presale permit from the authorities. The presale permit would not be granted to the developer until it has fulfilled certain conditions, including full payment of the land premium by the developer, commencement of the construction work, and completion of a significant percentage of the total investment of the development project. These conditions may vary from city to city as local authorities may impose more stringent conditions for a presale permit. Since presale (i.e., sale of real estates before completion of construction) is a common business model adopted by real estate developers in China, Chinese tax rules set out a "provisional collection and final settlement" approach in enforcing CIT collection on real estate developers. Provisional CIT is levied on a quarterly basis on presale proceeds of properties by a real estate developer based on the deemed profit rates which are generally ranged from 3% to 20%.

Withholding income tax (WHT) at 10% is applicable to a non-China resident (i.e., an overseas entity) which receives from China-sourced dividend, interest, rental, royalty, and other passive incomes such as the gains from the sale or transfer of real estate property, land use right, and shares in a Chinese company. WHT rate may be lower than 10% or exempted under a tax treaty. Land appreciation tax is levied on certain gains realized from real property transactions at progressive rates from 30% to 60%, based on the "land value appreciation amount" which is the consideration received from the transfer or disposition of real property less the "total deductible amount." For taxpayers engaged in a real estate development business, the "total deductible amount" includes the following:

1. The amount spent on obtaining land use right.
2. Costs of real property development and construction.
3. Finance expenses, such as interest, may be deducted in certain circumstances. Other real property development expenses (i.e., selling and administrative) are limited to 5% of the total amount expended to acquire the land use right and the costs of real property development and construction.
4. Taxes in connection with the transfer of real property (generally urban construction and maintenance tax, educational surcharge, and stamp tax).

5. For taxpayers engaged in a real estate development business, an additional deduction equal to 20% of the sum of the first two cost items noted above is allowed.

LAT is payable on a provisional basis in respect of sales made before completion of the real estate development project (i.e., presale) in the same manner of CIT as mentioned in Section "Stamp Duty" above. That is, LAT is also provisionally collected based on a certain percentage: say 1–2% of "presale" proceeds, followed by a later final settlement after the completion of construction of the entire project. For disposal of used properties, the deductible amount includes the assessed value of the used building and the taxes incurred upon the disposal. In July 2019, a new draft LAT law was issued by the Chinese tax authorities for public comments. This draft was introduced to improve the existing LAT rules and regulations, in particular, to propose for expanding scope of charge and offering wider exemption scope.

2 Investment Structuring

Since 2007, China has no longer allowed foreign investors to use an offshore entity to directly buy, sell, and hold real estate in China. Currently, foreign investors are mandatorily required to set up an onshore vehicle to hold, develop, or operate any new real estate project in China.

The onshore vehicle for foreign investment into the real estate market in China is generally referred as a foreign investment enterprise which can take one of the following three common forms:

1. Wholly foreign-owned enterprises (WFOE)
   A WFOE is a limited liability company wholly owned by the foreign investor. It gives the foreign investor 100% control over the real estate project invested without having to share with a Chinese partner.
2. Equity joint venture (EJV)
   EJV also has the legal status of a limited liability company where the Chinese and foreign partners share rights and obligations and profits and losses, according to their respective proportion of the registered capital contributed by each party. Generally, foreign investors own no less than 25% of the equity interest in an EJV.
3. Cooperative joint venture (CJV)
   A CJV can have two possible options of its legal status in China. Incorporated CJV has the legal status of a limited liability company, whereas unincorporated CJV does not have a legal person status. A CJV offers more flexibility, e.g., the share of profits is governed by the joint venture contract which can be disproportionate to their equity interest.

The above three common forms of onshore vehicle (i.e., WFOE, EJV, and CJV) are treated as China tax resident enterprise by the Chinese tax authorities. As a result, any income generated from real estate projects would be subject to corporate income tax at 25% in the hands of the onshore vehicle. Also, after-tax net income distributed by the onshore vehicle out of China to foreign investors in the form of dividend would attract China WHT at the time of repatriation. The use of offshore real estate holding vehicle to secure a lower 10% withholding corporate income tax rate on income (e.g., rental or capital gain) derived from real estate assets is not an option. This has significantly limited the flexibility on cross-border tax planning and cash repatriation on real estate projects in China.

3   Taxation on Onshore Project Company Level

Real estate business is highly capital-intensive, and significant funding is normally required at the initial stage of the projects. As compared to equity, debt financing appears to be a more flexible funding alternative to foreign investment in an onshore real estate project vehicle in terms of future offshore cash repatriation in this connection. Interest expense incurred by a real estate project company in China can attract 25% corporate income tax reduction. Also, interest paid during the development phase of real estate project can be claimed as part of its cost base in determining the accessible gain on LAT applied from future sales of real estate assets.

However, foreign investors are not permitted to push foreign debt down to their local real estate project companies since 2007. Cross-border borrowings cannot be arranged for an onshore real estate vehicle regardless of whether they are third party loans or shareholders' loan. As a result, foreign investors borrowing debts outside of China to finance real estate projects in China can only inject the fund into China by way of equity contribution to the project vehicle. Accordingly, interest expenses incurred on such foreign debts would be absorbed at the offshore holding company level and cannot be utilized to offset against the operating income earned by the onshore project vehicle from the underlying real estate assets This Chinese regulatory restriction on foreign debt being pushed down for Chinese real estate projects has created significant tax inefficiency for foreign investors as their onshore project vehicle cannot enjoy tax deduction on offshore funding costs for the purpose of both corporate income tax and LAT. Meanwhile, China real estate companies are still allowed to borrow onshore. Onshore financing can be arranged to reduce the tax base of the real estate project entity in China. In structuring intercompany loan for related entities in China, one also needs to observe the transfer pricing rules and thin capitalization tax rules which were introduced during the 2008 tax reform. Under these rules, excessive interest expenses may be denied for tax deduction where the intercompany interest rate is seen to be unreasonable as compared to the market rate or where real estate companies' related party debt to equity ratio exceeding 2:1 without reasonable excuse.

4   Offshore Intermediate Holding Structure

Foreign investors may consider establishing a single or multiple tiers of offshore holding vehicles to hold their investment in the onshore real estate project companies. Typically, one of the common business reasons for setting up these offshore holding structures is to enable foreign investors to have more flexibility to reorganize their interest in the underlying entities indirectly through restructuring its interest in the offshore structures. The option does not require a direct transfer of equity interest in the onshore entities, thus reducing the time and effort to secure various approvals from various authorities to effect the change.

Along with the potential restructuring flexibility under an offshore holding structure, the offshore holding entity, if properly arranged, may also allow the foreign investors to access relevant tax treaty benefit to reduce the PRC withholding tax on dividend repatriated from the onshore project company to overseas. The withholding tax rate under the corporate income tax law is 10%. Jurisdictions, such as Hong Kong, Singapore, and Luxemburg, have double tax treaties with China that offer preferential dividend withholding tax rate of only 5%. On the other hand, China tax authority also strictly controls the treaty benefit claim. In September 2015, the tax authorities issued Public Notice (2015) No. 60 to deal with the procedure of treaty benefit claim. The Notice mandatorily requires the nontax resident to go through self-assessment procedures and perform record filing with the tax authorities when claiming treaty benefits on dividends. Taxpayer would also need to pass the beneficial ownership test set out in Public Notice (2018) No. 9 and to prove the ownership and control over the dividend income. These requirements not only increase the compliance burden for the taxpayer but also put various uncertainties in practice.

Meanwhile, China has phased out all the favorable capital gain tax protection provisions in her treaty network in relation to sale of equity interest in a PRC real estate company. Barbados used to have a unique treaty benefit to protect capital gain tax on sale of equity interest in a Chinese real estate company, but such benefit has been removed in the renegotiated treaty effective 2011. From 2011 onwards, there is no longer any treaty-based structure that allows foreign investors to enjoy capital gain tax exemption on sale of a Chinese real estate project company.

5   Exit Structures

Exit of China real estate projects requires careful planning as it may trigger multiple levels of China taxes on both the sellers and the buyers. The most straightforward way of exit is the sale of onshore real estate which is one of the common exit routes in residential development projects targeting a large number of domestic buyers on residual housing units. This may not be considered as a tax efficient exit structure since a laundry list of potentially heavy Chinese taxes may be imposed on the seller, namely, a 25% PRC corporate income tax, a land appreciation tax ranging from 30% to 60% on the net appreciated value of the property, VAT on the sales price, stamp duty on the transaction documents as well as a 10% withholding tax on dividend repatriation by the onshore project company to distribute the net proceeds to the foreign investors. A further China tax problem may arise on an onshore sale of real estate asset where the foreign investor previously acquired the real estate project through the purchase of the onshore project company at a huge premium. The premium previously paid by the foreign investor on the acquisition of the project company cannot be used to step up the tax cost base in computing the net taxable amount of the onshore entity's asset sale for the purpose of corporate income tax, land appreciation tax, and VAT. The existing tax rules do not have a mechanism to allow the taxpayer to align this mismatched tax cost base, thus creating significant tax leakage.

An alternative exit route for foreign investors which intend to dispose of the entire PRC real estate project is to the sale of the equity interest in the onshore project entity. This alternative exit structure only exposes the foreign seller to 10% withholding tax on the capital gain and stamp duty on the equity transfer documents.

6   Offshore Divestment as an Alternative Exit

Exit through sale of the offshore holding vehicle of the project company is also seen to be very popular. If this exit route is structured properly, the offshore seller can take a position that the transaction should not be subject to any China tax on the grounds that the capital gain derived from the disposition of the offshore company is not a China-sourced income. However, China has introduced a series of anti-tax-avoidance rules focusing on offshore or cross-border transactions after its extensive tax reform in 2008. The tax Circular No. 698 (2009) is the landmark tax notice which confirms tax authorities' intention to attack tax-driven offshore exit transactions where the structure is considered abusive. The Circular has empowered the tax authorities, in certain circumstances, to disregard the corporate veil of an offshore intermediate holding vehicle and impose 10% capital gain tax on sale of the shares in such offshore company by deeming the transaction as a direct disposal of shares in the underlying project company. In 2015, the Chinese tax authorities have outlined a new landscape for tax treatment on offshore indirect equity transfer by the introduction of Public Notice No. 7 to replace Circular 698. Public Notice 7 sets out more guidance regarding the various factors for tax authorities to attack offshore exit transactions, voluntary reporting regime, tax withholding obligation, and safe-harbor rules to avoid anti-avoidance tax attack.

So far, there have been a number of widely reported tax cases where the tax authorities have successfully applied the principle under Circular 698 to tax offshore indirect disposal transactions. For example, one case, which was discussed in recent media report, involves a large single tax imposition on an offshore indirect disposal transaction, in which tax due of RMB403 million was recovered. Another case happens to be in relation to an indirect disposal of the real estate project companies by a Hong Kong-listed real estate group through the transfer of an intermediate holding company in the British Virgin Islands. The outcome of this case involves a tax payment of RMB300 million. In all these cases, the offshore disposal was attacked by the tax authorities on the grounds that the intermediate holding vehicles, whether single or multiple levels, do not have reasonable commercial and business substance. In particular, the intermediate holding structures in these cases appear to be special purpose holding vehicles without any business operations, employees, physical offices, and assets other than the investment in China.

Circular 698 and Public Notice 7 also impose a controversial obligation on the seller to notify the tax authorities with regard to the detailed information of the offshore, indirect exit transactions within 30 days after the conclusion of contracts on sale of the offshore intermediate holding company (which holds the project company) where the seller has concluded that the transfer may be seen as an indirect transfer of Chinese equity or immorally properties in China. The information reported by the offshore seller would be scrutinized by the tax authorities to determine whether the offshore indirect disposal transaction is undertaken for good commercial reasons or it is merely driven by tax motive. Meanwhile, Public Notice 7 also requires the buyer in the offshore exit transaction to withhold the relevant 10% capital gain tax from the payment of the sales consideration. It is now crystal clear that offshore indirect disposal transactions are under the radar screen of the tax authorities. Proper monitoring the economic substance of the offshore holding structures has become a heated tax topic for foreign investors intending to select offshore indirect disposal as its future exit strategy for their China real estate investments.

7   Cash Trap Problems

One of the biggest challenges faced by foreign investors in China real estate market is the cash trapped in their onshore project companies and the related tax costs for repatriation. This refers to a phenomenon where the real estate project has become cash rich but is unable to repatriate the excessive cash out of China because of sophisticated interactions among different layers of regulations governing outbound remittance, dividend repatriation, reserve accounting, and taxation. Dividend distribution is seen to be a simple and straightforward way to extract cash from project companies in China. However, this appears to be a tax inefficient repatriation strategy given that dividend is not tax deductible against the onshore project company's taxable profits, whereas such dividend is further subject to a 10% withholding tax on repatriation. This dividend withholding rate can be reduced to 5% under certain double taxation treaties. Notwithstanding this, an onshore project company's ability to pay dividend is also limited by its accounting profits which can be severely eroded by depreciation and other non-cash charges, including profit appropriation to various reserves.

Development of other tax efficient cash extraction strategies is always a priority of topics for real estate investors in China. Outbound payments on legitimate service fees and royalty charges, if structured properly, can be alternative solutions to cash trap and also attract a 25% corporate income tax deduction in China. These charges would, however, be subject to extensive queries by the PRC tax authorities where they are paid to related parties. In one of the recently announced cases, the tax authority in northern China conducted a tax investigation on a real estate company invested by a Hong Kong company and eventually denied a deduction from trademark payment with extra late payment surcharges of RMB currency of 5 million because of lacking of reasonable commercial substance. Moving excessive cash to other Chinese affiliates by way of intercompany "entrustment" loan can be another option. Again, this intercompany loan arrangement would be subject to close scrutiny by the local tax authorities and reasonable interest income needs to be allocated to the lender, i.e., the onshore project company, thus creating incremental tax costs on intercompany interest charges.

8   Real Estate as Part of Infrastructure Projects

It is common that real estate investments are bundled with infrastructure projects. For instance, urban metro projects may have significant commercial and residential real estate elements. Another example is the development of industrial and logistic real estate in a port project. China has a complex taxation regime on real estate development projects, with high effective tax costs arising from multiple layers of direct and indirect taxes in different stages of real estate development cycle. On the other hand, infrastructure projects are encouraged by the government and usually attract preferential tax treatments and incentives such as generous tax holidays and reduced corporate income tax rates. In some cases, early and proper craft-out of the real estate element from the infrastructure part of the overall project under separate vehicles may help to achieve overall tax efficiency. This craft-out ensures that the infrastructure project company, say a metro operator, could retain its preferential tax status without being tinged by real estate development activities, such as residential unit sales.

However, in certain special circumstances, it may be appropriate to keep real estate and infrastructure operation in the same vehicle so that the preferential tax policies on the infrastructure activities can be extended to real estate operations. For example, a port operator may try to characterize its logistic/warehousing real estate business to be part and parcel of the overall infrastructure project activities and secure the preferential tax treatment across the board.

9   The Way Forward

The past two decades have seen real estate investment in China a very rewarding business. Meanwhile, it is also one of the most regulated and heavy taxed industries for foreign investors. As China's real estate landscape is changing rapidly, new investment structures such as foreign-invested partnership, real estate investment trust, and real estate-backed securitization will become emerging business models in the China market. As a result, a series of new and uncertainty tax issues may rise and may have far-reaching impact on the future tax framework governing the Chinese real estate industry. On the other hand, the China tax environment is also undergoing significant evolution in response to various global tax initiatives, such as the OECD base erosion and profit shifting directives and local economic development policies, such as China's fiscal policy on urbanization. It is anticipated that the Chinese real estate tax regime will still be in the state of flux. Careful planning is suggested throughout the life cycle of different types of real estate projects. Meanwhile, the uncertain and constant changing practical environments also require foreign investors to form a robust implementation strategy to eventually achieve tax efficiencies.

Part III

Finance and Investment for Real Estate Development

The Leverage Game: From Offshore to Onshore

Dave Chiou, Joe Zhou, and Megan Walters

Abstract

In the years after China's housing reforms in 1998, demand for both residential and commercial properties soared, and developers responded by rushing into aggressive land bids and property construction to meet market demand. For most Chinese developers, residential development are always preferred over commercial assets, as residentials have a broader customer base and it is easier to apply a strata-titled sales approach to increase asset turnover and improve profitability. However, during the recent consumption boom, Chinese developers have transformed to include office and retail development in their portfolios. Aggressive project launches translated to high leverages for the Chinese developers. While traditional bank loans remain the main source of funding, in recent years Chinese developers are also adapting a more flexible approach in securing their working capital and lowering their cost of funding. In this chapter, an overview of the main funding mechanisms for Chinese developers is discussed, which includes offshore corporate bonds, onshore corporate bonds, perpetual bonds, trust firms, peer-to-peer (P2P) lending, crowdfunding, commercial mortgage-backed securities (CMBS) and asset-backed securities (ABS), real estate investment trusts (REITs), and joint ventures and strategic alliances.

D. Chiou (✉)
Colliers International, Shanghai, China

J. Zhou
CBRE Group, Shanghai, China

M. Walters
Allianz Real Estate, Singapore

© Springer Nature Switzerland AG 2021
B. Wang, T. Just (eds.), *Understanding China's Real Estate Markets*, Management for Professionals, https://doi.org/10.1007/978-3-030-49032-4_11

1   Recap of China's Residential Real Estate Market

Before the 1988 housing reforms, urban housing was allocated by employers on the basis of family size and seniority. From the early 1980s, China's central government began to experiment with the privatization of property rights. In 1988, the State Council allowed land-use rights to be purchased and traded, thereby creating a secondary market in which apartments formerly assigned by work units were allowed to be purchased and sold in the open market. That being said, China's welfare housing policy was not completely eliminated until a decade later in 1998, as the reforms were carried on by steps and met with strong resistance. Given the low base, China's property market demand was strong after the reforms, but property prices remained fairly stable, rising by a few percentage points higher than the nominal CPI, as disposable income remained fairly low before the turn of this century.

Driven by a robust economy with an average GDP growth of more than 10%, Year 2004–2010 marks an era where China saw a sharp rise in household disposable income and a desire to improve living standards, thereby pushing the nation's housing price and demand. Inward foreign direct investments (FDI) also increased from USD 60.6 billion in 2004 to USD 114.7 billion in 2010, or the equivalent of a 9.5% compound annual growth rate (CAGR). Coupled with an increase in disposable income and FDI, China's property market saw strong volume growth and a steep rise in prices. In 2008, China's property demand and prices declined in the latter half of the year during the global financial crisis but then quickly rebounded following the government's RMB 4 trillion (USD 581.4 billion) stimulus package in 2009 (Edwards and Yao 2012). In the second half of 2010, China was starting to feel the pain of surging property prices, fueled in part by speculative buying. With prices escalating, the Chinese government introduced new home purchase restrictions in 2011, restricting people from owning multiple homes by requiring greater down payments and applying higher mortgage rates to second homes (Hong 2011). Cross-border capital flows were also monitored to stop overseas speculative funds from buying up China's property market, and the city-level governments were also encouraged to increase land supply and speed up the construction of public housings. With these new measures enforced over a 3-year time span, this effectively put the reins on a surging market. In 2014, dragged by a weaker economy and tighter credits, transaction volumes declined in 2014, and prices dropped in a stronger magnitude as a result of high inventory.

Faced with a slowing economy and a housing inventory buildup, in March 2015 China's central government announced a series of relaxation measures, hoping to stimulate property demand. For the second home buyers, the minimum down payment has been cut to 40% from the previous 60–70%. For first-time home buyers, the down payment was lowered from 30% to 20% (Fung 2015). Also, from November 2014 to October 2015, China's central bank cut its benchmark interest rate six times in less than a year and pumped liquidity into the market by lowering the reserve requirement ratio (RRR) for banks. On back of a series of rate cuts, lower down payment requirements, and sector-supportive measures, transaction volume and prices were on an upward trend until early 2018, with property prices in tier-one and many tier-two cities reaching all-time highs. Since early 2018, however, China's property price and demand has stabilized as State authorities are now targeting overcapacity and planning to slow the pace of lending growth, especially in the real estate sector (Schrader 2018).

2   China's Commercial Property Market

In the years following the housing reforms, China's commercial real estate market has largely followed the trajectory of the residential market, with prices, demand, and supply growing at unprecedented rates. However, in the past four to five years, oversupply issues have led to high vacancy rates and yield compressions, especially for the retail sector that is experiencing fierce competition from online retailers. Chinese developers' unique strategy of strata-selling has only aggravated the situation, as units within the mall or office are sold individually, leading to limited property management or tenant mix strategy.

From 1988 to 2018, China's demand and growth of commercial properties largely followed the trend of the residential market. Commercial property demand in part came from China's urbanization, in which urban population increased from 25.8% in 1988 to 59.6% in 2018 (Fig. 1). Another contributing factor was a rise in disposable income in which consumers moved from a near-subsistence level to accelerated spending and consumption. Based on China's National Bureau of Statistics, the gross floor area (GFA) of completed commercial properties increased from 21.6 million square meters in 1995 to 151.4 million square meters in 2018, indicating

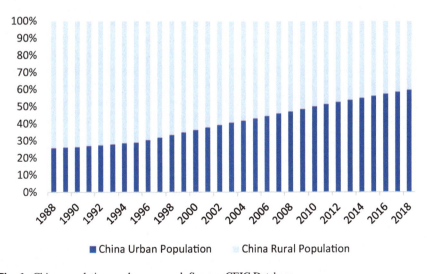

Fig. 1 China population—urban vs. rural. Source: CEIC Database

strong demand for retail and office space. Much like Hong Kong, owning a part of a floor in a building has been common practice in China (dubbed as "strata-title" ownership). The ability to subdivide property generates higher numbers of owners and smaller apartment or unit sizes. The reason why buildings are chopped up and sold in pieces is that a small unit size will increase the number of investors who can participate in the transactions, thereby allowing the developers a quick sell-through.

However, dividing up buildings on a floor-by-floor basis or selling off portions room-by-room benefits the initial seller and creates externalities that are borne both by neighbors and wider society. The division of buildings necessitates more complicated management and maintenance. The latter is often neglected due to the difficulty of getting multiple owners to agree on expenditure, and it only takes a couple of owners refusing to pay, to have the system and buildings break down relatively quickly. In addition, the costs of buying up the shares to redevelop the sites will be particularly high and slow in the future, leaving very poor property standing (Walters 2013). The net result of extensive strata titling for the commercial property market is a lack of debt in supporting continued ownership that can be bought and sold on a landlord and tenant system commensurate with commercial property markets in locations such as the USA, UK, and Australia. In some ways, it's a circular process with developers selling off floor-by-floor on the grounds as they cannot find an institutional buyer to take the whole block as an exit strategy. By contrast, institutional buyers and indeed western MNCs may not want to rent floors in buildings where they may have to deal with multiple landlords. The issue is even more difficult for retail malls. In a mall where units are sold off, there is no mall management or tenant mix strategy. Mall failure can be common, and it is costly to align the owners to sell and redevelop. The rise of e-commerce has done little to help strata-sold shopping malls.

China's e-commerce started to gain popularity in 2012. Starting from a low base, online retailing was a nonissue to the traditional retail channels until 2014, when total e-commerce sales grew 49.7% year-on-year, reaching RMB 2.79 trillion (USD 405.5 billion). In 2015, Chinese retail websites sold a total of RMB 3.88 trillion (USD 563.9 billion) worth of consumer goods, representing a 38.9% year-on-year gain (Tong 2016). In 2018, online retail sales continued its strong growth with a 25.4% year-on-year gain and accounted for 18.4% of all retail sales in China, a significant jump from 10.6% in 2014. With China's e-commerce market outpacing the overall retail market growth rate of 9.0% in 2018 (Fig. 2), logistics demand is increasing with retailers in need of more warehouse floor space. Traditional retail channels are now experiencing a decline in revenue, leading to an oversupply of commercial properties in China (Shanghai WOWeng 2016).

3   Developers' Offshore Funding

Bank lending used to be an important funding source for property developers, but after a spike in property prices in the years following the global financial crisis, China introduced a series of credit-tightening measures in 2011–2014, making it

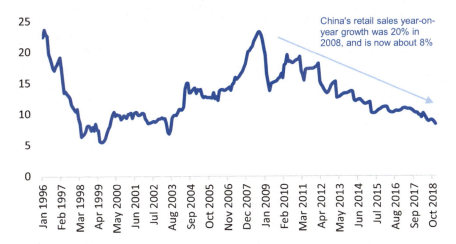

Fig. 2 China retail—year-on-year monthly sales (3-month moving average) in %. Source: CEIC Database

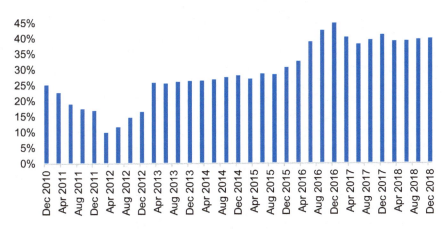

Fig. 3 China banks—real estate loans as a percent of total loans. Source: CEIC Database

difficult for real estate developers to borrow. Figures from China's National Bureau of Statistics show that developers accounted for 25.2% of the total new loans in the fourth quarter of 2010, but the ratio dropped significantly to 9.9% in March 2012. From 2011 to 2012, developers are finding it extremely difficult to get loans, as the domestic banks have only granted loans to a selected group of developers that have a strong brand recognition, a steady business operation, a solid balance sheet with relatively low leverage, and a good credit score. In March 2013, real estate loans rebounded to 25.8% of total new loans in China (Fig. 3), as banks were more willing to take risks and lend.

Despite banks' increased lending in 2013, property developers in China were generally still having difficulties getting credit lines from commercial banks. Apart from credit controls, the Chinese government had also prohibited developers sourcing funds from other channels such as nonpublic trust funds and real estate investment trusts (REITs). Added to the problem is that domestic banks were also encouraged to prolonged mortgage loan approvals to home buyers, leaving developers tight in cash to pay their contractors and suppliers (Chiang and Edwards 2012). The solution is alternative funding, as property developers were raising more money overseas. Offshore corporate bonds, or specifically senior notes denominated in USD, had become the mainstream among Chinese property developers as they offer the following advantages:

1. Offshore bonds offer an easy access of capital with lower rates. The US Federal Reserve started its first quantitative easing (QE) program in November 2008, and since then, the Federal Reserve would go on to issue two more QE programs that injected over USD 4.5 trillion of liquidity into the market (Wolfers 2014). This entails other central banks to follow the footsteps of the USA by launching more rounds of QE, which lead to lower yields globally. As global investors scramble to find higher investment returns, Chinese developers were able to funnel billions of USD from the international bond market at a lower interest rate than the onshore market.
2. Offshore corporate bonds provide a means of getting around strict domestic regulations. In July 2008, in efforts to cool down the property market, China's Banking Regulatory Commission (CBRC) issued a new policy banning the use of borrowed money to buy land. The policy was never tightly regulated since its announcement until 2011, when there were concerns of an overheated property market. In response, the Chinese developers raised money offshore, and the proceeds were remitted back as shareholders' equity to their subsidiaries, which would be used to buy land. In addition, as a highly regulated financial system, transferring money out of China has always been difficult (Keohane 2016). The accessibility of overseas funding has allowed Chinese developers to enjoy the flexibility of remitting money back home or keeping the money offshore to invest overseas.
3. An appreciating Chinese Yuan/Renminbi (RMB) has made debt payment less expensive for developers, as the offshore bonds were denominated in other currencies such as the USD or the HKD. Before 2015, the RMB had enjoyed a decade of steady appreciation against all major global currencies. From January 2011 to December 2014, the RMB gained 7.7% over the USD, and since developers receive RMB from its property sales, this makes its USD-denominated debt payment less expensive (Fig. 4).

In March 2015, Kaisa became the first Chinese real estate developer to default on USD-denominated debts, as the company did not make an interest payment on either of its bonds due in 2017 or 2018. Kaisa failed to pay the USD 16.1 million in interest on its 2017 bond and USD 35.5 million in interest on its 2018 senior notes, or a

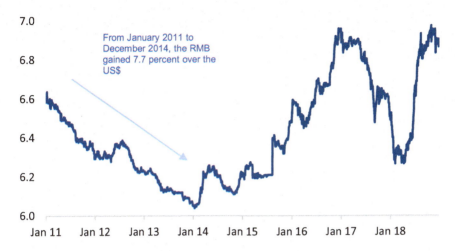

Fig. 4 Currency—USD to RMB exchange rate. Source: CEIC Database

combined of USD 51.6 million (Law 2015). The Shenzhen-based developer's default underscores the risks that Chinese developers face in a slowed economy and how a leveraged balance sheet could eventually backfire. Most developers in China are highly leveraged, with some companies having a debt-to-equity ratio of more than 1000%. The reason for this phenomenon stems from a unique presale business model that is widely adopted and accepted in China. Almost all of the new housings in China are presold, and the cash received from home buyers are used to finance the developers' activities. In China, home buyers typically pay 30% of the total transaction cost up front as a down payment, and the remaining 70% would be mortgaged. Once the loan has been bank approved, the mortgage loan proceeds would be wired to the developers. Since developers in China do not pay interest on the cash advances they collect, this cash transfer is effectively an interest-free loan. In the United States, presales are also common, but the home buyers' down payments and mortgage loan proceeds are put in a separate account managed by a third-party escrow agent. The money can only be transferred to the developer after the project has been completed and the government has issued an occupancy permit (Stefanac 2014). The Chinese developers' unique financing method boosts their balance sheets and understates the hidden risks.

Since Kaisa's default, Standard & Poor's and Moody's have downgraded the ratings of most of the Chinese developers in the following year (Stanton 2016). Among the ones downgraded or categorized as junk bonds include China's largest commercial property company Wanda Group and also Shanghai government-backed Greenland Holdings. With the ratings downgrade, Chinese developers are paying higher interest for their bonds, while finding it more difficult to raise money offshore (Fig. 5).

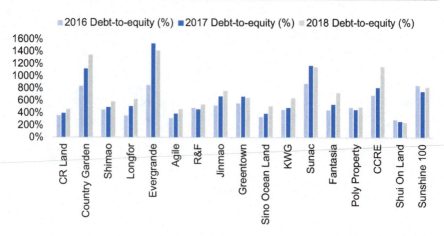

Fig. 5 China developers—debt-to-equity ratio (2016–2018). Source: Jones Lang LaSalle, Morningstar

4 Developers' Domestic Funding

Kaisa's failure and the rating agencies' downgrade have clearly dented investors' confidence since 2015. While developers will continue to issue offshore bonds to maintain their flexibility and relations with global investors, the trend since the second quarter of 2015 was a quick retreat back to the mainland bond market as the advantages of issuing a domestic corporate bond clearly outweigh the offshore option (Zhen 2016). These abrupt changes in preference provided an easy access of capital in the onshore market. After a series property sector-supportive measures and China's central bank cutting its benchmark interest rate six times in less than a year, the domestic market has been flooded with capital with limited places to go to. According to China's National Bureau of Statistics, total fixed asset investments in 2016 reached RMB 59.7 trillion (the equivalent of USD 8.7 trillion), or a 8.1% year-on-year gain, of which private sector growth was a mere 3.2% as a result of the slowed economy.

Added to the problem is a stringent capital flow control as the People's Bank of China attempts to defend the depreciating RMB (Xin 2016). The following new measures have been announced since January 2016 to tackle with a continuous capital outflow from China:

1. An increased scrutiny of overseas transfers: Banks are required to check whether individuals are sending money abroad by breaking up foreign-currency purchases into smaller transactions and if the amount wired exceeds the annual per capita limit of USD 50,000.

2. An effort in restricting foreign exchange purchases: Companies can only buy overseas currencies a maximum of 5 days before they make actual payments for goods, having previously been free to make their own decisions on timing.
3. Curbing offshore supply of yuan: The PBOC is discouraging onshore lenders offering cross-border financing to offshore counterparts and will suspend offshore yuan lending unless necessary.
4. Limited repatriation of earnings: The State Administration of Foreign Exchange (SAFE) made restrictions for international companies to repatriate their earnings made in China, and banks are required to review the transfers to check if they comply with regulations.
5. Outbound investment quotas frozen: New applications under the Renminbi Qualified Domestic Institutional Investor Program, which allows yuan from the mainland to be used to buy offshore securities denominated in the currency, are suspended. Also suspended are the new quotas for residents to invest in overseas markets via its Qualified Domestic Institutional Investor Program.
6. UnionPay debit-card clampdown: New measures are introduced to crack down the China UnionPay debit-card machines, which were suspected of being used to channel funds offshore via fake transactions.
7. Underground banking clampdown: The State Administration of Foreign Exchange (SAFE) indicated that it will crack down on illegal currency transactions, including underground banking.

With private capital receding and restrictions on capital flows, commercial banks in China have become more willing to take risks and lend to real estate developers. While the international credit agencies such as Standard & Poor's, Moody's, and Fitch have downgraded most of the Chinese real estate developers in the past 3 years, citing their stretched balance sheet and slowed economy as concerns, the domestic credit rating firms such as Golden Credit Rating International, China Cheng Xin International Credit Rating, China Lianhe Credit Rating, and Dagong Global Credit Rating, among others, have given most Chinese developers a high credit rating (Kynge 2016). The downgrades indicate that Chinese developers will have to issue their bonds at a discount in the offshore market while at the same time paying higher interest rates. However, the sharp difference by the investment grade credit ratings offered by the domestic banks has allowed Chinese developers to issue onshore bonds at a significantly lower interest rates, paying a mere 4–6% interest in 2016 or about half of the amount paid for an offshore ones. In the meantime, since July 2015, the Chinese yuan has depreciated over 10% on concerns of a slowing economy and being overvalued. This unexpected depreciation resulted in foreign exchange losses for Chinese real estate developers with heavy exposure to USD-denominated offshore bonds, prompting many to return to the mainland domestic bond market. Therefore, while onshore bonds have not completed replaced offshore funding, the trend is becoming more evident since early 2016.

5   Other Means of Financing

Depending on the government policies in China, the amount of liquidity available, and market interest rates, Chinese developers will continue to alternate their source of funding from either onshore or offshore markets. As China continues to relax its controls on the financial sector and free up cross-border capital flows, more financing options will be available to the developers in the future. The availability of new financing mechanisms will allow developers in China to secure their working capital, transfer part of the development risks, and possibly lower their costs of funding. In the following sections, an overview of the types of alternative funding and strategies will be discussed.

Given their large size and brand recognition, commercial banks in China consider lending to listed developers a low-risk business. However, with frequent changes in government policies, and faced with a leveraged balance sheet, Chinese developers are actively seeking new methods of funding their business. While bank loans and corporate bonds, either offshore or onshore, will remain the main source of funding for most developers, other funding channels or mechanisms such as perpetual bonds, trust firms, peer-to-peer lending, crowd funding, REITs, and joint ventures (JVs) have become popular options among Chinese developers.

5.1   Perpetual Bonds

Perpetual bonds or securities are a bond with no maturity date and are treated as an equity not debt, making it a popular financing tool among Chinese developers in recent years as they are converted into equity when a company becomes financially distressed. Theoretically, issuers pay coupons on perpetual bonds forever, and the principal is not redeemed. In China, perpetual securities come with call options to allow the company to redeem the notes after 5, 10, or 15 years. The coupon for the first 5 years of these perpetual bonds is determined through book building, a process by which the underwriters attempt to determine the interest rate at an initial public offering. At the first call date, the coupon will reset to the rate of the prevailing 5-year government bond and marked up additional 300–500 basis points (Fung 2014, Zhou 2018).

Chinese developers' indebtedness would be worse than what is shown on paper if the issued perpetual bonds are counted as debt. However, with limited disclosures on their interest rates and redemption terms, it would be hard to know the developers' actual leverage. The positive news is that with the current low interest rate environment and policies, the interest burden of the perpetual bonds is also manageable to the developers.

5.2   Trust Firms

Trust firms are nonbank lenders that raise money by selling high-yield wealth management products and use the proceeds to invest in equities, commodities, or real estate projects. The fund is raised through high-net-worth individuals, wealthy families, or retail and institutional investors, and the money is reinvested in high-risk businesses or borrowers that banks are reluctant to lend but are willing to pay higher interest rates. As of the end of 2015, according to China's Trust Association, total trust assets grew 16.6% year-on-year, reaching RMB 16.3 trillion, or the equivalent of USD 2.4 trillion.

Trust firms' wealth management products yield 4–7%, making them attractive to investors as the deposit rates in China are 200–400 basis points lower. However, the risk associated with these wealth management products is that they often package high-yield corporate debt (junk bonds), volatile small-cap stock funds, or risky real estate projects, and because the products are sold through commercial banks, investors assume they are backed by the government (Guilford 2014). China's trust industry is currently lightly regulated, but under the proposals from China's Banking Regulatory Commission (CBRC), trust firms' wealth management products could only be sold in banks with more than RMB 5 billion (roughly USD 726.8 million) of net capital, leaving only about 10% of the commercial banks in China qualified (Xie et al. 2016). The proposals, however, have not been passed as heavy regulation of the trust firms could dampen economic growth.

5.3   REITs

In May 2014, Penghua Asset Management listed China's first-ever REIT-like vehicle on the Shenzhen Stock Exchange. The REIT is backed by the rental income from commercial properties of China Vanke's properties in Qianhai, which is a special economic zone in Shenzhen. However, due to the absence of REIT laws in China, the trust does not resemble a fixed-income instrument. The Shenzhen-listed entity was only offered to a handful of institutional investors on a private basis and is subject to a finite investment horizon of 3–5 years, which does not conform to international standards for a REIT (Au 2015).

From a taxation standpoint, REITs should include additional tax credits or exemptions to attract investors. Apart from corporate tax, Chinese property developers pay land appreciation tax on taxable gains of 30–60% and real estate withholding tax of 12%. For potential REITs buyers, institutional investors do not pay tax on dividends but are required to pay 25% capital gains tax if they sell their stake. For retail investors, dividends from the REITs will be counted into personal income tax, which has an upper bracket of 45% for individuals making over RMB 80,000 a month (or the equivalent of USD 11,250). China property developers have long been studying the use of asset securitization to improve their funding structure and relieve repayment. However, Chinese REITs is unlikely to develop significantly in the short to medium term, even if regulations are loosened or tax benefits are given to investors, and the main reason is the low rental yields of 4% or less, which would be offset by developers' borrowing costs of 6–8%. Also, the excess supply of commercial properties and weak tenant mix will continue to weigh on rental yields, which make the properties of many Chinese property companies poor candidates for

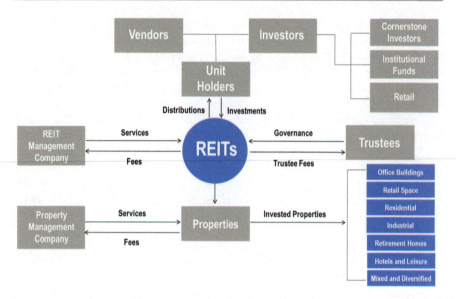

Fig. 6 REITs structure and investable properties. Source: Jones Lang LaSalle

REITs. In addition, the traditional development and financing business model in China is building real estate projects that are sold to investors or home buyers in pieces, which is also known as strata-title and en-bloc sales. When properties are sold off in bits and pieces, institutional tradable real estate assets are not created, making it difficult for China to develop a REITs market, as large income-producing assets used to generate yield are scarce in the market.

A significant discount on property valuation may be necessary to lure the REIT investors, but this is not an attractive option for property developers. Therefore, currently, REITs investment in China is a pure capital appreciation or speculation play, with limited funds interested to invest in this sector (Fig. 6).

5.4   CMBS and RMBS

Much like the REITs market, commercial mortgage-backed securities (CMBS) and residential mortgage-backed securities (RMBS) are in the early stages of development in China. In April 2015, the People's Bank of China relaxed rules for the sale of mortgage and asset-backed securities, and limited approval from regulators is now required (Chen 2015). The availability of CMBS and RMBS would allow developers or banks to transform their outstanding loans into tradable notes, thus allowing the developers to share some of the development risks with potential investors. In the case of banks, by freeing up their balance sheet, banks would be more willing and capable of lending money directly to property developers.

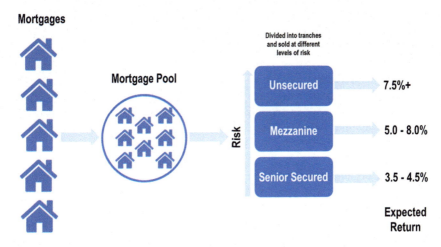

Fig. 7 Mortgage-backed securities—interest rate for different tranches in China (2015–2017). Source: Jones Lang LaSalle

Unlike REITs, CMBS and RMBS securitize on the debt of the underlying properties, rather than the equity part of the assets. These financial instruments are sophisticatedly structured and typically are targeted at institutional investors and sold through private placement. In 2016, for institutional investors, investing in CMBS and RMBS would yield 6–7%, making them attractive as the deposit rates in China are 300–400 basis points lower. Also, for CMBS and RMBS investors, these structured products usually offer a yield guarantee of up to 3–5 years. However, the absence of comprehensive CMBS and RMBS laws in China indicates high risks for investors, as these structured products are usually nonrecourse loans (Fig. 7). In China, CMBS and RMBS are sold almost all to institutional investors. The reasons why structured products are dominated by institutions include the following:

1. Increasing retail investor interests, but not savvy enough: Despite their higher returns and ability to offer diversified asset classes, structured products are often too complex and opaque for retail investors to understand. Even with enough disclosures, it is unlikely that most retail investors can understand the risk-return tradeoff and the costs being incurred in some of these complex financial instruments.
2. Absence of risk appraisal regulatory agencies: Unlike the US market, China currently has no guidelines or regulations on reasonable-basis suitability analysis, an appraisal that accesses the risks embodied in structured products before they are sold to individual retail investors. In addition, since structured products are new in the market, China has limited trained professionals and registered representatives that can adequately analyze the products and ensure the messages and risks are conveyed properly to retail investors.

3. Absence of guidelines on public fundraising: According to China's Securities Regulatory Commission, the line dividing public fundraising and private fundraising is issuing securities to more than 200 specific persons in the aggregate. While China did relax the rules for the sale of mortgage and asset-backed securities in 2015, the absence of public fundraising laws indicates the following: To avoid time-consuming regulatory approval, structured products would only be offered to a handful of institutional investors. Since there are no detailed and specific guidelines on public fundraising in China, even regulators are having issues finding the appropriate set of rules for approval.

4. Minimum investment requirement of RMB 1 million or above: Investing in structured products often requires a minimum investment amount. In China, one unit or one share of CMBS would range from RMB 1 million (USD 140,845) to RMB 10 million (USD 1.41 million), depending on the terms of the issuance. The higher investment entry barrier disqualifies most retail investors, leaving institutional and high-net-worth individuals as the dominant players.

5. No secondary market for structured products: Given the complexity of the financial products and the lack of retail participants, a secondary market for CMBS, RMBS, and ABS is nonexistent in China. For any investors to cash out before the bond maturity, these contracts can only be traded over-the-counter and privately between two parties, without going through an exchange or other intermediaries.

5.5   Peer-to-Peer Lending

Peer-to-peer lending is a group of investors lending to a person or business without the intermediary of traditional financial institutions. Investors are not related to and do not know the borrowers, and an online platform facilitates the loan transactions. P2P lending has gained popularity in China since 2013, and some real estate developers have actively cooperated with these online platforms by giving price discounts of 5–15% for all of their existing projects or other forms of subsidies. The size of China's P2P lending is estimated to be RMB 150 billion (USD 21.8 billion) at the end of 2015, with over 1400 platforms available (Alois 2016).

While developers do not use P2P lending as a source of financing, P2P platforms have helped the sales of their residential projects. In China, home buyers' down payment and mortgage loan proceeds are paid directly to the developers to finance their activities. More unit sales will translate to more cash advances that developers can collect, which is effectively interest-free loans as interests are not paid on these money. From a home buyers' perspective, P2P platforms will help when their existing homes have not been sold, but short-term funding is needed urgently to make a down payment for the new one. In addition, for second home buyers that are unable to enjoy interest rate discounts from commercial banks, with subsidies from developers, P2P funding costs could be as low as 5–6%, making it an attractive option.

Despite its benefits, default risk is P2P lending's major concern, as no collateral is offered. To tackle the issue, in April 2016, jointly with 14 other regulators and ministries, the State Council and People's Bank of China drafted rules to limit illegal lending in an effort to clean up the online financial sector. The new regulations restrict online platform activities that are not licensed, such as raising cash to fund real estate projects (Maras 2016).

5.6   Crowdfunding

Crowdfunding is the use of small amounts of capital from a large number of individuals to finance a business or a purchase. The major difference between crowdfunding and P2P lending is that crowdfunding is usually used for specific projects and not for personal loans. In China, crowdfunding has become advertising-oriented online campaigns to attract homebuyers, as price cuts and promised returns are offered to incentive home buyers. In September 2014, Vanke launched its first online crowdfunding trial, by offering one unit from its project named Vanke City in Suzhou City. To play the game, participants invest RMB 1000 (USD 145) per person to buy a stake in the unit that is priced at RMB 540,000 (USD 78,500) at that time. A month later, Vanke sold this unit via auction at RMB 775,000 (USD 112,600), and the profit is split among the investors, yielding 43.5% on their initial investment of RMB 1000. If the unit were sold below the list price of RMB 540,000, the losses would also be shared among investors.

Another form of crowdfunding in China comes with a promised investment return. In November 2014, Vanke launched a new crowdfunding campaign for 216 units for its project named North Vanke City in Guangzhou City. Under the program, home buyers will deposit RMB 50,000–135,000 (the equivalent of USD 7270–19,620) for 10 months for the right to buy the units at RMB 4800 per square meter (USD 688 per square meter), or a 13% discount from the current list price of RMB 5500 per square meter (USD 800 per square meter). Apart from price discounts, the deposits for 10 months will be given a 3% annualized return. This crowdfunding program allows the developer to sell a significant portion of the project in a limited period of time, which creates a sense of urgency for potential home buyers and thus giving developers the ability to raise prices.

5.7   Joint Ventures and Strategic Alliances

Land cost is the single most expensive item for developers, usually accounting for 50–70% of a project's total cost. In 2016, land auction prices continuously hit newspaper headlines in China, as developers with ample cash on hand were paying huge premiums outbidding each other. In July 2016, Gemdale Group outbidded 20 rivals paying RMB 8.8 billion (roughly USD 1.3 billion), or an eye-popping 286% premium over the reserve price, for a 140,252 square meter site at Shanghai's Pudong area (Esqueda 2016a). In the same month, Future Land Development paid

RMB 3.7 billion (roughly USD 537.8 million), or a 77% premium, for 19,959 square meters of land at Shanghai's Hongkou district (Esqueda 2016b). The list goes on with land auction prices in other cities going through the roof, as developers are betting that strong demand will continue.

With land costs rising to all-time highs, joint ventures (JVs) or strategic alliances with state-owned enterprises (SOEs) that have land on hand could become a popular option going forward as it alleviates developers' pain of paying huge premiums for bidding the land. There are limited developer-SOE JVs in China, and a standout is Tishman Speyer's JV with Shanghai government-backed Shanghai Lujiazui Group in September 2013. Together with Shanghai Lujiazui Group, Tishman Speyer will build a mixed-use building in Shanghai totaling 3 million square feet. The development is located in Shanghai New Bund, where it offers premium grade offices, upscale retail space, and high-end waterfront residential apartments (Kalinoski 2013).

Another risk-sharing approach for developers is to sell a portion of the stakes before the actual project development. In January 2015, Wanda Group raised RMB 24.0 billion (roughly USD 3.5 billion) from China Everbright, Harvest Capital Management, Sichuan Trust, and KuaiQian Payment and Settlement Service to build a portfolio of 20 mall-centered complexes having retail and hotel space alongside with high-end residential units for sale. Dalian Wanda will oversee the construction, leasing, and management of the properties, and rental income will be shared between Wanda and the investors. Wanda Group will adopt an asset-light business model in the future, with aims of capturing a faster growth and a higher return on equity (Cole 2015a). Following the footsteps of Wanda, in August 2016, commercial developer Joy City, which was previously named COFCO Land Holdings, agreed to sell a 49% stake in six mixed-use buildings in China to Singapore's sovereign fund GIC and mainland insurer China Life for RMB 9.3 billion (roughly USD 1.4 billion). The six properties sold include Beijing Xidan Joy City, Beijing Chaoyang Joy City, Shanghai Joy City, Tianjin Joy City, Beijing COFCO Plaza, and Beijing COFCO Landmark Tower. Joy City's deal appears to be part of the trend toward an asset-light development model in China, as commercial property firms look to share the financial burdens amidst pressures from rising land costs and risks of a competitive retail environment (Cole 2016).

6   Conclusion

While China's economic growth is unlikely to reach the double digits that it had enjoyed for a decade long, a targeted GDP growth of about 6%, if achieved, would still indicate relatively strong property demand for the next few years. However, the days of easy financing or refinancing could be over for the Chinese developers, especially after the US Federal Reserve has tapered off its quantitative easing (QE) programs, and China is now focusing more on deleveraging policies for the sector. There are limited indications that China would raise interest rates in the near term, but with property prices reaching record highs in 2016 and China's plans to divert the focus away from the real estate sector (Wildau 2018), the government could roll out new rounds of policies to discourage speculative buying and stabilize the sector. For developers to stay in the game, a combination of traditional financing in the form of bank loans or corporate bonds and alternative financing mechanisms would be required to secure the needed capital and lower funding costs in the future.

In the past Chinese insurers have remained sidelined, investing a fraction of their total assets in the real estate market. China's insurers were first permitted to invest in the domestic real estate market in 2009 and overseas in 2012. Under current regulations, China's Insurance Regulatory Commission (CIRC) allows insurers to invest up to 30% of their total assets in real estate and 15% into overseas investments. As of 2015, mainland insurance companies have invested limited into either categories, as only about 2% of their assets were employed (Cole 2015b). With lower interest rates in the domestic market and a need for insurers to diversify their portfolio, income-producing real estate such as office buildings, hotels, shopping malls, warehouses, long-term lease apartments, and senior housings will become a major investment for Chinese insurance companies in the years to come. Chinese insurers' involvement in real estate would come from buying commercial properties either in whole or in part or provide funds to real estate developers for co-development (Sito 2016).

The Chinese insurers have successfully bought commercial property overseas markets including Australia, the UK, and USA. The deal process and underwriting metrics used in those markets will be likely to be applied to their domestic market. One challenge the insurers will face is that similar to international investors looking at China, to find sufficient stock in single ownership that meets the underwriting requirements. The big opportunity from the China insurers buying domestically is the deepening and maturing of the pool of capital available to developers to exit by selling out to a single consortium, reducing the requirement for strata or subdivision sales. Despite China's real estate market demand and an abundance of liquidity in the market, Chinese developers remain heavily in debt, as they rush into the next cycle of investment by aggressive land bids and property construction. While low interest onshore bonds and other financing mechanisms will alleviate the short-term pain of a stretched balance sheet, in the long run, financial discipline, operational executions, and a well-managed land bank will be the key factors to the recovery of developers' credit profile. Some consolidation from developers can be expected as the market matures.

China's commercial property markets are maturing to a full landlord and tenant system, from an SOE owner occupied base in a relatively short time period. The ability of domestic insurers to provide the capital for developers to exit commercial property developments will improve underwriting standards and aid market liquidity; while in the residential market, there remains stable demand from end users as China's urbanization story continues.

References

Alois, J. D. (2016). *Report: China P2P lending topped $150 billion in 2015.* Accessed September 12, 2019, from http://www.crowdfundinsider.com/2016/01/79612-report-china-p2p-lending-topped-150-billion-in-2015/.

Au, D. (2015). *China's first public REIT set to go online in Shenzhen.* Accessed September 12, 2019, from http://www.asiaasset.com/news/chreit_da1606.aspx.

Chen, J. (2015). *China seen expanding mortgage bonds to revive housing.* Accessed September 10, 2019, from https://www.bloomberg.com/news/articles/2015-04-15/china-seen-expanding-mortgage-bonds-to-revive-housing.

Chiang, L., & Edwards, N. (2012). *Analysis: China developers launch funds to bridge finance gap.* Accessed September 12, 2019, from http://www.reuters.com/article/us-china-property-fund-idUSTRE80F05020120116.

Cole, M. (2015a). *Wanda goes asset light – creates RMB 24B partnership with 4 investors.* Accessed September 12, 2019, from http://www.mingtiandi.com/real-estate/china-retail-real-estate-news/wanda-goes-asset-light-creates-rmb-24b-partnership-with-4-investors/.

Cole, M. (2015b). *Chinese insurers expected to make $73B in cross-border real estate deals.* Accessed September 06, 2019, from http://www.mingtiandi.com/real-estate/china-real-estate-research-policy/chinese-insurers-expected-to-make-73b-in-cross-border-real-estate-deals/.

Cole, M. (2016). *Joy City sells stake in 6 mainland projects to GIC and China life for $1.4B.* Accessed September 06, 2019, from http://www.mingtiandi.com/real-estate/finance-real-estate/joy-city-sells-stake-in-6-mainland-projects-to-gic-and-china-life-for-1-4b/.

Edwards, N., & Yao, K. (2012). *China stimulus unnecessary, risks long-term damage.* Accessed September 12, 2019, from http://www.reuters.com/article/us-china-economy-stimulus-idUSBRE84T06U20120530.

Esqueda, A. (2016a). *Gemdale sets high mark for 2016 with RMB 8.8B Pudong land deal.* Accessed September 12, 2019, from http://www.mingtiandi.com/real-estate/projects-real-estate/gemdale-sets-high-mark-for-2016-with-rmb-8-8b-pudong-land-deal/.

Esqueda, A. (2016b). *Future land plans to sell Hongkou homes for RMB 120K/sqm.* Accessed September 10, 2019, from http://www.mingtiandi.com/real-estate/projects-real-estate/future-land-plans-to-sell-hongkou-homes-for-rmb-120ksqm/.

Fung, E. (2014). *Chinese property developers' new financing tool raises red flags.* Accessed September 12, 2019, from http://www.wsj.com/articles/chinese-property-developers-new-financing-tool-raises-red-flags-1409815273.

Fung, E. (2015). *China lowers down payments for buyers of second homes.* Accessed September 12, 2019, from http://www.wsj.com/articles/china-lowers-down-payments-for-buyers-of-second-homes-1427712176.

Guilford, G. (2014). *Five charts to explain China's shadow banking system, and how it could make a slowdown even uglier.* Accessed September 10, 2019, from http://qz.com/175590/five-charts-to-explain-chinas-shadow-banking-system-and-how-it-could-make-a-slowdown-even-uglier/.

Hong, S. (2011). *China expands home-purchase limits.* Accessed September 10, 2019, from http://www.wsj.com/articles/SB10001424052702304911104576445513471134364.

Kalinoski, G. (2013). *Tishman Speyer JV to build M-U development in Shanghai.* Accessed September 10, 2019, from https://www.cpexecutive.com/post/tishman-speyer-jv-to-build-m-u-development-in-shanghai/.

Keohane, D. (2016). *So you want to get your money out of China? Cut out and keep edition.* Accessed September 12, 2019, from http://ftalphaville.ft.com/2016/03/03/2155170/so-you-want-to-get-your-money-out-of-china-cut-out-and-keep-edition/.

Kynge, J. (2016). *China's domestic credit rating agencies see no debt problem.* Accessed September 12, 2019, from http://www.ft.com/cms/s/3/dca6f042-3ec8-11e6-8716-a4a71e8140b0.html#axzz4KsytE726.

Law, F. (2015). *Kaisa Group defaults on offshore debt*. Accessed September 12, 2019, from http://www.wsj.com/articles/kaisa-asset-freeze-sought-by-chinese-financial-organizations-1421042965.

Maras, E. (2016). *Chinese government cracks down on online P2P lending*. Accessed September 12, 2019, from https://www.cryptocoinsnews.com/chinese-government-cracks-down-on-online-p2p-lending/.

Qiaoling, Y. (2016). *Trust industry grew to more than 16 Tln Yuan last year: Report*. Accessed September 062, 2019, from http://english.caixin.com/2016-02-24/100912172.html.

Schrader, M. (2018). *Xi's economic deleveraging campaign and the limits of credit committees*. Accessed September 12, 2019, from https://jamestown.org/program/xis-economic-deleveraging-campaign-and-the-limits-of-credit-committees/.

Shanghai WOWeng. (2016, September 20). *Massive department store closings in Shanghai*.

Sito, P. (2016). *China's first public REIT set to go online in Shenzhen*. Accessed September 12, 2019, from http://www.asiaasset.com/news/chreit_da1606.aspx.

Stanton, D. (2016). *Asian rating downgrades hit highest level in years*. Accessed September 12, 2019, from http://www.reuters.com/article/asia-debt-bonds-idUSL3N17I25W.

Stefanac, M. (2014). *8 Tips When buying a house "for sale by owner"*. Accessed September 12, 2019, from https://www.trustedchoice.com/insurance-articles/home-family/buying-house-for-sale-by-owner/.

Tong, F. (2016). *China's online retail sales grow a third to $589 billion in 2015*. Accessed September 12, 2019, from https://www.internetretailer.com/2016/01/27/chinas-online-retail-sales-grow-third-589-billion-2015.

Walters, M. (2013). *Strata-spheric outcomes, Multiple ownerships in buildings encourage asset bubble formation*. Accessed September 06, 2019, from http://www.irei.com/publications/institutional-real-estate-asia-pacific/may-1-2013-volume-5-number-5/strata-spheric-outcomes-multiple-ownerships-in-buildings-encourage-asset-bubble-formation.

Wildau, W. (2018). *China easing threatens to derail debt-cutting measures*. Accessed September 14, 2019, from https://www.ft.com/content/54259f08-8ff1-11e8-b639-7680cedcc421.

Wolfers, J. (2014). *The fed has not stopped trying to stimulate the economy*. Accessed September 12, 2019, from https://en.wikipedia.org/wiki/Quantitative_easing.

Xie, H., Luo, J., & Zhang, D. (2016). *China said to weigh tighter rules on wealth-management products*. Accessed September 12, 2019, from http://www.bloomberg.com/news/articles/2016-07-27/china-mulls-tightening-wealth-product-rules-21st-century-says.

Xin, Z. (2016). *A trillion-dollar question on China's forex dilemma: Just how low should its reserves go?* Accessed September 12, 2019, from http://www.scmp.com/news/china/economy/article/1898978/trillion-dollar-question-chinas-forex-dilemma-just-how-low-should.

Zhen, S. (2016). *Chinese developers to increasingly tap onshore bonds*. Accessed September 12, 2019, from http://www.scmp.com/business/companies/article/1896966/chinese-developers-increasingly-tap-onshore-bonds.

Zhou, I. (2018). *China Inc. $287 billion perpetual bonds flash warning signs*. Accessed September 12, 2019, from https://www.bloomberg.com/news/articles/2018-10-28/china-inc-s-287-billion-perpetual-pileup-flashes-warning-signs.

Housing Financing at the Crossroads: Access and Affordability in an Aging Society

Friedemann Roy

Abstract

The property sector plays an important role within China's economy. The housing market accounts for about a quarter of Chinese GDP. Any swings in property prices have therefore a considerable impact on economic growth and stability in China. Despite having laid the foundations for a market-oriented housing and housing finance system, the government has remained a strong grip on the sector through administrative measures as well as a tight management of interest rates to influence the pricing of housing loans.

To date, despite rising house price inflation (HPI), the government has managed to avoid the building up of a property bubble, influencing banks' lending through tight regulations (especially interest rate fixings and loan-to-value limits). According to the latest research, it appears that challenging issues are supply-demand imbalances between smaller and larger cities due to restricted provision of land for construction of residential properties. Between July 2016 and March 2019, mortgage lending grew from RMB 16 billion to RMB 29.7 billion. It accounts for about 60% of total household debt and 19% of all bank loans (compared to 30% in Korea and 23% in Japan). The increased demand for mortgage loans is expected to place continued pressure on the housing market. With house prices still rising, the government may be encouraged to rethink this approach as lower income groups may face rising challenges to afford a home.

F. Roy (✉)
International Finance Corporation, Washington, DC, USA

© Springer Nature Switzerland AG 2021
B. Wang, T. Just (eds.), *Understanding China's Real Estate Markets*, Management for Professionals, https://doi.org/10.1007/978-3-030-49032-4_12

1 Introduction

China has experienced rapid economic growth in the last 20 years, propelling the emergence of a middle class with strong demand for new housing. Another factor for the increase in housing demand has been growing urbanization. The share of the population living in urban areas rose from 19% in 1980 to 60% in 2018. It has stimulated a significant construction boom across China and in Tier I cities in particular. Today, the construction sector accounts for about a quarter of GDP. In the United States, the ratio accounts for about 5%.[1] Any swings in the property market have therefore a considerable impact on economic growth of the country.

Housing policies and reforms have been adjusted and implemented to cater for changing demand patterns and to ensure continued affordability as house prices, especially in Tier I and Tier II cities, have soared, leading to frequent debates about growing and bursting bubbles among policy-makers, lenders, and researchers. To date, policy-makers have been capable of containing any form of excessive house price growth through a mix of changing lending standards or changes in the release of land. One point which has been overlooked in the current debate on China's housing sector is the question on how to ensure a continued supply of affordable housing finance in an aging society: it is likely that people will ask for a different form of housing. In addition, the current retirement schemes may not be financially viable because of changing demographics. Housing policies and housing finance solutions (e.g., reverse mortgages) are to be adjusted to ensure continued affordability and welfare. As a number of other countries face the same challenge (e.g., Germany, Vietnam, Russia, central and eastern Europe), China can offer valuable solutions and examples to policy-makers and lenders of these countries.

The objective of this article is to evaluate the role of housing finance within the ambit of China's real estate sector development and policies. The article is structured in the following way: first, it discusses the determinants of demand for housing in China; second, it looks at supply side measures to meet the growing demand for housing; third, it assesses the role of the financial sector to balance supply and demand. The next two sections discuss house price inflation, housing bubbles, and affordability. The last section focuses on future challenges for the housing sector which arise from the question on how to offer affordable housing in an aging society.

2 Determinants of Demand for Housing

Sustained economic growth since 1998 has been a major driver for rising incomes and increasing urbanization throughout China. Annual real GDP growth fluctuated between 14 and 7% between 2006 and 2015. In 2018, China's GDP increased by 6.6%. The following factors have contributed to a significant increase in the demand

---

[1]The most important contributor to GDP in the United States is the service sector which accounts for about 77% of GDP.

for housing: (1) The total urban population increased from 582.9 million in 2006 to 831.4 million in 2018. Figure 1 shows the growth of the urban population in absolute number as well as the share of people living in urban areas. The share of the urban population grew from 44% in 2006 to 60% in 2018. It is expected to increase to 70% by 2030. Rural to urban migration was the main cause for China's urban expansion. People from rural areas moved to cities as they could find better paid employment. Cities like Beijing or Shanghai have experienced a rapid growth of their populations. Between 2000 and 2010, Beijing expanded from 13.8 million to 19.6 million; Shanghai grew from 16.7 million to 23 million. (2) Rising incomes were another important factor in the development of the housing market in China. After 1998, household income among most social groups increased steadily: average salaries in 2014 were several times higher than in 1998 (see Fig. 2 for an illustration); the salary

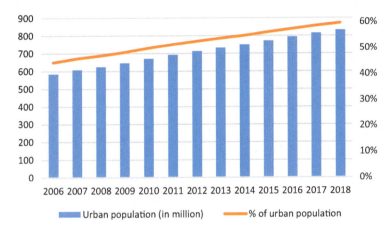

Fig. 1 Urban population growth in China 2006–2018. (Source: NBSC 2018)

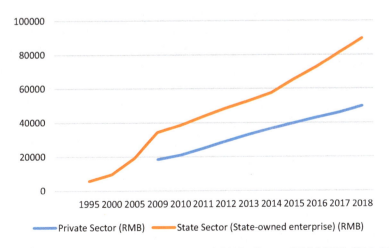

Fig. 2 Average salaries in CN¥ in urban areas (1995–2018). (Source: NBSC 2009, 2015, 2018)

increases in the public sector have been comparable to those in the private sector (or even slightly higher). (3) Changing demographics had an important impact on the demand structures for urban housing as people with higher incomes were looking for more space per person.

Since family planning patterns have also been changing, demand for smaller apartments in urban areas increased to house smaller families or singles. The average size of a household decreased from 4.41 persons per household to 3.10 persons in 2018. More young people have been in the position to obtain a university degree and have earned relatively higher salaries. The opportunity to earn a university degree or a diploma contributed to the expansion of the middle class because it allowed the graduates to receive higher salaries which allowed them to enter the housing market at an earlier stage and with a different purchase power (often supported by their parents). These young professionals have been taking up the lifestyle of the emerging middle class: as in most Western countries, owning a flat (or a house) and a car became a dream of many young professionals. Homeownership was regularly set as a precondition for marriage. This segment of the society created additional pressure on the urban housing market.

3   Supply Responses

The supply of housing in order to meet the increasing demand and changing demand patterns for housing is shaped by two phases (1) establishment and consolidation of a private housing finance system (1998–2008) and (2) support to the real estate market in response to the Global Financial Crisis of 2008 and large-scale development of social housing (since 2008); (Ping and Shao 2014). Before 1998, several reforms of the housing supply and distribution mechanism were implemented, aimed at commercializing urban housing provision. Housing was provided within three different categories:

1. Commercial housing. It focused on higher income groups (about 15% of the population). In this category, the government did not intervene in the pricing of the properties to individual buyers. Developer bought land from municipal governments at market prices.
2. Government-supported affordable housing was intended to cover about 70% of the population (low to middle incomes). To reduce the price of a housing unit, the government used a combination of subsidies (e.g., free land provision, loans to developers with favorable terms) and regulations (e.g., profit limits for developers, maximum size of housing units, qualifying criteria for home buyers).
3. Government-assisted rental housing. It targeted low-income groups (about 15% of the population) who had incomes below the official poverty line and lived in poor conditions.

The emergence of a commercial urban housing market was also accompanied by the establishment of a public and private housing saving system, a housing insurance system as well as a finance and mortgage loan system. These measures were aimed at supporting policy-oriented and commercial developments as well as market system of property exchanges, repairs, and management.

These reforms were also considered a response to the Asian Financial Crisis of 1997. For the first time since the early 1990s, China's GDP growth rate decreased due to a fall in exports. In 1999, it decreased to 7.62% and only reached two-digit levels in 2003 (10.3%). To stimulate the housing market, the government sought to increase domestic demand and consumption. Given the construction sector's role in job creation,[2] policy-makers believed that housing developments would generate demand in many other sectors and would create new employment opportunities (e.g., infrastructure, transport, and financial sector), increase investment, and accelerate consumption by urban residents. By abolishing the public welfare housing provision system, the reforms inaugurated in 1998 made therefore an important contribution to maintaining economic growth in the country.

Policy formulation and state intervention was influenced by the following events: as a result of the Global Financial Crisis of 2008, when exports slowed rapidly, the government's efforts to stimulate the economy targeted the housing sector because its growth was understood to balance the loss in exports. From September to December 2008, bank interest rates were cut five times from 7.74% to 5.94% to encourage borrowing and stimulate the purchase of housing units in the cities. Other measures included lower down payment requirements and a reduction of property taxes and property sales taxes. These policies had the desirable effect, and the country experienced a rise in construction and demand for housing which in parallel had a negative impact on HPI. From 2009 up to today, HPI increased and decreased, depending on policy measures of the government to avoid an overheating of the market.

China's 12th Five-Year Plan, which was rolled-out at the beginning of 2011, emphasized the provision of supported social rental and affordable housing. The goal was to bring 36 m social housing units to the market to increase the supply of affordable housing as low- and middle-income groups were struggling to pay for a housing unit given the composition and price structures of the urban housing markets. For 2011 and 2012, the target was to deliver 10 m homes each year and in the remaining 3 years of the 5-year plan to deliver 8 m homes each. Municipal governments were responsible for the delivery of these homes. Though the government did not meet the target ("only" 5.5 m homes were delivered in 2011), the program provided policy-makers with a tool to stimulate the housing market as it was needed to compensate for any negative developments in the economy (e.g., fall in exports, investment stimulus, or overheating property market).

Within two decades the government managed to create a mixed housing provision system with private homeownership as the main form. The homeownership

---

[2]According to calculations of the World Bank Group, for every housing unit built, about five new jobs will be created.

ratio increased from 56% in 1997 to 89.3% in 2015.[3] Although the privatization of the previously state-owned housing stock played a major role in reaching this ratio, about 38% have been purchased from the market (Yang and Chen 2014).[4] Those incomes groups who cannot afford may benefit from the government-assisted affordable housing programs or may be eligible for rental subsidies. These policies were considered necessary to mitigate a growing income inequality and social tensions among the different groups and thus maintain political stability in the country.

4   The Role of the Financial Sector

In a functioning housing market, financial institutions play an important role to balance supply and demand for housing through the offering of finance to developers and individual home buyers. The purchase of a house is usually the most important investment decision of a private household in its lifetime. In order to accomplish the investment, households are typically required to take out a loan. The availability of mortgage loans has therefore an important impact on HPI and the supply of housing. During the transition of the public housing system, reforms were aimed at establishing a market-oriented housing finance system in China. Beginning in 1994, the design of the housing finance system has taken shape. Today, Chinese households can access a housing loan through a bank or a housing provident fund (HPF).

The decision by Chinese households to take out a loan is driven by three main factors: (1) housing is considered an investment (especially for second or third homes) because there are only limited other alternatives (apart from bank savings and equities), and (2) it seems that there is an inclination among households to keep indebtedness levels low. As Fig. 3 shows, the share of mortgage debt to disposable income was below 30% in 2015. It has risen to 59% in 2018. In addition, actual loan-to-value ratios (LTV) are about 36% although banks would be willing to offer LTV ratios up to 70%. Interest fluctuations have influenced households' willingness to incur debt as they took on more debt when interest fell and vice versa. The recent increases of these ratios are due to the rising house prices. Despite falling interest rates, households have to borrow more to cover the house price rises. (3) Despite

---

[3]China does not regularly publish homeownership data that are comparable to the accounting in other countries. The "homeownership" rate published by the Ministry of Construction and Chinese National Bureau of Statistics is defined as the percentage of residential properties that are privately owned. In the United States and many other countries, the homeownership rate is defined as the share of households that own their homes. According to figures from Beijing and Shanghai, the homeownership rates in 1999 accounted for 48% and 56%, respectively (Barth et al. 2012; R. Arora 2005).

[4]There are huge homeownership ratio gaps across various age cohorts and regions. While in the bigger cities like Beijing or Shanghai, the homeownership of those below 35 years is about 60%, it accounts for more than 75% in other especially smaller cities.

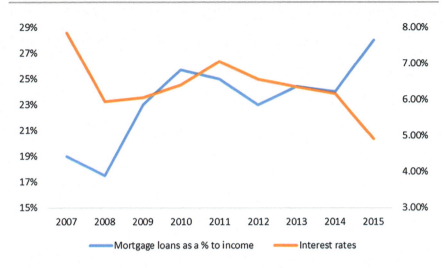

Fig. 3 Mortgage loans as a percentage to household disposable income and interest for mortgage loans from banks (for a term >5 years). (Source: Thomson, NBSC 2013)

Table 1 Mortgage loan conditions: HPFs versus banks

	Bank: mortgage loan conditions	HPF: mortgage loan conditions
Loan amount in Chinese Yuan Renminbi (RMB)	Varies according to borrower's individual creditworthiness (main determinants: credit history and stable income)	Maximum loan limits differ at individual HPFs
Term	Up to 30 years	Up to 30 years (actual: on average 3–9 years)
Loan-to-value ratio	70% for first-time buyer; for a second home the LTV ratio is 30%; no mortgages may be granted for the financing of a third apartment	70%
Payment-to-income ratio	Up to 30% (max: 50%)	Up to 30% (max: 50%)
Required security	Mortgage, may be other securities	Mortgage
Eligibility criteria	Borrower's creditworthiness	Minimum savings period (regularly 6 months) with HPF, individual creditworthiness

Source: Banks' and HPFs' loan conditions

some market orientation of the system, the regulators – the People's Bank of China (PBOC) and Chinese Banking Regulatory Commission (CBRC) – have kept a strong grip on the size and the conditions of the mortgage loans so that they can intervene in the market when necessary (Buitelaar 2014).

Mortgage loan conditions of banks and HPFs are very similar. Variations exist in terms of the maximum possible loan amount, the maximum LTV ratio, and the interest rate. Table 1 compares the mortgage loan conditions among HPFs and banks. Interest rates of HPF mortgage loans and bank mortgage loans will be adjusted according to the interest setting by the PBOC. Currently, HPF charge 3% for a mortgage loan with a term longer than 5 years (<5 years, the interest rate is 2.75%). Bank lending rates for a period longer than 5 years are higher than 5%. The PBOC, with approval from the State Council, sets base interest rates for the entire banking system, including nonbank financial institutions. It also defines the corridors in which commercial banks may offer loans. For all financial institutions, the floor on lending rates is 90% of the PBOC benchmark; a 230% ceiling applies to rural and urban credit cooperatives. Financial institutions may move their deposit rates below, but not above, the benchmark rate set by PBOC (EIU 2009, p. 46).

Typically, households purchase apartments from developers: The buyer identifies an apartment through the developer's website or sales department. In some cases, she/he is advised by a real estate agent. Once the buyer is satisfied with the apartment, she/he will reserve the apartment by making a deposit, usually 30% of the total apartment value; in some cases, the developer recommends a lender as she/he may have a relationship with the bank. To obtain a mortgage loan from a bank, it takes from 1 week to over a month; most banks need about 3–4 weeks to review the credentials; loan approvals by HPFs require more time. To improve the access to housing finance for ordinary urban households, the housing provident scheme was established in 1991 as a pilot and subsequently extended nationwide in 1994–1995. The HPF scheme aims to enhance people's housing purchasing power through a system of joint savings—with mandatory contributions from employees and work units. Contribution rates vary from 5% to 20% of an employee's monthly salary, i.e., the total contribution of one individual contributor (+ her/his employer's contributions) into her/his HPF saving account amounts to 10–40% of her/his monthly salary. These funds are accumulated in the saver's individual account. There is no centralized HPF for the whole country, but every city has its own HPF Management Center with its own policies and rules on contribution rates, maximum loan amounts, etc. The savings in these HPF accounts allow workers to apply for low-interest housing loans. The design of the HPF system was modeled after the Central Provident Fund in Singapore.

Although HPFs granted more than RMB 6 trillion in loans since their establishment, banks are main providers of housing finance to private households. Their outstanding loan volumes amounts to RMB 25.8 trillion – nearly five times as high as the loan volumes of the HPF's as per 2018 (see Fig. 4). Between 2005 and 2008, the market share of HPFs varied from 15% to 20%. Since 2009, the gap between banks and HPFs has continued to widen. One reason for the increasing gap is different loan volumes as a result of rising house prices. Banks do not face the same limitations as HPFs on maximum loan amounts. According to Fig. 5, the major providers of mortgage loans are the four state-owned banks (Bank of China, Industrial and Commercial Bank of China, Agricultural Bank of China, and China Construction Bank). They have a combined market share of 83% as per 2018 (in terms of mortgage loan values). Banks typically compete on service quality and to a minor extent on pricing as the PBOC's interest rate policy does not allow for huge variations in interest rate setting on individual mortgage loans.

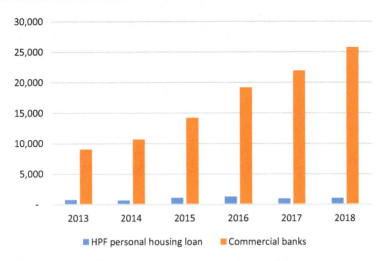

Fig. 4 Development of lending volumes at HPFs and commercial banks (in RMB billion). (Source: MOHURD, PBOC, The Economist, authors' calculations, China Citic Bank, Li and Yi)

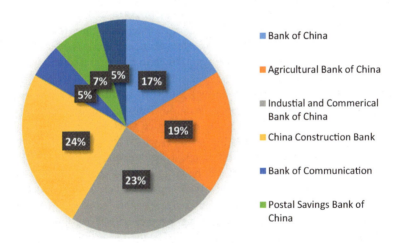

Fig. 5 Market shares of commercial banks. (Source: NBSC 2018)

To curb major rises of house prices, the PBOC instructed lenders to change the calculation of the interest rate. Banks are no longer allowed to give discounts to the benchmark lending rate when setting mortgage levies, a change from the ability to provide a discount as much as 30% under current rules. In practice, lenders usually provide discounts of as much as 10% (Bloomberg 26 August 2019). Due to the significant rise in mortgage lending, both LTVs and nonperforming loan ratios (NPL) increased as well. Some banks report an average LTV ratio of 62%. Additionally, NPL ratio rose from 0.3% in 2013 to 2% in August 2019 (according to data provided by PBOC and CBRC in 2013). Although a housing finance system has been established, which shows similar features to those of in the United States or in Europe, regulators still have a strong influence on the mortgage loan conditions and the pricing of the loans. In this way, it serves the policy goals, and it can be used to balance any excess in the supply of housing. Given the current strict lending conditions set by the government, it may be difficult for low-income households to access a loan (despite the introduction of lower interest rates). The government uses fiscal stimulus measures and does not rely on monetary policies to enable housing access to this group. In view of the experiences of the Global Financial Crisis of 2008, this policy orientation has some merit, but it comes at a considerable cost to the state budget.

5   The Conundrum Unresolved

A housing bubble is defined as a run-up in housing prices fueled by demand, speculation, and exuberance. Housing bubbles usually start with an increase in demand, in the face of limited supply which takes a relatively long period of time to replenish and increase.[5] Since 1998, house prices in China have continuously risen, with several short-term downward spikes in 2007, 2012, 2014, and 2016. When the government intervened through administrative measures (e.g., decreasing LTV ratios or changing purchase conditions for second or third home buyers) to curb HPI, however, house prices soon rose again, often to higher levels than before (see Fig. 6).

In 2017, HPI accelerated again throughout 2018. In 2019, average new house prices in China's 70 major cities rose 0.7% in May from the previous month, picking up from a 0.6% rise in April and the quickest pace since December 2018. On an annual basis, home prices increased by 10.7%. Higher prices were mainly driven by the smaller Tier 3 cities, up to 0.8% on a monthly basis compared with a 0.5% gain in April 2019. Those with rising inventories have quietly loosened restrictions on home buyers to prop up consumer confidence and demand (Chen et al. 2019). In 2015/2016 house prices have risen by 16% nationwide but doubled or even tripled in big cities (The Economist 2016). Although rising incomes and an ongoing urbanization would justify rising prices, an assessment whether the recent price rises indicate a housing bubble appears warranted. The following indicators serve to identify a housing bubble (Roy 2012).

Price-Rent Ratio
The development of the price-rent ratio is of particular interest for investors because a rising ratio suggests that an increasing share of an investor's expected return stems from expected capital appreciation, i.e., from potential future rental growth, rather than from current rental returns. This implies that speculative motives play an

---

[5]http://www.investopedia.com/terms/h/housing_bubble.asp

% change of a month earlier

Fig. 6 Development of house prices, newly built houses (2011–2017). (Source: The Economist, NBSC 2016)

increasing role. According to the Deutsche Bank Research, this indicator points to a sizeable overvaluation of house prices for most regions in China (Clemens et al. 2011).

House Price-Income Ratio
This measures the affordability of housing. An increasing ratio indicates declining affordability. According to Fig. 7, nominal and real-term disposable incomes of urban households as a whole have increased much more sharply than house prices.

In the 2007–2018 period, the nominal and real disposable income per capita rose by average of 10% and 7.3%, respectively, whereas the y-o-y house price increase was 6% on average. Even if this comparison were reduced to the four largest cities, it was only in Beijing that house prices outpaced disposable incomes for some years (between 2006 and 2009). In the other four cities, the trend corresponds to the nationwide development. According to Fig. 6, house prices fell nationwide by 6.83 percentage points and experienced an increase in 2016, though the steepest increase was in the top four cities (Beijing, Shanghai, Guangzhou, and Shenzhen). With house prices having increased further in 2017 and 2018, overall housing affordability will remain a challenge for policy-makers in the foreseeable future (Buitelaar 2014).

Supply Side Developments
The number of houses completed and vacancy rates are suitable indicators to describe changes in the supply of houses. House price rises and the increased availability of credit are poised to drive supply of housing. Although the government

Index 2007 = 100

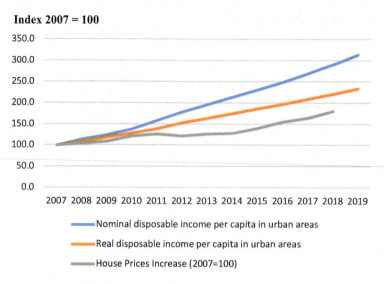

Fig. 7 Development of income and house prices. (Source: Thomson Financial, NBSC (House prices are based on unweighted average of house prices based on 70 cities))

aims to influence housing supply through administrative measures, more housing units have been built. In 2014, 0.81 billion square meter (sqm) of residential housing space was completed. The future incoming supply (= housing under construction and inventory) is estimated at 5.56 billion sqm (Chien 2015). According to Macquarie Securities, there is a severe imbalance in land supply. Smaller cities have plenty of land for building, but shrinking, populations. Big cities, on the contrary, where people want to live and work, have large land banks but releasing only small plots (The Economist 2016, p. 68).

Availability of Credit

The increased availability of housing credit has led to higher house prices. As already mentioned above, households have taken out more mortgage loans. Mortgage loans account for about 60% of households' debt. The ratio of mortgage loans to GDP increased from 10% in 2006 to 25% at the end of 2016. This ratio is relatively lower in comparison to the ratios in Western Europe or the United States. The mortgage loan-to-GDP ratio in the United States amounts to 62.58% (as per the end of 2018). Lending standards are understood to be prudent. However, these data may conceal a less positive picture. It is probably that property appraisal values in loan agreements have been overstated to allow for higher loan-to-value ratios and hence higher loan amounts. A sharp increase of wealth management products has fueled securitization. Banks move loans off-balance sheet and obtain capital relief by packaging them into wealth management products sold to investors through trust companies. This form of securitization is capable of hiding the true performance of loan portfolios and may distort data on defaulted loans. And the real exposure to public sector debt through "local government financing platforms" is difficult to determine. Not being allowed to borrow directly, many local governments circumvent the prohibition by establishing companies to borrow on their behalf, using land as collateral. If there is a sudden decline in land prices, the banks which lend to these companies could see their capital base eroding due to an increasing number of defaults from this source (B. Renaud 2011; J. Miles 2011).[6]

To date, the government policies have been effective in managing overall house price growth in the country. Overall, prices of newly built and secondhand homes across 70 cities slowed in November 2016 compared with the month before. Although the recent policy changes (e.g., restrictions to buy second homes and increased minimum down payment requirements) have their intended effect, a property downturn risks dragging down growth for the whole economy (Yang 2016). The effect on the banking sector of the recent measures is difficult to determine as the level of distorted property valuations of those properties offered as collateral is unknown and the debt levels of local governments are not disclosed.

Affordability, however, remains a continued challenge for housing policy-makers and cannot be solved through an increasing availably of housing finance. Continuous house price inflation and the discussion about emerging housing bubbles have made housing inequality an acute problem in cities and caused a great deal of concerns among observers and policy-makers. Many households voice concern about decreasing affordability and are often forced to increase their savings efforts to buy a housing unit (Yang et al. 2016).

However, urbanization is likely to continue to put pressure on the urban housing market for the foreseeable future. At present, about 60% of the population lives in cities. It is expected that by 2030, this ratio will increase up to 70% by 2030. Rising incomes, demographic changes, and access problems of lower income groups will create considerable demand for housing in cities and towns and will test the government's ability to manage urban property markets. A frequent critique has been the supply imbalances between bigger cities and smaller towns.[7]

Despite all the rush into the real estate market, the government has been successful in limiting an overborrowing of home buyers up to now. Given the considerable attachment of homeowners to their properties, it is unlikely that they will run away in case of falling house prices. This helps to ensure against the downward spiral of foreclosures and falling prices that have been quite detrimental to housing markets of other countries. However, the access to affordable housing is likely to remain an important factor in the policy formulation to compensate for an increasing income inequality and flawed distribution systems of land.

---

[6]The debt volumes of these companies are estimated at RMB 14,000 billion (Rabinovitch 2011).

[7]As the local municipal government depends on incremental land sales as a source of revenue, they tend to release only small plots of land to maintain a constant flow of revenues.

6   Future Challenge

As in most other Asian economies, economic growth and rising welfare has led to numerous demographic changes in China over the last 30 years. As result of lower fertility, higher mortality, and longevity, a significant aging of the population is emerging (Doling and Ronald 2014). China has been advancing this process through the introduction of the one-child policy which was introduced in 1979. Table 2 provides a number of key demographic indicators.

Life expectancy has been rising rapidly. It is now approximately 73 and is expected to be nearly 80 by 2050. As a result of sinking fertility and growing longevity, the share of the elderly has been constantly increasing (as Table 2 points out). By 2050, it is projected that the population ages 60+ and 80+ will reach 440 m and 101 m, respectively. Longevity coupled with the one-child policy is expected to deteriorate significantly after 2010. While the ratio of working age to non-working age was at 2.5 (i.e., 2.5 persons in relation to 1 person over the age of 65), it will decrease to about 1.6 by 2050. An aging society is associated with the following challenges:

1. Lower economic growth which is due to expected lower productivity of older people; the elderly population in general does not produce nearly as much as the working-age population, so the economic growth rate of economies with a high share of older people would seem likely to slow. Additionally, as the size of the population is shrinking, overall output is expected to decrease as there are fewer people available to be engaged in economic activity.
2. Increased expenses for medical care. According to anecdotal evidence, health cost will rise for people above 65 years. Additionally, there will be increased demand for special facilities for elder people. As a result, medical expenses for the whole economy will rise.
3. Deteriorating dependency ratio. It appears that a segment of the population (the elderly) that is relatively larger than in the past will have to be supported by a relatively smaller group of economically active adults. This has important consequence for the design and the affordability of pension schemes.

Table 2 Demographic indictors China

	1950	1980	1990	2000	2010	2016
Total fertility rate (births per 1000 women	6.11				1.56	1.62
Old dependency ratio		10.5			12.7	17
Share of population of people >65 years old in %		4.41	5.57	6.96	8.87	12
Share of population of people >80 years old in %		0.4	0.6	0.9	1.3	1.9 (2020 estimate)

Source: NBSC, UN, Economist, World Population Prospects

4. Changing housing preferences. Elder people require a different form of housing which accommodates for installation of medical facilities or facilities to cater for limited mobility (e.g., need for an elevator).

The aging society has the following impact on the structure and composition of the housing and housing finance market: on the one hand, housing policies have concentrated on the provision of affordable housing in order to ensure housing supply in growing urban areas as well as to provide housing to a growing population. A shrinking population will pose challenges for the treatment of the existing housing stock which may be in need to decrease (especially in rural areas due to the ongoing migration to urban areas). On the other hand, given expected pension deficits in China (Pozen 2015), elder people may not have enough income to pay for rising medical and living cost even if they are homeowners. In a worst-case scenario, they may be forced to abandon their homes. If house prices deteriorated, governments would face additional challenges to define appropriate housing policies. To complement a pension, however, a homeowner may use his home and convert it into a stream of cash flows to be paid out in regular installments. This is the concept on which the design of a reverse mortgage is based. The offering of these products may contribute to mitigate the negative impact of rising pension deficits.

A reverse mortgage is a special type of a home equity loan for older homeowners. In comparison to a conventional mortgage, a reverse mortgage does not require any monthly mortgage payments. The repayment of the loan will be deferred until she/he dies, sells, or moves out of the home. As there are no required mortgage payments on a reverse mortgage, the interest will be added to the loan balance each month. Table 3 shows the difference between a conventional mortgage and a reverse mortgage. The calculation of any given loan amount of a reverse mortgage is

Table 3 Comparison between a conventional mortgage and a reverse mortgage

Characteristic	Reverse mortgage	Conventional mortgage
Purpose	Provide funds to existing homeowners of advanced age	Facilitate purchase or construction of a housing unit
Eligibility requirements	– Minimum age – Equity in owner-occupied home; no existing mortgage on the home which is provided as a collateral for reverse mortgage	Capacity to repay mortgage
Loan amount determinants	– Value of the house – Borrower's age	– Borrower's income – Value of the housing unit – Borrower's credit record – Borrower's assets
Payout of funds	Typically, monthly payments over a given period	Complete payout of mortgage loan amount at the outset
Repayment requirements	Balance is due at death of borrower or permanent move-out	Typically, monthly payments until complete repayment of the mortgage

Source: Guttentag (hofinet.org)

determined by three factors: (1) Life length probability of the borrower on retirement. The longer she/he is expected to live, the lower will be the amount to be
paid out, (2) Future expected value of the housing unit offered as collateral. In order
to ensure the coverage of the loan amount plus the accumulated interest rates, lenders
will typically pay out between 50 and 70% of the appraised value of a housing unit,
and (3) Future expected development of interest rates. If the lender expects interest
rates to increase over time, payouts will be lower as well.

Reverse mortgages have been only offered in a few countries, especially in the
United States. One of the major reasons is that reverse mortgage products are
complex products and difficult for consumers to understand. The rising balance
and falling equity nature of reverse mortgages are particularly difficult for consumers
to grasp. Other reasons – according to experiences with reverse mortgages in the
United States – point to a misuse of funds or unwillingness of borrowers to comply
with the terms and conditions of the reverse mortgage. In comparison with previous
years, borrowers in the United States have been younger and have taken out
relatively higher upfront payouts. In the fiscal year 2011, nearly half of borrowers
were under age 70. Taking out a reverse mortgage early in retirement, or even before
reaching retirement, increases risks to consumers. By tapping their home equity
early, these borrowers may find themselves without the financial resources to finance
a future move – whether due to health or other reasons. In the same year, 73% of
borrowers took all or almost all of their available funds upfront at closing. This
proportion has increased by 30 percentage points since 2008. Borrowers who
withdraw all of their available home equity upfront will have fewer resources to
draw upon to pay for everyday and major expenses later in life. Borrowers who take
all of their money upfront are also at greater risk of becoming delinquent on taxes
and/or insurance and ultimately losing their homes to foreclosure.

Additionally, a large proportion of reverse mortgage borrowers (9.4% as of
February 2012) are at risk of foreclosure due to nonpayment of taxes and insurance.
Spouses of reverse mortgage borrowers who are not themselves named as
co-borrowers are often unaware that they are at risk of losing their homes. If the
borrowing spouse dies or needs to move, the non-borrowing spouse must sell the
home or otherwise pay off the reverse mortgage at that time (Consumer Financial
Protection Bureau 2012). The market for reverse mortgages in the United States is
very small. Only about 2–3% of eligible homeowners choose to take out a reverse
mortgage. Only about 582,000 reverse mortgage loans are outstanding as of
November 2011, as compared to more than 50 million traditional mortgages and
more than 17 million home equity loans and lines of credit.

But reverse mortgages have the potential to become a much more prominent part
of the financial landscape. Like China, people in the United States live longer and
have less children. On the other hand, pension funds will be unable to disburse what
they have promised. Therefore, it is likely that more households may be inclined to
use their home as a complement to their dwindling pension payments. The implementation of reverse mortgage loan products is likely to be difficult for a number of
reasons:

1. Collection of reliable data to calculate the appropriate loan amount in relation to the expected home value at the time of the repayment of the loan.
2. Loan amount to be expected from a reverse mortgage. In the United States, for example, the median home equity of the baby boomer generation whom the majority is becoming eligible for reverse mortgages amounted to about USD 108,000. Given the relatively high discounts, a baby boomer household may end up with a reverse mortgage loan amount of USD 54,000. This amount may be too low to complement a pension in a meaningful way. In China, at present it is difficult how house prices will develop over the next decades. If HPF continued to rise as in the previous years, homeowners might be in a position to borrow relatively higher amounts.
3. Level of subsidization required. In the United States, reverse mortgages under the Home Equity Conversion Program are guaranteed by the Federal Housing Administration (FHA).[8] If such an instrument is considered, subsidies may be required to ensure trust in the mortgage values given by the banks to determine the reverse mortgage amount.
4. Attachment to a home of a Chinese household. As already pointed out above, Chinese households appear to be highly attached to their homes. At this point, it is not clear whether they would be prepared to give up their homes instead of bequeathing them to their offspring.
5. Complexity of the product. As already mentioned above, reverse mortgages are considered complex financial products. If they are not implemented in a consumer-friendly way, they are able to provide harm to the growth of the whole housing finance industry.

In conclusion, reverse mortgages could be an option for households to use their home as an additional source of income to complement a pension. Given the deteriorating dependency ratio, demand for such products may rise rapidly especially among those homeowners whose pension is too small to cover for the rising living and health cost after retirement. Offering reverse mortgage is not without risks for borrowers. Products are considered complex and are difficult to design as they require superior knowledge and data of house price developments, interest rate movements, as well as life expectancy assessment. The implementation of these products may also contradict the argument in favor of homeownership (i.e., wealth creation and preservation) as reverse mortgage leads to elimination of capital. These arguments have to be weighed against a rising pension deficit and a support to more consumption to stimulate economic activity – an argument which may fall on fertile ground given the relatively high savings rates and the export orientation of the country.

---

[8]The FHA assumes two major reverse mortgage risks: (1) the lender will not be able to make payments to the mortgagor; (2) at the time of the termination of the reverse mortgage contract, the property value is not sufficient to repay the mortgage.

7   Conclusion

The property sector plays an important role within China's economy. The housing market accounts for about a quarter of Chinese GDP. Any swing in property prices have therefore a considerable impact on economic growth and stability in the country. The reforms of the housing sector, which have been started in 1998, have laid the foundations for a market-oriented system for the supply and demand for housing and housing finance. Nevertheless, the government has remained a strong grip on the sector through administrative measures as well as a tight management of interest rates to influence the pricing of housing loans. After 1998, reforms have been aimed at ensuring access to affordable housing to balance increasing inequalities and to implement countercyclical measure to stimulate the economy when exports fell (2007/2008 and 2014). To date, despite rising HPI, the government has managed to avoid the building up of a property bubble. According to the latest research, it appears that challenging issues are supply-demand imbalances between smaller and bigger cities due to restricted provision of land for construction of residential properties.

Future challenges for housing policy-makers are the reduction of income inequalities and the flawed distribution of housing as a result of the nature of housing reforms which emphasized the commercialization of the urban housing sector. The large-scale development of social housing, inaugurated in 2008, is a part of the strategy to rebalance the income distribution. Another challenge for the housing sector and the expansion of housing finance is likely to arise from the aging society. It may increase the demand for finance from an age cohort to accommodate for potentially limited mobility because the pensions may not be high enough to pay for the additional expenses of the home improvements. To date, no financial products have been introduced to serve this market gap. Reverse mortgage products may not offer a solution given their complex nature and their potential need for subsidization.

People have access to housing finance as shown by the significant increase in mortgage lending during the last 5 years. The modest importance of housing finance is partly due to the regulations (especially interest rate fixings and LTV limits). With house prices still rising, the government may be encouraged to rethink this approach as lower income groups may face rising challenges to afford a home.

Acknowledgment   The author is very grateful to Yuan Gao and Shuning Lu who supported the project as research associates. Yuan Gao works as a credit research Intern at CUNA Mutual Group in Washington DC. Shuning Lu works as a banking analyst at the European Bank for Reconstruction and Development (EBRD) at their London headquarters in the UK.

The views, findings, interpretations, and conclusions expressed in this paper are entirely those of the authors and do not necessarily represent the views of the World Bank Group, its Board of Executive Directors, or the governments they represent.

References

Arora, R. (2005). *Homeownership soars in China*. Accessed August 26, 2019, from https://news. gallup.com/poll/15082/homeownership-soars-china.aspx.

Barth, J. R., Lea, M., & Li, T. (2012, December). China's Housing Market: Is a bubble about to burst? *SSRN Electronic Journal*.

Bloomberg. (2019). *PBOC says new personal mortgage loan rate to be based on LPR*. Accessed August 26, 2019, from https://www.bloomberg.com/news/articles/2019-08-25/pboc-says-new-personal-mortgage-loan-rate-to-be-based-on-lpr.

Buitelaar, P. (2014). Chinese banks – risk and challenges. *DNB Occasional Studies, 12*(4).

Chen, Y., & Heath, N. (2016). China's pension funds under pressure with rising payments: Xinhua. *Reuters*. Accessed August 26, 2019, from https://www.reuters.com/article/us-china-economy-pensions/chinas-pension-funds-under-pressure-with-rising-payments-xinhua-idUSKCN11C137.

Chen, Y., Woo, R., & Zhang, M. (2019). China's home prices growth fastest in five months, raises policy challenge. *Reuters*. Accessed August 26, 2019, from https://www.reuters.com/article/us-china-economy-houseprices/chinas-home-prices-growth-fastest-in-five-months-raises-policy-challenge-idUSKCN1TJ04J.

Chien, J. (2015). *Perspectives of housing finance in China*. Presentation Uppsala, 2015.

Clemens, U., Dyck, S., & Just, T. (2011). *China's housing markets: Regulatory interventions mitigate risk of severe bust*. Frankfurt: Deutsche Bank Research.

Consumer Financial Protection Bureau. (2012, June 28). *Reverse mortgages – Report to Congress*.

Doling, J., & Ronald, R. (2014). Introduction. In J. Doling & R. Ronald (Eds.), *Housing East Asia – Socioeconomic and demographic challenges*. New York: Palgrave Macmillan.

EIU. (2009, August). *Country finance China*.

IMF. (2011). *People's Republic of China: Financial system stability assessment*. IMF Country Report No. 11/321.

Miles, J. (2011, June 25). Special Report on China: Rising power, anxious State. *The Economist*

Ping, Y., & Shao, L. (2014). Urban housing policy changes and challenges in China. In J. Doling & R. Ronald (Eds.), *Housing East Asia – socioeconomic and demographic challenges*. New York: Palgrave Macmillan.

Pozen, R. (2015). China's pension problems will not be solved by more children. *Financial Times*. Accessed August 26, 2019, from https://www.ft.com/content/d4ce82e4-937a-11e5-bd82-c1fb87bef7af#axzz3t0WmSFP8.

Rabinovitch, S. (2011, June 28). Emphasis on explicit debt hides extent of Beijing's local liabilities. *Financial Times*.

Renaud, B. (2011). *Housing bubbles in China: How do we analyze them?* Presentation given at SAIS course, Washington, DC.

Roy, F. (2012). Sustainable development of housing finance markets – An international perspective after the crisis. In G. Mennillo, T. Schlenzig, & E. Friedrich (Eds.), *Balance growth – finding strategies for sustainable development*. Heidelberg: Springer.

The Economist. (2010, May 27). Home truths – China's economic boom can survive a property bust.

The Economist. (2011, June 25). Special report on China: Rising power, anxious State.

The Economist. (2016). Chinese property: When a bubble is not a bubble. Accessed October 15, 2019, from https://www.economist.com/finance-and-economics/2016/10/13/when-a-bubble-is-not-a-bubble.

The National Bureau of Statistics of China (NBSC). (2009). *China Statistical Yearbook 2009*. Beijing: China Statistics Press.

The National Bureau of Statistics of China (NBSC). (2013). *China Statistical Yearbook 2013*. Beijing: China Statistics Press.

The National Bureau of Statistics of China (NBSC). (2015). *China Statistical Yearbook 2015*. Beijing: China Statistics Press.

The National Bureau of Statistics of China (NBSC). (2016). *China Statistical Yearbook 2016*. Beijing: China Statistics Press.

The National Bureau of Statistics of China (NBSC). (2018). *China Statistical Yearbook 2018*. Beijing: China Statistics Press.

Yang, Y. (2016). China braced for impact of property slowdown. *Financial Times*. Accessed August 26, 2019, from https://www.ft.com/content/fab25e94-ad6a-11e6-9cb3-bb8207902122.

Yang, Z., & Chen, J. (2014). *Housing affordability and housing policy in urban China*. Heidelberg: Springer.

Yang, Y., Mitchell, T., & Li, W. (2016, October 20). Beijing struggles to slow housing boom. *Financial Times*.

Listings and M&As of Chinese Real Estate Enterprises

Qingjun Jin

Abstract

Many domestic and foreign investors are paying great attention to the issues of real estate enterprises' listings and M&As within China. The Chinese supervisory authorities have made an effort to regulate the capital markets relating to real estate industry in order to improve transactional efficiencies and management of real estate development and investment activities. This chapter discusses the circumstances of the real estate industry's initial public offerings (IPOs), both domestically and overseas, based on an analysis of related laws and regulations issued by competent authorities. Some critical M&A matters in the real estate industry are also presented in this chapter to help readers understand the scenarios and situations before making plans to invest in real estate in China.

1   Listings

A listed company is a corporation whose shares are listed on and transacted through the stock exchange. The listed company can rapidly raise large amounts of capital and achieve large-scale production and operations by issuing shares publicly. Therefore, such a listing may help relieve the financial pressure real estate enterprises face while contributing to the needs of their business expansions. This article introduces the listing systems of Chinese real estate enterprises from both overseas and domestic aspects.

Q. Jin (✉)
King & Wood Mallesons, World Financial Center, Beijing, PR China

© Springer Nature Switzerland AG 2021
B. Wang, T. Just (eds.), *Understanding China's Real Estate Markets*, Management for Professionals, https://doi.org/10.1007/978-3-030-49032-4_13

1.1   Overseas IPO Listings

Overseas initial public offering (IPO) listings can be academically categorized as a direct listing and an indirect listing. An overseas direct listing is the mode of listing when a domestic company submits an application to register with the foreign competent security authority, issues shares at the same time, and applies to be listed on and transacted through the local security exchange. In this mode, shares are usually called H shares, N shares, S shares, etc. An indirect listing refers to listing under the name of an offshore company established by the domestic company to acquire the controlling power of the domestic assets through mergers or the exchange of shares. The offshore corporation applies for listing rights on the foreign security exchange through a backdoor listing or listing by a shell corporation (e.g., red chip).

1.1.1   Example of H Shares

H shares are approved by the Chinese Securities Regulatory Commission (CSRC). They are issued by corporations registered on mainland China, listed on Hong Kong market, and subscribed to and exchanged by foreign investors. This, section analyzes relevant issues about H shares by discussing the example case of Wanda Real Estate, which is listed on the Hong Kong Exchanges and Clearing Limited (HKEX).

According to the Special Provisions of the State Council Concerning the Floatation and Listing Abroad of Stocks by Limited Stock Companies and Supervision Guideline of Declaring Documents and the Procedure of Reviewing for Limited Stock Companies Issuing and Listing Overseas, the company, as a corporation was established in accordance with the Company Law of the People's Republic of China. By meeting the conditions for issuing and listing shares abroad, the company is qualified to submit an application for shares issuing and listing abroad to the CSRC. The required application documents include (1) an application report stating the history of the company and business profile, capital structure, corporate governance structure, financial situation and business performance, analysis of operation risk, development strategy, financing purposes, illustration of meeting the conditions for listing on the market, and an issuing and listing plan; (2) resolutions from the shareholders' general meeting and the board of directors; (3) articles of association; (4) the business license of the corporation and certificate of business license for a special permitted industry (if applicable); (5) supervisory opinions issued by the industry regulatory authorities (if applicable); (6) documents approved by the State-owned Assets Administration Department relating to the establishment of and the reducing or transferring state-owned shares (if applicable); (7) the examination, approval, and filling of documents for fund-financing invested projects (if applicable); (8) certificate of tax payment; (9) certificate of environment protection; (10) legal opinion; (11) financial statements and audit reports; (12) prospectus (draft); and (13) other documents required by the CSRC.

The preparations to list Wanda Commercial Properties took 10 years. The prospectus of Wanda REITs was approved in Hong Kong by the end of 2005. However, in July 2006, the regulation Opinions Concerning Regulating the Access to and Administration of Foreign Investment in the Real Estate Market (Circular No. 17 [2006] of the Ministry of Construction) issued by the State Administration of Foreign Exchange, the Ministry of Commerce, and other Ministries strictly restricted overseas companies acquiring the mainland properties; therefore the project of Wanda REITs had to be postponed. Wanda Commercial Properties officially initiated the process of listing on the A shares market in 2009; however, considering that real estate financing channels had been tightened, on March 20, 2013, Wanda Commercial Properties concluded an agreement with the controlling shareholder of Hengli Commercial Properties, and the parties agree that Chen Changwei would transfer 65% shares of Hengli Commercial Properties to Wanda Commercial Properties. Backdoor listing of Wanda's H shares was completed successfully in April 2013, but the company didn't revoke its application for an A shares listing. On July 2, 2014, Dalian Wanda Commercial Properties Co., Ltd. posted the statement to the public on its official website to confirm that Wanda Commercial Properties had terminated its A shares listing. Wanda Commercial Properties (03966.HK) was listed on the main board of the HKEX on December 23, 2014. Its opening price was 48 HKD, and Wanda Commercial Properties raised 28.8 billion HKD, putting an end to its decade-long work to be listed.

Wanda Commercial Properties ultimately chose to be listed on the Hong Kong market is because the requirements and environment of Hong Kong stock market were more beneficial to Wanda Commercial Properties. The Hong Kong capital market fully complies with the marketization issuing mode; there are no requirements on corporate profit results. Meanwhile, related transactions are also permitted to some extent. These circumstances address the two limitations Wanda Commercial Properties faced when trying to list A shares. Yet it should be noted that, with the influence of A shares listing of Chinese real estate enterprises, starting up refinancing, and overevaluation of A shares market, Wanda Commercial Properties issued The Notice of Issuance Concerning Voluntary Full Takeover Offer For the Acquisition of All H Shares Issued by Wanda Commercial Properties In Accordance With Article 3.7 of Takeover Rules and Insider Information Provision on March 30, 2016, which asserted that the controlling shareholder of the company, Dalian Wanda Group Co., Ltd., had notified Wanda Commercial Properties that it was considering offering an voluntary full takeover offer for its H shares. If the plan was carried out, it would lead to the privatization of Wanda Commercial Properties and result in the withdrawal of listing in HKEX.

1.1.2   Red Chip Listings

Red-chip listings refer to domestic companies that transfer their domestic assets in the form of shares exchange to an overseas registered company and hold domestic assets and shares in the overseas company. The domestic company is then listed in the name of the registered overseas company.

Before September 8, 2006, private enterprises like Mengniu, Gome, Ctrip and Shanda were listed by way of Red Chip listing overseas. However, the Ministry of Commerce and other six ministries and commissions issued the Provisions of the Ministry of Commerce on M&A of a Domestic Enterprise by Foreign Investors

(No. 10 [2006]) to influence M&As by foreign investors and Red Chip listings. Since September 9, 2006 when Circular No.10 came into force, there have been no domestic enterprises which have completed the establishment of Red Chip structure under the standards of Circular No.10 with its "M&A with related party" permitted by the Ministry of Commerce. Circular No.10 sets strict limitations on "M&A with related party"[1], and this blocks the way for listing offshore for the companies which had not completed the establishment of Red Chip structure.

In order to avoid the approval required by Circular No.10, pre-listing companies have adopted several strategies, including (1) from the point of time, taking advantage of the principle of non-retroactivity of the law; (2) from the relation of transaction, avoiding related-party relationships, such as holding shares by a third party; (3) from the mode of transaction, avoiding acquisition action, such as taking the mode of agreement controlling or VIE structure; and (4) from the related parties, avoiding being seen as supervised subjects, such as changing the nationality of the actual controlling person. Nevertheless, based on a series of regulations including Circular No. 171, Notice on Further Strengthening and Regulating the Examination, Approval and Supervision of Foreign Direct Investment in Real Estate Industry (No. 50 [2007] of the Ministry of Commerce) issued by the Ministry of Commerce and the State Administration of Foreign Exchange, Notice on Doing a Good Job in Archival Filing of Foreign Investment in the Real Estate Industry (No. 23 [2008] of the Ministry of Commerce) issued by the Ministry of Commerce, and Notice on Strengthening the Approval and Filing Administration of Foreign Investment in the Real Estate Sector (Circular No. 1542 [2010] of the General Office of the Ministry of Commerce) issued by the General Office of the Ministry of Commerce, the real estate industry has suffered more strict limitations on the acquisitions by foreign investors and return investment. It would be more difficult for real estate enterprises to list overseas under Red Chip structure. Logan Property is one of a few domestic real estate enterprises completing Red Chip listing after the issuance of Circular No.10. To avoid the approval concerning M&A with related party under Circular No.10, the company acquired the identity of foreign-invested enterprise by means of independent third party and finally listed in HKEX on December 20, 2013.

Compared with H shares listings, the regulations of Hong Kong Securities and Futures Commission concerning Red Chip listings are less strict for companies, and the cost of listing is lower. Furthermore, the ability of refinancing after listing is stronger as the company has the right to issue new shares to raise money 6 months after listing. More importantly, if the company is listed by means of Red Chips, the original shareholders can convert shares into cash (major shareholders can sell their owned shares as shown in the prospectus 6 months after the company listing on

---

[1] Article 11 "Where a domestic company, enterprise or natural person intends to take over its domestic affiliated company in the name of a company which it lawfully established or controls, it shall be subject to the examination and approval of the MOFCOM. The parties concerned shall not dodge the aforesaid requirements by making investments within China through the foreign-funded enterprise, or by other ways."

Hong Kong main board). H shares holding by Chinese shareholders cannot be circulated in the second market.

1.2   Domestic Listing

The main ways of real estate enterprises being listed for financing in the domestic market include direct listing and backdoor listing.

Direct Domestic Listing
Domestic listing for financing can be academically categorized into two ways: (1) domestic A shares IPO listing, that is, the real estate enterprise establishes a stock limited company and lists on domestic A shares market for direct financing; and (2) domestic B shares IPO listing, that is, the real estate enterprise establishes a stock limited company and lists on domestic B shares market for direct financing.

In April 2010, the State Council issued Notice on Resolutely Curbing the Soaring of Housing Prices in Some Cities (Circular No.10 [2010] of the State Council), which clearly stated that "For real estate development enterprises which have spare land or engaged in land speculation, commercial banks shall not grant loans for new development projects, the securities regulatory departments shall suspend the approval of their listing, refinancing and major assets restructuring." In February 2011, the State Council issued Notice of the General Office of the State Council on Issues Concerning Further Doing a Good Job on the Regulation and Control of Real Estate Market (Circular No.1 [2011] of the General Office of the State Council), and in February 2013, the State Council issued Notice of the General Office of the State Council on Continuing Improving Regulation and Control of the Real Estate Market (Circular No.17 [2013] of the General Office of the State Council); the above two orders prescribe that the above policies shall continue to be practiced.

After the issuance of Circular No.10 [2010] by State Council in April 2010, the CSRC suspended the approvals of listing, refinancing, and M&A of real estate companies. Three years later, on August 1, 2013, Xinhu Zhongbao issued the first refinancing plan of a real estate company for two markets, and immediately on September 4, 2013, the Listing Department One of the CSRC issued Notice on Filing Reports Concerning the M&A, Restructuring and Refinancing Relating to Real Estate Business to Shanghai Securities Exchange and Shenzhen Securities Exchange, which clarifies the scale of filing specific verification reports and requirements of application documents. On March 19, 2014, Zhongyin Co., Ltd. and Tianbao Infrastructure issued the notice that their applications of issuing A shares privately had been passed by the CSRC. This marks the beginning of the CSRC initiating the approval of refinancing of real estate companies since 2010.

The conditions of Chinese real estate enterprises listing on the main board and small and medium enterprise board in Chinese market include (1) the stock limited company is legally established and lasting; (2) the company has more than 3 years of continual operation; (3) the net profit positive cumulatively exceeds more than RMB30 million in the last 3 fiscal years; (4) the proportion of intangible assets of the last fiscal period compared to net assets is not higher than 20%, and there is no unremedied deficit; (5) the total share capital is not less than RMB30 million before issuance; (6) the main business has no material changes in the last 3 years; (7) the actual controller has not changed in the last 3 years; and (8) the directors and management personnel have not changed significantly in the last 3 years.[2]

Domestic Backdoor Listings

As for those real estate enterprises which don't meet the conditions of direct listing, backdoor listing is another financing channel by which the company can take advantage of listing and financing and can refinance by allotment and issuing new shares to constantly raise funds. Backdoor listing can avoid waiting too long and the complicated listing procedures. But it should be noted that in accordance with Measures for the Administration of the Material Asset Restructurings of Listed Companies (Measures for the Material Asset Restructurings) and Notice of China Securities Regulatory Commission on the Strict Implementation of the Standards of Listing for Initial Public Offering on the Approval of Backdoor Listing, if the plan of material asset restructuring of the listed company be confirmed as the situation regulated in Article 13[3] of Measures for the Material Asset Restructurings and be considered as backdoor listing, the assets purchased by the listed company shall be operated by a stock limited company or limited liability company, and the company shall abide by the conditions of issuance regulated by Measures for the Administration of Initial Public Offering and Listing of Stocks (Circular No.32 of China Securities Regulatory Commission). Besides, it cannot carry out the backdoor listing on the growth enterprise board. In the process of reviewing backdoor listing, the company shall strictly implement the standards of IPO listing.

The CSRC suspended the approval of listing, refinancing, and M&A of real estate enterprises in 2010. Subsequently, the CSRC approved applications of three real estate companies for backdoor listing in 2011, which include Beijing Macrolink Co., Ltd. listing through the shell of S*ST Shengfang on April 19 2011, later the same year, Yinyi Group Co., Ltd. restructured S*ST Languang on May 12, and ST Dongyuan absorbed Jinke Group Co., Ltd. by increasing issuance of 908 million shares on May 27. As for these cases, the related person of CSRC in charge

---

[2]Refer to Article 9, 12, and 26 of Measures for the Administration of Initial Public Offering and Listing of Stocks.

[3]Article 13, as of the day when change of control occurs, the total assets purchased by a listed company from the acquirer and the affiliates thereof account for 100% or more of the ending total assets as specified in the listed company's audited consolidated financial statements for the preceding fiscal year prior to the change of control; in addition to satisfy the requirements specified in Articles 11 and 43 of the Measures, the company listed on the main board (or the SME board) shall ensure that the target business entity is a stock limited company or limited liability company and shall meet other offering conditions as set out in the Measures for the Administration of Initial Public Offering and Listing of Stocks (Order No. 32, CSRC). If the assets purchased by the listed company are in the financial, venture capital, or any other specified industry, the governing provisions shall be separately developed by the CSRC. A company listed on the Growth Enterprise Market may not have the trading behavior specified in the preceding paragraph.

explained that these three real estate companies' applications of M&A and restructure had been accepted before the issuance of the restriction order. In the following days, there is no backdoor listing of real estate companies in A shares market other than the special case of Sanxiang Co., Ltd. On March 17, 2014, after suspension of trading for almost 9 months, Jinfeng Investment Co., Ltd. (600606) released its plan that the company was preparing for restructuring by purchasing assets and exchanging assets and issuing new shares, planning to acquire 100% equities of Greenland Group Co., Ltd, which was considered as backdoor listing. The CSRC permitted this transaction by issuing No.1226 [2015] CSRC Permission on June 12, 2015. On June 26, 2015, 100% equities of Greenland Holding Group Co., Ltd. had been transferred to Jinfeng Investment Co., Ltd, and this material assets restructuring had completed the closing obligation of assets placement, and the security abbreviation of the company had changed from "Jinfeng Investment" to "Greenland Holding" since August 18, 2015. On March 14, 2015, after suspension of trading for almost 5 months, Hubei Jinhuan Co., Ltd. (000615) launched its restructuring plan. The company intended to issue 179 million shares privately with the price of RMB8.3 per share to purchase 100% equities of King Hand Housing Group Co., Ltd. After the transaction was completed, King Hand Housing Group Co., Ltd. would accomplish backdoor listing. On September 21, 2015, Hubei Jinhuan Co., Ltd. received No.2139 [2015] CSRC Permission from CSRC. King Hand Housing Group Co., Ltd. acquired the reissued Business License of Enterprise from Beijing Industrial and Commercial Bureau on September 28, 2015. Hubei Jinhuan Co., Ltd. held 100% equities of King Hand Housing Group Co., Ltd, and therefore the transference procedure of the target asset had been completed. Therefore, two cases of backdoor listing of real estate companies appear in A shares market again. It is generally considered in the market that the backdoor listing case of King Hand Housing and Hubei Jinhuan might indicate the initiation of listing for real estate enterprises.

Under the background that Chinese real estate market facing unprecedented macro-regulation and control, the capital market is holding a more rational attitude to listing of real estate enterprises. The change of Chinese macro-policy and market environment will have a direct influence on the pace of Chinese real estate enterprises listing and financing on A shares market.

2   Mergers and Acquisitions (M&As)

In order to achieve corporate control of a domestic real estate company (i.e., the target company) in mainland China, a foreign investor with offshore funds may merge or acquire the target company by reaching equity purchase agreements with the company's shareholders or by subscribing the new shares. The target company would then be a foreign-invested company. This activity is referred to as foreign enterprise's M&A in real estate. However, several fundamental restrictions relating to foreign enterprises' M&As in real estate exist and are discussed in the following subsections.

Section 3, Part 5 of Guiding Opinions of the General Office of the Ministry of Commerce on the Work of Absorbing Foreign Investment in 2007 (No. 25 [2007] of the Ministry of Commerce) states that China "take[s] effective measures to restrict foreign investment in real estate strictly." Thereafter, restricting foreign investment in real estate was set up as a main principle.

According to Section 1, Part 1[4] of Circular 171 and Article 4[5] of Circular 50, foreign investors shall invest, develop, or operate a business in real estate industry by setting up or operating a foreign-invested real estate company. This is called the principle of business presence. The registration of foreign debt and settlement of foreign exchange underwent several policy changes, from a phase of complete prohibition in July of 2007 to a phase of conditional restriction in May of 2015. After the issuance and enforcement of Notice of the General Department of the State Administration of Foreign Exchange on Issuing the List of the First Batch of Foreign-Funded Real Estate Projects Having Passed the Procedures for Archiving with the Ministry of Commerce (No. 130 [2007] of the General Department of the State Administration of Foreign Exchange) in July, 2007, the State Administration of Foreign Exchange stopped proceeding the registration of settlement of foreign exchange for all foreign-funded real estate enterprises. According to Notice of the State Administration of Foreign Exchange on Repealing and Amending Relevant Regulatory Documents Involving the Reform of the Registration System for Registered Capital (No. 20 [2015] of the State Administration of Foreign Exchange) issued in May, 2015, the State Administration of Foreign Exchange would not proceed the registration of foreign debt or approve the settlement of foreign exchange for those foreign-funded real estate enterprises that did not obtain the state-owned land use certificate or not raised enough capital (35% of total investment) for developing projects.

According to Circular 50, foreign-funded real estate enterprise that failed to complete filing with the Ministry of Commerce shall not be allowed to handle formalities for the sales and settlement of foreign exchange under the capital account.[6]

---

[4]Section 1. An overseas institution or individual shall, when investing in China to purchase any not-for-self-use real estate, abide by the principles of commercial presence and apply, according to the relevant provisions on foreign investment in real estate, for establishing a foreign investment enterprise and may, upon obtaining the approval of the relevant department as well as completing the relevant registration, engage in the relevant operation according to its approved business scope.

[5]Article IV. Overseas investors engaging in the real estate development or operation business in China shall observe the principle of commercial presence, apply for establishing foreign-funded real estate enterprises according to law and engage in the relevant business within the authorized business scope.

[6]VI. No administrative department of foreign exchange or designated bank of foreign exchange may handle formalities for the sales and settlement of foreign exchange under the capital account for any foreign-funded real estate enterprise that fails to go through the formalities for filing with the Ministry of Commerce for record or failing to pass the annual joint inspection on foreign-funded enterprises.

According to Circular 23,[7] the Ministry of Commerce transfers the authority to verify archival materials of foreign-funded real estate enterprises to the competent provincial departments of commerce. Article 3[8] of Circular 50 regulates that a merger with or investment in domestic real estate enterprises (including by the same actual controller) by means of returning investment shall be under strict control. Circular 23[9] and Circular 1542[10] also require that commercial departments carefully identify and prohibit returning investment in foreign-funded real estate enterprises. These restricting policies remain unchanged.

In Catalogue of Industries for Guiding Foreign Investment (2015 Revision) [Effective] (Circular 22 of the National Development and Reform Commission and the Ministry of Commerce), supervision departments cancelled three restrictions listed in the "Real Estate Industry" of Catalogue of Industries for Guiding Foreign Investment (2011 Revision) (Circular 12 of the National Development and Reform Commission and the Ministry of Commerce). The three cancelled restrictions are as follows:

1. Development of tracts of land (limited to joint ventures or contractual cooperation)
2. Construction and operation of high-class hotels, high-class office buildings, and international exhibition centers

---

[7]I. The Ministry of Commerce shall authorize the competent provincial departments of commerce to check the archival materials on foreign investment in the real estate industry. After legally approving the matters on foreign investment in real estate (including but not limited to formation of enterprise, increase of capital or shares, share transfer, merger and acquisition), the competent local departments of commerce shall submit the materials, which should be submitted to the Ministry of Commerce for archival purposes, to the competent provincial departments of commerce for checking.

[8]III. The merger of or investment in domestic real estate enterprises by way of return on investment (including the same actual controller) shall be placed under strict control. No overseas investor may evade from subjecting foreign investment in the real estate industry to examination and approval by means of changing the actual controller of any domestic real estate enterprise. Where the administrative department of foreign exchange finds out that any foreign-funded real estate enterprise is illegally established by adopting such illegal means as malicious evasion or false statement, the department shall investigate its behaviors of illegally remitting outward capital and the incomes therefrom and subject it to the liabilities for obtaining foreign currency under false pretenses and not turning over foreign currency owed to the government.

[9]II. The competent provincial departments of commerce shall check the legality, authenticity and accuracy of the following materials in accordance with the requirements of Documents No. 171 and 50 and the relevant provisions:...4. The materials provided by the company prove that the foreign shareholder is not a company formed abroad by a domestic company/natural person and all shareholders of the company are not affiliated each other, or subject to a same actual controller.

[10]IV. Commerce departments across the country shall, jointly with the State Administration of Foreign Exchange and other relevant departments, carefully sort out and strictly examine and approve real estate enterprises that engage in round-tripping investments and strictly control the establishment of domestic real estate enterprises in the form of round-tripping investments.

3. Real estate secondary market transactions and real estate intermediary or brokerage companies

Moreover, Catalogue of Industries for Guiding Foreign Investment (2015 Revision) (Circular 22 of the National Development and Reform Commission and the
Ministry of Commerce) does not have any other restriction or prohibition in real
estate industry. Therefore, the restrictions on "market access to foreign investment in
real estate industry" no longer exist.

2.1 Domestic M&As

As the purpose of domestic M&A in real estate industry is mainly to acquire
properties, and the transactions are easily influenced by state economic macro-
control policies, therefore, domestic enterprises may encounter many legal risks in
the transaction. The main risks of M&A in real estate industry include "current
situation risks" and the risk of noncompliance with the regulatory conditions of
transfer. The former one refers to the risks that the ownership, the demolition
situation, or the geographical condition of the real estate may have some legal issues.
The latter one refers to the risk that may affect the M&A agreement's validity if the
requirements of real estate transfer regulated under Article 37–39[11] of the Urban
Real Estate Administration Law of the People's Republic of China are not met. As
such, it is important to determine whether property ownership is clear and whether
the land use right is established separately in compliance with Article 136 of the
Property Law. At the same time, it is also necessary to examine whether the
demolition is completed or whether the acquirer needs to take the responsibility of
demolition compensation, or whether there is a dispute or potential crisis of violating

---

[11] Article 37. Transfer of real estate shall mean the move of the ownership of a real estate from the
original owner to another person through sale, donation and other lawful means. Article 38. Real
estate with following conditions shall not be transferred: (1) The acquirement of the right of land use
through lease does not comply with conditions as prescribed in Article 39 of this law; (2) The title to
the real estate has been sealed up or restricted in any form upon ruling or deciding of judicial
authorities or administrative departments in accordance with the law; (3) The right of land use has
been taken back in accordance with the law; (4) Without a written consent of other owners as under
joint ownership; (5) There are disputes on the title; (6) Those which have not been registered and
obtained title certificates in accordance with the law; and (7) Other condition that the transfer is
forbidden according to the law or administrative rules.
Article 39. The transfer of real estate with the right of land use shall comply with the following
conditions: (1) All the fees in concern with the lease of the right of land use have been paid in
accordance with provisions prescribed by the contract for the lease and the certificate of the right to
use the land has been obtained; and (2) Investment and development have been done in accordance
with the provisions prescribed by the contract for the lease; for housing construction projects,
25 percent of the total investment has gone through; for development of large tracts of land, land has
been available for the construction of industrial or other projects. When a real estate is transferred
with a finished building, title certificate for the building is also needed.

the regulation "Relationships of Adjacency" in Chapter VII of the Property Law. Finally, it is necessary to confirm whether all the legal conditions of transfer are met.

Risks in real estate enterprises industry are mainly debt risks, which mean the balance sheet of the enterprise cannot reflect the occurred or potential debt. The range of properties available for security regulated by the Property Law and the Guarantee Law is wide, among which the guaranteed debt of the target company needs extensive attention. During due diligence, the financial reports of the target company, the signed external contracts, and the implementation of these contracts (especially guarantee contracts) are the key points of inspection; and the condition of guaranty to other parties should be individually verified by the relevant departments.

The real estate market can be greatly influenced by state macro-control economic regulations and policies. The policies related to market access to real estate, land use, financial support, credit support, and tax may change frequently. In different phases of M&A in real estate, the enterprises may encounter various political circumstances, which may lead to risks. Each party in an M&A should be fully aware of these risks, respond actively to any changes in state policy in a timely manner, and if necessary consult with law firms or professional institutions. Tax items related to Chinese real estate industry are complicated. Taxation regulations are regional, so the parties in M&A should pay attention to tax arrangement.

Like M&A in other industries, taxation relating to M&A in real estate industry generally includes business tax and income tax. It also includes land value increment tax and title deed tax. In accordance with Article 2 of the Interim Regulation of the People's Republic of China on Land Value-added Tax, units and individuals are obliged to pay land value-added taxes for their income derived from transference of right of use of State-owned land or buildings along with their attached installations. It is regulated in Article 1 of the Provisional Regulations of the People's Republic of China concerning Title Deed Taxes that unit or individuals to whom titles of land or houses have been transferred within the territory of the People's Republic of China shall pay title deed tax. It is worth noting that our country is in an experimental reform of replacing business tax with value-added tax. In the Government Work Report for the annual session of NPC and CPPCC in 2016, Premier Li Keqiang put forward that a nationwide implementation of the tax reform of replacing business tax with value-added tax will set up from May 1, 2016. The sectors related to this reform include real estate. Therefore, enterprise's value-added tax for newly added real estate will be deducted. To ensure a successful realization of the reform target, financial and taxation departments have issued a number of notices.[12]

---

[12]The Ministry of Finance and the State Administration of Taxation issued the *Notice on Doing a Good Job on Full Implementation of Pilot Program of Replacing Business Tax With Value-added Tax* (No.32 [2016] of The Ministry of Finance and the State Administration of Taxation) on March 7, and the State Administration of Taxation issued the Notice on *Carefully Executing the Full Implementation of Pilot Program of Replacing Business Tax With Value-added Tax* (No.32 [2016] of the State Administration of Taxation) on March 8.

2.2   Overview of China's Real Estate M&A Funds

In recent years, China's real estate industry has consistently ranked at the top of the list of M&A funds according to the number of M&A cases and the transaction sizes of these cases. This is because China's entire real estate market is continually evolving, and the in-depth control and regulations are not fully established with a corresponding financial system. The financing costs at times are too high, resulting in some real estate enterprises facing tight budgets and they have to sell properties and projects under construction in order to obtain capital. Meanwhile, real estate enterprises with abundant financial resources plan to expand under this circumstance which provides real estate M&A funds a great opportunity to develop. From a regional perspective, M&A funds that mainly invest in real estate enterprises are located in first-tier cities, including Beijing, Shanghai, Guangzhou, and Shenzhen, or in some developed provinces, such as Jiangsu, Zhejiang, and Guangdong. At the same time, thanks to a policy encouraging Chinese enterprises to "go global", the United Kingdom, Singapore, and other countries with mature capital markets are gradually becoming the appealing choices for investment. From a risk prevention perspective, the development of domestic M&A funds has a short history, and some fund managers lack adequate experiences. Therefore, the risks facing M&A funds warrant further attention so fund companies can improve the capacities to restructure its governance and generate profits after M&As.

Scenarios of Real Estate-Backed Securitization and Financing

Dave Chiou

Abstract

With constant shifts in government policies, Chinese developers are finding it increasingly difficult to make projections on how future projects will be financed. As a result, in the past 4 years, asset securitization is becoming a relatively popular option for Chinese developers. This chapter provides details on China's asset securitization policies and the regulatory hurdles that need to be addressed. Examples are also highlighted to reveal how commercial mortgage-backed securities (CMBS) products are packaged in China and why some developers are choosing CMBS over traditional bank loans. While China is still in the early stages of asset securitization and CMBS, the market potential for such products could grow substantially over time.

1   Introduction

Since late 2016, China has aggressively rolled out policies aimed at curbing the overheated property market. Some policies targeted home buyers and others aimed at property developers. The policies imposed on developers are intended to avoid excess capital flowing to the land market, which results in higher bid prices for land auctions and home prices. As a result, in 2017, while some developers have successfully issued bonds based on quotas obtained a few quarters earlier, most new issuances have been reprimanded by regulatory authorities.

As sources of funding dried up, China's securitization market has blossomed with commercial mortgage-backed securities (CMBS), residential mortgage-backed securities (RMBS), and asset-backed securities (ABS) becoming a major financing

D. Chiou (✉)
Colliers International, Shanghai, China

© Springer Nature Switzerland AG 2021
B. Wang, T. Just (eds.), *Understanding China's Real Estate Markets*, Management for Professionals, https://doi.org/10.1007/978-3-030-49032-4_14

mechanism for those large-scale developers and asset owners. Despite its relatively recent introduction, with limited market liquidity, China's CMBS, RMBS, and ABS markets will likely grow in the next few years as developers reach out for flexible means of financing.

2   Securitization

Mortgage- or asset-backed securities are securities which are based on pools of underlying assets. These assets are usually illiquid and long-term, and through pooling and securitization, they are made available for investment to a broader range of investors. When assets are securitized, a special-purpose trust or intermediary is set up which takes title to the assets, and the future cash flows of the assets are passed through to the investors in the form of an asset-backed security. The types of assets that can be securitized range from commercial mortgages to residential mortgages, to car loans, to account receivables, to future cash flows of a theme park, and even to music royalties. These asset-backed securities are then rated based on the risks of the underlying assets and are divided into different risk tranches.

In April 2015, the People's Bank of China (PBOC) relaxed rules for the sale of mortgage- and asset-backed securities, and limited approval from regulators is now required. The emergence of CMBS, RMBS, and ABS in the past 3 years in China has changed the market for mortgage lenders, property developers, and institutional investors. Banks no longer have to keep the assets or mortgages on their balance sheet for the duration of the loan, as they could sell the stream of interest and capital payments to investors, freeing up capital for other lending and investing business activities. Borrowers, on the other hand, benefit from improved loan availability and competitive rates (Fig. 1).

For investors, CMBS, RMBS, and ABS offer some notable and favorable characteristics:

1. Better yield potential: The returns of these structured products are reflected in their higher spreads over corporate bonds, which makes them an alternative option for investors seeking higher returns.

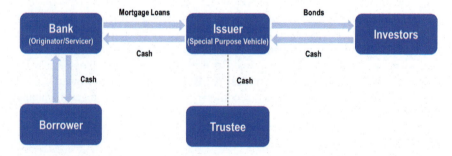

Fig. 1 Asset securitization—CMBS, RMBS, and ABS structure. Source: Jones Lang LaSalle

2. Diversification of portfolio: For CMBS and RMBS, the diversity of property locations, property types, tenants, and borrowers represented in each pool of loans would allow investors to effectively spread the risks.
3. Alternative asset exposure: For CMBS and RMBS, credit performance is determined by how well the underlying commercial or residential real estate properties perform. For ABS products, investors have a wide range of options, as investing in leases, credit card debts, car loans, accounts receivables, and royalties is all available. These products provide an easier access to invest in commercial mortgages and loans, with asset classes capable of meeting a wide range of risk-return preferences.

2.1 Benefits of Securitization

When an asset or loan is pooled for securitization, the borrower must abide to strict rules and guidelines for a specific time period. These loans have strict prepayment penalties and yield maintenance requirements to lending institutions or bond investors. They also place restrictions on what the property owners can do with the asset during the life of the loan. Because of these limits, borrowers would find it difficult to prematurely exit CMBS, RMBS, or ABS loans, unless they go through a loan defeasance process. Defeasance is a form of paying off loans without violating the terms of a securitization agreement. To defease a loan, the borrower must replace that loan with a similar yielding asset that has little potential for losing its value over time.

Despite the restrictions, there are certain benefits for asset owners to securitize their assets. Through securitization, borrowers are now able to tap into larger pools of capital with potentially lower interest rates. In addition, other benefits of securitization include (1) a nonrecourse loan to the parent company; (2) to release value while retain future growth potential of the underlying asset; and (3) to provide off-balance sheet financing, thereby lowering the debt-to-equity level of the parent company (Table 1). The ability for CMBS, RMBS, and ABS products to unlock asset values while allowing asset owners to keep part of the future growth potential is probably the single biggest attraction. When assets are securitized in China, apart from the debt, the future cash flows and a portion of the asset appreciation for a specific time period are often bundled into the financial product. This allows the asset owners to unlock the asset value, and use the proceeds to pay off debt and lower their leverage, or the money could be utilized for other investment opportunities.

2.2 Risks of Structured Products

Depending on the terms of the securitized products, interests could be paid monthly, quarterly, semiannually, or annually. The cash flows received from all the pooled loans are paid to investors, starting from investors holding the highest rated bonds (tranche one or senior secured bonds), until all accrued interests on those bonds are

Table 1 Comparison of financing mechanisms

	Bank loans	Share placement	Structured product
Fund source	Debt	Equity	Debt
Investors	Commercial banks	Retail and institutions	Institutions and high-net-worth individual
Advantages	Easy and quicker in arranging finance Lower arranging cost	No interest cost Fast and efficient to raise capital	Lower interest rates Nonrecourse to originator Release asset value and retain future growth potential
Disadvantages	Interest expenses cut into corporate earnings Require higher corporate ratings Stringent loan covenants	Dilution effect in both earnings and net asset value per share Unfavorable in a depressed market with low valuations	Complex deal structure Relative costly funding arrangements A limited pool of investors

Source: Jones Lang LaSalle

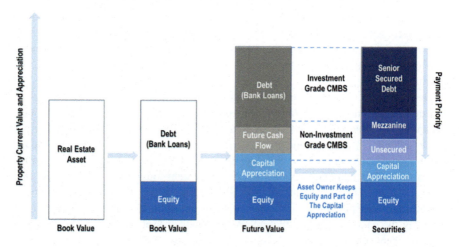

Fig. 2 Securitization—mortgage-backed securities issuance in China. Source: Jones Lang LaSalle

paid. Then interest is paid to holders of the next highest rated bonds, and unsecured bond holders are usually the least protected (Fig. 2). The same "waterfall" concept applies to principal payments.

As a result of the different risks involved, senior secured bond holders usually require the lowest yield, while unsecured bond holders would require a risk premium for holding these securitized assets. In China, in 2016 and 2017, the yield for senior secured bond holders would be 3.5–4.5%. For tranche two or three bond holders or mezzanine debt investors, the required return would be 5.0–8.0%. In the case of unsecured bond holders in China, the running rate in 2017 was 7.5% or above. The different risks and returns of these securitized products allow investors to choose from a wide range of asset classes capable of meeting their risk-return preferences.

2.3   A Lack of Retail Investors

Similar to the US market, CMBS, RMBS, and ABS products in China are sold mostly to institutional investors. The reasons why structured products are dominated by institutions include:

1. Increasing retail investor interests, but not savvy enough: Despite their higher returns and ability to offer diversified asset classes, structured products are often too complex and opaque for retail investors to understand. Even with enough disclosures, it is unlikely that most retail investors can understand the risk-return trade-off and the costs being incurred in some of these complex financial instruments.
2. Absence of risk appraisal regulatory agencies: Unlike the US market, China currently has no guidelines or regulations on reasonable-basis suitability analysis, an appraisal that accesses the risks embodied in structured products before they are sold to individual retail investors. In addition, since structured products are new in the market, China has limited trained professionals and registered representatives that have the ability to adequately analyze the products and ensure the messages and risks are conveyed properly to retail investors.
3. Absence of guidelines on public fundraising: According to China's Securities Regulatory Commission (CSRC), the line dividing public fundraising and private fundraising is issuing securities to more than 200 specific persons in the aggregate. While China did relax the rules for the sale of mortgage- and asset-backed securities in 2015, the absence of public fundraising laws indicates: To avoid a time-consuming regulatory approval, structured products would only be offered to a handful of institutional investors. Since there are no detailed guidelines on public fundraising in China, even regulators are having issues finding the appropriate set of rules for approval.
4. Minimum investment requirement of RMB 1 million or above: Investing in structured products often requires a minimum investment amount. In China, one unit or one share of CMBS would range from RMB 1 million (USD 140,845) to RMB 10 million (USD 1.41 million), depending on the terms of the issuance. The higher investment entry barrier disqualifies most retail investors, leaving institutional and high-net-worth individuals as the dominant players.
5. No secondary market for structured products: Given the complexity of the financial products and the lack of retail participants, a secondary market for CMBS, RMBS, and ABS is almost nonexistent in China. For any investors to cash out before the bond maturity, these contracts can only be traded over-the-counter (OTC) and privately between two parties, without going through an

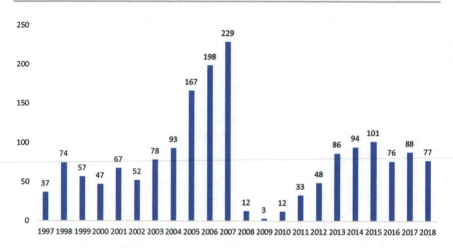

Fig. 3 CMBS market—US CMBS new issuance in US$ billion. Source: Commercial Mortgage Alert

exchange or other intermediary. Compared to the USA, China is still in the early stages of CMBS, RMBS, and ABS issuance, as regulations were only relaxed recently. According to Commercial Mortgage Alert, in 2018, the USA accounted for 93% of global CMBS issuance, making it the single largest market in the world (Fig. 3). Given China's market size of real estate, and banks and developers' need for alternative financing, CMBS, RMBS, and ABS products should see more popularity and issuance in the years to come.

3   Case Studies of CMBS and ABS

Case Study: Asia Pulp & Paper CMBS

In December 2016, Asia Pulp & Paper's (China) investment affiliate launched its first CMBS product in China, with Sinolink Securities being the lead book runner. The total deal size is RMB 7.8 billion, of which RMB 5.46 billion is Senior Secured Tranche A bonds, RMB 1.54 billion is Tranche B bonds, and RMB 800 million is an unsecured zero-coupon bond. The coupon rates for Tranche A and B bonds are fixed and undisclosed and are callable and rate adjustable once every 3 years for a total of 24 years. The Shanghai Arch, a mixed-use building consisting of retail and office spaces, is the underlying asset of Asia Pulp & Paper's CMBS and located in Hongqiao area of Shanghai City. The building is operated primarily by Asia Pulp & Paper (China), and the 28-floor building constitutes a total GFA of 260,000 square meters. Located at a decentralized part of Shanghai, Shanghai Arch's daily rent for its office space is RMB 6.5–RMB 7.0 per square meter, and the whole mixed-use building has an annual rental income of roughly RMB 460 million. Asia Pulp & Paper (China) securitized the asset primarily to pay back its long-term debt. Shanghai Arch has a current market value of about RMB 4.2 billion, but through

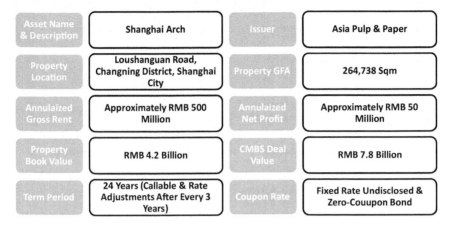

Asset Name & Description	Shanghai Arch	Issuer	Asia Pulp & Paper
Property Location	Loushanguan Road, Changning District, Shanghai City	Property GFA	264,738 Sqm
Annulaized Gross Rent	Approximately RMB 500 Million	Annulaized Net Profit	Approximately RMB 50 Million
Property Book Value	RMB 4.2 Billion	CMBS Deal Value	RMB 7.8 Billion
Term Period	24 Years (Callable & Rate Adjustments After Every 3 Years)	Coupon Rate	Fixed Rate Undisclosed & Zero-Couupon Bond

Fig. 4 China CMBS—Asia Pulp & Paper CMBS. Source: Jones Lang LaSalle

securitization, Asia Pulp & Paper was able to fetch RMB 7.8 billion (Fig. 4), as part of the future cash flows of the building and appreciation value are all bundled in the bond valuation.

Case Study: Everbright Group ABS

In August 2016, Everbright Asset (EBA), the real investments consultancy of Everbright Bank, through a partnership with one of its affiliates Everbright Prestige (EBP), launched their first ABS product in China. The total deal size is RMB 1.6 billion, of which the interest rate for the RMB 1.3 billion Senior Tranche A bond is 3.8% and the Senior Tranche B bond worth RMB 300 m has a 4.3% interest rate. Officially called the IMIX Park REIT and listed on the Shenzhen Stock Exchange, Everbright Group's "REIT" product is actually an ABS product, as the securitized asset is based on the cash inflow or rental income from Guanyinqiao IMIX Park. Guanyinqiao IMIX Park was originally owned by EBA and a consortium of local developers in Chongqing, and in 2011, EBA teamed up with a local company to take over the asset from the rest of the ownership. Although located in Chongqing's CBD, due to poor management, the property had been struggling for years with loses. EBA's then-partner failed to turn it profitable after a major overhaul that transformed the site from an apparel wholesale market into a shopping mall. This forced EBA, originally a debt-financing investor, to take over the asset and start the property management in 2013. Managed by the retail section of EBA, the seven-floor mall occupies a total GFA of 130,000 square meters and enjoys a stable occupancy rate of 97%, with an annual rental income estimated to be about RMB 120 million (Fig. 5). With numerous properties on hand, IMIX Park REIT is just one of the projects that Everbright Group is involved, as the group is looking for more opportunities to securitize its assets and free up cash flows for other investment opportunities.

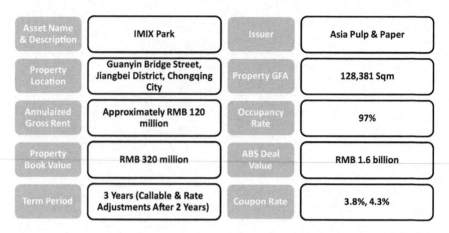

Asset Name & Description	IMIX Park	Issuer	Asia Pulp & Paper
Property Location	Guanyin Bridge Street, Jiangbei District, Chongqing City	Property GFA	128,381 Sqm
Annulaized Gross Rent	Approximately RMB 120 million	Occupancy Rate	97%
Property Book Value	RMB 320 million	ABS Deal Value	RMB 1.6 billion
Term Period	3 Years (Callable & Rate Adjustments After 2 Years)	Coupon Rate	3.8%, 4.3%

Fig. 5 China ABS—Everbright Group ABS. Source: Jones Lang LaSalle

4   REITs: The Next Big Thing in China?

In 2004, the China Banking Regulatory Commission (CBRC) issued a consultation draft or a set of guidelines to manage trust companies, which was the first time that REITs were openly discussed. More than a decade later, China has yet to see a REIT issuance as regulatory hurdles such as tax benefits or incentives, and other issues such as low property rental yields, lack of sophisticated retail investors, and capital flow restrictions remain unsolved. Unlike CMBS, RMBS, and ABS products that are structured for institutional investors, REITs are catered for both institutional and retail investors. With a possible retail participation, China's securities regulators have pursued a deliberate procrastination strategy on REIT issuance, cautiously analyzing the effects of REITs while touching upon topics such as retail investors' protection and other social and economic goals. It would be a couple of years away before the Chinese government formally approves a REIT issuance, but once all regulatory hurdles are cleared, Chinese developers with a leverage balance sheet will find REITs a welcoming idea as it is an alternative solution to fundraising.

A real estate investment trust (REIT) is a company, trust, or association that owns, and in most cases operates, income-producing real estate. The types of assets owned by REITs include office buildings, retail spaces, apartment buildings, warehouses, hospitals, and even timberlands. REITs can be publicly traded on major exchanges, public but non-listed or private. As a collective investment scheme, assets of REITs are professionally managed, and the revenues generated, which come primarily in the form of rents, are distributed at regular intervals to unit holders. As unit holders, investors share the benefits and risks of owning a portfolio of property assets. REITs normally have regular cash flows as their revenues are derived from rental payments under contractually binding lease agreements with specific tenures, making them stable income-producing vehicles for long-term investors. Similar to structured products, REITs offer investors a diversified portfolio of real estate or mortgage assets. However, unlike CMBS, RMBS, and ABS, REITs securitize on the equity of the underlying properties, rather than the debt of the assets. In this article, discussions on debt-focused REITs would be omitted as they are usually financed by institutional pooled funds or asset management companies, and not by cash-strapped but asset heavy real estate developers. In May 2014, Penghua Asset Management listed China's first-ever REIT-like vehicle on the Shenzhen Stock Exchange. The REIT is backed by the rental income from commercial properties of China Vanke's properties in Qianhai, which is a special economic zone in Shenzhen. However, due to the absence of REIT laws in China, China Vanke and Penghua's REIT does not give ownership of the underlying assets to the trustee, and the trust does not resemble a fixed-income instrument. The Shenzhen-listed entity was only offered to a handful of institutional investors on a private basis and is subject to a finite investment horizon of 3–5 years, which does not conform to international standards for a REIT. China's property developers have long been studying the use of asset securitization to improve their funding structure and relieve repayment. However, Chinese REITs are unlikely to develop significantly in the short to medium term, even if regulations are loosened or tax benefits are given to investors.

The traditional development and business model in China is building real estate projects that are sold to investors or home buyers in strata-titled sales. Much like Hong Kong, owning a part of a floor in a building has been common practice. The ability to subdivide property generates higher numbers of owners than would be found in a city of comparable size where buildings are wholly owned in single ownership. The reason why buildings are chopped up and sold in strata-title is to increase the number of investors who can participate, thereby allowing developers a quick exit. However, the division of buildings necessitates more complicated management and maintenance. In addition, the costs of buying up the shares to redevelop the sites will be particularly high and slow in the future, leaving poor property standing.

The net result of extensive strata titling for the commercial property market is a lack of debt in ownership that can be bought and sold on a landlord and tenant system commensurate with commercial property markets in locations such as the USA, the UK, and Australia. In some ways it's a circular process with developers selling off floor by floor on the grounds they cannot find an institutional buyer to take the whole block as an exit strategy. By contrast, institutional buyers and multinational companies (MNCs) may not want to rent floors in buildings where they may have to deal with multiple landlords. The issue is even more difficult for retail malls. In a mall where units are sold off, there is no mall management or tenant mix strategy. Mall failure can be common, and it is costly to align the owners to sell and redevelop. The rise of e-commerce has done little to help strata sold shopping malls. When properties are sold off in bits and pieces, institutional tradable real estate assets are not created, making it difficult for China to develop a REIT market, as large income-producing assets used to generate yield are scarce in the market. As a result of a slowed economy, China is now experiencing a broad-based yield compression for real estate properties, with many assets yielding 4% or less. Also, the excess supply of commercial properties and weak tenant mix will continue to weigh on rental yields, which make the properties of many Chinese property companies poor candidates for REITs. A significant discount on property valuation may be necessary to lure the REIT investors, but this is not an attractive option for property developers. Therefore, currently, REIT investment in China is a pure capital appreciation or speculation play, with limited funds interested to invest in this sector.

From a taxation standpoint, REITs should include additional tax credits or exemptions to attract investors. Apart from corporate tax, Chinese property developers pay land appreciation tax on taxable gains of 30–60% and real estate withholding tax of 12%. For potential REIT buyers, institutional investors do not pay tax on dividends, but are required to pay 25% capital gains tax if they sell their stake. For retail investors, dividends from the REITs will be counted into personal income tax, which has an upper bracket of 45% for individuals making over RMB 80,000 a month (or the equivalent of USD 11,251). China's high tax burden on asset owners and investors is also a key reason why the REIT sector has not flourished. REIT managers and professionals are essential in the operations of a REIT, as they actively manage the properties to maintain high occupancy rates, achieve strong rental growth, and maximize the net income. REIT manager works closely with the property managers to drive organic growth and build strong relationship with tenants as well as seek property enhancement opportunities. However, in China, currently there is a lack of the needed talent to perform either REIT or highly professionalized property management. Despite their higher returns and ability to offer diversified asset classes, REITs are often too opaque for retail investors to understand. In addition, since capital gains from the stock market are tax-free while dividends from REITs are incorporated into the personal income tax, Chinese investors are more likely to opt for short-term trades and gains. The lack of investment-grade stock looks set to remain a fundamental problem, largely due to market mentality. Even if asset owners are willing to securitize their properties and sell the REIT overseas, China's stringent capital flow control would make it hard for the REIT to pay dividends to offshore foreign investors.

5   Conclusion

While China's economic growth is unlikely to reach the double-digits that it had enjoyed for a decade long, a targeted GDP growth of about 6%, if achieved, would still indicate relatively strong property demand for the next few years. However, the days of easy financing or refinancing could be over for the Chinese developers, especially after the US Federal Reserve has tapered off its quantitative easing (QE) programs. China is now focusing more on the policies of deleveraging for the real estate sector. There are limited indications that China would raise interest rates in the near term, but with property prices reaching record highs in 2016 and China's plans to divert the focus away from the real estate sector, the government could roll out new rounds of policies to discourage speculative buying and stabilize the sector. For developers to stay in the game, a combination of traditional financing in the form of bank loans or corporate bonds and alternative financing mechanisms would be required to secure the needed capital and lower funding costs in the future.

Despite China's real estate market recovery and an abundance of liquidity in the market, Chinese developers remain heavily in debt, as they rush into the next cycle of investment by aggressive land bids and property construction. While low interest onshore bonds and other financing mechanisms will alleviate the short-term pain of a stretched balance sheet, in the long run, financial discipline, operational executions, and a well-managed land bank will be the key factors to the recovery of developers' credit profile. Some consolidation from developers can be expected as the market matures. For asset owners such as banks or insurers, alternative financing would allow them to transfer some of the risks to investors while at the same time free up cash flows for other investments.

CMBS and other forms of asset securitization have become popular options among developers in the past 2 years, as it is an efficient method of financing and unlocks asset values. China is still in the early stages of CMBS issuance, with only a handful of issuances a year valued at less than RMB 20 billion (or about USD 2.81 billion), which is a fraction compared to the US market. Given China's market size of real estate, developers' urge to access cheaper and easier financing, and growing demand from domestic institutions, CMBS issuance and demand should grow significantly in China in the next few years. Among all the possible financing mechanisms via capital markets for developers in China, REIT is attractive and could still be a solution. Across Asia, REITs are still a new asset class, with only Japan, Singapore, Hong Kong, and Taiwan of the Greater China area having an established REIT market. Despite continuous discussions since 2010, China mainland has yet to have a REIT product, as legal and procedural hurdles are preventing REITs from taking off. The market for REITs is evidently there, as Chinese investors lack investment channels offering them a variety of choices. While China's stock market is a hot topic in the past 3 years, the market volatility is often too high for most investors seeking a long-term steady income.

From the perspective of developers and asset owners, REITs could also be a solution to lower debt leverage and secure long-term funding. However, in China, most developments have been built with the primary aim of sales, and this build and strata-sell approach is a considerable hurdle for REIT development in China. Even for developers or asset owners that are willing to develop investment-grade properties, the urgent need to see immediate returns to recover high land costs and financing costs will deter them from doing so. Despite the hurdles, with government relaxations and a different mindset from investors, developers, and asset owners, REITs could be the solution in the long run, as they offer stability, return, and diversification that no other asset classes could mimic.

The Development of REIT Markets in Greater China

Bing Zhu

Abstract

This chapter provides an overview of the development of real estate investment trusts (REITs) in Greater China. Prior to 2015, there was no established REIT market in Mainland China. However, since the Chinese regulators approved the mainland's first REIT investment structure in June 2015, it has been open to selected institutional investors. An alternative way for private individuals and other small-scale investors to gain exposure to specific Chinese real estate assets is through offshore RMB-REITs. This chapter considers the regulatory structure of REITs with a focus on Hong Kong and Taiwan. It also analyzes the current performance of offshore RMB-REITs, Hong Kong and Taiwan REITs, and summarizes the opportunities for and current obstacles to the development of REITs in China.

1 Introduction

Real estate investment trusts (REITs) have a long and successful history in the United States and have now become one of the most important indirect property investment vehicles. Asian REIT markets have also been expanding rapidly over the past decade. In November 2000, the first Asian REIT was launched in Japan, and, in July 2002, the first Singapore REIT—CapitaMall Trust—went public. Taiwan saw its first successful REIT launch in March 2005. Furthermore, after some initial legal difficulties, in November 2005, Hong Kong launched its first REIT—the Link— which, at the time, was also the largest REIT IPO (initial public offering) in the world.

B. Zhu (✉)
Technische Universität München, München, Germany

© Springer Nature Switzerland AG 2021
B. Wang, T. Just (eds.), *Understanding China's Real Estate Markets*, Management
for Professionals, https://doi.org/10.1007/978-3-030-49032-4_15

In 2003, Fortune REIT became the first portfolio of Hong Kong assets to be listed on the Singapore Exchange as a REIT. In 2005, the launch of Link REIT led to the rise of REIT listings on the Hong Kong market, and HK-REITs experienced particularly steep growth during the 2005–2007 periods. Subsequently, due to the global financial crisis that originated from the US real estate market, the growth of HK-REITs slowed down. However, after the crisis, the HK-REIT market recovered strongly and resumed its rapid expansion. As Fig. 1 shows, the number of listed HK-REITs rose to 12 in 2018. The sector's market capitalization also increased, from USD51 million in 2003 to over USD30 billion in 2018. During the financial crisis, the market capitalization decreased slightly, but it recovered and ultimately doubled from 2009 to 2018.

In Taiwan, Fubon No. 1 was the first local REIT, established in March 2003 and listed on the Taiwanese Stock Exchange in July 2006. Compared to HK-REITs, TW-REITs have not been overly active, and there have only been three to date. Their market capitalization did not expand as rapidly as in Hong Kong, growing by only 14% (from USD1.2 billion to USD1.4 billion). In fact, overall, the growth prospects for TW-REITs remain somewhat limited because of their closed-end structure.

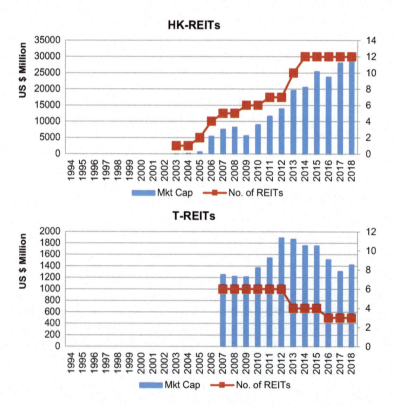

Fig. 1 Market evolution of HK-REITs and TW-REITs. Source: Authors' calculations based on data from the SNL database and datastream

Prior to June 2015, there was no established REIT market in Mainland China. Since the Chinese regulators approved the mainland's first REIT investment structure, it has been open to selected institutional investors. On July 26, 2015, the first Chinese REITs (C-REITs) went public on the Shenzhen Exchange. However, the legal framework for C-REITs is still in its infancy.

As an alternative, retail investors can choose offshore RMB-REITs to hold Chinese real estate assets. Such REITs allow private individuals and other small-scale investors to gain exposure to specific Chinese real estate assets such as shopping centers and office buildings. The listing of Hui Xian REIT in April 2011 was a significant step toward the development of the RMB-REIT market. All of its investment properties are located in Mainland China, including the Beijing Oriental Plaza Hotel and the Sheraton Shenyang Lido Hotel. As shown in Fig. 2, in 2018, the number of offshore REITs with exposure to Chinese (Mainland) real estate markets rose to 5, and the total market capitalization rose to over USD10 billion. With the rapid expansion of the Chinese (Mainland) real estate market, offshore RMB-REITs become a serious alternative for private investors wishing to invest in the Chinese real estate market.

Listed real estate operating companies (REOCs) provide further access to the real estate market in Mainland China. Most of them are listed in Hong Kong exchange. Different from REITs, REOCs are not exempted from corporate tax but are also not be subjected to rules and restrictions applied to REITs. Since 2005, Chinese REOCs developed rapidly. In 2018, the total number of Chinese REOCs rose from 2 to 35, with a total market capitalization of USD5 billion (Fig. 3). The remainder of this chapter is organized as follows. Section 2 introduces the regulatory structure of REITs, with a focus on Hong Kong and Taiwan, while Sect. 3 summarizes their performances so far. Section 4 concludes the chapter.

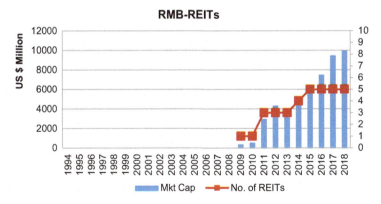

Fig. 2 Market evolution of offshore RMB-REITs. Source: Authors' calculations based on data from the SNL database and datastream

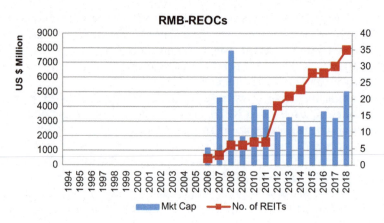

Fig. 3 Market evolution of offshore RMB-REOCs. Source: Authors' calculations based on data from the SNL database and datastream

2   Regulatory Structure

Table 1 provides a summary of two REIT structures. While the legal frameworks for REITs vary across the markets in Asia, they are nevertheless converging toward a generally less restrictive system.

2.1   Mainland China

Until now, there has been no legal framework for REITs in Mainland China. The first attempt to implement a Chinese REIT regime was in 2004. The China Banking Regulatory Commission (CBRC) issued a consultation draft governing companies that engage in REITs, but the program was abandoned in 2007. In 2008, the Chinese government reconsidered introducing REITs, and a number of listed companies submitted applications to the State Council for approval. In 2015, the first C-REIT (Penghua Qianhai Vanke REIT Closed-End Hybrid Securities Investment Fund) was listed on the Shenzhen Exchange. It is China's first public real estate investment fund. However, different from a standard REIT securitization product which invests directly in real estate by means of property or mortgage loans, 50% of the assets of Penghua Qianhai Vanke REIT Closed-End Hybrid Securities Investment Fund were used to purchase the equity of target companies and the other half invested in the shares, bonds, and money market instruments of listed companies (Zhang and Yuan 2016). Thus, it is not a standard REIT. In terms of tax incentives, it is not exempted from double taxation. In other words, both the company and the individual investor are still obliged to pay tax and cannot be exempted because of transmission.

Table 1 HK-REIT and TW-REIT legislation overview

	HK-REITs	TW-REITs
Year introduced	Aug-03	Jul-03
First REIT established	Nov-05	Mar-05
Structure	Unit trust	Trust (real estate asset trust or investment trust)
Management structure	Internal/external	Internal/external
% invested in real estate	Over 90%, mainly invest in real estate	75%, cash, government bonds, property, property-related rights, beneficiary securities, or ABS issued under Real Estate Securitization Act/Financial Asset Securitization Act must be at least 75% of NAV
Geographical restrictions	No	No restrictions under RESA, but subject to approval
Other restrictions	Minimum 2-year holding period	Single property not allowed
Property development	Generally prohibited, but HK-REITs may acquire uncompleted units as long as they comprise less than 10% of NAV	Allowed for urban renewal, infrastructure, or public amenities construction; investments must not exceed 15% of asset value
Foreign development	No	No
Asset valuation frequency	Annually	Every 3 years
Gearing limit	45% of the total gross asset value	35%
Leverage	Capped at 45% of gross asset value	Equal to or less than 10% of NAV
Minimum initial capital	No	US$10 million to US$60 million
Payout	At least 90% of the annual net income after tax	At least 90% of distributable income
Tax treatment at the REIT level	Income tax: HK-REITs are subject to property tax for property held directly. Dividend income from SPVs is exempted from profit taxes. No capital gains tax	Income tax is exempted at the fund level. Income generated by trust is treated as "interest income"
Tax treatment at the shareholder level	Investors receive tax credits that can be used against personal income tax obligations. No withholding tax	Income tax for dividends paid to unitholders. 10% withholding tax for domestic unitholders; 15% for foreign unitholders

Sources: Linklaters (2004), Pham (2014), and APREA (2014)

Apart from that, investors can launch overseas REITs with a geographic focus on Mainland China. There are two mainstream channels: (1) in the form of a joint stock limited company or a limited liability company and (2) in the form of a mature overseas real estate investment trust management company. However, both conflict with existing Chinese legislation. For example, Chinese company law regulation stipulates that a firm's external investment shall not exceed 50% of its net assets. This would limit a joint stock company wishing to acquire new real estate projects (Zhang and Yuan 2016). If investors choose to issue REITs in the form of a mature overseas real estate investment trust management company, a potential conflict with the Securities Investment Fund Law may arise, as the Securities Investment Fund Laws state that the fund supervisors "shall not mix their existing assets or a third party's assets with fund assets as their securities investment" (Zhang and Yuan 2016). Accordingly, legal and procedural hurdles prevent a significant growth of the C-REIT sector.

2.2 Hong Kong

On July 30, 2003, the Securities and Futures Commission ("SFC") published the Hong Kong Code on REITs (the "Code"), which allows both unit trusts and mutual funds to invest in real estate.

Structure of HK-REITs
The Code permits HK-REITs to acquire and hold properties in two primary ways:

1. Direct ownership of real estate assets via REITs. When a HK-REIT directly acquires and holds real estate assets, the unitholders subscribe for units in an initial public offering and receive income/capital from the HK-REIT in return. As Fig. 4a illustrates, the management company, trustee, and property manager are employed by the HK-REIT (Linklaters 2004).
2. Ownership of real estate assets via a special-purpose vehicle (SPV). When a HK-REIT acquires and holds real estate assets through an SPV, the unitholders subscribe for units in an initial public offering and receive income/capital from the HK-REIT in return. However, in contrast to REITs, in this case, the property manager is employed by the SPV (although the management company and trustee are employed by the HK-REIT) (Linklaters 2004). Shares in the SPV are wholly owned by the REIT, and the REIT receives all dividends paid by the SPV. Figure 4b illustrates how a listed HK-REIT is typically structured.

A)

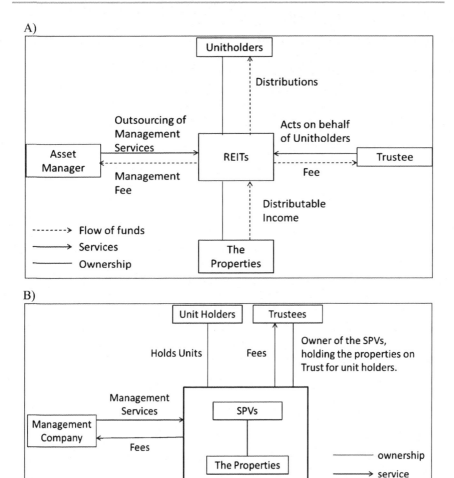

B)

Fig. 4 Typical structure of a listed HK-REIT. (**a**) Direct ownership. (**b**) Ownership through special-purpose vehicles. Sources: Pham (2014), Linklaters (2006)

Permissible Investments

The Code contains a list of investment restrictions, including the following (Linklaters 2004):

1. HK-REITs are generally permitted to invest only in an income-generating real estate. A non-income-generating real estate must constitute less than 10% of the total net asset value.
2. HK-REITs are prohibited from investing in vacant land and from engaging in property development activities, except for refurbishment, retrofitting, and renovation.

3. HK-REITs are only permitted to acquire limited-liability assets.
4. HK-REITs are subject to a minimum asset holding period of 2 years.

Mandatory Outsourcing of Operations and Conflicts of Interest

According to the Code, HK-REITs must be structured in the form of a trust, with a trustee appointed by the HK-REIT. Trustees must be functionally independent of HK-REIT management, in order to ensure they will act in the best interest of unitholders. According to Linklaters (2004), examples of suitable trustees are as follows: (1) Banks licensed under Section 16 of the Hong Kong Banking Ordinance, (2) Trust companies that are subsidiaries of such banks, and (3) Banking institutions or trust companies incorporated outside Hong Kong that are otherwise acceptable to the SFC.

The management company of the HK-REIT must be licensed under Part V of the Securities and Futures Ordinance and specifically approved by the SFC to manage the HK-REIT. HK-REITs should also employ at least two responsible officers with track records of at least 5 years managing collective investment schemes. Key managers should be professionally qualified to manage real estate [e.g., approved by the Hong Kong Institute of Surveyors (HKIS) or the Royal Institution of Chartered Surveyors (RICS)] and should also have at least 5 years' experience. In order to fully develop HK-REIT management expertise, the Code permits overseas REIT managers to be considered. Furthermore, the Code also requires that party transactions be approved by unitholders through an ordinary resolution at an extraordinary general meeting (EGM) (unless the total transaction value is less than 5% of the latest net asset value of the REIT, as disclosed in the most recent published audited reports).

Minimum Initial Capital

There is no minimum initial capital requirement for HK-REITs.

Gearing Limits

The Code restricts the borrowing of an HK-REIT (either directly or through its SPV) to less than 45% of its total gross asset value.

Taxation

HK-REITs are not granted any preferential tax treatment and are taxed according to the same principles as ordinary companies. This does not imply they are taxed twice in Hong Kong, however, because Hong Kong employs an imputation tax system, rather than a double one. This means that, although income is taxed at the firm level, individual shareholders can obtain tax credits to offset their personal income tax. Thus, tax transparency is not as important as it would be in, for example, a double taxation system such as the United States. However, in contrast to other stock types, HK-REITs that own properties directly (the primary type of structure) do not provide any additional tax benefits for investors. Holding real estate through an SPV provides tax advantages at the trust level. In such a structure, the HK-REIT may pay a profits tax, as opposed to a property tax if the HK-REIT owns the real estate directly. The HK-REIT may be able to deduct many of its expenses against its profits, including debt interest payments and management fees. Moreover, under existing Hong Kong tax rules, individual investors are not subject to capital gains or dividend income taxes.

2.3   Taiwan

Initially announced on December 13, 2001, and finally passed on July 9, 2003, the securitization of real estate property bill (the "Securitization Bill") in Taiwan enabled the real estate statute (the "Statute"), which was implemented on July 23, 2003. The Statute permits the establishment of special-purpose trusts ("SPTs"), which can issue securities backed by underlying real estate assets. Prior to the Statute, the Financial Assets Securitization Statute (the "Securitization Statute") was passed on June 21, 2002, and implemented on July 24, 2002. The Securitization Statute permits securities backed by underlying financial assets to be issued by special-purpose companies and SPTs.

Structuring SPTs
SPTs in Taiwan can be either open- or closed-ended, and listing on the Taiwan Stock Exchange is optional. Two types of SPTs are permitted: REITs and real estate asset trusts ("REATs"), described as follows: (1) REITs are based on the US model and enable SPTs to raise funds from investors and invest in real estate and related assets. In return, investors receive beneficiary certificates representing their interests in the trust assets and (2) REATs, in contrast, are based on the Japanese model and enable SPTs to acquire real estate and related assets from their proprietary owners. REATs also issue beneficiary certificates to investors, thus representing their interests in the trust assets. Figure 5 illustrates the structure of T-REATs.

Permissible Investments
SPTs in Taiwan are permitted to invest in real estate (including real estate in the process of development); rights relating to real estate, such as mortgages; the securities of companies engaged in real estate activity; and certain other investments, as allowed by the Ministry of Finance in Taiwan. Single property holding is not allowed. The investment properties must constitute diversified portfolios.

Mandatory Outsourcing of Operations and Conflict of Interest
The Statute does not mandate any specific provisions with regard to the asset management or administrative functions of the SPT. However, SPTs should be managed by a trustee or a custodian.

Minimum Initial Capital
Depending on the business scope, the minimum initial capital ranges from USD10 million to USD60 million. The minimum paid-in capital for a trust company engaging only in REIT business is USD10 million. The minimum paid-in capital for a TW-REIT is USD30 million.

A)

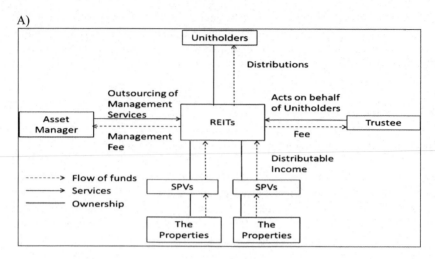

B)

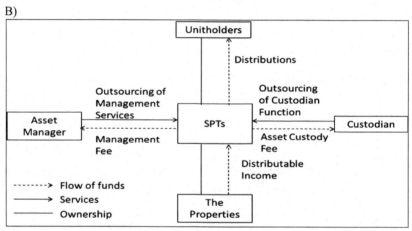

Fig. 5 Typical structure of a listed TW-REIT. (**a**) TW-REITs. (**b**) T-REATs. Source: Pham (2014)

Gearing Limits

The Code restricts the borrowing of a SPT to not more than 35% of the total gross asset value of the scheme.

Taxation

Any dividends paid to investors who purchased beneficiary certificates issued by the SPT are subject to income tax, with domestic unitholders taxed at 10% and foreign unitholders at 15%. The SPT is also subject to income, land, and housing taxes. However, investors and SPTs are exempted from securities transaction taxes when the beneficiary certificates are traded.

3   Performance of REITs in China

Although Mainland China does not have its own REIT market, offshore RMB-REITs enable retail investors to effectively access China's real estate portfolios via the Hong Kong, Taiwan, and Singapore markets, and the markets have performed well. Revisions to the HK-REIT Code in 2005 eased the geographic limitations on assets held in HK-REITs, which helped foster cross-border deals. An increasing number of REITs now hold Chinese assets. Table 2 reports the main RMB-dominated REITs which focus on the real estate markets in Mainland China. RMB-REITs have spanned many real estate asset classes, including retail (one REIT), office (one), hotels (two), and diversified (two). The diversified REIT has the largest total market capitalization at close to 47%, followed by retail and hotel.

The RMB-REIT Hui Xian was the third largest RMB-REIT in Hong Kong, ranking as 11th in Asia in 2015 (Zhang and Yuan 2016). Its primary purpose is providing direct exposure to rental growth in Mainland China through the listed securities market. Hui Xian REIT originally focused on the Beijing real estate, but has since diversified to other geographical areas like Shenyang. It is a hybrid REIT that has properties across various sectors, including offices, serviced apartments, retail properties, and hotels. Hui Xian REIT is actively managed by implementing asset-enhancement initiatives to unlock more profits from its existing portfolios and yield-accretive acquisitions. Jinmao (China) is another HK-REIT that focuses on property in Mainland China. It was the fourth largest REIT in Hong Kong in 2015 (Zhang and Yuan 2016), with a market capitalization of USD4.4 billion in 2018. Its underlying properties include seven hotels located in Lijiang, Pudong, and several other cities throughout China. Yuexiu REIT is also a RMB-dominated REIT listed in Hong Kong. It has a market capitalization of USD1.7 billion and also covers several sectors including offices, retail properties, and hotels. CapitaLand Retail China Trust (CRCT) is the first REIT in Singapore consisting of Chinese assets. The underlying assets initially consisted of seven shopping centers in Beijing, Zhengzhou, Huhehaote, Anhui, and Shanghai. According to Zhang and Yuan (2016), CapitaLand Retail China Trust ranks as the 28th largest REIT in Asia in 2015.

Table 2 Profiles of listed RMB-REITs as of year-end 2018

REIT name	Listed date	Issuance place	Property sector	Market cap	No. of properties	Asian rank in 2015
Hui Xian REIT	Apr-11	HKex	Diversified	2295	7	11
CapitaLand Retail China Trust	Dec-06	SGX	Retail	934	7	28
Jinmao (China) investments	Jun-14	HKex	Hotel	4464	7	–
Yuexiu REIT	Dec-05	HKex	Diversified	1711	6	35
Spring	Dec-13	HKex	Office	525	2	–
Total				9931	29	

Source: Authors' calculations based on data from the SNL database. Ranking is from Zhang and Yuan (2016)

The non-RMB-REITs include HK-REITs and TW-REITs. By the end of 2018, the Hong Kong REIT market was the third largest in Asia, after Japan and Singapore, with a total market capitalization of USD26 billion (see Table 3). HK-REITs have spanned many real estate asset classes, including retail (one REIT), office (one), hotels (one), lodging (one), and diversified (two). The retail REIT has the largest total market capitalization at close to 73%, followed by office (14%) and diversified (6%). Among the 12 HK-REITs (4 of them are RMB-dominated REITs), Link REIT is the largest in Hong Kong and Asia, with a market capitalization of USD18 billion in 2018. Its portfolio consists of 131 properties with an internal floor area of over 11 million square feet of retail space.

Regarding Taiwan REITs, the breakdown by real estate asset class shows that all Taiwan REITs are diversified REITs. There are three currently listed TW-REITs with USD2.1 billion total market capitalization, which accounts for 1.2% of the Asian REIT market. As shown in Table 3, all the currently listed TW-REITs were launched before 2007, and all have relatively small capitalizations, averaging USD472 million and holding from three to six properties. Unlike open-end funds, which can tap additional investor funds by issuing more shares, Taiwan's REITs have a closed-end structure. Thus, secondary offerings are not permitted, even if they locate additional new investment opportunities. As a result, their growth prospects are relatively restricted.

Table 3 Profiles of listed non-RMB-REITs as of year-end 2018

REIT name	Listed date	Property sector	Market cap	No. of properties	Asian rank in 2015
Hong Kong					
Link REIT	Nov-05	Retail	18,007	131	1
Champion REIT	May-06	Office	3918	2	8
Langham Hospitality Investment Trust	May-13	Hotel	765	3	45
Sunlight REIT	Dec-06	Diversified	1115	16	54
Regal REIT	Nov-05	Lodging	908	9	57
Prosperity REIT	Dec-05	Diversified	557	7	78
Taiwan					
Cathay No. 1 REIT	Jul-06	Diversified	629	6	41
Shin Kong No. 1 REIT	Jul-06	Diversified	522	6	56
Fubon No. 1 REIT	Jul-06	Diversified	264	3	76
Total			26,685	183	

Source: Authors' calculations based on data from the SNL database. Ranking is from Zhang and Yuan (2016)

3.1   REIT Performance

Table 4 shows the performance of RMB-REITs,[1] HK-REITs, and TW-REITs based on cross-sectional and time series REIT data. US- and European REIT performance (including the United Kingdom) are also reported for comparison purposes. Note that from 2006 to 2015, average annual total RMB-REIT returns, HK-REIT returns, and TW-REIT returns were 9.7%, 14.27%, and 8.22%, respectively, while the annualized returns of their stock markets were only 7.5% and 6.41%, respectively. Moreover, the REIT stocks also exhibited less volatility than general stocks in the two regions, with a slightly lower standard deviation. Although HK- and TW-REITs have lower dividend yields than US- and European REITs, the RMB-REITs provide investors with a higher dividend yield.

The superior performance of REITs in the Greater China area than US- and European REITs was quite obvious during the global financial crisis (GFC). The US real estate market crash was regarded as the root of the crisis; Asian real estate markets, especially in China, were not seriously affected. In contrast to US- and European REITs, which exhibited negative annualized returns amounting to over −15%, REITs in China remained quite stable. Although REITs are listed on stock exchanges, the majority of their income derives from the performance of their underlying real estate assets. Because these are fixed in location and less liquid than the general market, real estate markets tend to be less vulnerable than stock markets to any international contagion effects.

The divergent performance between REITs and other equities in Hong Kong and Taiwan during the 2006–2016 periods, especially during the GFC, implies that investing in HK- and TW-REITs can provide diversification benefits to investors. The correlation coefficients of REITs and their respective equity markets range from 0.39 to 0.52, much lower than those in Europe and the United States. One reason for this finding could be that the performance of HK- and TW-REITs is determined largely by the value of their underlying assets, and therefore, they are less affected in general by shocks to the stock market. Thus, REITs in Hong Kong and Taiwan can serve as suitable alternatives to equity investments.

This conclusion can be confirmed further by using the Capital Asset Pricing Model (CAPM) analysis. The alpha in CAPM measures the unpredictable part of REIT returns that cannot be explained by general equity market returns; the beta shows the sensitivity to risks in the equity market. HK-REITs yielded a significantly positive alpha during the 2006–2016 periods, which indicates that HK-REITs exhibit a superior performance over equities. Furthermore, RMB-, HK-, and TW-REITs are much less vulnerable to general stock market risks than European or US-REITs. During the GFC, HK-REITs even exhibited an insignificant beta, which implies they are essentially immune to downside risk in the equity market.

---

[1]In this section, RMB-REITs only include RMB-REITs listed on the Hong Kong stock exchange. The comparison with the local equity market refers to a comparison with the Hong Kong stock market.

Table 4 Performance of RMB-REITs, HK-REITs, and TW-REITs from January

	RMB-REIT	HK-REIT	TW-REIT	E-REIT	US-REIT
Overall period (January 2006 through December 2015)					
REIT annualized returns	9.7%	14.27%	8.22%	0.23%	6.34%
Equity market annualized returns	7.5%	7.5%	6.41%	4.32%	7.32%
Standard deviation of REIT stocks	7.5%	5.71%	4.32%	7.69%	9.56%
Standard deviation of equity	6.7%	6.7%	5.67%	6.43%	5.19%
Yield	5.49	3.90	3.67	4.04	4.24
Correlation with equity market	0.48	0.39	0.52	0.81	0.81
Correlation with US-REIT returns	0.07	0.22	0.46	0.77	–
Alpha of REIT stocks	0.0044	0.0093*	0.0043	−0.0033	−0.0023
Beta of REIT stocks	0.596***	0.338***	0.398***	0.973***	1.45***
Crisis period (January 2008 through December 2009)					
REIT annualized returns	4.20%	11.12%	10.9%	−17.34%	−18.9%
Equity market annualized returns	8.76%	8.76%	3.62%	−3.30%	−5.47%
Standard deviation of REIT stocks	11.20%	6.83%	3.51%	10.45%	15.78%
Standard deviation of equity	9.29%	9.29%	8.32%	8.68%	7.23%
Yield	6.62	4.30	4.38	5.33	5.20
Correlation with equity market	0.73	0.23	0.64	0.83	0.88
Correlation with US-REIT returns	0.38	0.07	0.60	0.85	–
Alpha of REIT stocks	0.0052	0.0081	0.0011	−0.011	−0.0070
Beta of REIT stocks	0.637***	0.163	0.434***	1.00***	1.93***

Source: Authors' calculations based on data from datastream
Note: Alpha of REIT stock and beta of REIT stock are based on the CAPM model and compare the performance of REIT stock and general stock. RMB-REITs only include RMB-REITs listed in Hong Kong. The comparison of RMB-REITs with the local equity market refers to the comparison with RMB-HK-REITs and Hong Kong stock index
***, **, and * stand for the estimated alpha or beta which is significant at the 10%, 5%, and 1% levels

Investing in Asian REITs can also help international investors diversify away risk in the international REIT markets. The correlation between RMB-REITs and US-REITs was only 7% over the period from 2006 to 2015. The correlation coefficients of HK- and US-REIT returns were less than 30% from 2006 to 2015 and were only 7% during the GFC. The correlation coefficients of TW-REIT and

US-REIT returns were higher, amounting to 46%, but were still lower than European REITs, which exhibited a 77% correlation with US-REITs. During the GFC, this correlation dropped to 7%, while that between European and US-REITs rose to 85%. Thus, REITs in China could provide diversification benefits for international investors.

3.2   REITs in Mainland China

The emergence of REITs in Asia provides investors with opportunities in professionally managed real estate portfolios that feature attractive dividend yields. The introduction of REITs would inject much-needed liquidity and capital, so as to bring the real estate sector back to life. On the supply side, REITs offer an attractive method for corporate real estate owners to divest their noncore real estate assets. Besides, for developers holding many high-quality properties, REITs can also be an ideal exit mechanism. Through securitization, shares in a project are converted to cash, so as to ease financial pressure for development in new developments, at the same time retaining control of the developed property. REITs are also used by the government to divest its assets. For example, in Hong Kong, REITs have provided a divestment of publicly owned assets that allowed the government to contain its fiscal deficit. This was particularly helpful for the Hong Kong government, because revenue from land sales and property transactions has dwindled since 1997.

On the demand side, REITs are characterized by high dividend yields with prospects for long-term capital growth. Therefore, REITs offer a defensive position in the volatile equity market while complementing other investment products. Increased liquidity, stricter corporate governance, and greater transparency make REITs appealing to international investors who are interested in institutional-grade real estate, but find direct ownership of these properties problematic. REITs provide an attractive opportunity to own, albeit a small stake, in a landmark property, a prospect that is appealing to many retail investors in Hong Kong, Taiwan, and even Mainland China. In addition, REITs are also attractive to institutional investors such as insurance companies and pension funds. REIT products have a higher liquidity than direct real estate property investments and can thus help investors diversify their investment risks by offering them different investment channels in real estate (Zhang and Yuan 2016).

The main obstacle to investing REITs in Mainland China is the lack of a clear legal status for REITs. Without a specific legislation for REITs, it does not make much sense to regulate and manage the structure of assets, sources of income, profit distribution, and taxation policies. Thus, the establishment and support of the corresponding laws and regulations have been vital to the development of REITs in mature markets. Investing in offshore RMB-REITs has become a serious alternative for private individuals and other small-scale investors wishing to gain exposure to specific Chinese real estate assets. However, these products may contain many additional risks, due to differing accounting standards and tax systems. Differences in accounting standards between Mainland China and foreign markets may lead to lower distributable profits. Also, the profits to be made from the underlying property holding vehicle in China are determined in accordance with Chinese accounting standards, which differ from those estimated using Hong Kong or international financial reporting standards. The complexity of the tax system in Mainland China can mean that different real estate projects, or the same project in a different period, are subject to different taxes and rates. This may affect the estimation of dividends for offshore RMB-REITs. The implementation of the enterprise income tax reform in 2008 means that offshore RMB-REITs are subject to turnover taxes (value-added tax) and a land value appreciation tax. The concurrent rise in regulations governing the conditions for tax treaty benefits will significantly influence the future income of offshore RMB-REIT investors (Deloitte 2013).

4   Conclusion

Real estate investment trusts (REITs) provide a valuable investment alternative for real estate investors. They help improve the liquidity and the efficiency of the real estate market, as well as the corporate governance of real estate organizations. In a multi-asset portfolio, REITs can also serve to reduce investors' overall level of risk. Hence, REITs have become increasingly popular among investors, banks, and financial institutions.

Thus far, Asian REITs have enjoyed relatively rapid development. However, direct investing in real estate via the vehicle of REITs is still prohibited in Mainland China. In Hong Kong and Taiwan, although REITs have developed steadily, they still lag behind those of Japan and Singapore. In Hong Kong, due to the high levels of restrictions and the lack of tax transparency, HK-REITs are facing a much tougher operating environment than in regional markets such as Singapore and Malaysia. Therefore, Hong Kong and Taiwan should aim to strengthen their advantages in view of the rapid growth of wealth that both countries are experiencing, as well as the compelling need for investment products to cater for the growing retirement savings market. In Mainland China, gaining vital support from the governing authority for a less restrictive REIT regime, with favorable tax transparency status, would play a central role.

Overall, the opportunities for further development of the REIT market in mainland China are significant. Since the beginning of the twenty-first century, the real estate industry has been the most important sector in China. With the development of asset securitization, the huge potential of the real estate market will no doubt attract investors to join in this market.

References

APREA. (2014). *Asian Pacific REITs: A comparative regulatory & tax study*. Accessed January 19, 2017, from http://www.aprea.asia/file/Asia%20Pacific%20REITs%20-%20a%20comparative%20regulatory%20&%20tax%20study.pdf.

Deloitte. (2013). *China Real Estate Investment Handbook – The details that make a difference.* Deloitte Report. Accessed January 19, 2017, from https://www2.deloitte.com/content/dam/Deloitte/cn/Documents/real-estate/deloitte-cn-re-realestate-investment-handbook-2013-en-250713.pdf.

FSDC. (2014). *Developing Hong Kong as a capital formation centre for real estate investment trusts.*

Linklaters. (2004). *REITs in Asia.* Accessed January 19, 2017, from www.linklaters.com/pdfs/Insights/REITs_part1.pdf.

Linklaters. (2006). *Executing REITs in Hong Kong.* Accessed January 19, 2017, from http://www.linklaters.com/Insights/Publication1481TechnicalBulletin/Pages/Index.aspx.

Ong, S. E., Ooi, J. T. L., & Sing, T. F. (2000). Asset securitization in Singapore: A tale of three vehicles. *Real Estate Finance, 17*, 47–56.

Ooi, J. T. L., Newell, G., & Sing, T. F. (2006). The growth of REIT markets in Asia. *Journal of Real Estate Literature, 14*, 203–222.

Pham, A. K. (2014). *The development of REIT markets in Asia.* Working Paper.

Zhang, S., & Yuan, S. (2016). *REITs in China: Opportunities and challenges.* RICS Research Report. Accessed January 19, 2017, from http://www.rics.org/de/knowledge/research/research-reports/reits-in-china-opportunities-and-challenges-/.

Real Estate Private Equity Investing in China: From a Practitioner's Perspective

Christina Gaw

Abstract

Being the second largest economy in the world, China is a complicated assemblage of many different sub-markets. For investors, it is essential to be on-the-ground in China or have a team with similar capacity in order to fully comprehend the investment opportunities and be successful. This chapter highlights insights and observations by a private equity real estate fund management team in its 20 plus years of on-the-ground real estate investing experience. Some of these experiences include revitalizing neighborhoods and not just focusing on buildings, forming an in-house team from the ground up, and nimbly and creatively bringing together best practices from both west and east to make it work. These observations are informed by actual investment projects, three of which are presented as case studies. Based on experience and observations, seven "immutable" principles are suggested, from a practitioner's perspective, for succeeding in China's real estate industry.

1 Introduction: Passion, Responsibility, and Creativity

Investors can't help but notice two kinds of news coming out of China these days. One tells a story of near-panic-driven stock market declines, a falling currency, high and rising debt levels, and a rapid slowdown in growth—all adding up to evidence of a so-called hard landing for the world's second-largest economy. The other type of news portrays a confident, rising superpower that is setting up institutions to rival the World Bank and the International Monetary Fund, a country whose companies are embarking on a record-breaking spree of

C. Gaw (✉)
Gaw Capital Partners, Hong Kong, PR China

© Springer Nature Switzerland AG 2021   221
B. Wang, T. Just (eds.), *Understanding China's Real Estate Markets*, Management
for Professionals, https://doi.org/10.1007/978-3-030-49032-4_16

offshore acquisitions while its wealthy elite drive up property prices from Manhattan to Mayfair. (Cheng 2016)

Just like what Charles Dickens wrote in *A Tale of Two Cities*: "It was the best of times, it was the worst of times, it was the age of wisdom, it was the age of foolishness...," the years of 2016–2018 were a fascinating and dynamic time for China, as together they were indeed a time of seeming economic contradictions. The current trade war between the United States and China certainly adds more chaos to the complicated situation. On the one hand, there have been dramatic and nerve-wracking stock market gyrations and concerns about debt while, on the other hand, stability and projections of China's soft power such as the establishment of the Asian Infrastructure Investment Bank (AIIB), the winning of the Beijing 2022 Winter Olympics (the first city to win bids for both a summer and a winter games), and endless headlines of China's outbound acquisitions.

But which narrative is the real China? Is it a country with a tenuous financial situation or is it the world's second largest economy on an unstoppable and unflappable path forward to the top spot? Based on reporting from the international media, it's difficult to know what, in fact, is happening on the ground. This chapter is about private equity investments in China's commercial real estate industry and the immutable learned rules for how to be successful in China's real estate market by an experienced team. It can be regarded as a case study of how one company, in this case, Gaw Capital Partners, the author's firm has been able to leverage the recent volatility and apply knowledge and "ground game" in order to be successful.

2   China's Economic and Real Estate Dynamics

Even with the "China confusion," China's economy remains strong. China is poised to serve as President of the Group of 20 in 2016, has a GDP of USD 14.2 trillion, and is leading across a number of soft power fronts: Mainland China remains a source of growth and strength for the global economy with its global trade totaling USD 4.61 trillion in 2018, the world's largest trading nation. Its prospects are only set to get better as China's GDP is expected to overtake that of the United States in 2026 at the 2030 target growth rate of 6.5%—outpacing the United States' anticipated 2% GDP growth to 2030 (Bloomberg 2016). Even with RMB volatility and as the downturn in the commercial property market goes into its third year, China presents potential. That being said, undeniably there has been a slowdown which is not new—the economy has not grown by more than 8% since 2012.

2.1   Not a Systematic Decline

Quite simply: China is relatively stable and not in a systematic decline. The economy of the country is healthy—even with the current trade war and the "New Normal."[1] However, the media likes to paint it as a slowdown. It takes a firm which is operating in China, has assets in China, and does its own asset management to come up with its own description of on-the-ground reality.

President Xi Jinping is a strong, stable, and centralized leader; some reporters depict him being probably the strongest leader since Deng Xiaoping. The rationale for the optimism toward China is based on the following:

1. While stock market gyrations usually foretell a pending major economic correction or collapse, equities account for only about 9% of household wealth in China, compared to over 30% in the United States.
2. The private sector now accounts for almost 50% of the urban workforce as opposed to that of the state-owned enterprises (SOEs).
3. China's upper middle class (with annual earnings of USD 16,000–34,000) is expected to expand from 14% to 54% of the population between 2012 and 2022.

China's growth is to be in the medium to longer term. Volatility in the short term is always something that one can't predict minute to minute, but real estate is a physical asset and it is for the long term. We believe the recent volatility of RMB is moving to its equilibrium. As currency is a reflection of the economy and balance of trade, from this point of view, China is very healthy. Prices for homes in China have risen on average by 9% every year between 1999 and 2019 and increasing as much as 9.9% year-on-year in 2019.[2] This reflects a strong demand seen across all asset classes in the country.

At the time of the book publishing, we are in the midst of a US-China trade war. However the tactics used in this trade war are not new. The US government has been using them for years on Brazil, India, Russia, Japan, South Korea, Taiwan, and even mainland China before. As the emerging China gaining more muscle, competition between the United States and China is unavoidable. The relationship between the two super powers for sure will have its ups and downs in the years to come.

By looking at the assets under management by Gaw Capital Partners, including commercial office assets, retail assets and outlet malls, the assets of hospitality sector, as well as platform investments in medical, education, and data center, it seems that our reality check for how the domestic economy is doing is indeed different from how most of the western media has been covering it. For example,

---

[1]China's "New Normal" is a political and economic concept espoused by the Chinese leadership to describe expectations of 7% annual GDP growth for the foreseeable future and the need for a new model of economic growth that places less emphasis on investment-led growth and focuses more on consumption, especially domestic consumption.

[2]National Bureau of Statistics of China.

Gaw Capital's retail outlet platform in China, Florentia Village, is experiencing continuous growth of 25% year on year in 2018 compared to the 3.8–4.4% growth of US retail sales overall (Reuters 2019). It is clear that the mindset of China's domestic consumer is confident with a strong domestic labor market and a low unemployment rate of 3.67% in Q1 2019 (Trading Economics 2019), which is helping to pave a solid foundation for President Xi Jinping to continue his reform. Given the unforeseeable outcome at this time with the turbulent trade war, Gaw Capital opted to look for opportunities in the real estate sectors that would be resilient to these global macro-trends that might tend to have short-term volatility but remained focused on sectors that serviced the broader domestic economy. The target thematic platforms include medical, education, data center platforms backed by real estates. These platform investments in the livelihood industries would further tie in the domestic economy and the new technological evolution age and provided stable return with long shelf life. The reality check sustains our position that there is a long-term story to China, a domestic consumption story with the creation of more service sector jobs and beyond just manufacturing labor.

2.2   On-the-Ground in China

On the ground, we as well as our investors see that China today is truly a tale of two economies: Northern China has witnessed the lowest growth rate due to its historical economic conditions, lack of government initiatives, and population structure. The "rust belt" of China (industrial-heavy regions in Northeast China) posted just 4–5.1% GDP growth year on year in 2018 (Xinhuanet 2018). Despite China's debt to GDP ratio increasing from 130% to 297% (from 2008 to 2018), industrial sector contribution to the GDP has decreased from 46% to 40.7%. Credit extended to the state-owned enterprise dominated "old economy" no longer drives GDP growth. On the other hand, the Pan-Beijing, Pan-Shanghai, and Guangdong Province Area (the metropolitan areas of Tier 1 cities) still deliver the highest growth rates. Key Tier 2 economic clusters such as Pan-Wuhan, Pan-Chengdu, and Western China areas have seen the strongest growth, with Tibet ranking first with year-on-year GDP growth in 2016 of 11.7% and Chongqing, which ranked second, seeing 9.1% in 2018 (Xinhuanet 2018). The service sector, requiring far less investment, rose in total GDP contribution from 40% to 52% in 2018.

However, what is interesting is that despite the significant slowdown of the so-called old economies (e.g., mining, steel, cement, factories, construction) which have resulted in the traditional "rust belt" generating only 5% of China's GDP growth, China's new economy (e.g., tourism, services, E-commerce, entertainment) is actually generating strong growth to help take the economy to its 16.1% targeted GDP growth (Xinhuanet 2019), despite starting from a much smaller base. This indicates that China is shifting from a manufacturing, construction, energy and labor-intensive economy into a service, skill-intensive, technology and innovation-driven economy.

China is still fully employed: despite a year-to-year drop in real GDP last peak in the quantitative easing induced peak of 12%, China's labor demand-supply ratio continues to post double-digit imbalance with demand outweighing supply at 28% in Q1 2019 (ceicdata 2019). The private sector now accounts for almost 50% of the urban workforce as opposed to SOEs.

It is likely to be a painful and volatile transformation for China from a fixed asset investment and export-led economy of the past to the domestic consumption and service sector-driven future in the near term; and the murky world economy with the result of the Brexit referendum, Trump as the President of the United States, and the ascendance of trade protectionism are certainly not helping. How the Chinese government is dealing with short-term volatility is critical, but real estate is long term, and one should not be distracted by short-term emotional volatility. While the next 2–3-year outlook may be cloudy, the 5–7-year view should be quite bright. The fact that the views from investors and economists are so divergent also means that opportunities should be more abundant with reduced competition. Gaw Capital's investment philosophy is well presented by Chairman Goodwin Gaw: "I always tell my investors, if you don't believe in China, don't invest. But don't short China. Because if you try to short China, you're going against the government. And the government has way more bullets and way more time than you."

2.3 Main Drivers of China's Real Estate Market

Urbanization and the rising of the middle class have been the key drivers of China's real estate market or rather the economy. In order to decrease the gap between the rich and the poor and increase the stability of the society, the Chinese government has been trying to move the population from the countryside to the cities by creating jobs. Companies like Foxconn[3] are given tax incentives to set up factories in Henan and Sichuan, as examples.

China has been doing the almost unthinkable feat of shifting its people from the countryside to cities—urbanization—in a way no other country has done. China's urban population is now nearly 700 million and is expected to rise to over one billion people in just over a decade. This move from an agriculture-based economy to an urban-driven economy has had the greatest impact on China's real estate market, more than any other factor. As a point of reference, China has had the entire population of the United States move from the countryside and into cities over the past 20 years. This has created a huge boom in what we call Tier 2, Tier 3, and Tier 4 cities, cities with growing populations. According to a McKinsey report: "By

---

[3]Hon Hai Precision Industry Co., Ltd., trading as Foxconn Technology Group, is a Taiwanese multinational electronics contract manufacturing company headquartered in New Taipei City, Taiwan. Foxconn is the world's largest contract electronics manufacturer and the third-largest information technology company by revenue. They are the main manufacturer of Apple.

2025, China will have 221 cities with one million—plus inhabitants—compared with 35 cities of this size in Europe today—and 23 cities with more than five million. For companies in China and around the world, the scale of China's urbanization promises substantial new markets and investment opportunities."

According to McKinsey's report "Mapping China's Middle Class" (Barton et al. 2013): "The explosive growth of China's emerging middle class has brought sweeping economic change and social transformation—and it's not over yet. By 2022, our research suggests, more than 75 percent of China's urban consumers will earn 60,000 to 229,000 RMB (9,000 to 34,000 USD) a year . . . In the decade ahead, the middle class's continued expansion will be powered by labor-market and policy initiatives that push wages up, financial reforms that stimulate employment and income growth, and the rising role of private enterprise, which should encourage productivity and help more income accrue to households. Should all this play out as expected, urban-household income will at least double by 2022."

Here at Gaw Capital, we spotted the trend and have followed the government's direction for our investment strategy since 2007. We invested in mass market residential development in Tier 2 and Tier 3 cities, such as Chengdu and Xuzhou back in 2008, and mass market retail malls and outlet malls from 2011 to 2013. Recently, we put more focus on hotels in the Asia Pacific region as the income level of the middle class in China started to empower them with options to travel abroad. COVID19 however has temporarily suspended tourism. In the years to come, urbanization and consumer behavior of the middle class will continue to be the main direction for our investment strategies in China.

2.4   High Barrier to Market Entry

Despite the opening up of the real estate market to foreign investment over the past decades, there are still regulatory hurdles. China remains top of the high barrier-to-entry market list of Asian real estate investment due to the less transparent real estate regulations. In addition, China's government tends to impose new regulations whenever it needs to "regulate" the market, either to cool it down or stimulate it depending on the economic needs at the time. Therefore, regulations on foreign investment in the property industry can be loosened or tightened overnight. A number of significant restrictions (listed below) were issued on foreign investment in the Chinese real estate market in 2006 and 2007 in order to restrict property speculation and control rapid price appreciation. In the wake of the global financial crisis, Circular 23 was issued in June 2008 to ease up the regulatory environment.

If investors follow the government's direction closely, they can generally navigate how the policies will play out, and having a local team in China to monitor such regulatory changes and review investment strategy regularly is highly essential.

As an example, in 2008, it was difficult for foreigners to set up a real estate QFII (qualified foreign institutional investor) scheme in China due to the tightening up of the market. It was almost impossible for foreigners to invest in Tier 1 cities, so we targeted our investment at Tier 2 and 3 cities where the local governments welcomed us with open arms and helped us to overcome regulatory challenges. The key is again to have team on the ground so you would be able take a pulse of the situation first-handedly.

The following is a brief summary of the key measures forming the regulatory framework governing foreign investments in the Chinese real estate sector based on *China Real Estate Investment Handbook* by Deloitte.[4] The regulations referred to as Circular 171 was released in July 2006 targeted at direct foreign investment and foreign-invested enterprises ("FIE") involved in China's real estate sector. It comprised a range of measures to control the flow of foreign capital, including provisions regulating the purchase of real estate, new minimum capital requirements, restrictions on debt financing, and a number of other measures. Two circulars (Circular 50 and Circular 130) were issued in 2007, aiming to discourage speculative foreign investment in the country's real estate market. The two circulars affected a number of critical areas, including project approval and the requirements necessary to form a project company and project financing. Circular 186 was issued in 2010 to further restrict foreign investment in China's real estate market. The Catalogue of Guidance on Foreign Investment Industries was revised in 2011 and then in 2015. The latest version of the Catalogue (2015 Catalogue) became effective on April 10, 2015. The previous restrictive regulations on land plot development and construction and operation of high-end hotels, office buildings and international exhibition centers, etc. have all been lifted under the 2015 Catalogue and become easier for FIEs to participate.

Holding Structure
Circular 171, effective on January 1, 2008, requires all foreign investors to establish an onshore "commercial presence," i.e., incorporate a FIE (foreign-invested enterprise). For new investments, direct ownership of real property by a foreign investor offshore is no longer possible, though pre-Circular 171 structures can still be found. In China, any one of a number of legal entities can be considered FIEs including equity joint ventures (EJV), cooperative joint ventures (CJV), wholly owned foreign enterprises (WFOE), and foreign-invested companies limited by shares (FCLS).

Project Approval Conditions
Circular 50 imposes that approval to set up a foreign invested real estate company ("RE FIE") will be granted only if the investor has obtained land use rights, or building ownership, or has entered into a sale and purchase agreement to obtain such tights or ownership. Circular 50 also provides the approval of a local MOC office on the establishment of a RE FIE needs to be filled with the national level MOC. Prior to the completion of these approvals, the SAFE and its designated banks will not process any foreign exchange settlement for this FIE.

---

[4]China Real Estate Investment Handbook, Deloitte, June 2013.

Investment Funding

Circular 171 imposed new minimum capital requirements for real estate investments. A RE FIE with a total investment size that equals or exceeds USD 10 million must have a registered capital equal to no less than 50% of its total investment amount, whereas it was possible to maintain a debt-to-equity ratio of up to 2:1 previously.

License and Land Use Rights

A temporary business license of 1-year validity will be issued to a RE FIE upon completion of incorporation. The official business license with a term equivalent to the approved operation period would be issued only after the RE FIE has settled the full payment for the land use right and has obtained the relevant land use right certificate. The maximum tenure for land use rights is determined based on the usage of the land: 70 years for residential use; 50 years for industrial, educational, scientific, etc.; and 40 years for commercial, tourism, and recreational use.

3   Observations: Real Estate Investing in China

By learning from the experience of over 20 years of investing in real estate globally and observing how the economic/real estate cycles play in China and beyond, the principals of Gaw Capital believe that for investors, it is critical to know how to enter and exit the market at the right time, seize the short windows, and ride with the arc of opportunities. Operations are crucial; it's good to talk about investment, but at the end of the day, you need to deliver, and one can only deliver through management. Some companies opt to build their own in-house asset management team which could help to provide cost control over projects—a key competitive advantage that can differentiate them from their peers.

With such asset management operating teams handy on the ground, you can then dare to consider the best time to invest is probably when there is uncertainty and volatility. Uncertainty creates a better entry. Our asset management capacity covering all aspects of the development and management of retail, commercial, and hospitality properties along with residential developments in China allows us to look into investments where heavy asset management is required and most of other competitors shy off.

> Investing cynics may be leery of China's shaky real-estate market but one contrarian institutional real-estate investor is still making aggressive bets. Hong Kong-based private-equity fund manager Gaw Capital Partners is planning to invest more in China's major cities this year, even as the downturn in the commercial property market overall goes into its third year. The firm is on the hunt for underused properties that it can turn into trendy locations for shoppers, office workers and tourists. (Fung 2016)

3.1   Revitalizing Neighborhoods, Not Just Buildings

One investment strategy that was placed into practice for us is to go into areas where there is a transportation link as traffic brings people and people are essential in real estate. Look for buildings and areas that are not yet discovered, mismanaged, up and coming, or an iconic assets/neighborhoods that have lost their previous luster. There are certain areas that used to be very vibrant, and we like to go into these areas in Tier 1 and Tier 2 Chinese cities and revive them. The rule of thumb for China investing is to work with city governments and regional governments and persuade them that the success of your buildings will make their surrounding/community better: not just reviving a building but revitalizing an entire area; that's how one gains their support. Gaw Capital considers and focuses on the direction the entire neighborhood is heading in and what will be needed to facilitate the neighborhood's transformation.

It requires the out-of-the-box vision when planning for repositioning of a building. How not to limit our creativity by the status quo of the building is critical in our operation. We look at the need and development trend as well as potential of the neighborhood and then reference our observation of other similar locations globally before coming up with a new concept. As a result, we tend to revive and revitalize not only the acquired buildings but the entire communities surrounding them; Plaza 353 in discussion below illustrates this point.

3.2   East-West Connectivity

Same as all international firms operating in China, we try to stay slightly ahead of the market with our creative concepts, and we also bring in a lot of new practices into our investments in China. However we need to be mindful as China plays by its own rules; we need to apply the values and experience learned in western markets but tailored for the east. Gaw Capital's focus on east-west connectivity and east-west positioning has benefitted the firm greatly. To be successful in China, a real estate firm needs to improvise, to be able to draw from western experiences while at the same time be nimble and apply creativity to make it work in China. Simple replication of western models will not work for China.

One of our strategies is to act as a bridge between western and eastern cultures; it's essential to understand how the Asia region works and also have the ability to represent Western capital coming to Asia. We believe we're niche and creative; we don't just replicate Western ideas but try to create investment strategies using our on-the-ground experience. Usually one does not find many restaurants in outlet malls elsewhere in the world other than those in East Asian realms where we noticed in the first phase of our first outlet mall that shopping in an outlet mall is a recreational activity for the entire family, and we increased the restaurant tenants right away in the second phase expansion of our outlet mall. The restaurant tenants of outlets malls in China usually generate substantial cash flow income.

3.3   Integrated Operating Platforms

Gaw Capital noticed through experience that if it intended to bring something unique, niche, and different to its business, many local third-party operators wouldn't understand its model, positioning, and approach, especially when it went outside the comfort zone of Tier 1 cities. Gaw Capital decided to grow its own in-house team, and this has become a significant point of differentiation for the firm. One of the reasons Gaw Capital grew its asset management team is that partner risk can be quite significant in China. Long-term interests between partners are difficult to align, and quality service providers in the Tier 2 and Tier 3 cities are hard to find. Gaw Capital learned from experience and thus created its own asset management team; the firm now has three operating platforms for the management of commercial properties and hospitality properties respectively along with a platform for residential developments. We have also subsequently developed dedicated logistics asset management team as well. These integrated platforms give the firm expertise that is top-down, controlled in-house; therefore, during times like the financial crisis or down market times, the firm is able to control the project delivery, the cost, and the execution and ultimate business plan execution better than if the firm was to use a third-party operator. This operating model provides the control and the local knowledge needed to be successful.

4   Case Studies

4.1   Plaza 353

Plaza 353 is a pedestrian shopping mall housed in a landmark building on Shanghai's famous shopping promenade, East Nanjing Road. Whenever people ask about the most memorable deals—this one stands alone. It's within our hearts. Plaza 353 was our first deal in China and is emblematic of our other deals as it captures our philosophy of reviving a community and not just a building. The building is an art deco, eight-story retail mall dating back to the roaring 1930s of Shanghai. Since the early 1900s, East Nanjing Road has been the single most important and popular retail destination in Shanghai, if not the entire China. The building was designed by Chinese architect Zhuang Jun in the fashionable art deco style of the day, embellished with Bauhaus, art nouveau, and renaissance influences. It opened in 1932 as the Continental Department Store, offering two retail levels topped with four floors of offices and has been a heritage landmark property on Shanghai's Municipal Protection List for a few decades. The building practically laid dormant for more than 10 years prior to its 2-year restoration by Gaw Capital along with the specialist heritage architectural firm, Woods Bagot.

Ideal Timing for Acquisition
Even though the frontage of the building commands 100 m long, 1/10 of the entire pedestrian section, this retail building has not been successful for the past 20 years

with frequent changes of hands. The biggest issue was that nobody from the street side could even tell (just by looking at it) that there was an entire shopping mall behind the three ground floor tenants occupying the entire frontage, namely, a state-owned bookstore, a McDonald's, and a fast food noodle shop. There was only a small passage entry in the front leading into the mall. The shopping mall was entirely hidden and dwarfed by these three ground floor tenants. The headline back in 2006 was "Gaw Capital Acquires Bermuda Triangle Mall in Shanghai"; in other words, the market thought we couldn't succeed, and it was a hopeless case. The previous owner, a local merchant, tried to chop up the building through strata title selling with a theme of jewelry town, but the plan was thrown out by the government, disapproving of having multiple owners of an historical building. As a result, the previous owner was desperately trying to sell the building. It was a bit of a challenge to buy the property from a local merchant as there was culture shock on both sides; we knew the seller may not like the complicated Sales & Purchase agreement, but we didn't compromise our standards. Even after all the negotiations were done and the price agreed to, the seller almost walked away, seeing how complex the agreement was. "What's with all the documents? I thought we were brothers. Why can't we just shake hands and get the deal done the old way?" complained the seller. Luckily, our chief legal counsel who speaks fluent Mandarin sat him down and explained the whole agreement line by line.

Location, Location, Location

One of the main reasons which attracted us to this building was its prime location. The history of Nanjing Road can be traced back to the year 1845. At the beginning of the twentieth century, eight big department stores were established along the street. A series of franchised stores were also set up at that time. When we were acquiring the building, neighborhood foot traffic could have easily been a million per day. Even though the government "pedestrianized" that section of East Nanjing Road, trying to bring back its formal glory of the "No. 1 shopping street in the Far East," the retail scene of the whole neighborhood was still very "local": hundreds of thousands of pedestrians walked by the street, and they were mostly middle-aged domestic tourists from the other parts of China. The street was mostly shops selling gold jewelry, watches, cameras, and inexpensive clothing catering to domestic tourists from the hinterlands of China. We saw beyond that and envisioned a pedestrianized retail area that had the potential to be the equivalent of Harajuku and Shibuya in Tokyo, Myeong Dong in Seoul, and Ximending in Taipei which are all retail and cultural hubs for youngsters. Given enough time, East Nanjing Road would evolve just like its other Asian siblings, especially given the vast public transportation network in the neighborhood, and we felt its location couldn't be wrong.

Aligned with the Government's Interest

The Huangpu District government carried out major renovations on East Nanjing Road in 1999 including widening and pedestrianizing the street and upgrading the civic facilities. They engaged McKinsey, the global leading consulting firm, to prepare a research report and recommendation on how to revitalize the area's walkways. According to the study by McKinsey, the east end of the street where Plaza 353 is located was suggested to skew more toward young and fashionable people, and they proposed this area to link up with the Bund area, one of the most famous international tourist spots in Shanghai. We happened to share the same view about how to position our mall. And, because Plaza 353 had such a long frontage, commanding an entire city block and one tenth of the entire pedestrian street, the success of Plaza 353 would be critical to the government's plan to revitalize the neighborhood, and we knew we could leverage it to gain assistance from the local Huangpu District government.

Problem-Solving

One might wonder: if the location was good and the only problem was the frontage being blocked, why didn't we just relocate the tenants? That's exactly what needed to be done, but how? McDonald's and the noodle shop were easy, as there were commercial leases with expiration dates and relocation penalties that could be qualified. The state-owned bookstore was an entirely different story. After the Communists took over China in 1949, real estate properties in China became state-owned, and the state assigned usage right to users. Most of the urban entities used assigned office space, and urban citizens lived in assigned welfare housing (to be accurate). The users only had the right to use the property as long as the state allowed it, and the use right of the storefront at Plaza 353 was assigned to the bookstore.

After China's economic reform in 1979, the privatized land use right was reintroduced despite the land still being state-owned. However, none of the previous owners of Plaza 353 had wanted to touch on the historical issue and sign a lease with the bookstore for the past 30 years. In other words, the bookstore had the right to use the storefront for free indefinitely and without a lease even though we paid for and owned the building. In addition, the bookstore was not the only "squatting tenant" in that building. We tried to resolve the issue by reasoning with them and coming up with an agreeable compensation, but without much success. We then tried to resolve the issue through legal measures by dragging one of these types of tenants to court, after the "Real Right Law of the People's Republic of China" was enacted in 2007. But we received a call from the judge telling us he would not rule on the case to avoid setting a precedent, and we were kindly requested to withdraw the case. He said there were too many similar cases in China, and we should try to negotiate our way out.

By that time the renovation had already started with the interior gutted; the site was pretty much like a "war zone," but the bookstore was still in full operation. Our leasing team was busy pre-leasing the building, and we had already secured a major international brand in "fast fashion" (when designs move from the catwalk quickly to retailers to capture the current fashion trends) who was interested in the bookstore space. We asked them if they would be interested in the storefront next to the bookstore in case we couldn't relocate the bookstore. An email from the brand's Spanish HQ indicated they would not consider the building at all if the bookstore remained on the frontage as it wasn't a desirable neighbor for them. Without a better solution, we asked the district government for assistance. Our view was that if we couldn't relocate the bookstore, the last chance to revitalize the building and the neighborhood would be gone. And we'd only be able to run the building with the same shops that were already located on this street, selling watches, cameras, gold jewelry, and cheap clothing. With a 5-year letter of intent to lease from a major international fast fashion brand in hand, we finally convinced the district government to intervene on our behalf. As a number of our state-owned squatting tenants were at the city level, they would not acknowledge orders from district government. We went to negotiate with their higher ruling bureaus with introductions from the district government. One by one, we managed to resolve the 30-year squatting tenant issue after a whole year of effort and countless meetings and, of course, many sleepless nights. The building was finally entirely ours, and the market value of the property doubled overnight.

Grand Opening

After careful market studies and 2 years of painstaking renovation, we transformed Plaza 353 into a hip urban concept mall to engage China's influential youth market through an inspired mix of twenty-first-century retail and dining concepts along with high-tech creative platforms. With small design boutique shop where up-and-coming designers could sell their clothes directly to consumers and a DJ booth playing its own music as opposed to regular mall "muzak" plus the hippest designs from mainstream established brands and edgy lesser-known labels, Plaza 353 redefined a whole new retail experience.

Levels one to three featured "city vogue" fashions by trend-setting global brands, including Zara, Guess, Mango, Fila, Lyle & Scott, Lacoste, and Nike. Latest "urban trend" offerings in technology, cosmetics, sports, casual wear, and accessories were showcased on the fourth and fifth floors, including Nike, New Balance, Dickies, and Etude. Levels six and seven were cool dining and family stores. Along with children's retailers Toys "R" Us and Goodbaby, there were three restaurants and a 600-seat Food Loft, with a mix-and-match fusion of international flavors.

We held this property in our Gateway Fund I until 2012—and it was a very good exit. We sold it 6 years later to a large sovereign wealth fund with a double-digit IRR and a more than two times multiple. In addition to the satisfying return, what delighted us the most was the change we brought about to the neighborhood. When we were pre-leasing in 2007–2008, we had a difficult time to convince the young and trendy brands such as Zara and Mango to move in. When they looked at this area, they saw a very local and old-fashioned retail scene. The trendy shops were on the other end of the pedestrian street, and we had to lower the rent to lure them in. After 4 years of operations, Apple opened its Shanghai flagship store directly across the street from our mall, Gap was in the mall next to us, and a China flagship store of Forever 21 was just down the street. We cannot help but think that our success contributed to this neighborhood revitalization, through our persistence and creativity (Fig. 1).

Fig. 1 Entrance of Plaza
353—East Nanjing Road/
Shandong Road crossing—
before (up) and after (down)
renovation. Source: Own
illustration

4.2   Embassy House

Embassy House is a luxury residential tower in Beijing's central embassy district,
neighboring the trendy Sanlitun nightlife area. In a city where location is everything,
Embassy House's enviable location has attracted tenants including many executives
of Beijing's multinational corporations, and there was a long waiting list to move
into the building during our management.

Timing

This is a case where we were able to play the "right cycle, right timing." The
property was one of the last projects in a fund managed by another manager that
needed to be exited due to the life of the fund, and the seller conducted an open
bidding. This asset was nicely managed, very well occupied, and turning out
excellent cash flow—a prime building in a prime area of Beijing. There were lots
of bidders for this property, and the highest bidder was actually 10% above our
highest bid. The picked buyer actually reneged on the deal due to the 2008 financial
crisis and didn't go through with it. After 6 months of frustrating negotiation with no
success, the seller came back to Gaw Capital in 2009 asking if we were still
interested and had the funding to make the acquisition. There was one more clause
form the seller—we had to be able to close the deal, including arranging the
mortgage within 45 days. Given the distressed situation of the seller, we were able
to renegotiate the price to our favor. At the end, we managed to acquire the property
with more than a 20% reduction from our original bid in 2008. Our acquisition team

and finance team worked around the clock and closed the deal within the 45-day limit, a testament to our efficiency and bond with our professional partners such as banks and lawyers.

Value Adding
The service apartment was nicely maintained and had been doing well with its superb hardware and impeccable location. Most of the other owners might have run the project as a core plus asset, but Gaw Capital managed to find a way to provide value adding through aggressive asset management without massive renovation. After our hospitality asset management team, GCP Hospitality, took over the property, we put in a more sophisticated hotel management aspect into the operation. We provided further services such as a monthly organic farmers market, adding a small deli where children of the residents could easily purchase/charge to their apartment by showing their room keys, among other enhancements. The management also established a more aggressive system for rent increases using the same yield management concept from hotels and airlines. During the 7 years of holding the property, we managed to boost the occupancy from 70% to 97% and increased the rent by 30% (Fig. 2). Gaw Capital maintained Embassy House and the cash flow improved leading up to the building's sale on December 31, 2015, to an RMB-denominated fund with more than 25% of IRR and a 3.5 times multiple. This exit showed substantial liquidity onshore in China, but not everyone would have access to this liquidity unless they are in the market and have an on-the-ground presence like ours.

4.3 Project Telephone

Gaw raised eyebrows in 2014 when it paid $928 million for Pacific Century Place, a mixed-use retail, office and residential complex in Beijing's affluent Sanlitun area. At that time, it was the most expensive single asset purchase by a foreign private-equity firm in China, and there was skepticism about the deal given the property's need for major renovations. But Gaw has jazzed up Pacific Century and increased its occupancy of its retail space to 75%, up from less than 20% when it purchased the property. (Fung 2016)

Bold and Daring Acquisition
Pacific Century Place is a 1,829,900 square feet mixed-used complex with two office towers and two serviced apartment towers, all sitting on a retail podium and basement parking garage. The complex is located within walking distance from Tuanjiehu metro station on East Beijing's 3rd Ring Road and adjacent to the trendy Sanlitun area, the most sought-after office and retail location in Beijing. The complex was once a Beijing office and retail landmark but has been going downhill in recent years.

There were a few reasons for the "raised eyebrows" for this deal. The seller was another experienced investor who had been selling a series of large real estate

Fig. 2 General view of
Embassy House. Source: Own
illustration

properties in China starting in 2014, which caused the market to suspect the seller
was "cashing out" of China. And, the property had been for sale on the market for the
past 3 years. If this well-connected seller with substantial experience was not
optimistic about the market and the property, people thought we must have been
lack of insights to have acquired it. The second reason for the "raised eyebrows" was
that the property's retail podium had been empty for 3 years since the well-known
Pacific Department Store moved out. Being diagonally located across the street from
one of the biggest and most successful malls in Beijing, Tai Koo Li, it was very
difficult to bring in a retail concept that would attract shoppers to venture over to the
other side of the street. What could Gaw Capital do to fill up the 807,000 square feet
of space with less than 20% occupancy at the time of acquisition?

Your Poison, Our Meat
Being a nimble investor, we discussed all the abovementioned issues during the due
diligence period. The reason why we were willing to acquire this property that had
been on the block for 3 years was because we came up with a creative solution to
better utilize the retail space and to boost the rent before we entered the purchase
agreement. The most difficult part of operating a vertical mall is how to draw
shoppers to go beyond the third floor. Hence, the rents for the fourth floor and

above in a vertical mall are usually a quarter or less of the ground floor. As the office rental prices in Beijing grew higher and higher, our team came up with an unexpected idea during the due diligence period to convert the upper floor of the mall into office space. Taking advantage of the higher ceilings and wider distances between columns, the former retail space was ideal to convert into a creative loft office setting. But would China be ready for it? While the acquisition team was negotiating price, our asset management team quickly put together a schematic rendering for the conversion and started approaching potential tenants. By the time the acquisition team nailed down the purchase price, the asset management team had already signed the letter of intent for 100,000 square feet of creative office space converted from the retail mall and the rental price for the space doubled. Twelve months later, the converted office space had been fully leased, and 80% of the tenants for the creative office moved in while we were currently finishing up the renovation of the façade and ground floor.

Reposition + Renovation
In addition to the upper floor of the retail podium, the rest of the complex went through major renovation and repositioning. The lobby, along with the elevator lobbies and toilets on each floor in the two office towers were low-hanging fruit. And, we had plenty of experience in how to carry out such a renovation in an office tower with over 89% occupancy. The two service apartment towers were also undergoing complete transformation. Based on our understanding of the market, obtained from operating another serviced apartment in the same neighborhood, we planned to reconfigure the size of the apartments and beef up the amenities to meet the needs of our target clients: young expatriate executives with no children or preschool-aged children. A state-of-the-art gym and rooftop garden was also added to complete the whole offering. The new product would be branded as Residence G, a brand which carries the same simple chic and modern comfort found in all of our other life-style hotels and serviced apartments. Due to the rise of ecommerce in China and the deep penetration of ecommerce behemoth, Taobao, the performance of shopping malls in China has been sliding in recent years. Being on the opposite side of the street from a major landmark shopping mall, it was very difficult for the retail podium of Pacific Century Place to continue to be operated as a shopping mall. Even though the upper floors were converted into a creative office, we still have the basement and the bottom three floors in the retail podium. As the project is located on a main street with busy traffic, we created more vertical transportation such as elevators and divided the street-facing side into six mini-blocks with triplex storefronts, each of which had their own individual entrance, vertical transportation, and outdoor signage. The six blocks were sold like hot cakes to car show rooms, experience centers for e-retailers, and financial industries alike. Together with the creative office transformation, the average rent for this previously near empty retail podium more than doubled (Fig. 3). The renovation of Pacific Century Place was completed in early 2017. Certified as LEED Gold, Pacific Century Place becomes another Beijing landmark and a textbook case study for conversion from retail property to office. The renovation project also received multiple international

Fig. 3 Pacific Century Place atrium before (up) and during (down) renovation. Source: Own illustration

recognition, such as "Asia Deal of the Year 2014" by Global PERE Awards and "Best Refurbished Building" by MIPIM Asia Awards in 2017 (Fig. 4).

5   The Seven Immutable Principles

This chapter reflects Gaw Capital's experiences in investing in real estate in China. Below are seven key points that have been "field-tested":

1. "Boots on the Ground" in China
2. Understand Chinese culture: It may surprise you that being fluent in Chinese language is only secondary but the reality is with advances in technology that being able to communicate in Chinese is less important than having an understanding and appreciation for Chinese culture; people call this skill EQ.
3. Align with the Chinese government's macro-level economic planning: It's imperative to be aligned with the direction of the market in China. As the real estate market has strong influences from the central and local government's economic planning, it's essential to "go with the flow" of those planning priorities. First, one needs to identify the economic direction the government is taking the market

Fig. 4 Pacific Century Place—Office "blocks" in the atrium. Source: Own illustration

and then to align with that direction. As an example, Gaw Capital has opened shopping malls in areas where domestic consumption and service sector job growth is a priority and encouraged by local governments, and these projects have performed well.

4. Leverage transportation links: Urbanization is a major trend in China and there is a boom in Tier 2, Tier 3, and Tier 4 cities. When choosing real estate projects in China, it is essential that there are adequate infrastructure and transportation links, i.e., roads leading to these cities! China's high-speed rail, with stops in smaller cities, has created tremendous real estate opportunities.

5. Select the right partner: Partner risk is highest in China; you have to select your partner very carefully and rely on your own team's execution.

6. Have your own team and invest in your team: Have your own team and grow your own team (see rule #1: Be in China)! In our view, partner risk is the highest type of risk in China, and it is difficult to maintain interest alliance among partners on a long-term basis. Therefore, having your own team is crucial; in case the partnership runs into difficulties, you can still ensure your needs are met, and it can also help with on-the-ground issues such as finding qualified service providers outside of Tier 1 cities.

7. Have your Own DNA: Gaw Capital's DNA is passion, responsibility, and creativity (PRC); it is essential to have your own points of differentiation.

6 Conclusion

Gaw Capital is long-term positive on China's economy and the direction of its real estate industry. This confidence comes from many years of on-the-ground experience and many macroeconomic indicators about the Chinese consumer and the direction of the economy and real estate sector. Gaw Capital relies on the company's own DNA: passion, responsibility, and creativity in selecting projects, investing in assets, and building its own team from the ground up.

References

Barton, D., Chen, Y., & Jin, A. (2013). Mapping China's middle class. *McKinsey Quarterly*. Accessed May 28, 2016, from http://www.mckinsey.com/industries/retail/our-insights/mapping-chinas-middle-class.

Bloomberg. (2016). Accessed May 28, 2016, from https://www.bloomberg.com/graphics/2016-us-vs-china-economy/.

CEICDATA. (2019). *China city labor market: Demand-supply ratio.* https://www.ceicdata.com/en/china/city-labor-market-demandsupply-ratio.

Cheng, A. (2016). China confusion: Ascendant power or troubled economy? *Institutional Investor*. Accessed December 14, 2016, from http://www.institutionalinvestor.com/article/3540753/banking-and-capital-markets-banking/china-confusion-ascendant-power-or-troubled-economy.html#/.WKV2KNJ96dF.

Fung, E. (2016). Family firm seizes on Chinese property downturn. *The Wall Street Journal*. Accessed May 28, 2016, from https://www.wsj.com/articles/family-firm-seizes-on-chinese-property-downturn-1456852175.

Reuters. (2019). *U.S. retail sales expected to top$3.8 trillion in 2019: NRF*. New York: Reuters.

The World Bank. (2017). *Household finale consumption expenditure*. Accessed February 2, 2017, from http://data.worldbank.org/indicator/NE.CON.PETC.ZS.

Trading Economics. (2019). *China unemployment rate*. Accessed January 19, 2019, from http://www.tradingeconomics.com/china/unemployment-rate.

Xinhuanet. (2018). China Focus: Economic recovery building up in China's rustbelt. Accessed August 13, 2019, from http://www.xinhuanet.com/english/2018-11/22/c_137624191.htm.

Xinhuanet. (2019). *Economic Watch: China's new economy coming to the fore*. Accessed August 15, 2019, from http://www.xinhuanet.com/english/2019-07/29/c_138267595.htm.

YCharts. (2016). *US retail sales*. Accessed January 19, 2017, from https://ycharts.com/indicators/retail_sales.

Part IV

Real Estate as a Physical and Social Asset Type

Sustainable Buildings and Practice in China

Sean Chiao and Nancy F. Lin

Abstract

Sustainable building, or more commonly referred to as "green building" in China, is an integral part of the country's path toward sustainability. There are both opportunities and challenges in China's green building market. Opportunities lie in both architecture and building engineering, as well as planning and urban development areas. The recently appeared WELL building concept may also be promising in China. On the other hand, the development of green building in China faces challenges in economics, professional capability and awareness, and regulatory standards. Moving forward, the certification-focused developers shall introduce new technologies to increase the added value of green building labels. For technology-focused developers, they will need to combine their advanced core technology with the existing ones to capture larger shares of the market, particularly in the residential area. The ideas and concepts that may bring about technological integration will be the main drivers in the market.

1 Introduction

"Sustainable building" is more commonly referred to as "green building" in China, and these two terms are sometimes used interchangeably. Although the idea of sustainability was already known in China in the 1980s, it had minimal influence then. The concept of green building on the other hand was brought into China in early 2000s by multinational companies (MNCs) as they invested in the country and required their offices or manufacturing facilities to meet green building standards. This resulted in developers building office buildings in first-tier cities like Beijing

S. Chiao (✉) · N. F. Lin
AECOM, Shatin, Hong Kong SAR, China

© Springer Nature Switzerland AG 2021
B. Wang, T. Just (eds.), *Understanding China's Real Estate Markets*, Management for Professionals, https://doi.org/10.1007/978-3-030-49032-4_17

and Shanghai using internationally recognized green standards in order to attract MNC tenants.

The first building in China to receive the internationally recognized US Leadership in Energy and Environmental Design (LEED) certification was the eight-story office of the Ministry of Science and Technology in Beijing, completed in 2004. This gave rise to adopting LEED as a benchmarking and rating system for green buildings at the time when there was no Chinese institutionalized or formal standards available (Nelson 2012).

In the following years, green building was instituted and defined in detail by the Chinese Green Building Evaluation System (CGBES) under the governance of China's Ministry of Housing and Urban-Rural Development (MoHURD), requiring the real estate practice of developing buildings to provide a healthy, applicable, and effective environment, while to conserve resources (energy, land, water, and materials), protect the environment, and reduce pollution as much as possible and thus to remain harmonious with nature throughout the life cycle of a building. With a population of 1.4 billion, how to achieve energy efficiency in buildings is undoubtedly one of the most critical factors for buildings. Hence, green buildings in China have generally focused on improving energy efficiency, conserving natural resources, and using new environment-friendly building materials. More recently, focuses have also been made on making revolutionary changes in the concept of design and procurement and management processes of real estate development in order to reduce the impact of buildings on the overall environment (Chau et al. 2010).

Before policies and regulations were enforced in 2009, green building concept did not translate to the China market well, however. Under rapid urbanization, construction decisions were frequently made with short-term goals in mind. It usually takes 5–10 years for a developer to make back the initial investment in a green building (Nelson 2012), while the decision-makers expect a 3.2 years payback on building efficiency measures (Qin 2015). For many Chinese developers, they would even prefer to save the money for new developments or at least expect to make back the investment in 1–2 years. Since developer and builder do not usually operate buildings after they are built and sold to the market, the perceived economics of green buildings are not necessarily there as savings from occupancy in energy costs don't incentivize builders; green building market in China remains in its infancy stage (Zhang 2016). Although back in 2003, there was an appraisal handbook for eco-housing and construction guidance for green Olympic buildings, it was not until 2005 that informal guideline books finally turned into national standards when Design Standard for Energy Efficiency of Public Buildings (GB50189-2005) was published. This standard first provided a definition, the technical specifications, and then the assessment framework for green buildings. Due to vast territory and differentiated climatic zones between east and west, as well as the northern and southern part, of China, adopting technologies, materials, and methods that are suitable for local circumstances has been advocated by the central government. This inevitably led to many local standards and definitions.

China's own green building label (GBL) was only introduced in 2006 by MoHURD (Ministry of Housing and Urban-Rural Development and then Ministry of Construction) and later revised in 2014. This 3-star system and LEED have become the most widely recognized green building standards in China. They coexist with BREEAM, CASBEE, and others, and often the same building would seek accreditation from multiple rating systems due to the fact that GBL is not as comprehensive as other standards in addressing indications responding to climate change, region-specific requirements, quantitative indications, and innovative green technologies[1] (Geng et al. 2011).

In 2007, China's National Development and Reform Commission (NDRC) announced to build a resource-efficient and environment-friendly society. In December 2009 when signing the climate change agreement in Copenhagen, China declared to cut carbon intensity per capita of GDP by 40–45% by 2020 on the basis of 2005 and increase its renewable energy share to 15% by 2020 (National Development and Reform Commission 2007). To achieve this goal, the government has set up a number of high-level energy and environmental targets, many of which are directly related to the building sector since energy consumption by buildings have increased from 10% of national total four decades ago to an estimated total of 35% for heating and cooling of buildings alone by 2020 (Qin 2015).

It was not until 2013 that green building requirement in China was first institutionalized at a national level. Under the 12th Five Year Plan, MoHURD issued the Green Building Development Plan, specifying targets for the industry and its plan to realize a new development mode. Not only demonstration programs on green development were established in 100 new urban zones, 400,000 energy-efficient demonstration houses were set up in rural areas; and also green building standards were required for government-funded projects and large public works and subsidized residential apartments from 2014 onward; as well as green building standards were to be adopted for over 50% of new real estate projects in cities directly under the central government (Beijing, Tianjin, Shanghai, and Chongqing) and cities in eastern coastal provinces from 2015. Subsequently, as a signee of the Paris Accord at the Paris Climate Change Conference (COP21) which concluded in late 2015, China agreed in striving to achieve reduction of carbon dioxide emissions per capita of GDP by 60–65% by 2030 compared to the 2004 numbers. With the mandate from the 12th Five Year Plan and the commitments with Paris Accord, green building became a legitimated concept, and it is the confirmed direction for future developments.

---

[1]*Green Practices in the Chinese Building Industry: drivers and impediment* studied the evolving process and influence of the national policies within the green building industry. The Institute for Building Efficiency took another angle and researched more on the local policy in different parts of China in their report of *Green Building in China: Conception, Codes and Certification*. EU SME Center also published a related report on *The Green Building Sector in China*, which paid attention on the international rating system adopted by China, and comparison of different rating systems was analyzed.

2   Key Market Drivers

AECOM, along with other international design consulting companies like Mott MacDonald, WSP, and ARUP, were the first players in China's green building market, working with their MNC clients. It is not surprising that 8 out of the first 15 LEED-certified buildings in China back in 2009 were all designed or built for the multinational companies driven by global corporate's social responsibility policies. Early LEED buildings generally took the form of owner-occupied, single-tenant buildings and corporate headquarters since it would give those responsible all the long-term benefits of the green features.

In 2006, Plantronics was the first multinational to seek LEED certification in China, for its factory and office in Suzhou. Its new manufacturing and design center in Suzhou became the first manufacturing facility in China to achieve LEED certification with Gold rating. Since then, Nokia has followed suit with its LEED Gold campus in Beijing, and GM, Coca-Cola, ExxonMobil, Siemens, BHP Billiton, Boeing, Carrefour, Carrier, Otis, and Rockwell were among other early adopters to start designing and constructing their own LEED-rated green buildings in China. In 2009, AECOM assisted Coca-Cola to obtain LEED certification for Coca-Cola's Global Innovation and Technology Center (GITC) in Shanghai. This was a critical milestone in the development and promotion of green buildings in China that since then, Coca-Cola required all its new offices and factories in China to apply for LEED standards. MNCs implement green buildings for projects all over the world because real estate portfolio affects corporate image, ability to attract and retain employees, and reduction of operating costs and environmental liability. Unexpectedly, demanding green space by the MNCs started transforming the real estate market in the late 2000s.

When it was completed, the Gold-rated Prosper Center[2] constructed by Chinese developer was the only rentable green office space available in Beijing. Despite the rent was the highest in Beijing then, CBRE, the world's largest commercial real estate services company, chose Prosper Center as its office location to address company policy to occupy LEED space where available. To build for the demand and attract MNC tenants in office buildings, both local and international property developers started building rentable LEED-certified buildings. Most notable was Tishman Speyer, the US-based real estate developer. Although Tishman Speyer estimated meeting LEED requirements adds around 3–5% to the cost of building in China, Tishman Speyer was constructing three LEED projects at the same time in 2009 to conform to a company-wide policy adopted in 2007 to achieve certification of all new buildings so as to entice foreign tenants (Lewis 2009).

On the other hand, many global design consultants were also motivated to design their offices and occupied buildings with LEED certification not only for corporate social responsibilities and commitments to the environment but also to use their own

---

[2]Fraser Place Shekou in Shenzhen, Prosper Center in Beijing, and Lac Song Shopping Plaza in Harbin were the first projects to apply for any green labels in China.

offices as an effective way to communicate their design concepts, demonstrate key aspects of green building, and showcase their capabilities.[3] Together, the MNC clients, high-end property developers, and design consultants drove the developments of the first wave of green projects and promoted sustainable design, green building standards, and certifications.

2.1   Residential Developments

Although MNCs helped to boost the idea of green building and standards, most of the buildings considered were industrial and commercial buildings catering for MNCs' own needs in manufacturing facilities or office spaces. Changes in the residential sector have been lagging behind due to lack of economic drive. Most progress made in advancing residential buildings in sustainable design was contributed by large local developers of which Vanke is the most representative. Vanke has been leading investments in green buildings to distinguish themselves and justify a quality premium in projects they developed since 2008. They are also among the first to incorporate green strategy into the company's vision, rolling out quantifiable goals in 2009 to achieve 100% green architecture standards by 2014.

In order to reduce construction waste and water and energy usage, Vanke standardized and mass-produced building parts and implemented in situ construction. Efforts were also made in material selections and construction methods from architecture to interior fit-out. For example, steam is used instead of water to cure concrete, and building parts were cast in centralized areas to reduce water usage and water pollution and improve efficiency in recycling polluted water. Steel formwork was also used to replace the traditional wood formwork, allowing reuse rate of formwork from 2 to 200 times. Furthermore, innovation was sought through in how residential units were sold. Providing design options and solutions to customize for individual needs and allowing fit-out components to be assembled by owners on-site were new concepts introduced to reduce construction waste. From Vanke's study, fit-out contributed to one of the largest portions of construction waste, of which new home owners knocking down walls, partitions, and interior fit-out in newly constructed buildings to suit their individual requirements worsen it further.

Some of Vanke's prominent green residential projects include Vanke City Phase 4 in Shenzhen, Langrun Gardens in Shanghai, and Dongli Lake Resort in Tianjin. Vanke led the aggressive promotion of GBL 3-star certification across China. In 2010 alone, nine Vanke projects with a total area of 757,000 m^2 received GBL 3-star certification (Wang et al. 2011). Moreover, Vanke established experimental sites to test different strategies, materials, and climate differentials. An example is Changyang Project in Changyang County, Fangshan District of Beijing. Alternative energy, material science, and biotechnology were tested under cold weather in Changyang Project to achieve green targets in various environmental and energy

---

[3]AECOM's own offices in Guangzhou and Shanghai achieved LEED Silver and Gold certifications.

aspects.[4] Additionally, Vanke Center, Vanke's headquarter office in Shenzhen, designed by Steven Holl and opened in 2009, was built as a demonstration building for sustainable design. It is one of the first LEED Platinum-rated buildings in southern China. Microclimate is created integrating the building and landscape with rectangular cooling lakes fed by a gray water system. The building itself has a green roof with solar panels and widely uses sustainable materials such as bamboo. Porous louvers were incorporated into the glass to protect it against the sun and wind.[5]

The commitments and impacts Vanke's developments exerted in China's early stage of green development are evident from the sixfold increase in its total built area for green buildings within 3 years from 2007 to 2010. Its 3-star green label developments in 2010 were more than 50% of the total built areas receiving 3-star green label in China's entire residential market. According to Shanghai Branch of China Academy of Building Research, the average incremental costs for China GBL 1-star, 2-star, and 3-star buildings stand at 2.7%, 6.2%, and 9.3% of the overall construction costs, respectively (Sun 2011). With such investment, Vanke has ranked no. 1 among China's developers for seven successive years since 2009 and its market share increased to 3% in 2015 (Xinhua News 2016), a historical high of the industry in China. These set new benchmarks for other developers competing in the premium real estate markets.

Meanwhile, it is important to note that demand-side drivers are accompanying this trend. According to the official data published by the National Bureau of Statistics of China, the average disposable income of urban residents has increased over seven times from 5425 CNY in 1998, when China launched housing reform and apartments became a commercial commodity, to 39,251 CNY in 2018. During these two decades, the green building concept was introduced in the country and increasingly accepted by the people, especially those live in big cities.

2.2   Eco-city and Urban Planning

According to the Asian Development Bank, as early as the mid-1990s, Chinese government already began encouraging development of sustainable communities.

---

[4]The Beijing Changyang Project has a total land area of 154,076 m^2, FAR 2.17, and total floor area is 374,487 m^2. It achieved 30% greenery coverage with 50.8% of outdoor areas being water permeable. It increased energy efficiency by 65–72% and 65% of housing units adopted solar heating system. It used gray water for irrigation and decreased water usage by 50–70% compared to traditional irrigation system; it promoted water recycling and satisfied as least 30% of water demand; and it put in place safe and environment-friendly collection and disposal system for solid waste.

[5]Vanke Center is a long building as long as the Empire State Building, with a total size of over 120,000 m^2. It won numerous awards including 2010 Good Design, Good Business China Award for Best Green project, 2010 Architectural Record Best Green Project in China, 2011 AIA Honor Award in the USA, and 2014 Federation Internationale Du Beton, Switzerland.

Hundreds of eco-projects or eco-cities were planned scattered throughout China, aiming to establishing new cities of 250,000 to 500,000 people. China's push to develop more sustainable communities undoubtedly influenced green building's future in the country. It is not by coincidence that China has the largest number of LEED for neighborhood development (LEED ND) projects outside of the USA,[6] focusing on walkability, energy efficiency, water usage, and adopting alternative energy for communities. The most prominent example of sustainable planning is Tianjin Eco-city (Nelson 2012).

Tianjin Eco-city is a collaboration project between Singapore and Tianjin governments in 2007 to transform a former uninhabitable swamp into a residential area for 350,000 residents, as a satellite city of Tianjin. Its vision is to be "a thriving city which is socially harmonious, environmentally friendly, and resource-efficient—a model for sustainable development". Occupying a total site area of 30 km^2, the master plan was jointly developed by the China Academy of Urban Planning and Design, the Tianjin Urban Planning and Design Institute, and the Singapore planning team led by the Urban Redevelopment Authority, to promote water and energy conservation, mixed-use development, and comprehensive public transport.

During the planning phase, various design consultants were also brought in to study alternatives and provide guidance to help the Tianjin government in assessing the practicalities and potential challenges on their developing master plan. Different parcels and zones were then commissioned by the Sino-Singapore Tianjin Eco-city Administrative Committee to different teams. For example, the conceptual landscape design focusing on creating an urban environment which is sustainable, ecological, and livable was provided for the three water bodies within the Tianjin Eco-city: the Ji canal, the old water channel, and the Qingjing Lake.[7] Sustainable strategies that were recommended created diversities in habitats, water management systems, and water-related experience spaces were integrated with landscape.

---

[6]LEED ND revaluates an entire community looking at walkable streets and reduction in dependence on cars and energy efficiency for buildings and infrastructure in terms of usage of renewable energy sources and reduction in water usage.

[7]Legacy EDAW, now AECOM, completed the project in 2009. The project site area is 1080 ha. The water strategy included utilization and management of storm water and waste water and measures for flood control and water recycling. The ecological restoration strategy included the creation of an ecological corridor, a wetland habitat, and planting was based on an investigation into existing wildlife communities. The team proposed a new circulation system and added a waterborne transportation route and theme tour routes. In riverine slope treatment and existing wetlands were preserved while new ones were created, resulting in a variety of shorelines that are well integrated with leisure and recreational programming. Soil and vegetation restoration was considered as well. To establish the project as an exemplary case in economic, ecological, energy-saving, and environment-friendly goals, the design utilized advanced measures to convert wind energy, solar energy, and thermal energy into electricity and put into use.

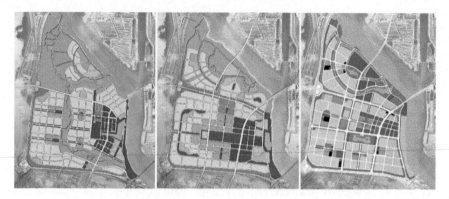

Fig. 1 Options for Beitang New Town development using SSIM. Source: AECOM

Another example is the master planning of Beitang New Town in Tanggu District of Tianjin.[8] Inspired by the popularity of "sustainable planning," the local authorities have committed to achieving greener development as they aim to become the new commercial center of northern China. To provide measurable sustainable master planning for the client, AECOM used the Sustainable Systems Integration Model™ (SSIM) to create several alternative options for this new town development (Fig. 1).[9] The quantified sustainable master plan provided a suitable and feasible implementation guideline for the decision-makers, helping them to determine which sustainability measures are possible within a reasonable cost range (Fig. 2) (Table 1).

2.3   Government Incentives and Regulations

To achieve the aggressive goals China committed at COP21, the Chinese government implements energy labeling programs, provides subsidies for energy-efficient technologies, and releases policies to support carbon and energy reduction goals. Local governments began introducing plans and incentives to grow the green

---

[8]Situated on approximately 1000 ha land, the Beitang New Town project's existing conditions consist of residential development, limited commercial development, and significant portions of environmentally degraded, undeveloped land. The Tanggu District has a history of industrial development that has seriously affected the environmental condition of the area, which was once home to healthy wetlands.

[9]Several "sustainability indicators" were chosen to provide a comparison through which a preferred master plan alternative could be chosen. Once the best performing and thus preferred alternative was chosen, the cost and benefit of various system (water, transport, energy, etc.) measures were modeled individually to determine the highest performing measures with a parallel cost-benefit analysis. Finally, SSIM measured the overall environmental and cost impact of all systems combined into various sustainability program alternatives and determined which program met the goals of the client, while ensuring the greatest financial benefit for the initial and long-term investment.

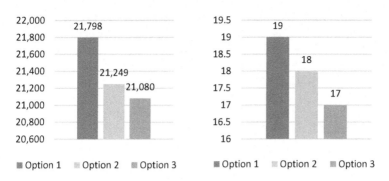

Fig. 2 SIMM analysis for energy use per person. Energy use per person in kWHr per year (left); Carbon emissions per person in MT per year (right). Source: AECOM

Table 1 SIMM cost analysis for different key indicators

	Performance of preferred master plan/master program	% Reduction	Change in capital cost	Total additional cost of development
Residential building energy use	1.4 billion kWh/year	56	+5%	CN¥ 292 million (4.6% of total development cost)
Nonresidential building energy use	460 million kWr/year	51	+3%	
Transportation: private car use	439 million VKT/year	50	+¥255 million	
Water use	9 million m³	40	−¥16 million	
Greenhouse gas emissions	1.8 million MT CO₂ Eq/year	36	Absorbed in overall cost	

Source: AECOM

building sector, especially in developed eastern provinces like Jiangsu, Zhejiang, and Guangdong. Green developers are given priorities for land access in order to initiate change, and green buildings become a means to boost project image and are viewed as high-end.

With MoHURD's institutionalization of green building requirement on a national level, both central and local government subsidies are provided to green building developments, although these usually only apply to buildings that meet China's own GBL standards. The central government provides subsidies to GBL 2-star and 3-star buildings at the level of 45 and 80 CNY/m², respectively (Ministry of Finance 2012). Some local government, such as Beijing, covers certification fees for 1- and 2-star buildings[10] and provides additional subsidies of 22.5 and 40 CNY/m^2 for GBL 2-star and 3-star certified buildings. These subsidies are surely beneficial in promoting green building development; though such measures are top-down and of temporary nature, they helped close the gap of the average construction cost increase of 100–150 CNY (USD13–19)/m^2 for green building when comparing to a standard building in 2009 (Lewis 2009).

Though China's national GBL standards are non-compulsory, quite a few local governments have issued regulations to enforce local GBL standards as mandatory. Jiangsu Province was the first locality to issue a Green Building Regulation in 2015 to require all new civil buildings in the province to meet GBL 1-star standards and all those invested by the government to meet 2-star standards.[11] Since then many provinces and municipalities have followed suit. As of January 2019, GBL standards are mandatory in Beijing, Tianjin, Shanghai, Chongqing, and Shenzhen, Zhejiang, Jiangsu, Shandong, and Hebei provinces, etc. Many other local governments are in the process of developing similar regulations to make GBL "hard" standards in their jurisdictions. These regulations will be an important and effective driver to popularize the GBL standards throughout the country.

3   Market Outlook and Opportunities

Green building certifications had a significant success in the first decade of its introduction not primarily due to social responsibilities or promoting green design but as a fast way to be labeled with "green design." Within 10 years after China's own green building standards and rating system was introduced in 2006, nearly 4000 projects with a total building area of 460 million m^2 received China's GBL (Chinese Society for Urban Studies 2016). By the end of 2017, over 10,000 projects with a total building area of 1 billion m^2 received GBL certification (Chinese Real Estate Association 2018). Such exponential growth over the past 2–3 years was partly a result of the gradual enforcement of mandatory green building regulations in quite a few cities and provinces since 2015.

Since 2015, LEED market in China began to grow at an accelerated rate, with over 8 million m^2 incremental areas certified in 2015 and 2016, respectively, and by 2017, 1211 projects with 47 million m^2 building area received LEED certification in China. Although LEED-certified building area in China is not as large as the country's own GBL, China has been consistently the largest market for LEED outside the USA in terms of gross square meters since 2010 (CBRE 2017). At the same time, China's certified LEED professionals have also more than doubled from

---

[10]According to Beijing Municipal Government, the municipal government covers the certification fees for GBL 1-star and 2-star projects, which is around 8000–10,000 CNY per project.

[11]The Green Building Regulation of Jiangsu Province was passed by the 15th Standing Committee Meeting of the 12th Provincial People's Congress on March 27, 2015, and became effective on July 1, 2015.

about 1300 in 2014 to over 2800 in 2017 (USGBC 2014, 2017), another perspective for China's booming LEED market. It is predicted that the growing trends for both GBL and LEED certification will continue and the clientele will evolve from mostly MNCs to larger number of local companies in China.

Initial green building projects were primarily dealing with a single building focusing on the mechanical, electrical, and plumbing design (MEP) and performance on energy savings. Frequently, green design did not necessarily start from the pre-design stage. As sustainability concepts are understood and accepted, the next market opportunity for green buildings resides with high-end office development projects consisting of multiple-building complex, building cluster center, or a campus where offices, commercial spaces, restaurants, and parking structures are integrated. Investments on green building gradually increase not only that green concept and design will initiate from before and during design phase but more projects and developments started seeking for higher-level rating and services on certification and LEED specific consultancy. Sustainability strategy services are sought by clients separately and in addition to the traditional building engineering services.

Taking Beijing Raycom InfoTech Center as an example, LEED consulting services including technical assistance in document preparation and management services on MEP design and audit report submission before and during design phase were performed between 2009 and 2011. The project successfully achieved LEED Platinum certification in March 2016.[12] It purchased renewable energy for 35% of its annual total electricity usage and adopted 100% low-emitting materials to reduce harmful indoor air contaminants (Ramanujam 2016). More recently, new services also came into demand to assist clients strategizing in design options to optimize in terms of reducing environmental impacts such as pollution emission, energy and resource usage, and waste generation in a practical and cost-effective way. Project like Beijing's Volkswagen Brand Center[13] is one example (Figs. 3 and 4). However it is worth noting that green building certification is no longer a high-end service now as it was a decade ago. Competition from local design and consulting companies has drastically cut down the service fee and made the market unattractive to international design and consulting firms that were key stakeholders in development of promoting green building certifications.

It is also evident that the government, as well as real estate industry leaders, began to shift their focus to the quality of the green building design, rather than the overall

---

[12]Raycom Information Technology Center is a high-end office development project in Zhongguancun area in northwestern Beijing. The Center comprises four buildings, and the project site is Building B, which is 118 m tall with a total construction area of 85,000 m^2 (58,000 m^2 aboveground and 27,000 m^2 underground). AECOM provided LEED consulting services both before and during the design phase between 2009 and 2011.

[13]Volkswagen Brand Center is located in Chaoyang District, Beijing. The site is in close proximity to 798 Art Zone and between the INDIGO mixed-use development and the Bahe River. The project's total aboveground area is 18,161 m^2, and it aims to achieve LEED Silver certification.

Fig. 3 Volkswagen Brand Center in Beijing (1). Source: AECOM

Fig. 4 Volkswagen Brand Center in Beijing (2). Source: AECOM

quantity of certified buildings. This created another market area for international design and consultancy firms with professional capabilities and rich experiences in green building. Two examples are the new office building of Administrative

Fig. 5 TEDA Administrative Commission office building with BIPV panel. Source: AECOM

Commission in Tianjin Economic-Technological Development Area (TEDA)[14] and Beijing Aether Plaza.[15] Advanced green design was incorporated throughout the construction process, and both projects have received multiple green building certifications. These illustrated the fact the clients are looking for more stringent KPIs in their sustainability design (Fig. 5).[16]

Yet, the market for green certification will continue to grow because of the sheer size of China's economy and the pace of its development. By 2020, builders are expected to construct 215 billion ft^2 (20 billion m^2) of new construction in the country. According to preliminary estimates, with the National New Urbanization Plan (2014–2020) released in 2014, projecting the number of green buildings in China is set to increase from 2% of total new constructions in 2012 to 50% in 2020. When green building becomes the mainstream in the construction field, construction

---

[14]AECOM provided structural, MEP, and sustainability consulting services to the TEDA project. The frame of building's south façade is made of building integrated photovoltaic (BIPV). Natural ventilation, sun shading devices, and solar tube are widely adapted in entrance hall and office tower. On top of the podium, solar heating panel provides domestic hot water for the whole building. Besides renewable energy, energy-efficient systems such as ground source heat pump, capillary tube radiant cooling and heating, and lift power regenerative motor help bring the building's annual energy consumption and carbon emission 35 and 30% lower than national building code.

[15]In the design scheme, by using energy modeling, AECOM helped the project team to integrate high-performance strategies, such as good façade system, highly efficient lighting system and chillers, chilled beam, free cooling, demand ventilation and PV facilities, etc.

[16]The TEDA project has been certified for LEED Gold, BREEAM Very Good and GBL 3 star, and LEED Platinum and Beijing Aether Plaza for LEED Platinum and Green Mark Platinum.

waste will be reduced by 83%, and energy savings will increase by 50% (Zhang 2016; CBRE 2016).

3.1   Beyond Singular Buildings

As the concept of green building became more mature, it evolved beyond merely looking at secluded structures but rather as integral parts of their surrounding environment and the city at large from a planning perspective. Demands shifted into seeking cross-disciplinary sustainability design and planning consultancies especially from MNC consultants since many professionals in the green building practice were building service engineers with little or no technical competency in the environmental and ecological fields. First examples that considered site design were New World Guiyang mixed-use development[17] and Foshan Metropolitan mixed-use development (Figs. 6 and 7).[18]

To proactively contribute to the sustainability design and planning profession in China, and to assist the public sector to speed up the development in green building to achieve beyond just green building certification, AECOM initiated scenario planning to assess China's green building market. During 2011–2012, AECOM identified 17 driving forces for China's sustainable development in the coming 10 years. One of the most powerful yet unpredictable factors was extreme climate change and environmental incidents.

Even though earlier in 2006–2007, EDAW (now AECOM) was already engaged in developing a feasibility study, planning framework, and demonstration project for the Beijing Urban Storm Water Runoff Management System (BUSWRMS), the project did not get carried into implementation. Geographical information system and hydraulic modeling software were utilized to accurately predict stormwater runoff volumes and manage diversion into overflow detention and treatment facilities, and prototype facility for the Yizhuang District was proposed to test and to verify the system's preliminary design. Despite the study was well received, the importance of stormwater management was underlooked at the time.

---

[17]The project site is located in the north of the Jinyang New District in Guiyang, capital city of Guizhou province. AECOM designed an ecosystem for the community green belt, the jade lace, that connected four neighborhoods together as well as with nearby Jiang Jun Hill. Water-sensitive urban design principal was applied to integrate the regional water cycle, including storm water, groundwater, water supply, and wastewater management into environmental design to minimize environmental degradation and improve esthetic and recreational appeal. Rainwater garden, bio-swale, and other best practices not only reduce storm water runoff but also reserve and create ecological habitat for local animals. Bird feeder, butterfly wall, and squirrel nest also enhance the communication between residents and their environment.

[18]The project site is located in Foshan, southern Guangdong province with a total land area of 300 ha, and is planned for residential buildings, hotels, and retail facilities. The developer wishes to make the project a landmark low-carbon community in southern China. AECOM consulted on sustainable solutions including design review and adjustment recommendations, renewable energy, waste management, and on-site gray water reclamation and rainwater management.

Fig. 6 Foshan Metropolitan mixed-use development (1). Source: AECOM

Fig. 7 Foshan Metropolitan mixed-use development (2). Source: AECOM

The deadly storm that killed 37 people in Beijing on July 21, 2012, served as a wake-up call, and preparedness for extreme weather came under spotlight. Then Beijing Party Chief Jinlong Guo admitted that the tragedy revealed major problems in the city's planning, infrastructure, and emergency response and significant improvement is needed. The incident also initiated nationwide discussion on stormwater management. On December 12, 2013, President Xi Jinping called for development of sponge cities in China in his speech on urbanization work. Within a year in December 2014, the central government of China introduced pilot programs on sponge city development, with a central fund of 400–600 million CNY for each pilot city. In October 2015, the State Council of China issued Guiding Opinions on Promoting Sponge Cities Development, which specified that by 2020, at least 20% of urban areas shall be capable of absorbing and utilizing 70% of the stormwater and by 2030, 80% of urban areas shall meet the standard. Sponge cities have become a real national priority and generated opportunities for urban planning and sustainability consulting firms.

3.2   Evolving Connotations of Sustainable Building

All green building evaluation systems had primarily focused on the relationship between the building and the environment, i.e., how we can reduce the negative impacts of the building on its surrounding environment. In recent years, we saw the evolvement of the connotations of sustainable building, and more focus has been given to the relationship between the building and the people, i.e., how we can enhance the positive impacts of the building on the people who live in and utilize the building space. The pioneer in this regard is the newly emerged WELL building evaluation system.

After its first launch in October 2014 in the USA, the International WELL Building Standard (IWBI) was introduced to China in March 2015 by Paul Scialla, founder of IWBI. This further elevated the consciousness of enhancing people's health and well-being through the built environment. The seven categories of building performance, air, water, nourishment, light, fitness, comfort, and mind, place emphasis on the relationship between people and building and the human experience in the building.

As China's economy enters the "new normal" stage after China's economic slowdown since 2014, more attention is now placed on consumer experience and quality of life. The WELL Building Standard becomes the new trend in discussion of sustainable design. Progressive and forward-looking developers, such as Luneng Group, began seeking consulting services and partners on R&D and implementations of demonstration projects from late 2015. The Luneng Diaoyutai MGM Loft Apartments Project[19] is an example of first WELL building projects in

---

[19]The project covers a total land area of 121,320 m^2 with gross floor area of 406,467 m^2 in Beijing. The project will include villas, serviced apartments, commercial and financial facilities, schools, and other types of properties. AECOM has been involved since June 2016 to use WELL standards to optimize the relationship between the buildings and the well-being of the occupants and create a healthy and vibrant neighborhood. The lighting system, for instance, divides a day into five time intervals according to the 24-h circadian rhythms of people. LED light is used to present the diurnal changes to enhance residents' stable biological cycle and good sleeping quality. In addition to

the country. By 2017, China was already a world leader in WELL certification with over 1 million m^2 of building areas being WELL certified or pre-certified (CBRE 2017).

Currently, many companies are keen to adopt WELL standards besides looking into LEED or GBL certifications. Haworth Shanghai Showroom in Kerry Center is already LEED Platinum-certified, but they also became the first commercial interior in Asia to receive WELL Building Certification in September 2016. Sino-Ocean Land is another proactive company in seeking WELL certification. For its 230,000 m^2 development project in Guangzhou that comprised ten residential buildings, one commercial mixed-use building, kindergarten, primary school, and sports facilities, Sino-Ocean Land announced in December 2015 to adopt WELL standards—the first residential community in China to do so.

4   Challenges

The real estate market in China is like no other, and the huge yet constantly growing demand for housing is also rarely seen in the world. Green building is of course perceived as a good thing, but does it make economic sense for the developers and users in China?

For commercial real estate, maybe. Office buildings are the largest clientele for LEED certification in China and studies have shown the offices with LEED certification enjoy a 25% premium in terms of rental fees as compared to those uncertified. However, it must be noted that the 25% figure is an average; there are also cases where green certification does not make much a difference or even brings about a surprising disadvantage. For example, in Houhai area in Shenzhen, Nanjing Xilu area in Shanghai, and Financial Street in Beijing, all core CBD areas in China's first-tier cities, the rental fees of LEED-certified offices are 11.3, 10.7, and 2.0% lower than the uncertified ones in the same areas, respectively (CBRE 2017).

For residential buildings, the situation is even more discouraging. First, there is a clear disconnection between the certification standards that focus on reduction of energy use and environmental pollution of the building as a whole and the personalized needs of the residents for healthy and comfortable indoor environment. Compared with price and location which the home buyers are most sensitive to, the greenness of the building has minimal impact in their decision-making. Second, the apartments that might seek green certification are of very good quality in themselves and will sell well anyways, whether or not the building is designed and built to the green standards and/or green certified. Third, since 2016, the Chinese government launched measures to control the rapid growth of housing price, and many cities have issued price caps for the apartments. Under such circumstances, being green

---

adopting WELL standards for the whole community, the main building also aims for WELL Platinum certification.

might be a pure additional upfront investment without meaningful economic returns for the developers, who will be naturally discouraged from doing so.

A related problem is that the supply chain for green building industry in China is not robust enough. It is estimated that green building materials only represent 10% of the total building materials market in China (Industry Research Information Bank 2016), while the government aims for 40% ratio by 2020 (MoHURD 2017). Since the market is still considered in its very early stage, green building materials are difficult to source and sometimes not readily available in the country. Furthermore, the implementation of building codes varies from place to place in China; some developers will have little incentive to use expensive authentic green materials, and suppliers may also verify materials without strictly complying with relevant requirements. As a result, the qualities of green building materials are not guaranteed. These economic factors impeded the development of green buildings in China, and more regulation and incentives are needed in this regard.

4.1 Professional Capability and Awareness

As the dimensions of green buildings continue to evolve, the practice now requires professionals from different backgrounds. Conventionally, the concept of green building had a focus on energy and water use reduction; thus architects and designer would only need to work with engineers to make the building "green." As sustainability takes on a much broader meaning to include the well-being of people and additional aspects such as the surrounding environment, life cycle footprint, sustainable sourcing of building materials, and physical and mental health of people, not only cross-disciplinary engineering professionals are required, but also health professionals and physiologists will need to be incorporated. Moreover, to translate a good design concept into reality, skillful construction workers who truly understand what is needed and build the structure to the exact specifications of the design is critical. However, there is insufficient supply of professionals who are equipped for performing integrated design services, and the construction workers in China lack the basic knowledge of green building. Also, most training materials on sustainability and green buildings are not designed in the way that the workers can easily comprehend.

For the general public, their environmental awareness has been significantly raised over the past years, especially in the wake of major disasters such as the July 21 storm in Beijing, which gave rise to the concept of sponge cities, and the 2013 smog incident in Beijing that popularized awareness on PM2.5. These pushed the government to issue new national air standards. Nevertheless, on the green building front, people's understanding remains limited. Many still simply think of green buildings as those that use less electricity and water, rather than a holistic system that reduces the negative impacts on the natural environment and human health. It is imperative to educate the public on what green building really means and how they can help enhance their lives. Ultimately, the true market demand will be driven by the general public, who are also the end clients of green buildings and sustainable environment.

4.2   Regulatory Standards

Compared to the developed countries such as the UK or the USA, where green building standards are constantly evolving to set benchmark for integrated approach to sustainable developments, China's green building practice remains at the level of getting green labels with compliance to a basket of various national standards, mostly in the fields of energy conservation, water use reduction, and volatile compound levels in building materials.

In the UK, in addition to BREEAM, standard and codes have evolved to be carbon oriented, and the government has developed Energy Performance Certificates, Display Energy Certificate, and Code for Sustainable Homes which will be replaced by Nearly-Zero Energy Building by 2018 (Department for Communities and Local Government 2015). These codes are the foundation for green building development and serve as benchmark for developers. In the USA, besides LEED, there are other widely accepted standards, such as Energy Star by the Department of Energy, WaterSense and IAQ Label for the Homes by the Environmental Protection Agency (EPA), and so on. The American Society of Heating, Refrigerating and Air-Conditioning Engineers (ASHRAE) is also an important player in this field. In 2014, ASHRAE published Standard 189.1, which provides total building sustainability guidance for designing, building, and operating high-performance green buildings. From site location to energy use to recycling, this standard sets the foundation for green buildings by addressing site sustainability, water use efficiency, energy efficiency, indoor environmental quality, and the building's impact on the atmosphere, materials, and resources.

But it is very encouraging to see the Chinese government to publish a draft revision of GBL standards in September 2018 for public comments. In this draft revision, the indictors were restructured to cover six aspects, including safety and durability, convenience of use, health and comfort, environment and livability, resource conservation, and management and innovation (MoHURD 2018). This revision addresses the issue of sustainability from a more comprehensive and people-first perspective and hence is more aligned with international green building standards, including LEED and WELL.

However, this revision is still a draft; when and whether it will be issued remains a question. We look forward to the promulgation and implementation of more integrated codes and standards so that the development of green buildings in China can be elevated to the next level.

5   Moving Forward

Looking back at the passing years, it is easy to see the scope of building sustainability in China has been expanding, from singular green building to green neighborhood and now green district and even green cities. The 2008 Beijing Olympic Village is a key example as the first LEED neighborhood development Gold project in China and one of the first in the world (Ginsberg 2016). More recently the development of Tongzhou District as Beijing's subcenter provides ample opportunities in building and urban sustainability. Besides being appointed as a trial district for sponge city development, Tongzhou also aims to become a Near Zero Emissions Demonstration District, which requires to reduce carbon emission sources, improve energy efficiency in industrial and service sectors, and adopt carbon sink compensation measures. In addition, green transportation coverage in Tongzhou will need to reach 80% by 2020, which is higher than the 75% target for Beijing's central urban areas (Beijing Municipal government 2016).

Moving forward, it is certain China's building and urban sustainability market will continue to grow and bring about abundant opportunities for both types of players in China's green building market, including developers that focus on green building certification and those that focus on technological innovation.

For the developers that pursue green building certification, they have gone through an evolving process over the past 10 years during which period certification was first introduced and then grew rapidly and finally reached maturity. As green building services focusing on certification have entered the phase of price competition, it also means the added value of green building labels have diminished. For products at the maturity phase, differentiation is a key path to maintain their added value. China is currently promoting sponge city development and has introduced policies for energy conservation and pollution reduction. Looking ahead, it can be predicted that environmental management system (EMS) focusing on energy efficiency and enhanced performance and site stormwater management are some of the differentiation areas that can satisfy client needs, generate added value, and become new drivers of the green building certification process.

For the developers focusing on technological innovation, they have strived to provide comfortable, energy-efficient, and high-performance buildings for the high-end market. This group not only appreciates the importance of environmental protection and energy efficiency but also demands comfortable and safe living environment. New technologies are accepted as long as they can provide higher levels of comfort. For technology-centered developers, core green building technology has to be integrated with other relevant technologies to bring a whole product solution that promises comfort, health, and value.

The Jin Mao Group is a forward-looking group that has taken action. The core technology of the company is radiant ceiling, also termed as "ecological air conditioning system." Compared to the traditional stand-alone heating system and independent air conditioners, the radiant ceiling employs ceiling blocks with piping system imbedded inside, along which hot or cold water runs through and provides heating or cooling for the building through radiation. Additionally, the company also offers other supporting technologies, including independent fresh air system, low energy consumption system, noise reduction system, same floor drainage system, smart home system, new media system, and home security system. These eight systems combined can provide an integrated solution for comfortable, energy-efficient, convenient, and safe living environment. Another example is Modernland Group, whose core technology is the same radiant ceiling, but they put forward a technological system that features constant temperature, humidity, oxygen level, and quietness. They also combined their core constant temperature technology with other technologies to provide integrated home solutions.

Recent environmental studies suggested that about 40% of carbon emissions currently are from buildings and roughly half of new buildings going up in the world are in China. As the world's largest carbon emitter and energy consumer, China has added more than 3 billion m^2 of building floor areas annually, and the floor areas in China today exceeds that of the USA and the EU combined (Yu 2015). The commitment China provided in COP21 illustrated the determination China has on enforcing policies and regulations to reach its goals. This is supported by the survey published in February, World Green Building Trends 2016 SmartMarket Report, a research done by Dodge Data and Analytics and US Green Building Council. Although only 5% of their current China's projects are green, 28% reported they expect to be doing over 60% of their projects as green building within 3 years.

Undoubtedly, protecting natural resources, improving air quality, and enhancing health and well-being through green building and developments are key priorities for China. New commercial, high-rise residential buildings and sustainable communities are expected to have high growth. Notably, out of 35 responding nations, China has the highest percentage at 35% responded that they expect to work on sustainable mixed-use developments combining residential and commercial building (Benjamin 2016).

Furthermore, with energy consumption of buildings in China growing year after year, attention has been paid to retrofit and renovate existing buildings to improve energy efficiency. In 2011, the government strengthened its obligation by requiring a 10% reduction in energy consumption per square meter for commercial buildings and a 15% reduction for large commercial buildings with more than 20,000 m^2 of floor area by the end of 2015. More than 400 million m^2 in residential homes and all eligible commercial buildings in the northern heating zone are anticipated to be retrofitted by the end of 2015 and 2020, respectively (Hojjati 2015). Without mention, three recently LEED-certified Platinum buildings under LEED v2009 for Existing Buildings, Operations and Maintenance (LEED's EBOM), AZIA Center in Shanghai,[20] Beijing

---

[20]AZIA Center is the first office building in China to be certified LEED Platinum under LEED v2009 for Existing Buildings: Operations and Maintenance. The project is 11-year center; 500 m^2 of plant area was added to improve the environment; submeters were installed to monitor consumption to improve water and energy efficiency; new landscape irrigation system was installed to enhance rainwater collection and irrigation. Air-handling units and fresh air unit filters were replaced.

IFC Building[21] in 2015, and Chengdu IFS in July 2016[22] (Cruz 2016), show the county's awareness in retrofitting existing buildings to improve sustainable performance. Since it can take up to 80 years to make up for the environmental impact of demolishing an old building and constructing a new one, converting existing buildings to use less energy, water, and natural resources, and improving the indoor environment and building operations, the existing buildings present the green building industry with a great opportunity (Xue 2016).

To sum up, going forward, the certification-focused developers will introduce new technologies to increase the added value of green building labels. These new technologies will need to echo the Chinese government's call on energy efficiency and pollution reduction and aim to resolve current environmental challenges, such as air quality and urban storm management. For technology-focused developers, they will need to combine their advanced core technology with the existing ones to capture larger shares of the market, particularly in the residential area. The ideas and concepts that may bring about technological integration, such as smart home and home energy management system, will be the main drivers of the market. Strengthening technical capabilities in integrated delivery services beyond traditional architecture and engineering will be inevitable for design and engineering professionals in the green building industry because sustainable design is a legitimated concept. For both types of developers and the design and engineering professionals in the industry, the trends of increasingly tighter government regulations on green buildings, with more and more localities to enforce green building standards by law, and the shifting focus of the green building standards from energy and environmental considerations to broader sustainability requirements have never been so clear. Every one of us has a good reason to believe that green buildings will further grow in China and support the country to march toward a more sustainable future.

References

Beijing Municipal Government. (2016). *Major infrastructure development plan of Beijing during 13th Five Year Plan Period (2016–2020)*.
Benjamin, H. (2016). *World green building trends 2016: Focus on China*. Retrieved October 29, 2016, from http://www.usgbc.org/articles/world-green-building-trends-2016-focus-china

---

[21]Beijing International Finance Center (IFC) increased outdoor air ventilation rates for all air-handling units serving occupied spaces by at least 30% to help prevent particulates from entering into the building; smoking was prohibited in the building and within 75 m of entryways, outdoor intakes and operable windows were installed, and an indoor air quality management plan for facility additions and alteration phases were developed and implemented to protect construction workers' occupant's health.

[22]Chengdu International Finance Square (IFS) is a 760,000 m^2 development by The Wharf (Holdings) Ltd. It achieves a 35% higher energy efficiency than the average for buildings and overshoots Platinum standards by 7 points.

CBRE. (2016). *China major report—Towards excellence—Market performance of green commercial buildings in the Greater China region.*

CBRE. (2017). *China major report—China green building report 2017.*

Chau, C. K., Tse, M. S., & Chung, K. Y. (2010). A choice experiment to estimate the effect of green experience on preferences and willingness-to-pay for green building attributes. *Building and Environment, 45*(11), 2553–2561.

Chinese Real Estate Association. (2018). *China Green Real Estate Development Report 2018.*

Chinese Society for Urban Studies. (2016). *China green building 2016.* Beijing: China Architecture & Building Press.

Cruz, A. (2016). *Could green building finally be taking off in China?* Retrieved September 7, 2016, form http://www.property-report.com/how-green-buildings-are-gaining-appeal-in-the-worlds-biggest-co2-emitter/

Department for Communities and Local Government. (2015). *2010 to 2015 government policy: Energy efficiency in buildings.* Retrieved March 28, 2016, from https://www.gov.uk/government/publications/2010-to-2015-government-policy-energy-efficiency-in-buildings

Geng, Y., Dong, H., Xue, B., & Fu, J. (2011). *An overview of Chinese green building standards.*

Ginsberg, M. (2016). *Reflections from the second U.S.—China climate leaders summit.* Retrieved August 20, 2016, from http://www.usgbc.org/articles/reflections-second-us%E2%80%93china-climate-leaders-summit

Hojjati, B. (2015). *Today in energy—Chinese policies aim to increase energy efficiency in buildings.* U.S. Energy Information Administration (EIA).

Industry Research Information Bank. (2016). *Development stages and outlook of green building materials.* Retrieved May 30, 2016, from http://www.irinbank.com/analyst/110/11196.shtml

Lewis, G. (2009). *Building the future. China international business article on LEED in China Wednesday.* Retrieved August 30, 2016, from http://chinagreenbuildings.blogspot.tw/2009/02/china-international-business-article-on.html

Ministry of Finance. (2012). *Opinions on accelerating green building development in China.*

Ministry of Housing and Urban-Rural Development (MoHURD). (2017). *13th five year plan for construction industry development.*

Ministry of Housing and Urban-Rural Development (MoHURD). (2018). *Notice on soliciting public comments on the draft revision of green building assessment standards.*

National Development and Reform Commission. (2007). *Middle and long term development plan for renewable energy.* Retrieved May 26, 2016, from http://www.sdpc.gov.cn/zcfb/zcfbghwb/200709/W020140220601800225116.pdf

Nelson, C. (2012). *China's green building future.* Retrieved March 14, 2016, from http://www.chinabusinessreview.com/chinas-green-building-future/

Qin, Y. (2015). *Green building industry in China.* International City/County Management Association.

Ramanujam, M. (2016). *Leaders across China are creating a more sustainable future for millions.* Retrieved October 28, 2016, from http://www.usgbc.org/articles/leaders-across-china-are-creating-more-sustainable-future-millions

Sun Daming. (2011). *The incremental cost research & survey on green buildings in China.* Retrieved October 5, 2016, from http://wenku.baidu.com/link?url=e3QNspD9nH5h5ED37vKvUr6NeSBIF6eGSmg3o_MIkDjSmc7FxqUirPcp8lpVOr6GLflKccpcCgSqmfdMUOV5AZpSZvyVcgi73cov5rKQe1m

USGBC. (2014). *LEED in motion: Greater China.* China, Hong Kong, Taiwan

USGBC. (2017). *LEED in motion: China.*

Wang, Y., Yang, G., & Shi, Y. (2011). Research and practice of Vanke on green building. *Construction Technology, 7*, 34–36.

Xinhua News. (2016). *Vanke released 2015 annual report.* Retrieved November 19, 2016, from http://news.xinhuanet.com/house/yz/2016-03-16/c_1118350416.htm

Xue, Z. (2016). *In China, LEED makes existing buildings greener.* Retrieved September 21, 2016, from http://www.usgbc.org/articles/china-leed-makes-existing-buildings-greener

Yu, S. (2015). *China policy institute: analysis. The future of green construction in China*. Retrieved September 15, 2016, from https://cpianalysis.org/2015/11/23/the-future-of-green-construction-in-china/

Zhang, Y. (2016). *Green building: The future of construction*. Retrieved November 17, 2016, from http://www.china.org.cn/business/2016-08/29/content_39186867.htm

Thoughts on China's Real Estate Policies

Baoxing Qiu

Abstract

This article shares the author's suggestions to the orientation of public policies regarding real estate industry and market. Highlighting the importance of avoiding broad-brushed centralized policies for all without consideration of local specifications and providing a policy focusing on equality, the author advocates a legalized structure of effective tax mechanism to curtain speculation and encourage location-based guidance to real estate industry operation.

1 Introduction

Real estate regulation should be people-oriented. That is to say, real estate regulation should effectively restrain housing speculation in order to promote fair allocation of spatial resources and thus wealth and to make housing affordable for low- and middle-income households and in the meantime to gradually eliminate real estate bubbles that endanger national financial stability and security.

As China's urbanization enters its second stage, real estate regulation has also entered a critical phase. The polarization of the Chinese real estate market is evident and is getting worse. Housing inventory, including government-funded social housing, has been increasing in second and third tier cities. The pressure of reducing existing real estate inventory has been increasing. This is the result of the current regulations that are based on short-term approval of land conversion, restrictions on

---

I wrote this article to reflect my thoughts on real estate policies in 2017. In retrospect, many of the ideas stated here have been reflected and implemented in the current real estate policies in China.

B. Qiu (✉)
Ministry of Housing and Urban Rural Development, Beijing, PR China

© Springer Nature Switzerland AG 2021
B. Wang, T. Just (eds.), *Understanding China's Real Estate Markets*, Management for Professionals, https://doi.org/10.1007/978-3-030-49032-4_18

housing purchases according to locations of household registration, and the imposition of property transaction taxes. This type of regulation would not serve the purpose of restraining speculation and reduction of existing inventory. As international speculative money flows into China, market polarization could become even worse, and the volatility of housing prices could be especially exacerbated in some regions. More seriously, if real estate regulation is not able to stabilize the expectations of the public and developers alike, conventional regulative policies could lose efficacy, resulting in unrealistic expectations of housing prices, and thus prices and large-scale speculation could become out of control. If housing prices fluctuate at double-digit levels, the capital originally invested in manufacturing could be squeezed and shift to the real estate sector. This would have negative effects on economic recovery and long-term economic structural adjustment. Therefore, it is urgent to establish medium- and long-term mechanisms and policy solutions for the real estate market and its industry with Chinese characteristics that aim to smoothly transition from the current short-term-oriented policies. I suggest that these mid- to long-term policies comply with the following seven principles.

2   Principle of "Homes for All"

During the process of China's urbanization, real estate has been perceived as a pillar industry by local governments due to the fact that it drives the broad growth of various industries. However, the successes and especially failures of developed countries demonstrate that real estate should be the means for the distribution of living space in essence, and thus the principle of "Homes for All" should be upheld. Real estate should not be treated as a long-term pillar industry that is depended upon to expand consumer demand or be promoted as a permanent driver of economic growth, unless there is a need for real estate to support the economy in the short run during serious economic recessions. Otherwise, the promotion of real estate could exacerbate inequality of wealth, heighten unnecessary speculation, and shrink fundamental industries, which would fundamentally undermine stable long-term economic growth of a society. On the other hand, the main source of wealth of most households is indeed home ownership. Any broad-brush unified regulations would be resisted by many due to their possible adverse effect on the interests of the majority of the society. So the government should exercise extreme caution in policy orientation, which should restrain real estate speculation but not adversely affect basic housing demands.

Decentralize location-based regulations
The advantages of current housing purchase restrictions based on household registration are their clarity, feasibility, and swift short-term effects as well as their direct link to migration policy in Chinese megacities. On the other hand, the disadvantages are that they could conflict with the direction of gradual household registration reform and could undermine those fundamental need-based demands, such as

retirees joining their only child, and cities' ability to draw talent from various locations. Therefore, such regulations should be replaced by indirect regulations such as residence-based credit and taxation; of course, the means can vary for selected megacities. Due to the criticality of real estate regulations for the overall market, policies should focus on the establishment of long-term mechanisms and avoid negative effects based on rigidity.

Differentiate Basic Housing Needs

Housing has dual attributes of investment and consumption. In the medium and long run, housing policy should restore its nature as a shelter to meet basic human needs. The following three differentiated principles for policies should be adopted:

The first principle is to achieve deleveraging by providing various housing credits to people with different income and wealth levels, including offering differentiated support toward an individualized housing providence fund. The second is to replace the single channel of social housing supply with multiple channels for social housing construction and especially to diversify channels for building public rental houses and urban old neighborhood regeneration. The third is to eliminate excessive housing speculation through the establishment of comprehensive real estate taxes, including a consumption tax, a vacancy tax, a transaction tax, and a property tax.

Furthermore, all policies falling under these three principles should be progressive and experimental before finalization, with details guiding nuances instead of a rigid overall cookie cutter orientation.

Achieve Comprehensive Tax Mechanisms

The advantages of creating a real estate transaction tax are to achieve a long-term balance of capital wealth, to restrain excessive speculation, and to raise revenue for local governments. However, its disadvantages are insignificant regulatory effects on housing vacancy and homeownership of excessive residential units, and on restraining housing prices, and even on increasing housing prices due to the constraining of second-hand housing supply. It would also trigger negative practices such as fraudulent divorces to increase allowable purchases of housing units.

Governments should adopt systematic regulation, similar to the practice by developed countries, on restraining housing speculation through a progressive consumption tax, property tax, vacancy tax, and transaction tax. The effect of incremental regulation on households is lower than that of inventory regulation. Therefore, regulations should be enacted on a trial basis before national implementation.

Promote Proactive Management

In 2011, in 9 out of 40 major cities in China, including Sanya, Shenzhen, Wenzhou, Beijing, Xiamen, Shanghai, Hangzhou, Fuzhou, and Taiyuan, the observed house price-income ratio was above 10, and in 19 major cities, including the above 9, the house price-income ratio was above 8. If the government adopts measures to restrain housing prices, for example, setting the price increase target lower than one-third of household income growth for major cities, and if the house price-income ratio is over

8, it could take advantage of the current wave of urbanization and avoid overly fast-rising housing prices and bring the ratio back to a normal level through a time-for-space strategy. Thus, it could avoid a Japanese-style financial crisis caused by insufficient demand for housing during the later stages of urbanization.

Establish the Nationwide Real Estate Law

Real estate policy tools, such as a real estate consumption tax, a transaction tax, and a vacancy tax, and current restrictions imposed on housing purchases, may be effective for sustainable development of real estate. But such policies are not prescribed in legislation, hard to apply with appropriate nationwide scale, and could cause future disputes. In the long run, real estate regulation must be legalized and normalized. Therefore, the government should promptly formulate real estate laws and formalize some effective regulations. Furthermore, national legislation should make clear the principles of regulation, while local legislation, according to the local circumstances, stipulates details of tax categories and rates, effective time framework, procedure, and so on. This would offer local government regulation toolkits and make clear local governments' duty of avoiding excessive real estate speculation and thus achieve housing price control. The central government should strictly supervise and evaluate the performance of local governments.

Mobilize Local Governments

The discrepancies in social and economic development among various regions in China are significant. It is inappropriate to adopt broad-brush regulations. The national government should mobilize local governments to formulate their own regulations with initiative and creativity. If regulation was effective, the central government could summarize and promote it. Short-term regulations could be integrated into medium- and long-term ones through implementation of different approaches and phases, based on local circumstances.

The first level of policy implementation can be at a subtle level: continuation of housing purchase restrictions already in place for the permanent residence population in some coastal megacities but gradual abolition of such restrictions in other cities as housing price targets are reached. Measures can also include raising the down payment ratio and interest rate for second homes and extending the scope of the comprehensive real estate tax.

The second level of policy implementation can be a moderate intervention, which includes implementing housing purchase restrictions, except for the permanent resident population, and tightening housing purchase limitations on people without household registration. For residents who live in prefecture-level cities where housing prices might be rising too fast, housing purchase limitations need to be broadened to include those who do not have household registration but still contributing to social insurance and taxes locally; for residents in large cities, housing purchase limitation needs to focus on raising real estate tax rates, levying a vacancy tax, and restricting the issuance of residential loans for purchasing second homes.

The third level of policy implementation can be a strong policy intervention: to enhance restriction of housing purchases in large cities where targets of housing price control are absent or missed, to prohibit loans for the purchase of second homes, and to further raise real estate taxes and vacancy tax rates and to levy a progressive consumption tax.

All three levels of policy implementation can be adjusted according to local market situations. As such, policy intervention guidance could assign clear responsibility to governments at all levels and could have adjustable regulation scope, strength, and flexibility. It then could achieve an effective connection between short-term regulation goals and medium- and long-term ones.

3 Conclusion

In brief, whether real estate regulation can be effective and successful is directly related to domestic and global economic situations and public attitudes because it involves an interaction of complex political, economic, and social factors. When formulating real estate policies, the demands of the public, especially those with low and medium income, should be respected, as should local governments' spirits of initiative and creation and domestic and international historical experiences and lessons. If incremental regulation is effective, there should not be regulation on existing stocks. If partial regulations such as those on cities with uncontrolled housing price increases and on an irrational house-income ratio are effective, there should not be universal regulations for the whole country. If regulations can be handled by local governments, the potential risks should not be borne by the central government. More importantly, the formulation of central and local regulations should be people-oriented, highlighting coordination between short-term regulations and medium- and long-term policies, between local government initiatives and central government supervision, and between regional experiments and overall implementation. China's real estate regulation should have a macro-level design. However, if the macro-level design is too specific, it cannot effectively resolve complicated and volatile market circumstances and diversified local regulation needs. It would thus involve unnecessary risks. Therefore, real estate regulations and policies should be flexible and leave room for adjustments according to local needs. China's real estate policies should be transformed from being reactive to a progressive and fully legalized model. All regulations should have legal bases through their formulation and implementation based on the laws of real estate. This would enable individual local governments to effectively implement legal toolkits for real estate regulation.

Minding the Strategies: A Progressive Development Model

Haijun Xia

Abstract

Based on its rapid economic growth of the past four decades, China has the largest real estate market in the world. However, given the sheer number of domestic and foreign real estate enterprises operating in China, it also boasts one of the fiercest industrial competitions worldwide. The real estate enterprise Evergrande has the largest scales of real estate development operation in the country, and its business strategies of the recent 20 years have followed progressive stages—namely, choosing the right scale for residential units, expanding into second-tier cities, returning to first-tier cities, and promoting diversified business operations.

1   Introduction

Evergrande, established in 1996 and listed as a public company in Hong Kong in 2009, has developed into a real estate-focused enterprise with assets totaling RMB 757 billion. It expanded its affiliated business into diversified industries such as finance, technology, health care, and cultural tourism. It has more than 400 real estate projects in over 170 major Chinese cities throughout the country, with a land reserve of 156 million square meters. Since being listed, Evergrande has maintained its rapid growth and achieved an increase in contracted sales volume, growing from RMB 30.3 billion in 2009 to RMB 551.3 billion in 2018, at a compounded annual average growth rate of 37%. Its net profits have increased from RMB 1.1 billion in 2009 to RMB 72.2 billion in 2018. Subsequently, its cash balance has increased from

H. Xia (✉)
Evergrande Group, Shenzhen, PR China

© Springer Nature Switzerland AG 2021   273
B. Wang, T. Just (eds.), *Understanding China's Real Estate Markets*, Management
for Professionals, https://doi.org/10.1007/978-3-030-49032-4_19

RMB 14.4 billion in 2009 to RMB 164 billion in 2015, at a compounded annual average growth rate of 50%.

2   Implementing the Scale Priority Strategy

In 1996, when Evergrande was established in Guangzhou, the city was already home to more than 2000 real estate companies, some of which had quite considerable scale and competitive strength. As a latecomer to the industry, Evergrande expanded its scale rapidly, benefitting from China's rapid urbanization. Accordingly, Evergrande's strategy of scale priority emerged at a historic moment. In response to market conditions at the time, Evergrande adopted the business model of building residential units with relatively smaller usable areas and thus lower total purchase prices for customers to ensure rapid sales and speed up the capital turnover, thereby expanding its operational scale rapidly. To better achieve its goal, in 2000 Evergrande started to integrate its resources more effectively, standardize its development process, and focus attention on management to promote its operating efficiency and performance. Such efforts enabled it to support its future development.

Evergrande soon successively developed many Jinbi Series building projects, forming the prototype of product standardization, and established a complete system from middle-end products to middle- and high-end products to high-end products and then to the tourist real estate products, enriching and diversifying the overall product line. During this period, a series of initiatives with profound influence on the future were gradually implemented. For instance, in 2004, Evergrande developed a set of rigorous construction standards to ensure high-quality construction throughout the process, thereby laying the foundation for a long-term product quality advantage. Evergrande also established more than 6000 technical documents guiding project construction, with strict requirements for each physical detail, and required the management team to develop a thorough understanding of the enterprise and process of real estate and construction operations, in order to provide strong support for the company's expansion throughout the country.

At the same time, Evergrande established and improved a set of target plan mechanisms at the core of its management system. It further implemented talent cultivation by adopting a forward-looking approach, allocating several managers, deputy managers, and manager assistants without limit in a department. With the establishment of each regional company, Evergrande dispatched exceptional team members to form the core of these regional companies to carry out Evergrande's management style and company culture. The company's first batch of professional teams seeking land projects was dispatched to major provincial capitals during this period, laying a solid foundation for the company's expansion of land reserves throughout the country.

By placing scale of operation as a priority in strategy, Evergrande increased its number of projects from one when the company was established to more than ten simultaneous projects in 2005; it also grew its number of employees from approximately ten at the beginning to 2000 people responsible for annual sales of RMB 2.1 billion, thereby becoming one of the top ten real estate enterprises in China.

3   Expanding into Second-Tier Cities

Over the years, China's real estate industry has increasingly matured, and Guangzhou where Evergrande's headquarters was located for many years as well as other first-tier cities, has gradually become saturated with increasingly fierce competition among various real estate developments. In contrast, the market of second-tier cities was still at the initial development stages, meaning that it not only had a huge market capacity but also had the potential to become the subject of numerous preferential policies by the government, providing extremely favorable conditions for companies like Evergrande to implement the next strategy of the country's urbanization development.

After 2 years of planning, Evergrande officially started its nationwide rollout in 2006, with the most potential second-tier cities in China being the main focus in which to expand the enterprise development space in an all-round manner. To adapt to the deep expansion in second-tier cities nationwide, Evergrande established an intensive and collectivized management model under the control of the headquarters to ensure that regional companies could reduce the risks without detours, that the excellent project model could be duplicated throughout the country, and that the enterprise culture could be inherited around China.

Under such a management mindset, Evergrande implemented a standardized operational model. For example, Evergrande's headquarters implemented standardized operations in its regional companies throughout the country, including the standardization of every aspect of the development process, from the management model, project selection, planning and design, material selection, and bidding to the engineering management as well as marketing, so as to minimize the operating risks from the nationwide expansion and ensure effective cost control and excellent project construction. "Such a standardized operational model gradually became a basic element of Evergrande's rapid growth".

Thanks to the collectivized management and standardized operation, Evergrande utilized its scale advantage to implement the uniform bidding and tendering of projects throughout the country. Construction and building materials could be supplied through centralized purchasing, and Evergrande thus substantially reduced the material and equipment prices under the precondition of guaranteed quality. Meanwhile, by relying on the nationwide unified purchasing and delivery system to deliver materials and equipment directly to the construction site, Evergrande effectively reduced transportation and warehouse costs in the supply chain, thereby putting an end to the counterfeit and shoddy products and guaranteed product quality.

After successfully implementing the strategy of full-scale expansion into second-tier cities, Evergrande achieved remarkable unconventional scale and growth in more than 20 cities, including Guangzhou, Shanghai, Tianjin, Shenyang, Wuhan, Kunming, Chengdu, Chongqing, and Nanjing, with a land reserve of 54.98 million square meters—the most provincial capitals throughout China—and fully formed a strategic pattern for nationwide expansion, laying a solid foundation for the future rapid enterprise development, with an unprecedented sales volume of more than RMB 50 billion.

Due to the constant improvement in sales performance, Evergrande was favored by flagship international capital investors. During this period, Evergrande introduced strategic investments from Deutsche Bank, Temasek, and Merrill Lynch, with accumulative funds totaling more than USD1 billion raised in the international capital markets. On November 5, 2009, Evergrande was successfully listed on the Hong Kong Stock Exchange and, on the same day, achieved a closing stock price 34.28% higher than the issued premium, with the aggregate market value of HKD 70.5 billion. Thus, Evergrande became a real estate enterprise of the largest market value in the Hong Kong exchange that was originated in mainland China.

4   Developing Third-Tier Cities

As China's urbanization advanced, the huge market space of third-tier cities emerged, offering low land prices and great market potential. Since 2010, Evergrande has worked to develop third-tier cities such as Foshan, Zhongshan, Ezhou, Nanchong, Anshan, Qujing, and Chenzhou to increase the proportion of projects in these cities and seize this broad market. At the time, residents of third-tier cities did not have a deep understanding of commercial residential building and community life and did not know much about the Evergrande brand. Thus, product quality promised to be the best stepping stone into the market. Therefore, while seizing the opportunities offered by third-tier cities, Evergrande further improved the product quality and implemented some important initiatives, such as fully refined interior fitting out, before building delivery and high-quality residential facilities and amenities with garden environments.

Evergrande remains the sole enterprise in China, providing fully refined interior fitting out and decoration before building delivery, highly consistent with the house-purchasing requirements of the population in third-tier cities, where all decoration materials used are high-quality and well-known brands. By being the sole enterprise to adopt this approach, Evergrande was able to firmly establish its market shares within a relatively short period of time.

The upgrading of the community gardens is a realistic reflection of a continually improving social life and is an urgent demand in China. Evergrande has consistently designed and constructed residences for everyday consumers based on the climate, natural environment, and supporting facilities, gradually forming the garden theme with a lake scene as the core of residential communities. This landscape-conscious approach has led to the development of the community gardens into a healthy ecosystem by making the best of terrain, topography, and local natural resources, which nowadays have become an outstanding feature of Evergrande's real estate development so that the company's market competitiveness is greatly improved.

Along with seizing the opportunity offered by third-tier cities, Evergrande has substantially increased the number of its projects in related cities. Given the huge space of the local real estate market, Evergrande formed models of the efficient construction process, standardized large-scale development, rapid market sales, and fast turnovers, using standardized operation and powerful execution to ensure that project sales could be started within 6–8 months of land acquisition. This process helped the company realize a high turnover and increase its capital utilization rate. In addition, this initiative ensured that Evergrande could have salable buildings throughout the year—an optimal strategy for seizing the broadest market share of third-tier cities successfully.

It would be impossible to seize the broad market of third-tier cities without sufficient capital strength. Therefore, Evergrande took full advantage of its listed position in Hong Kong and in the international capital markets to expand the financing channels. In 2010, the company successfully issued international bonds totaling USD 2.75 billion, creating a record in terms of the scale of global bond issuance among China's real estate enterprises. By virtue of the consecutive implementation of the two discussed strategies (i.e., expansion into second-tier cities in 2004 and seizing the opportunities offered by third-tier cities in 2010), Evergrande became a leading enterprise in these cities early on in China and rapidly completed its nationwide strategic positioning, developing more than 800 projects in 220 major cities throughout the country, including 84 projects in second-tier cities and 97 projects in the third-tier cities in 2018. Such efforts created a solid foundation for the large-scale growth of Evergrande's sales performance.

5   Returning to First-Tier Cities

Those focusing on China's economy might remember that, since the end of 2009, the macro-control over the country's real estate market has continually been tightened; as a result, the real estate market has cooled down to some extent. However, China's developed first-tier cities, with their centralized public resources, were always hot spots with net population inflows where the demand for market-rate residential buildings exceeded the supply. Along with the constantly powerful self-strength and the increasingly solid capital strength, this situation brought Evergrande the idea of returning to the first-tier cities in a large-scale manner.

Starting in 2013, Evergrande increased its investments in first-tier cities to realize a more balanced nationwide positioning as well as to further optimize the regional standards for all projects. In 2013, Evergrande developed projects in the first-tier cities such as Beijing, Shanghai, Guangzhou, and Shenzhen, winning three projects in Beijing for the first time, five projects in Shanghai, and two projects in Guangzhou and Shenzhen consecutively.

To match the increasing investment in first-tier cities, Evergrande innovated financing channels and methods to uniquely promote large project financing during this period, raising more than RMB 50 billion and effectively solving its financial challenges for developing first-tier cities on a large scale and winning high-quality projects. In addition, Evergrande initiated the Red Chips Company to issue China's domestic debts in 2015, further solidifying its capital strength. At present, Evergrande has a cash balance of more than RMB 164 billion, thereby providing a guarantee for a future steady development.

To adapt to the macro-economic conditions of slowing growth in China, Evergrande developed ten indicators for quantitative assessment, with a strict assessment of the top ten key tasks, including sales refunds and project quality, to promote a substantial increase at the enterprise management level. Such efforts provided an internal guarantee for the overall positioning in the first-tier cities. Thus, during the period of strict macro-control that prioritized first-tier cities, Evergrande adopted bold strategies to focus on first-tier cities.

Soon after Evergrande's positive business orientation focusing on first-tier cities, the constantly and dynamically adjusted macro-control policies were relaxed to some extent, and the population affected by the house purchase quota policy gradually met the house purchase conditions. The market in first-tier cities was the first to recover. Due to its quick actions, Evergrande's sales performance experienced rapid growth again, despite the recent international economic depression, slowed economic acceleration in China, and overall industrial downturn. Driven by the strategy of returning to first-tier cities, Evergrande's sales performance was significantly superior to that of its peers, surpassing RMB 200 billion and a net profit of RMB 17 billion in 2015. As a result, it became the largest real estate enterprise in the world, with the total assets of RMB 757 billion.

6   Engaging in Diversified Development

In 2014, considering its long-term enterprise development, Evergrande engaged in diversified development to cultivate new business growth trajectories while sustainably consolidating its main business (i.e., real estate). Diversified development has been widely adopted by mega-corporations throughout the world, particularly the top 500 enterprises. GE, Samsung, Siemens, DuPont, and even Cheung Kong Holdings in Hong Kong are outstanding as the diversified enterprises. Evergrande took into full account its strengths, opportunities, and macroenvironment while moving forward with its diversification strategy. Its scale, management, and brand advantages built over the years help establish the optimal foundation for its diversified development.

As judged from the development experience in the main business real estate over the years, business trajectories closely related to the daily life of ordinary people would be an optimal development direction. Consequently, Evergrande spared no effort to develop the health industry, not only providing consumers with spring water, grains and oils, dairy products, and other green healthy products but also developing existing resources for entry into the medical health field. Its subordinate-listed platform Evergrande Health (HK.0708) on Hong Kong Exchange, with the online community hospital, international hospital, pension industry, and medical cosmetology as the main businesses, has become one of the listed companies.

In addition, Evergrande has engaged in high-tech industry, including online community services by taking advantage of owning more than 400 real estate communities throughout the country, in collaboration with Tencent to establish the listed platform HengTen Networks (HK.0136), whose business covers three basic areas (i.e., property service, neighborhood social contact, and life service) and two value-added areas (i.e., Internet household and community finance), thereby adding value to increase the competitiveness of its main business while developing new industries.

Evergrande already exploratorily entered into the football and culture industry before officially engaging in its diversified development strategy. Its subordinates officially logged into the "New Third-Board Market"[1] in 2015 to link with the capital markets for better development. Today, Evergrande has become a diversified large-scale enterprise owning five listed companies. Cultural tourism also generated a significant development in this stage. The world-class century cultural tourism project China Hainan Ocean Flower Island, with an investment of RMB 160 billion, created three world records: sales volume of RMB 12.2 billion, the sales area of 1.36 million square meters, and 100,000 pledged chips when the sale of vacation products was first initiated. This project covers 8 km^2, which is 1.5 times the size of Dubai Palm Islands, the largest artificial island in the world. The project engages the design work by 600 internationally well-known architects, focuses on the establishment of 28 business categories (including tourism, culture, conference, exhibition, and commerce), and protects high-quality ecological resources such as the 40-km Gold Coast and the natural island Dachanjiao.

---

7   One-Body-Two-Wings Strategy

The diversified enterprise development is now injecting a continuous new growth impetus for Evergrande. At this point, it is striving to develop a great pattern with real estate as the main "body" and finance and high technology as its "two wings", accompanied by the synergetic development of other industries. This development pattern is nearly identical to the China's new economic development situation and is highly consistent with the direction of China's decision to promote the "Internet+" era and encourage financial innovation with the broadest prospects.

In the one-body-two-wings development strategy, real estate is constantly consolidated as the main business and foundation of the company. At present, due to the ongoing strengthening of the recovery momentum in China's real estate market plus the intensified industrial division, lots of excellent merger and

---

[1]The "New Third-Board Market" is China's OTC market, established in 2006. Compared to China's Main Board Market and the Second Board Market, it attracts start-up companies needing financing with lower listing requirements.

acquisition opportunities have emerged. Recently, Evergrande invested more than RMB 160 billion in land purchases, including the acquisition of high-quality projects with a total buildable area of more than 17 million square meters from New World, Chinese Estates Holdings, Sino Land, and other well-established Hong Kong enterprises. As a result, the company's main business has been greatly strengthened.

With respect to the financial industry, Evergrande established the Financial Group in 2015. Its subordinate insurance company, Evergrande Life Insurance, achieved premiums totaling more than RMB 30 billion on the current scale and will surpass 100 billion this year. Its subordinate asset management company is aimed to achieve more than RMB 150 billion in asset management this year. In addition, Evergrande participated in Shengjing Bank, becoming its first and largest shareholder, and it plans to merge with a security company this year. Along with the initial formation of the business structure of the "one-body-two-wings" development strategy, each industry has realized its developmental formation, and each core business is expected to continue to grow and strengthen the synergy from various business focuses.

China's Housing Markets

Tobias Just and Hannah Levinger

Abstract

House price growth in Chinese metropolises has been impressive for the last three decades, to say the least. Long-term trends, most of which are still intact, have been fuelling housing demand. Therefore, it is unlikely that the demand for urban residential units will weaken in the near future. Much of this momentum is backed by fundamental factors such as income growth, urban population growth and access to capital. However, at the same time, affordability and rental yields have deteriorated over the last few decades. Thus, the risk of housing market bubbles is elevated, and this applies particularly to housing units which were built about 20 years ago and which do not fulfil the quality demands of the rising middle class today.

1 Introduction

Housing is one of the most important services for a household, as it provides shelter and comfort and very often serves as an investment. What is more, due to its immobility, housing is an essentially local service. It is also a very lumpy product. For most households, buying a house or apartment is the largest expenditure in their entire life. For tenants, rents frequently account for the major share of a household's monthly budget. Finally, it is impossible to substitute housing services with other goods or services. In cities, it is often possible to substitute ownership of a car by using public transport or riding a bike. But, with regard to housing, it is only possible to compromise on the size or quality of a unit.

T. Just (✉)
IRE|BS, University of Regensburg, Regensburg, Bavaria, Germany

H. Levinger
Deutsche Bank AG, Frankfurt am Main, Germany

© Springer Nature Switzerland AG 2021
B. Wang, T. Just (eds.), *Understanding China's Real Estate Markets*, Management for Professionals, https://doi.org/10.1007/978-3-030-49032-4_20

All these factors determine the development of housing markets. When key drivers of residential demand are concentrated on a limited number of locations, rents and prices rise. Due to the abovementioned characteristics, the options for households to adapt to market forces are limited. This applies particularly, when the supply side cannot react fast enough to demand growth, for example, because of a lack of space.

In their famous but brief book on China, Woetzel and Towson (2013) define six megatrends for China. Two of them, urbanisation and the rise of Chinese consumers, have impacted directly and strongly on residential demand over the last few decades. In fact, all other long-term trends mentioned in Woetzel and Towson's book (manufacturing scale, monetary growth, brainpower, Chinese internet) have also impacted indirectly on the residential demand, as these trends are driving economic growth, especially in cities, and income growth is the most important driver of residential demand.

Though these trends have backed strong house price growth over the last 30 years, many national and international market observers are concerned about housing bubbles and the deterioration of affordability in China's cities. This development is also inevitably a key concern for policy makers, considering the importance of housing services for private households. In this chapter, we analyse the key drivers of housing demand and the relative development of regional house (apartment) prices.

2   Demand Factors Driving Growth

At present, according to the UN Population Division (2019), there are more than 1.4 billion people living in China. This compares to 1 billion in 1982 and "only" 544 million in 1950. Of course, this remarkably strong population growth has been driving the demand for living space in China. Yet, this isolated trend underrates the demand growth in the last three decades for three main reasons. First, for residential demand, household growth matters more than population growth, and household growth has been significantly stronger than population growth. Today, there are more than 450 million households in China, approximately twice as many as in 1982 and four times as many as in 1950. This means that the average household size has been declining from approximately five people per household in 1950 to roughly 4.4 in 1982 and three today. Note that there are still significant regional differences. While the average household size in Tibet is still above four people per household and in Hainan, roughly 3.6, the average household size in Beijing and Shanghai is merely 2.5 (National Bureau of Statistics 2018).

Second, the average floor space per inhabitant has been rising due to strong income growth. According to data collected by the London School of Economics and the Alfred Herrhausen Society (LSE/AHG 2016), the residential floor space in Shanghai rose from 6.6 m^2 in 1990 to more than 24 m^2 in 2015. These households live in roughly 415 million housing units, according to National Bureau of Statistics' data (Huang 2015). Slightly more than half of this housing stock is in urban areas, i.e. 261 million units with a gross floor area of 21 billion m^2. The urban vacancy rate is comparatively high and stands at almost 20%.

Third, the government has relaxed the restrictions for mobility within China over the last years. This has led to significant migration from rural to urban areas, particularly to cities on the east coast. Today, more than 50% of the Chinese population live in cities; in 1982, the urban percentage in the total population was roughly 20%, dramatically lower. All these trends are poised to continue, partly because the catch-up potential of China is still large. Considering that GDP per capita is not even half the Western European level and that living space per capita in China is still about 50% lower than Western European levels and also considering that China's average household size is still approximately 50% higher than in Europe, it is very likely that floor space per inhabitant will continue to increase and that average household size will continue to fall further. Hu and Peng (2015) estimate that the number of households in China could reach 500 million, somewhere between 2035 and 2040, even though the population will have started to decline many years earlier. This forecast is conservative, however, as it implies that the average household size will barely fall further within the next 20 years. Given that the average household size is a function of urbanisation, ageing, income growth and fertility rates (Just 2013) and given that the outlook for these factors points to falling household sizes, it is likely that the number of households will top 500 million by 2035 and will not peak before the middle of the century.

At the same time, the demand structure for housing will change as the population ages. At present, 10% of the population are older than 65. This share has doubled since 1982 and will continue to rise to more than one quarter of the population by mid-century. This will not only impact on the average household size but also call for a significant increase in the provision of nursing homes and low-barrier homes. Finally, the pent-up demand remains significant. This applies to qualitative as well as quantitative aspects. For example, about 50% of all urban apartments have no more than two rooms (Huang 2015), and the share of "low-quality housing" is large (see Fig. 1), even if we allow for some impreciseness in the definition of what constitutes low quality.

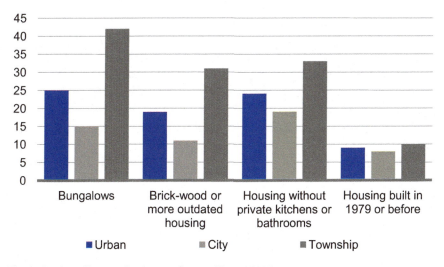

Fig. 1 Portion of low-quality houses. Source: Huang (2015)

3   The House Price Boom: National and Regional Breakdown

Residential prices have increased markedly over the last two decades. Since the late 1990s, national average residential prices have risen by more than 200%, according to data from China's National Bureau of Statistics (see Fig. 2). Even after correcting for consumer price inflation, real house price growth has been significant, considering that inflation has rarely exceeded 4% in the past 10 years and has not exceeded 10% in any single year during the past 20 years. Prices for newly built housing units have risen faster than for existing stock. However, the difference is not large. This indicates that much of the house price boom can be attributed to a lack of specific supply. Given the big vacancy rate of approximately 20% in urban areas, this lack of supply is rather a specific than a general issue.

For some regions, it is even reasonable to measure the growth momentum in factors other than growth rates; in Beijing and Shanghai (nominal), residential house prices are presently 10 times higher than in the late 1990s; in Shanghai prices are almost 13 times higher, while prices in Gansu "only" quadrupled within the last 30 years. However, caution is advised when analysing regional long-term data, as average growth rates mask extremely volatile movements. In the case of Hainan, for example, the comparatively low average growth rate is the mean of two very different phases; in the late 1990s, residential prices in Hainan fell by roughly 75%. Since then, residential prices have increased by a factor of 15—even more than in Beijing or Shanghai. Nonetheless, by and large, regions with higher average house price growth have also been more volatile.

With regard to current house price levels, regional differences are pronounced. While an existing housing unit in the economically weaker provinces like Gansu or Guanxi costs approximately 4300–5000 RMB, residential prices in Shanghai and Beijing range between 27,000 and 36,000 RMB/m^2. Prices for houses in advance are

Fig. 2 Nominal house price growth in China (national average) in % year-on-year, smoothed. Source: National Bureau of Statistics (2019b)

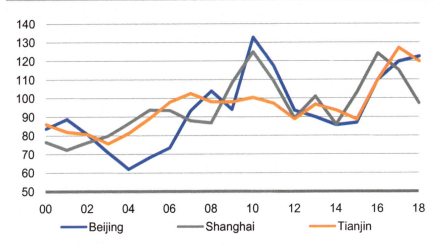

Fig. 3 Price-income ratio trends up. Average house price in relation to disposable income per capita; long-term average = 100. Source: own calculation, National Bureau of Statistics (2019b)

typically 10–30% higher than prices for existing buildings. Again, regional differences are pronounced: in the region of Qinghai or Shanxi houses in advance cost as much as 70–80% more than existing houses.

Even though incomes have been rising strongly too, house price growth has exceeded income growth in Tier 1 cities (see Fig. 3 and Fang et al. 2015). It is important to note that the sharp drop in house price to disposable income in Shanghai can be attributed to a sharp decline in prices in 2017 that has been compensated only in the previous 2 years, i.e., affordability in Shanghai has rapidly deteriorated again until mid-2019. However, this is not captured in the data yet. As income growth has been much more stable than house price growth, the price-income ratio is also very volatile. Fang et al. (2015) also show that the deterioration of affordability is stronger in Tier 1 cities than in Tier 2 or Tier 3 cities and that the implied financial stress is larger for low-income households than for middle-income ones. What is more, according to data collected by the private research platform Numbeo (2019), China's price-income ratio is among the highest in the world, with the price-income ratio in Beijing being significantly higher than the respective values for Tokyo or London. Even so, Fang et al. (2015) also argue that a very high down payment ratio of 40–50% and close family ties buffer the risk of financial stress for the buyers as well as for banks.

4   Development of Supply Side: Housing Completions

China has experienced tremendous growth in the dwelling stock over the last 30 years. In the 1980s, the dwelling stock grew annually by more than 8%. In the following two decades, the growth rates declined, but at 4% p.a., supply-side growth

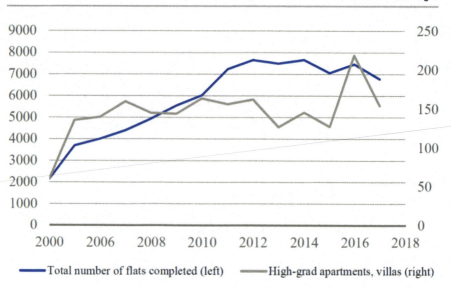

Fig. 4 Residential construction activity in China, in 1000 units. Source: National Bureau of Statistics of China (2018)

is still very strong (D'Arcy and Veroude 2014), considering that in Western economies, the dwelling stock grows at about 1 or 2% p.a. However, technical depreciation rates in China are probably higher than the depreciation rates in Europe or the United States. And what is more, vacancy rates have sharply increased in China's metropolises.

After some very strong growth years in the early 2000s, annual construction volume has stabilised at a high level in the last few years (see Fig. 4). While the nationwide construction volume fell moderately in the last few years, there have been striking regional differences. In Beijing, Guangdong or Henan, construction activity has tumbled by more than 20% in Jiangsu or Yunnan, it rose considerably.

In fact, construction activity in the luxury segment stabilised more than 10 years ago. Given the comparatively high vacancy rates in many cities, this is not surprising. Such development also reflects the transaction volume in the prime segment: In this market segment, the number of transactions has rather trended downwards until 2015, while the transaction volume in the other market segments has continued to rise (see Fig. 5). Only in the last 2 years, the transaction volume has also picked up sharply in the prime segment again.

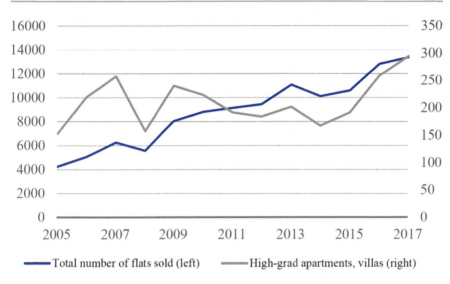

Fig. 5 Residential transactions, in 1000 units. Source: National Bureau of Statistics of China (2018)

5   Conclusion

China's residential property market largely reflects the country's economic performance during the last few decades; income growth, urbanisation and demographic changes have fostered a rapid improvement improvement of the Chinese housing stock. With slightly more than 50% of the Chinese population living in cities today (i.e. 837 million people) and another 250 million urban inhabitants expected by 2040, the growth story of China's housing market is by no means over. Above and beyond quantitative growth, the qualitative growth will most likely matter even more in the future, that is, investment in private bathrooms, private kitchens and more spacious apartments with better installations. As Chinese cities are already comparatively compactly built, this demand growth will further drive up property prices. However, this development will hardly be linear, and severe cycles are likely. In the past, the Chinese government has repeatedly attempted to cool market exaggerations by severe measures (Just and Dyck 2011).

At present, the risk of a new downward cycle seems to be rising. Fang et al. (2015) have already named three major risk factors for the Chinese residential real estate markets a couple of years ago. First, given that much of the current price level can be justified by expectations of private households about future income growth, any economic slowdown that forces households to adjust their expectations downward would result in temporarily falling house prices and might also yield in rising non-performing loans for China's banks (Wan 2018). This, however, need not imply distress for the banks, as mortgage lending is still modest. Second, China is ageing quickly; in fact, the number of people between 30 and 49 years, i.e. the typical home buyer cohort, has started to shrink nationally. This will not necessarily dampen house prices everywhere, as regional migration will constrain this downward pressure in economically strong regions. However, the impact of the shrinking home buyer cohort will then be even stronger in outward migration regions. Third, any new tax levies on property will exert a negative impact on house price growth. In particular, if tax receipts fall during an economic slowdown, local governments might be tempted to either increase taxes or try to increase their receipts by selling land, which would increase the housing supply and thus vacancies. Zhi et al. (2019) found that 10 out of 35 cities exhibited significant overvaluation, and Pan (2019) concludes that most of the Tier 1 cities have been experiencing several bubbles and the longest-lasting bubble still ongoing.

References

D'Arcy, P., & Veroude, A. (2014, March). Housing trends in China and India. *Reserve Bank of Australia Bulletin*, pp. 63–68.
Fang, H., Gu, Q., Xiong, W., & Zhoug, L. A. (2015, December 18–19). *Demystifying the Chinese housing boom*. Paper presented at the international symposium on housing and financial stability in China. Chinese University of Hong Kong, Shenzhen.
Hu, Z., & Peng, X. (2015). Household changes in contemporary China: An analysis based on the four recent censuses. *The Journal of Chinese Sociology, 2*(9), 2–20.
Huang, H. (2015, December 18–19). *Discussion on China's housing market: What we know? What we don't*. Paper presented at the international symposium on housing and financial stability in China. Chinese University of Hong Kong, Shenzhen.
Just, T. (2013). *Demografie und Immobilien*. München: Oldenbourg.
Just, T., & Dyck, S. (2011). *China's housing markets—Regulatory interventions mitigate risk of severe bust*. Frankfurt am Main: Deutsche Bank Research Current Issues.
LSE/AHG. (2016). *Conflicts of an urban age*. Retrieved February 17, 2017, from https://urbanage.lsecities.net/events/conflicts-of-an-urban-age
National Bureau of Statistics of China. (2018). *Statistical yearbook*. Retrieved July 14, 2019, from http://www.stats.gov.cn/tjsj/ndsj/2018/indexeh.htm
National Bureau of Statistics of China. (2019a). *Statistical Yearbook*. Retrieved June 27, 2020, from http://www.stats.gov.cn/tjsj/ndsj/2019/indexeh.htm
National Bureau of Statistics of China. (2019b). *Monthly housing statistics*. Retrieved July, 12, 2019, from http://data.stats.gov.cn/english/easyquery.htm?cn=A01
Numbeo. (2019). *Property prices*. Retrieved April 11, 2019, from https://www.numbeo.com/property-investment/
Pan, W.-F. (2019). Detecting bubbles in China's regional housing markets. *Empirical Economics, 56*(4), 1413–1432.
UN Population Division. (2019). *UN world population prospects*. The 2019 Revision. Retrieved July 14, 2019, from https://esa.un.org/unpd/wpp/Download/Standard/Population/
Wan, J. (2018). Non-performing loans and housing prices in China. *International Review of Economics and Finance, 57*, 26–42.
Woetzel, J., & Towson, J. (2013). *The 1 hour China book*. Cayman Islands: Towson Group.
Zhi, T., Li, Z., Jiang, Z., Wei, L., & Sornette, D. (2019). Is there a housing bubble in China? *Emerging Markets Review, 39*, 120–132.

Hotel Markets and Development in China

Michael A. Crawford

Abstract

Over the past ten years, the five-star hotel market in China has grown at a pace of 11.8% a year. While growth was predominantly driven from the Tier One cities such as Beijing, Shanghai, Guangzhou, and Shenzhen, there is now a push to develop key resort destinations as well as Tier Two cities. Key to this growth has been a focus on the high-net-worth Chinese consumers. According to the Global Wealth Report in 2019 by Credit Suisse, there were 100 million Chinese among the world's top 10% of richest people, compared with 99 million in the United States. Together with a continually emerging middle class, this has prompted greater liquidity in the market, resulting in travel for both business and leisure, increasing at the highest growth rate in the world. Developers have attempted to replicate the hotel market existing in other more developed economies throughout the world. In addition to this trend, the Chinese market itself has undergone a significant transformation. With the focus on eliminating corrupt government officials, the development market has been challenged with a reduction toward luxury hotel use for government functions. An unstable regulatory environment creates difficulty in receiving timely approvals of development submissions. This chapter explores the importance of cultural differences in this market and how companies intending to enter the high-end hotel business must be prepared not only to develop and operate differently but also to have patience in adapting to local policies and practices.

M. A. Crawford (✉)
Hall of Fame Village & Media Co., Canton, OH, USA

© Springer Nature Switzerland AG 2021
B. Wang, T. Just (eds.), *Understanding China's Real Estate Markets*, Management for Professionals, https://doi.org/10.1007/978-3-030-49032-4_21

1   Assessing Market Readiness

In preparing to embark upon hotel development in China, desired product type must first be understood. Secondly, the level of economic return expected and appreciation for the location in terms of its consumer spending power require careful analysis. China for all purposes is more of a continent than a country. There is great diversity in language, economic development, social stability, regulatory environment, and infrastructure quality. China has multiple economic capabilities with each province/city establishing their projected growth targets (Fig. 1).

As a developer and operator of luxury hotels, Four Seasons evaluates multiple drivers of business, to support the evaluation of market readiness. We consider our cost structure in the context of service levels, product offerings, and development costs associated with the building of each hotel. In many cases, this level of detailed analysis is required to provide critical input to a pro forma development process. Market evaluation in this case also includes a study which helps better understand the level of revenue possible, along with guest patterns of spending on each type of revenue category. Room rate, food and beverage average spend per guest, business

Fig. 1 China GDP by provinces: A Union of Developed + Developing countries based on GDP estimates in 2020 (projected but without taking consideration of the impact by Covid19). Source: HSBC, CEIC, IMF, CIA

and social event spending, spa spending, etc. all help formulate a final perspective on the market's potential to drive the top line in terms of gross revenue (Chap. 1). From city to city, there are different factors to consider by way of revenue categories:

1. Meetings and convention business activity
2. Inbound leisure tourism volume
3. Average room rate of existing luxury hotel supply
4. Competitive occupancy and room rate revenue per available room
5. Competitive project pipeline for new luxury hotel product
6. Other unique travel behaviors which may influence length of stay and total spending patterns while staying at the hotel

In addition, there have been multiple government initiatives designed to help support the business economics of new luxury product development. One example would be special economic zones (SEZs) of China. There are currently 7 SEZs and 14 coastal development areas, all supporting business development through tax regulation, land pricing consideration, and additional guidance in completing the regulatory process more efficiently.

Despite slower economic growth, crackdown on gifting, and a weaker currency, China delivered more than half the global growth in luxury spending between 2012 and 2018 and is expected to deliver 65% of the world's additional spending heading into 2025 (McKinsey & Company 2019). Companies that consider China as a "great new opportunity" to expose their product and brand must also be aware that, with any emerging market, patience is critical. China's Tier One cities are rapidly becoming higher quality in terms of construction standards, as well as a greater level of financing sophistication. However, a majority of the country is still experiencing growing pains. If companies are considering luxury hotel construction, deal term flexibility will be important. Understanding risk tolerance, both in terms of short- and medium-term returns, is also paramount. It takes time to build a high-quality property in China, but it also takes time to establish a new brand. These issues coupled with economic risk and potential changes in government regulation should be part of the awareness building process a developer needs to contemplate.

2   The "China Mode" of Conducting Business

Over time, investors, companies, and individuals learn how to adapt their business practices to be successful in China. Localizing doesn't have to mean compromising standards or ethics. However, the way in which business gets conducted is very different both culturally and in terms of your expected outcome. Most companies entering the Chinese market for the first time try to replicate their business practices in other parts of the world and are soon hit by a unique set of constraints and challenges. Education is critical, and finding the right local partner is even more important. These individuals or consultants can help navigate the waters of change.

They can also help support the education process back to corporate headquarters located in the Western world.

As a leading luxury hospitality company, we knew that compromise on our service standards, product quality, or brand integrity was not an option. We believed the consistency in our approach to treating guests as they wanted to be treated, and the need for authentic and personal service was paramount to establishing our credibility in China. Over the years we learned this was not only about taking our global standards and localizing them but more importantly developing standards that were relevant to the market itself.

Lastly, while sometimes the path from deal execution to project completion may be long and hard, patience is critical to long-term success in China. A company must be willing to engage in social interactions and building relationships with your partners, ultimately promoting trust and understanding. Luxury hotel companies are typically very good at developing relationships, but most do it according to their own corporate culture practices. Relationships must be formed at the highest level to promote the trust and enable efficient decision-making at lower levels. The Four Seasons model of hotel management, where others own the asset, is an example of how transparency and trust are invaluable to successful partnerships. Owners agree to allow our company to run the hotel and invest in the asset on their behalf. Most of the luxury hotel companies have a management model vs. self-owned and operated in China. For such an asset-light model, relationships need to be formed over time and through open and direct communication.

3   Finding the Right Partner

The Chinese market is full of both wealthy individuals and large domestic corporations looking to diversify their investment portfolio. Critical to the long-term success of building luxury hotel assets are aligning interests with investors and developers and ensuring common goals in terms of returns for potential assets. There are multiple types of investors to consider:

1. Wealthy Chinese individuals
2. Government-backed enterprises
3. Major investment funds (Chinese and foreign)
4. Foreign developers and investors looking to break into the Chinese market
5. Foreign developers and investors with clear experience in the Chinese market

Ideally, an investment partner is someone who brings credibility to a project and bridges the gap of knowledge, capital, and network required to build a luxury product in the Chinese market. When selecting a Chinese partner, consider their knowledge of luxury product as first tier of evaluation. The level of investment and reinvestment required to build and maintain an asset at the highest level is sometimes overlooked by local investors. Also, it's important to be aligned on return requirements for the operation of the luxury hotel. You will find many investors like to build "trophy assets" and then request unreasonable returns for the market. Early alignment on market dynamics against return expectations is critical to help guide an investor who wants to build a new hotel beyond what the economics of the deal will support. There are many new luxury hotel brands trying to build assets that are beyond reasonable economic viability. At Four Seasons, we look for hotel deals that last multiple decades, so long-term returns are critical to the success of a partnership.

While a local Chinese partner may certainly bring expertise and knowledge of local business practices, be careful to not fall into the trap of believing they can produce results faster in a system that is still very regulated and ever-changing. In fact, consider timing of project delivery to be the same if not greater than building with a foreign company. Local partners will also request, and sometimes require, luxury hotel companies to do business with vendors and suppliers not accustomed to producing high-quality products. There are many instances where furniture, fixtures, and equipment must be reproduced due to defects or substitution of quality materials for lower-cost replacements. Again, early alignment on quality expectations with local partners is critical. The right of approval and control over acceptance of all items will drive the quality of product building in market. This allows the hotel company to generate the type of "brand representative" product they need.

Foreign partners can be beneficial in terms of business approach but also require a great deal of education concerning doing business in China. While the upfront negotiation may be easier when working with a foreign partner who truly understands what a luxury product looks like, and will generate in returns, unless they have market experience in China, they are not bringing local expertise to the table. Foreign partners require more education along the development process in China, more management by way of delivery timing expectations, and may also not fully understand the impact of government personnel and policy changes may have on project timeline and returns. Currently Chinese major cities are all growing their stock of five-star rooms. Beijing leads the way with about 42,000 five-star rooms in 2019, followed by Shanghai, Macau, and Hong Kong (Knight Frank Research May 2020). The luxury portfolio consists of differing operating models, both self-owned and operated, some are under management contracts in partnership with specific owners, and others are franchised to local partners to operate on their behalf.

An assessment of a company's long-term goals in China is critical in choosing a partner. Multiple partnerships may diversify your portfolio risk in this market but can also make it difficult to operate and align interests around a "shared service" model of operation. To explain further, there are certain aspects of the hotel business which may be more efficient when aligned with volume. Marketing and sales efforts, as an example, provide opportunities to leverage funding and human resources in order to more broadly brand and sell a hotel portfolio in China. With multiple partners, there is always concern about each feeling underrepresented. When selecting partners, a company must document the need for this type of business model while providing the legal rights to do this in the daily operation of a hotel business. Stand-alone luxury hotels typically drive 7–15% return on investment, and partners want greater returns but with pricing following market standards, with a little premium, leaving only the operating model to ensure it's working as efficiently as possible. Partners need to be in support of this type of cost-sharing model.

In addition to partners that want to build assets in China, there are local partners looking to expand their development footprint outside the country as well. Considering this in partner selection could be equally as important, especially in the search for partners that can help grow a luxury brand in other parts of the world. At Four Seasons, part of our global strategy is to frame a process of building, marketing, and operating hotels that will attract an outbound Chinese luxury traveler. China remains the world's biggest market in outbound tourism with nearly 170 million outbound visits made by Chinese travelers in 2019, up 4.5% year-on-year (National Bureau of Statistics 2019). Chinese outbound travelers are projected to increase to 400 million by 2030 (COTRI/Ctrip report 2018). A local partner can help provide access to Chinese consumer trends, educate a company on appropriate operating standards, and help position brands as "Chinese-friendly" among the most demanding group of consumers. This drives greater potential to capture a higher percentage of outbound travelers, so there is also strategic value in partnering with local Chinese investors in building luxury hotels around the world. Some Chinese investors claim they are interested in partnering with high-profile luxury hotel companies to help expand their development investments to "where the Chinese are going."

Lastly, setting clear expectations around how to nurture Chinese partnerships inside a foreign company is very important. Cultural differences in communication, legal environment, and resolving differences are key to a successful relationship with a Chinese entity. This takes time and various approaches to better understand a partner. There is the formal relationship where business is conducted, and then there is the social aspect of the relationship where trust and understanding are formed. Senior company leaders play a critical role in the daily operation of the business. Many corporate leaders will "fly in and out" of China for a few days a year, hold a meeting or have a lunch with their partner, and then leave until the next encounter. Companies must invest in understanding local customs, holidays, business practices, etc. and then act upon those on a regular basis. Social engagement is a strategy many companies forget when selecting and developing a partnership in China. While this is important everywhere in the world, it's a baseline principle allowing a preferred working relationship in China. In times of conflict, social relationships resolve issues faster, while formal letters and legal action will be difficult and costly for foreign companies to implement as a way of managing through any misunderstandings around business agreements. Most Chinese partners will view a contract as a "guideline" to managing the business and not apply the same level of rigor around its implementation as foreign companies are used to in Western legal systems.

4   Executing a Standard for Development and Service

In the mid- to late 1990s, Chinese consumers equated luxury hotels to the saying "the bigger the better," and the more ostentatious the hotel designs were, the more the hotels were perceived to be very high-end luxury. Not unlike other markets around the world, the consumer lacked sophistication as major hotel companies entered a market that was not as familiar with branded luxury hotels. Travel abroad was not as prevalent, so exposure to different styles of luxury design had not been experienced by most of the wealthy individuals who would be able to travel and stay in premium hotels. Over the last decade, the perception of luxury hotel development standards has evolved. All of the Tier One cities have been exposed to the most influential hospitality brands in the world, and today travel abroad is easier for Chinese consumers. There has also been an evolution of product designs for this market that take into account space planning, dining preferences, and overall guest sentiment around amenity and room layout preferences. At Four Seasons, we've continued to perfect designs that include public space size and layout, unique room design and materials, and the mix in food and beverage, all with a focus on how to create an emotional connection through personalized and authentic service. In addition we have also taken typical service amenities commonly found in the Chinese market, like spas, and providing high-quality programming and at a price premium.

It all starts with the exterior design and architectural statement being made. There is great fascination with unique buildings and facades that stand out among the many different new and different structures dotting city skylines. Another critical factor in exterior design has been sustainability and quality of maintenance standards applied. Many of these new architectural statements, while unique in look and feel, have been proven to be difficult to maintain and are also inefficient in space planning. When working with designers, it's important to find the balance in materials, layout, and construction capabilities of contractors to deliver on the design vision. We look for materials that are functional and allow the high-end crafts workers to build using techniques and materials they have become accustomed to working with in each market. This does vary, and when selecting a design architect, consider the experience they have in each market, and look for buildings they have designed to determine how the construction has held up over time. More and more, hotel companies are looking to deliver on the promise of luxury inside the box while keeping the exteriors simple and aligned with market planning guidelines in terms of building look and materials.

The goal in China is to have the guest walk in and immediately feel immersed in a distinct environment removed from their daily hustle and bustle. Whether looking at an urban hotel or creating a unique resort environment, luxury must look and feel special yet comfortable at the same time. Consumers are also looking for something to "brag and write about" while connecting with friends and family through social media. Product differentiation in standards from market to market is a critical consideration. Luxury in Tier One Chinese cities is much easier to define for guests, as these markets have been evolving with both domestic and international travelers. Entering Tier Two and lower cities, executing a new standard of high-end luxury becomes increasingly challenging. Material selection becomes more important as designers begin to imagine a product for these markets. Realizing investment is an important part of the return equation; luxury hotel companies have still continued to provide for product that is best in market but allow for slight differences in quality of things like marble, tile, carpet, etc. selection. Many hotel investors have accepted this as a necessary change, while maintaining a level of programming and quality commensurate with their brand standards. There is clearly a need to only consider development in markets that can support the quality of development that enhances your luxury brand. Tier One cities are safer bets still in China, as rates support a higher level of investment. As of the second quarter of 2018, the average daily rate (ADR) of five-star hotels in first-tier cities in China amounted to around 860.9 yuan per day (Statista Research Department 2019).

In addition to focusing on design, project management and project delivery are skills lacking in the Chinese market. Construction quality is a significant challenge in most markets, including major cities. In many instances, the quality of materials prescribed by designers is substituted for lower-level materials for both cost savings and availability. Onsite project leadership is necessary to ensure key milestones are met, and the quality of building construction is in line with agreed upon programming. Luxury hotel standards are higher than typical construction work, so proper management with a Chinese partner is important and also helps ensure no misunderstandings in managing development issues during project delivery. Foreign companies working in China must have a local partner with a project management organization overseeing the integrated delivery model that respects construction capabilities in market but also doesn't compromise on design standards while building the hotel. A "protector" of the product will help ensure what was designed is what gets built. This also allows for reduced quality control issues once the operating team takes possession of the facility. Often operators are saddled with a building hastily constructed with quality issues forcing additional operational maintenance on a regular basis. While the construction cost may be less with lower quality, luxury standards require a building to perform at the highest level. Operating deficiencies can create a negative guest perception of their experience and also force lower economic return when refunds or lower room rates are required to deal with poor operating quality.

Throughout the entire development process, multiple factors create challenges in delivering a luxury hotel product. Construction is driven by the permitting process, and as China continues to evolve on the regulatory front, change-out in government personnel causes change in policy and, in some cases, reversal in decisions. Project oversight is critical to monitor this changing environment and adjust scheduling of the critical path to account for delays caused by government approvals. Without this type of onsite management, there can be impacts on funding requests and timing of land or building permitting vs. timing of key construction milestones. Most contractors continue with building construction in an uncertain environment, and this too can cause delivery challenges as regulatory changes can also drive building codes. High-end hotel projects are continuing to be impacted by this changing landscape, hotels on average take 4–6 years to develop in China.[1]

---

[1] Average development cycle for a Four Seasons hotel in China is 6.2 years. Average development cycle for a five-star hotel is 4–5 years.

5   Creating Synergy and Success Through Asset Mix

Stand-alone hotels can be profitable, but more and more developers and investors are looking to "double down" on their bet and create economic return through a diverse product offering. China is still a challenging economic environment driven by a large supply of luxury hotel product under construction. In lower-tiered markets, the average daily rate of luxury hotel rooms can range from USD 100 to 170. In many cases consumers also expect additional services and amenities to be provided at this price, such as breakfast or airport pickup services. Over the last decade, margins of five-star hotels have dropped sharply, with an average profit margin of approximately 32%.

Mixed-use developments are now more prevalent in China. Investors are intrigued by the upfront returns on new components of a lifestyle development. Living accommodations, specifically branded residences with services, are now catering to ultra-high-net-worth individuals. In the case of this type of addition to a hotel development, the upfront generation of capital off the sales of the residential units generally helps the developer receive a larger return on the overall development investment, as well as generate cash flow for payment of the other components of the mixed-use developments. Typically, Four Seasons has seen about 50–70% of its new development opportunities in China having a branded residential component to the requested master plan. While this also provides economic diversity, it allows for ongoing cash flow through the management of these facilities as well. Management fees of 10–14% of Home Owners Association costs help flatten some of the "lumpiness" of unit sales throughout the life of the project. Branded residences have also become a great extension for companies looking for ways to reach consumers through their everyday living. Selling the commodity of time, with access to services like travel booking, 24-hour concierge, housekeeping, food service, etc., allows for these wealthy individuals to be more efficient with how they live, work, and play. We find this to be more important, along with the prestige of living in a facility that has a great brand and also delivers luxury amenities and services.

In addition to residences, mixed-use developments are now starting to include other amenities which cater to both domestic and international travelers and citizens. Including office space and commercial development such as retail and dining venues balances the overall demand for new developments in all types of cities and environments in the country. While mixed use is an attractive way of balancing risk, there are additional considerations regarding the emerging Chinese market. No longer can luxury hotel operators predict with single accuracy the timelines of their own building construction; they now need to monitor the overall progress of every component of the developer's commitment. Just as previously discussed regarding the challenge of changes in regulatory environment, this risk profile becomes much bigger with an integrated development which requires a much larger project management effort, as well as a larger land footprint and funding requirement. At times, achieving all of these is difficult in more mature development environments, but in China this just beginning to be understood. A lack of sophistication in the regulatory environment and construction quality makes creating these synergies more difficult to achieve.

6   Considerations for Success

As previously stated, many luxury hotel companies found difficulty understanding the Chinese market, making financial returns challenging to achieve. The belief that China will be the growth engine for most hotel companies is still the case; however I believe many have realized that a more balanced and measured approach is necessary. Five key takeaways to remember: (1) Be open-minded to doing business differently, yet maintain balance in standards and policies; (2) Relationships at every level of the government and with a partner are critical to the success of luxury development and operation over time; (3) Project oversight and delivery management will ensure quality and lessen delivery and ongoing operating risk; (4) Local talent development should be a critical focus. Balancing culture carriers with individuals who understand the Chinese market defines a longer-term success model; and (5) Whoever said "patience is a virtue" was truly defining the approach Western companies must take in conducting business in China. Everything must be done with a balance of economic return and long-term success. Be prepared for project life cycles to take twice as long as normal and the stabilization of your business to take 2–3 years longer than in other parts of the world.

While China is clearly an economic and political superpower, in many respects, it is still an emerging market. The unique combination of communism and capitalism takes time to figure out, and the balance is still being developed within the government and the country. Do not take for granted the investment it will take in building a brand, a company's profile in the community, and the economic viability of your business in this important part of the world. Just as a business can represent a brand in China, loyalty and emotional connection with the outbound Chinese traveler will continue to grow. There are no shortcuts in this business, and as the Chinese proverb says, "you can only cross the river touching one stone at a time".

References

China Tourism Academy and Ctrip. (2019). *2018 Chinese outbound tourism big data report* (in Chinese).
Credit Suisse Research Institute. (2019). *Global wealth report*.
Knight Frank Research. (2020). *Greater China hotel report*.
Kowano, S., Lu, J., Tsang, R., & Liu, J. (2015). *The Chinese tourist boom*. Goldman Sachs report. Retrieved May 30, 2016, from http://www.goldmansachs.com/our-thinking/pages/macroeconomic-insights-folder/chinese-tourist-boom/report.pdf
McKinsey & Company. (2019). *China luxury report 2019: How young Chinese consumers are reshaping global luxury*.
The National Bureau of Statistics of China. (2019). *China Statistical Yearbook 2019*.
Statista Research. (2019). Retrieved March 14, 2020, from https://www.statista.com/statistics/1045164/china-5-star-hotel-adr-by-city-tier/

The Rise of Platform-Based Networks: Outlook for the Real Estate Brokerage Industry

Hui Zuo

Abstract

The evolution of the real estate brokerage industry is characterized by the ever-emerging, expanding, and evolving network effect. Historically, the real estate brokerage industry developed in different countries around the world in three general forms of agent networks: the multiple listing service (MLS)-centered cooperation network among independent agents that is typical in the United States, through which a real estate listing service is created for and by real estate brokers to inform each other in selling their clients' properties; the random stochastic informal cooperation network based on an Internet information platform, such as those utilized in Australia and Britain; and an internal closed cooperation network within individual brokerage firms, which is typical in Japan. Despite the differences, all three modes rely on the basic institutional guarantee of the exclusive listing agreement that is based on an "exclusive right to sell" contract where the listing broker receives a payment if the home is sold during the listing period regardless of who finds a buyer for the home. Meanwhile, due to the rapid penetration of the Internet, the boom in consumers' demand for quality service, and the special backgrounds of open listing agreements, through which a broker has the nonexclusive right to sell the home and receive payment but other brokers or the seller may also sell the home without any payment to the listing broker, China is steering toward a completely different approach to brokerage, featuring a platform-based limited opening cooperation network.

H. Zuo (✉)
Beijing Lianjia Real Estate Agency Co. Ltd., Beijing, China

© Springer Nature Switzerland AG 2021
B. Wang, T. Just (eds.), *Understanding China's Real Estate Markets*, Management for Professionals, https://doi.org/10.1007/978-3-030-49032-4_22

1 Introduction

China has experienced a boom in its real estate market since the real estate reform in 1998. Today, there are more than 200 million housing suites in inventories, exceeding one suite per household on average and a living area per capita of more than 36 square meters. Since the end of its housing shortage phase, China has seen a slowing down of the newly built housing era predominated by incremental housing development, whereas an era of second-hand housing trading is emerging. In 2017, the trading volume of second-hand houses surpassed four million suites, involving transactions totaling more than six trillion RMB, which is roughly equivalent to the annual average of transaction value in the United States. Although China's housing inventory is twice as large as that in the United States, the circulation rate[1] is merely half of that in America, suggesting considerable space for further growth for China. Given this background, China's real estate brokerage industry is witnessing a boom amid the fast rise of the second-hand housing market, a standardizing and maturing trend from its early stage that was featured by the small number and scattered distribution of the second-hand houses and disorderly market environment. By the end of 2017, an estimated more than 1.5 million agents were working in more than 150,000 brokerage outlets in the real estate industry, with the largest brokerage company employing more than 150,000 agents in more than 8000 brokerage offices, accounting for 15% of the market.[2] Another feature of the market is that a batch of nationally directly run and franchised brands have been established and gained dominance in the industry. These figures suggest that the world's largest brokerage industry and march of agents have taken shape in China.

Looking into the future, three dominating trends promise to reshape the structure of the Chinese real estate brokerage industry. The first is the expanding influence of the Internet. China is witnessing a "population migration" from the offline to the online world that is more extensive today than ever before in human history, inevitably leading to a natural and faster trend of the online service availability of the brokerage industry. The second is consumers' pursuits of quality-oriented services accompanying their rising incomes due to rapid urbanization. Consequently, sufficient and accurate information, safe and efficient guarantees for transactions, and trustworthy professional agents will become integral to high quality. The third is the rise of the platform-based network. Only large platforms equipped with the capacity for infrastructure export can empower agents and the industry as a whole, thereby ensuring the industry's more efficient operations and consumers' better access to services as well as agents' higher level of professionalism. These three factors are, arguably, continually changing forces that are

---

[1]Circulation rate is the percentage ratio of second-hand housing transaction volume to total housing inventory.

[2]Lianjia's 15% market share data cited in this article is computed and provided by the Lianjia Research Institute based on public housing data and residential real estate brokerage offices at the national scale in 2017.

redefining the existing brokerage models and developing a unique model with Chinese characteristics.

2   Three Types of Networks

As the experiences of different countries have shown, the nature of the real estate brokerage industry is built on the ever-emerging, expanding, and evolving network effect. Due to its very nature, the real estate brokerage industry involves the integration of matching information and transactions. In general, during the early formative stages of the industry, transactions involving existing homes were limited in size, within limited geographical ranges, and even between acquaintances, thereby resulting in humble network effects. As the market evolved, information interactions and matching saw a sharp rise in the complexity of the transactions, with the expansion of existing home markets, increases in the trading volume and market scope, and extension of the geographical boundaries of transactions contributing to the natural emergence and expansion of a larger transaction network rising above the limitations of geography and acquaintance connections. This network, enabling cooperation and competition among professional agents, makes it possible for the transmission of information on sellers' housing sources as well as the most precise response and matching of buyers' preferences, thereby contributing to positive feedback among the buyer, seller, and agent.

Through comparative studies of various evolutionary paths of the brokerage industry in different countries, it becomes evident that three agent networks dominate the industry's process: the MLS-centered network, an Internet platform-based network, and a company-centered internal network (Table 1).

Table 1 Comparison of three types of networks

	Background	Market characteristics
MLS-centered network	Exclusive commission and unilateral agreements Independent agents Comprehensive rule system	Low value of brands Small and localized firms
Network centered on internet-based platform	No MLS Exclusive commission Uniform Internet information platform	Value of company higher than American companies
Company-centered internal network	No MLS Open listing agreements No guarantee for agents' interests	High value of brokerage company Big company-led industry landscape

Source: Compiled by author

2.1   MLS-Centered Network

This network stands out for several reasons. First, the MLS is a central vehicle. As the MLS originated in the United States, it is not surprising that the United States represents the best model in the practice worldwide. Countries like Japan, Canada, and Australia have all made various efforts to replicate the MLS, but generally with very limited or no success. For this reason, this model can be regarded as one that is specific to the United States. Currently, approximately 900 localized MLS networks in the United States function to support the cooperation and divisions among 1.2 million brokerage agents while facilitating the resale transactions of roughly five million houses each year.

Second, the core of the MLS lies in its exclusive commission and unilateral agreements, which ensure cooperation and division, respectively. In general, 90% of sellers choose to entrust their housing sources exclusively to their corresponding agents, while 85% of buyers also turn to their specific agents as sources of housing searches and negotiations on their behalf. Conditional on the conclusion of deals, commissions are paid by sellers and divided equally between the buyer and the seller agents. As an industry-based institutional infrastructure, the MLS puts in place the mechanism for cooperation, division, and assignment among agents. This American model is generally perceived to be committed to the independent agent model, as agents' operations seem independent and liberal. However, this perception overlooks the essence of the MLS's emphasis on the rules. Indeed, the MLS operates under a comprehensive rule-based system in many aspects, such as the release of housing sources, collection of commissions, operations of agents, and transaction contracts. The enforcement of these rules fundamentally ensures the "lightness" of agents' work.

Third, in the MLS-led network structure, brokerage firms and franchised brands are of relatively low value and are continuously on the decline. Brokerage firms are typically small and predominantly localized firms staffed with fewer than 10 people, thereby providing limited availability of services to support individual agents; meanwhile, the companies receive 20% to 30% of the total commission income earned. Even well-known franchise brands such as twenty-first century, KW, and RE/max still have limited value, earning merely 5% to 10% of total commission income.

2.2   Network Centered on Internet-Based Platform

This model, which exists mainly in Australia and Britain, has the following core features. First, an Internet-based platform is designed as a uniform approach to information release and spread, such as REA and Domain, two major platforms in Australia, and Rightmove and Zoopla, two major platforms in Britain. The Internet plays three significant roles. For sellers, it serves as a boundless and around-the-clock platform for the spread of housing source information. For buyers, as a housing source search platform online a 24×7 basis, it also allows for the evaluation and screening of agents, enabling buyers to gain comprehensive and timely access to the information necessary for identifying trustworthy agents. Finally, for agents, it acts as a source for finding clients; it also provides a series of service means, meaning such a platform ensures not only agents' contact with clients but also various operational means necessary for their services, thereby generating higher work efficiency among agents.

Second, the growth of an Internet-based platform is based on two prerequisites: exclusive listing agreements, ensuring the genuineness of house information, and the absence of an MLS. Unlike the cooperation mechanism based on the traditional MLS network in America, industrial environments led by an Internet-based platform do not typically promote cooperation in a real sense. The more common mode concerns seller-entrusted agents publishing housing source information on the Internet, where buyers spend much time surfing and searching on their own before establishing direct contact with the agents to schedule in-person visits after locating possible housing options. Eventually, buyers finish the process by purchasing the housing best matched to their expectations, with the sellers paying the relevant commissions to the sellers' agents.

Finally, in the same vein, due to the industrial structure led by an Internet-based platform, although companies can report a slightly higher value than those in America, they report no higher value in the main industry, mainly stemming from the availability of services provided for agents related to hiring and training, workplace, contract text, advertisements, operation tools, etc.

2.3   Company-Centered Internal Networks

This model, mainly involving countries and regions such as Japan, Taiwan (China), Hong Kong (China), and Mainland China, includes several core features as well. First, without a uniform MLS platform or dominant Internet-based information platform, it is impossible to enable cooperation between companies and agents throughout the industry. As a result, housing source information is spread within the company or covered by individual agents, not in an open, genuine, timely, and complete manner, which prevents consumers' uniform access to such information.

Second, the industrial system typically features open listing agreements. A seller tends to trust companies or agents more, meaning agents' interests are not guaranteed, resulting in income security. This situation leads to a high turnover rate among agents and lower service quality. In general, the industry is plunged into typical negative feedback featuring repeated lower-level cut-throat competition and almost the complete absence of cooperation—or at least requiring a much higher threshold for cooperation.

Finally, in this model, companies report much value. If a company can guarantee the genuineness of information and secure transactions with service-related commitment and proper entry for agents, it garners more recognition among consumers and a high premium from them. In Japan and China, the industrial structures are practically led by large companies. In Japan, three large companies report high market shares: Mitsui, Sumitomo, and Nomura Real Estate. In China, the largest brokerage firm reports a market share of up to 15%, with the total market share of the top five brokerage firms exceeding 35%, a rare case worldwide.

3   An Alternative Choice: A Platform-Based Network

Looking into the future of brokerages in China, we will see a radical change from a company-based network to a platform-based network. For example, Lianjia, a company founded in 2001 that had more than 150,000 agents and more than 8000 company-operated brokerage offices as of 2017, is currently committed to transforming from a singular company to a cross-company and cross-brand Internet platform in the next few years. In other words, under the direct run model, Lianjia invests in brokerage offices and hires professional employees to operate brokerage offices around China, but in order to better promote cooperation among brokerage firms and improve industry transaction efficiency, it is establishing a new brokerage Internet platform named *Beike* to accommodate housing listing information from a variety of brokerage companies. In this way it aims to help manage customer relationships and business processes.

Unlike a company-based network, a platform-based network has the following key distinctive features. First, a platform-based network will extend beyond the company based on its commitment to developing more extensive connections, interactions, and cooperation across companies and brands. In the next three years, China is expected to see the emergence of a large cooperative network, reporting transaction amounts of up to 3 trillion RMB and a market share of more than 40% by connecting 0.5 million agents. Second, although a platform-based network is open, it is conditional and restrictive. The process of "platformization" is essentially the process of establishing trust and cooperation among companies sharing common values and brands; such a process must identify clear rules for entry and exit. Only in this way can it ensure the genuineness of housing sources and quality of services while giving a strong boost to cooperation and division. Third, the core capacity of a platform-based network lies in its commitment to infrastructure, good service quality, and professionalism of agents. Only with a strong capacity for infrastructure, especially for data and technology, can it empower the industry and all agents, guarantee service quality, and ultimately promote agents' professionalism to impress consumers in practice.

Furthermore, under the industrial structure of a platform-based network, the value of a company and brand will remain, but will be on the decline, with the value of agents and outlet owners increasing. A platform with a specific network effect will partly replace the role of traditional companies and engage in more and deeper direct interactions with agents and consumers.

Therefore, compared with the MLS network, a platform-based network is built on the Internet as an online (rather than off-line) product to enable cooperation and promote good services. Compared to an Internet-based cooperation network, a platform-based network in China features seriousness as it involves putting in place rules, constructing infrastructure, giving commitment to service, making arrangements for transactions, and even directly engaging in agents' training, thereby enhancing the quality of the service supply chain. Compared with a traditional internalized company-based network in China, a platform-based network plays an open and relatively neutral role across company boundaries as it is oriented to industrial efficiency and consumers' interests. Essentially, a platform-based network is built on the basic context featuring open listing agreements in China and the core capacity for Internet and big data, with a view to creating a larger and more efficient cooperation network among different companies and brands.

This is the blueprint of this unique industry, and it is also Lianjia's top agenda that defines the company's commitment and vision. In the future, if twenty-million home buyers, 300 million renters, and 700 million urban consumers in China can gain access to accurate information and rich contents someday while having good experiences when interacting with the well-organized and standardized information platform, or if half a million brokerage agents and 50,000 outlets in China have access to a unified network and have confidence in consistent professional values and philosophy in service, we can argue that China has established a platform-based network and we have transformed this industry.

References

Armstrong, M. (2002). *Competition in two-sided markets*. London: University College. Revised 2005.

Hendel, I., Nevo, A., & Ortalo-Magné, F. (2009). The relative performance of real estate marketing platforms: MLS versus FSBOMadison.com. *The American Economic Review, 99*(5), 1878–1898.

Jullien, B. (2001). *Competing in network industries: Divide and conquer*. Toulouse: IDEI and GREMAQ, University of Toulouse.

Miceli, T. J. (1988). Information costs and the organization of the real estate brokerage industry in the U.S. and Great Britain. *AREUEA Journal, 16*(2), 173–188.

Rochet, J. C., & Tirole, J. (2003). Platform competition in two-sided markets. *Journal of European Economic Association, 1*(4), 990–1029.

Rowley, J. (2005). The evolution of internet business strategy. *Property Management, 23*(3), 217–226.

Yavas, A. (2007). Introduction: Real estate brokerage. *The Journal of Real Estate Finance and Economics, 35*(1), 1–5.

Zumpano, L. V. (2003). Internet use and real estate brokerage market intermediation. *Journal of Housing Economics, 12*, 134–150.

Printed by Printforce, the Netherlands